AF814574

All in One®

Recommended by **Teachers**
Trusted by **Toppers**

HISTORY

Class 11

EVERYTHING YOU NEED TO SCORE

- Simplified Theory
- NCERT, Diksha & Other Imp. Ques.
- CBQs; MCQs, A-R, Source Based
- Sample Question Papers

CBSE Exams 2026

Author
Charu Tripathi

arihant
SUCCESS AND NOTHING LESS

arihant
SUCCESS AND NOTHING LESS

ARIHANT PRAKASHAN
(School Division Series)

卐 *ADMINISTRATIVE & PRODUCTION OFFICES*

Regd. Office
'Ramchhaya' 4577/15, Agarwal Road, Darya Ganj, New Delhi -110002
Tele: 011- 47630600, 43518550; Fax: 011- 23280316

卐 *Head Office*
Kalindi, TP Nagar, Meerut (UP) - 250002, Tel: 0121-7156203, 7156204

卐 *SALES & SUPPORT OFFICES*
Agra, Ahmedabad, Bengaluru, Bareilly, Chennai, Delhi, Guwahati, Hyderabad, Jaipur, Jhansi, Kolkata, Lucknow, Nagpur & Pune.

PO No : TXT-XX-XXXXXXX-X-XX

Published By Arihant Publications (India) Ltd.

For further information about the books published by Arihant, log on to www.arihantbooks.com or e-mail at info@arihantbooks.com

Follow us on

卐 *PRICE* ₹300.00

PRODUCTION TEAM

Publishing Managers	*Cover Designer*	*Inner Designer*
Mahendra Singh Rawat & Keshav Mohan	Salman Shaikh	Ankit Tyagi
Project Head	*Page Layouting*	*Proof Reader*
Shivam Gupta	Jashoda	Priya

Index *cum* Study Planner

SECTION A Early Societies

SECTION B Empires

SECTION C Changing Traditions

SECTION D Paths to Modernisation

One Book- Endless Features

to Help you Succeed

Complete Theory

Each chapter has Complete, Easy to Understand and Simplified theory covering latest syllabus and rationalised NCERT Textbook.

1

CHAPTER

Writing and City Life

This chapter deals with some of the earliest cities of Mesopotamia i.e. present day Iraq. Sources like archaeological evidence, remains of old settlements, written material have been used to know about the history of people who lived in Mesopotamia.

YOUR STUDY GOALS

1.1 Mesopotamia
1.2 Urbanism in Mesopotamia
1.3 Life in the City
1.4 The Development of Writing

1.1 Mesopotamia

- The name Mesopotamia is derived from the Greek words *mesos* meaning middle and *potamos* meaning river.
- Mesopotamia is the land between the **Euphrates** and the **Tigris** rivers which is now part of the Republic of Iraq.
- Mesopotamian civilisation is famous for its prosperity, city life, its vast and rich literature, its mathematics and astronomy.

Quick Test

To make students understand the chapter in a smooth part-by-part manner, Quick Tests have been given in each chapter. These help students to assess the understanding of related concepts at regular interval.

NCERT Folder

Intext Questions

1. **Many societies have myths about floods. These are often ways of preserving and expressing memories about important changes in history. Find out more about these, noting how life before and after the flood is represented. (Pg. 10)**

Ans. Life before and after the flood as represented in different myths such as

- As per Bible, God was angry with humanity's misdeeds and thus flood was a reversal of creation. He asked a man named Noah to build ark (boat) to save some species so that life continued after the flood. Before flood, animals and humans coexisted in peace but after flood, God gave mankind control of animals so that they can now eat animals by removing blood.
- Another mythical story among indigenous inhabitants of Andaman Islands tells how Puluga the creator, stopped visiting the people when they stopped following commands given to them at the creation. Without warning, he sent a devastating flood and only four people survive. When they landed they found that they had lost their life and all living things had died. Puluga then created the animals and plants but did not return fire to the survivors.

3. **Why do you think Assurbanipal and Nabonidus cherished early Mesopotamian traditions? (Pg. 27)**

Ans. Assurbanipal and Nabonidus cherished the Mesopotamian traditions because of the following reasons

- **Legitimacy of Rule** By honouring ancient traditions, both kings strengthened their authority by connecting their reigns to the greatness of earlier rulers.
- **Cultural Continuity** They preserved ancient knowledge and traditions to ensure the rich heritage of Mesopotamia continued through their rule.
- **Religious Respect** Both kings believed that following ancient religious practices would bring divine favour and help secure their kingdoms.
- **Historical Awareness** They valued Mesopotamia's long history and saw themselves as protectors of its culture, preserving the wisdom and achievements of the past.

Answer in Brief

1. **Why do we say that it was not natural fertility and high levels of food production that were the causes of early urbanisation?**

Ans. It is often said that natural fertility and high levels of food production were not the only causes of early urbanisation. There were other causes also which are as follows

NCERT Folder

Complete explanations of all the questions of NCERT Exercises.

Quick Test 1

1. Which two rivers define the land of Mesopotamia?
2. After 2000 BCE, which regions adopted the Mesopotamian writing system?
3. Which kingdom was established in the North around 1100 BCE?
4. What significant archaeological work began in Mesopotamia in the 1840s?
5. The date-palms bear fruit in which season?

One Book- Endless Features

to Help you Succeed

Exam Pattern Questions

This section has all types of questions; Objective Type Questions, SA, LA Sources & Map Based Questions.

Exam Pattern Questions

Objective Type Questions

Multiple Choice Questions (MCQs)

1. The term used for Southern region of Mesopotamia was
   (a) Babylonia (b) Assyrian
   (c) Mesopotamian (d) None of these

2. Which one among the following is the main cause for the development of urbanisation in the Mesopotamia? **CBSE Diksha**
   (a) Slave trade
   (b) Employment generation
   (c) Expansion of trade
   (d) Decline of agricultural production

SELF ASSESSMENT TEST

Objective Type Questions

1. Who was the last ruler of Babylon city?
   (a) Nobopolassar (b) Nabonidus (c) Alexander (d) None of these
2. .... was a king of Mesopotamia.
   (a) Enmerker (b) Zimrilim (c) Gilgamesh (d) All of these
3. In Mesopotamia, the .... family was the norm.
   (a) nuclear (b) joint (c) patriarchal (d) None of these
4. What type of communities filtered into Mesopotamia?
   (a) Urban communities (b) Nomadic communities
   (c) Maritime communities (d) Agricultural communities
5. Who were put to work for the temple or the ruler?
   (a) Only local people (b) War captives and local people
   (c) Only skilled artisans (d) Only farmers

Mind Map

A quick revision visual tool for the complete chapter.

Self Assessment Test

Complete Test of chapter in Exam format.

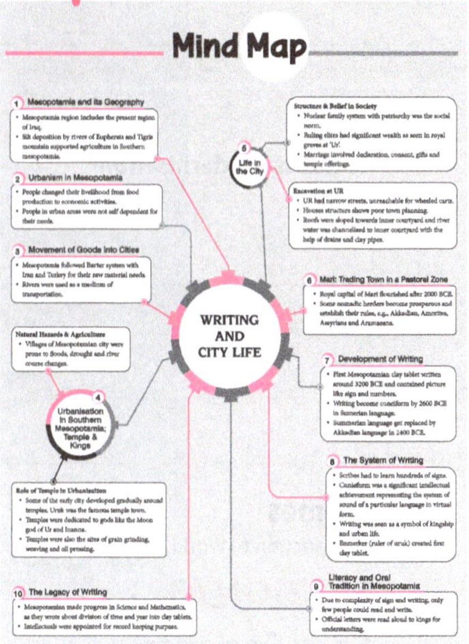

Sample Question Papers

To make students practice of examination in real sense, there are 3 Sample Question Papers at the end. All these Sample Questions Papers are exactly prepared on the latest syllabus & pattern of examination.

SAMPLE QUESTION PAPER 1

A Highly Simulated Sample Question Paper for CBSE Class XI

(SOLVED)

HISTORY

General Instructions

- Question paper comprises five Section: A, B, C, D and E. There are 34 questions in the question paper. All questions are compulsory.
- Section A: Question numbers 1 to 21 are MCQs of 1 mark each.
- Section B: Question numbers 22 to 27 are Short Answer Type Questions, carrying 3 marks each. Answer to each question should not exceed 60-80 words.
- Section C: Question number 28 to 30 are Long Answer Type Questions, carrying 8 marks each. Answer to each question should not exceed 300-350 words.
- Section D: Question number 31 to 33 are Source Based Questions with three sub questions and are of 4 marks each.
- Section E: Question number 34 is Map based, carrying 5 marks that includes the identification and location of significant test items. Attach the map with the answer book.
- There is no overall choice in the question paper. However, an internal choice has been provided in few questions. Only one of the choices in such questions have to be attempted.
- In addition to this, separate instructions are given with each section and question, wherever necessary.

Time : 3 hours **Max. Marks : 80**

Section A (1 × 21 = 21)

(Objective Type Questions)

1. Identify the European astronomer who brought the elements of turning point in European science, with the help of following information. (1)
   - He believed opposite of what Christians had believed about the Earth.
   - He asserted that the planets including the Earth, rotate around the Sun.

   (a) Nicolo Martini (b) Martin Luther (c) Copernicus (d) Galileo Galilei
2. Who among the following crowned Charlemagne as Holy Roman Emperor? (1)
   (a) Pope Leo I (b) Pope Leo II (c) Pope Leo III (d) Pope Leo IV

Latest Course *Structure*

Section Title	Theme Title	Marks
Reading of World History	Introduction of World History	-
Early Societies	Introduction Timeline I (6 MYA to 1 BCE)	-
	Writing and City Life	10
Empires	Introduction Timeline II (C. 100 BCE to 1300 CE)	-
	An Empire Across Three Continents	10
	Nomadic Empires	10
Changing Tradition	Introduction Timeline III (C. 1300 to 1700)	-
	The Three Orders	10
	Changing Cultural Traditions	10
Towards Modernisation	Introduction Timeline IV (C. 1700 to 2000)	-
	Displacing Indigenous Peoples	10
	Paths to Modernisation	15
	Map work of the related Themes	05
	Theory Total	80
	Project Work	20
	Total	100

Themes

Introduction to World History

SECTION A

Early Societies

1. **Writing and City Life**

   Focus: Iraq, 3rd millennium BCE

   (a) Growth of towns

   (b) Nature of early urban societies.

   (c) Historians' Debate on uses of writing.

Learning outcome with specific competencies

- Elucidate the interwoven social and cultural aspects of civilisation in order to understand the connection between city life and culture of contemporary civilisations through their writings.
- Analyse the outcomes of a sustained tradition of writing.
- Explain the connection between the growth of human civilisation and the tradition of writing.

Themes

SECTION B

Empires

2. An Empire across Three Continents

Learning outcome with specific competencies

- Explain and relate the dynamics of the Roman Empire in order to understand their polity, economy, society and culture.
- Analyse the implications of Roman's contacts with the subcontinent empires and discuss about slavery.
- Examine the domains of cultural transformation in that period & the impact of slavery.

3. Nomadic Empires

Learning outcome with specific competencies

- Identify the living patterns of nomadic pastoralist society.
- Trace the rise and growth of Genghis Khan in order to understand him as an oceanic ruler.
- Analyse socio-political and economic changes during the period of the descendants of Genghis khan
- Distinguish between the Mongolian people's perspective and the world's opinion about Genghis Khan

SECTION C

Changing Traditions

4. Three Orders

Learning outcome with specific competencies

- Explain the myriad aspects of feudalism with reference to first, second, third and fourth order of the society.
- Relate between ancient slavery and serfdom.
- Assess the 14th century crisis and rise of the nation states.

5. Changing Cultural Traditions

Learning outcome with specific competencies

- Analyse the causes, events, and effects of the Renaissance, Reformation, Scientific Revolution, and Age of Exploration.
- Relate the different facets of Italian cities to understand the characteristics of Renaissance, Humanism and Realism.
- Compare and contrast the condition of women in the Renaissance period.
- Recognise major influences on the architectural, artistic, and literary developments to understand the facades of Renaissance.
- Critically analyse the impact on later reforms.
- Evaluate the Roman Catholic Church's response to the Protestant Reformation.

SECTION D

Towards Modernisation

6. Displacing Indigenous People

Learning outcome with specific competencies

- Evaluate the process of displacements of the native people which led to the development of America and Australia to understand their condition.
- Analyse the realms of settlement of Europeans in Australia and America.
- Compare and contrast the lives and roles of indigenous people in these continents
- Analyse the domains of Japanese nationalism prior and after the Second World War.

7. Paths to Modernisation

(Note-Keeping inview the importance of the themes i.e. Japan, China and Korea; it is advised that all must be taught in schools).

Learning outcome with specific competencies

- Summarise the nationalist upsurge in China from Dr Sun Yat Sen to Mao Zedong to understand the era of Communism.
- Analyse the Chinese path to modernization under Deng Xioping and Zhou enlai in order to understand the transformation from rigid communism to liberal socialism.
- Deduce the histories of China and Japan from the phase of imperialism to modernization.
- Analyse the domains of Japanese nationalism prior and after the Second World War.

Question Paper Design

Class 11

Section	Theme	MCQ mm-1	SA mm-3	LA mm-8	Source Based mm-4	Total
I Early Societies	Theme 1	3	1	0	1	10
II Empires	Theme 2 Theme 3	4	0	2	0	20
III Changing Traditions	Theme 4 Theme 5	6	2	0	2	20
IV Towards Modernisation	Theme 6 Theme 7	8	3	1	0	25
MAP						5
Total		**21×1=21**	**6×3=18**	**8×3=24**	**4×3=12**	**80**

All in One

SECTION A
EARLY SOCIETIES

Chapter 1 Writing and City Life

TIMELINE I (6 MYA to 1 BCE)

This timeline or period focuses on the emergence of humans and the domestication of plants and animals. It highlights some major technological developments such as the use of fire, metals, plough agriculture and the wheel. Other processes that are shown include the emergence of cities and the use of writing.

1

CHAPTER

Writing and City Life

This chapter deals with some of the earliest cities of Mesopotamia i.e. present day Iraq. Sources like archaeological evidence, remains of old settlements, written material have been used to know about the history of people who lived in Mesopotamia.

YOUR STUDY GOALS

1.1 Mesopotamia
1.2 Urbanism in Mesopotamia
1.3 Life in the City
1.4 The Development of Writing

YOUR PRACTICE GOAL

- Objective Type Questions (29 Qs ; MCQs, A-R, Matching, Picture Based)
- Subjective Questions (22 SAs, 8 LAs)
- Source Based Questions (6 Qs)
- Map Based Questions (3 Qs)

1.1 Mesopotamia

- The name Mesopotamia is derived from the Greek words *mesos* meaning middle and *potamos* meaning river.
- Mesopotamia is the land between the **Euphrates** and the **Tigris** rivers which is now part of the Republic of Iraq.
- Mesopotamian civilisation is famous for its prosperity, city life, its vast and rich literature, its mathematics and astronomy.
- After 2000 BCE, the regions like the **Eastern Mediterranean, Northern Syria** and **Turkey** started to communicate in writing to one another and to the Pharaoh of Egypt in Mesopotamian script.
- The urbanised part of South Mesopotamia was called **Sumer** and **Akkad**.
- After 2000 BCE, Babylonia, the Southern region of Mesopotamia, became important.
- From 1100 BCE, the region in the North came to be known as **Assyria** when the **Assyrians** established their kingdom.

- **Sumerian** was the first language of the land. It was replaced by Akkadian around 2400 BCE which was used till about Alexander's time (336-323 BCE).
- From 1400 BCE, Aramaic language came to be used which was similar to Hebrew. It is still spoken in parts of Iraq.

Archaeology of Mesopotamia

- Archaeology in Mesopotamia began in the 1840s at sites like **Uruk** and **Mari**.
- Archaeological sources included buildings, statues, ornaments, graves, tools, seals and thousands of written documents.
- Mesopotamia's references are mentioned in the first part of the **Bible Old Testament**. For example, the Book of Genesis of the Old Testament refers to **Shimar** (meaning Sumer) as a land of brick-built cities.
- In 1873, a British newspaper attempted to search for a tablet narrating the story of 'Noah and the Flood', mentioned in the Bible. This story was similar to the story in Mesopotamian tradition, where the main character was called Ziusudra or Utnapishtim.
- By the 1960s, scholars understood that the stories of the Old Testament may have been a way of expressing major historical changes.

Geography of Mesopotamia

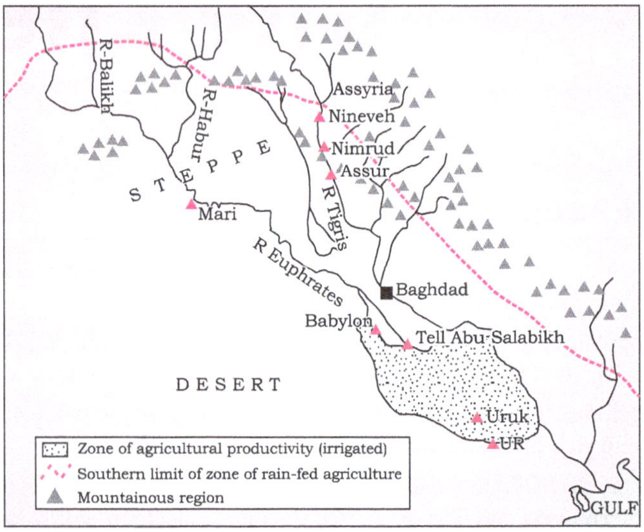

▲ *Geography of Mesopotamia*

- In the North-East, Iraq has green undulating plains. These plains gradually rise to tree-covered mountain ranges with clear streams and wild flowers.
- Mesopotamia receives enough rainfall to grow crops. Agriculture began here between 7000 and 6000 BCE.
- **Animal herding** is done for livelihood in a stretch of hilly land called a steppe in the North.
- In the East, tributaries of the Tigris provide routes of communication into mountains of Iran.
- The South is a desert where the first cities emerged. It is because the rivers Euphrates and Tigris which originate in the Northern mountains, bring a lot of silt (fine mud) and deposit in this region. The water from these rivers makes the silt fertile and suitable for agriculture.
- The water from the Euphrates river flows into small channels which worked as irrigation channels in the past.

Agriculture and Other Activities in Mesopotamia

- Agriculture of Southern Mesopotamia was most productive as compared to all the ancient systems including the Roman Empire, even without enough rainfall.
- Apart from agriculture, Mesopotamian sheep and goats produced meat, milk and wool. They grazed on the steppe (grassland), the North-Eastern plains and the mountain slopes.
- Fish was available in rivers and date palms gave fruit in summer.
- The agriculture in Mesopotamia faced both natural and man-made hazards. **Natural hazard** included the Euphrates river having too much water, which resulted in flooding crops. **Man-made hazards** included diversion of the water from the upstream stretches of channel by the people who lived there which affected villages downstream. Removal of silt was also ignored from the stretch of channel leading to blockage of the flow of water.

Quick Test 1

1 Which two rivers define the land of Mesopotamia?
2 After 2000 BCE, which regions adopted the Mesopotamian writing system?
3 Which kingdom was established in the North around 1100 BCE?
4 What significant archaeological work began in Mesopotamia in the 1840s?
5 The date-palms bear fruit in which season?

1.2 Urbanism in Mesopotamia

- Different economic activities like **trading, manufacturing** and **food production** were carried out by the people living in towns.
- **Division of labour**[1] was a feature of Mesopotamian city where people were more specialised in their field of work and became interdependent rather than being self-sufficient.
- Various things like fuel, metal, various stones, wood, etc, came from different places for city manufacturers. Food supplies coming from village need to be stored and distributed. Different types of bronze and stone tools must be available to different people.
- Social organisation and storage of written records were needed in urban economy.
- Some people were involved in this economy who give commands and others obey.

Movement of Goods into Cities

- Mesopotamia was rich in **food resources** but it lacked mineral resources. Most parts of South lacked stones, wood and metal.
- Mesopotamians could have traded their extra agricultural produce for wood, metals and stones with **Turkey, Iran or Across the Gulf**.
- The earliest cities in Mesopotamia dates back to 3000 BCE which also relates to the Bronze Age.
- The bronze was imported from long distance which sustained activities like carpentry, drilling, digging, etc. Bronze is an alloy made up of copper and tin.
- Beside crafts, trade and services, an efficient transport is needed for urban development. The cheapest mode of transport is over water through river **boats** or **barges**[2].
- The **canals** and **natural channels** of ancient Mesopotamia were important transport routes between large and small settlements.

Urbanisation in Southern Mesopotamia

From 5000 BCE, settlements began in Southern Mesopotamia. Following are the kinds of cities that were developed

(i) Cities that gradually developed around temples
(ii) Cities that developed as centres of trade
(iii) Imperial cities

Development of Temples

- Temples were the residences of various Gods like **Moon God** of Ur and **Inanna**, the Goddess of Love and War.

1 **Division of labour** It refers to the system where people are assigned task according to skill. This increase their productivity and efficiency.
2 **Barge** A long narrow boat with a flat bottom that is used to carry goods or people on a canal/river.

- Earliest temple was a small shrine made of unbaked bricks. Gradually, temples became larger with more rooms around open courtyards.

▲ *A Temple of Period c. 3000 BCE*

- Temples had their outer walls going in and out at regular intervals.
- The focus of worship was God and people brought grain, curd and fish as offerings. The floors of some early temples had thick layers of fish bones.
- God was considered as the owner of the agricultural fields, fisheries and herds.
- Gradually, temple became the main urban institution for the processing of produce, e.g. oil pressing, grain grinding, spinning and the weaving of woolen cloth.
- They also became center of production, employer of merchants, keeper of written records of distribution and allotments of grains, plough animals, bread, beer, fish, etc.

Role of Kings in Development of Temples

- In early periods, there were continuous wars in the region. After winning the war, the chiefs would distribute the loot to their followers. They would take prisoners from defeated group and employ them as their servants or guards.
- Victorious chiefs began to offer precious things to the gods and used them for beautifying the community temples.
- Temples were used to distribute wealth in an efficient way by keeping accounts of everything. This gave the king high status and authority to command.
- The leaders encouraged the settlement of villagers close to themselves so they could help them in recruiting army.
- War **captives**[3] and local people were to work for the temple or directly for ruler. In return, people were paid rations like grain, oil and cloth.
- People had to fetch stones or metal ores, make or lay bricks for temple and go to other countries to get suitable materials.

Development in Urban Economy

- Uruk, one of the earliest temple towns of Mesopotamia, grew significantly around 3000 BCE. It expanded to 250 hectares in size, which was twice as large as the **Mohenjodaro** site.
- The site was continuously occupied from about 4200 BCE to about 400 CE. It had expanded to 400 hectares by about 2800 BCE. It also had a defensive wall around it.
- Around 3000 CE, technical advances were evident at Uruk like bronze tools came into use. Architects learnt to construct brick columns to bear the weight of the roof of large halls. People worked to make and bake clay cones that were pushed into temple walls. They painted it in different colours creating a colourful mosaic. Sculpture using imported stone was also started to be made.
- An important technological development was the invention of **potter's wheel**. It enabled to produce similar pots at a large scale.

---

3 **Captives** A person who is confined, especially a prisoner of war.

The Seal - An Urban Artefact

In India, early stone seals were stamped. Until the end of the first millennium BCE, cylindrical stone seals were used.

A hole was made at the center of the seal in which a stick was fitted and then it would rolled over wet clay so that a continuous picture was created.

Seals were carved by very skilled craftsmen. Sometimes, the name of the owner, his god, his official position, etc were written on them. A seal on a letter written on a clay tablet, became a mark of authenticity.

▲ *Five early cylinder seals and their impressions*

Quick Test 2

1. What economic activities were carried out by people living in the towns of Mesopotamia?
2. Which types of cities were developed in Mesopotamia from 5000 BCE?
3. Who was the Goddess of love and war?
4. What is the name of the earliest temple town ofMesopotamia?
5. Which type of seals were used during first millennium BCE?

1.3 Life in the City

Ur and Mari were the most important imperial cities of Mesopotamia.

Ur Town

- Ur was one of the earliest cities excavated in the 1930s.
- Ur had **narrow twisted streets**, so wheeled carts might not have reached many houses. Donkeys would have been used to carry sacks of grains and firewood.
- The narrow streets and house plots with irregular shapes in the town also indicates that there was **no town planning** in the city.
- Ur did not have street drains like those of Mohenjodaro. The **roofs of the houses** in Ur were **sloped inwards** and rainwater flowed through the clay and drain pipes into sumps[4] in the inner courtyards.
- People used to throw all the household waste onto the streets which raised the level of street. The level of houses had also to be raised, so that no mud would flow inside after the rains.
- Light came into rooms through doorways but not from windows. This would also have given their families their privacy.
- There were some beliefs about how the houses are built, like
  - A raised threshold (a strip of wood or stone forming the bottom of a doorway) would bring wealth.
  - A front door that did not open towards another house was lucky.
  - If the main wooden door of the house opened outwards, the wife would be a mental suffering to her husband.
  - Graves of royal and commoners were found at the town cemetery. Some individuals were also buried under the floors of ordinary houses.
- In Ur, there is evidence of precious things buried with some kings and queens in large numbers. These included jewellery, gold vessels, wooden musical instruments inlaid with white shell and lapis lazuli, ceremonial daggers of gold, etc.

4 Sumps It is a covered basin in the ground into which water and sewage flow.

Mari : A Trading Town in a Pastoral Zone

- The royal capital of Mari flourished after 2000 BCE. It was located upstream on the Euphrates.
- Both agriculture and herding were done in the town but most of the territory of Mari was used for pasturing sheep and goats.
- Herders exchanged animals, cheese, leather and meat in return for grain, metal tools and manure of flock, with farmers.
- Sometimes **herders** and **farmers** were also involved in conflict when animals destroyed the crop while crossing a sown field to reach water.
- Settled groups might deny access to the pastoralists to river and canal water in some places.

Mari as an Important Trade Centre

- The trade was carried out using boats along the Euphrates, between the South and the uplands of Turkey, Syria and Lebanon.
- These boats would stop at Mari for inspection by the officers. They would charge a part (one-tenth) of the value of goods before allowing them to go further.
- Various goods like wood, tin, bronze, oil and wine were traded. Copper from **Alashiya**, the islands of **Cyprus**, was also an item of trade.

The Palace at Mari of King Zimrilim (1810-1760 BCE)

- The great palace of Mari was the residence of the royal family. The palace was the hub of administration and production, especially of precious metal ornaments.
- The palace had a large structure, with 260 rooms and covered an area of 2.4 hectares.
- Large quantities of food were presented each day for the king's table like flour, bread, meat, fish, fruit, beer, wine, etc.

Cities in Mesopotamian Culture

- Mesopotamians valued city life, where people from various communities and cultures lived together.
- Even after cities were destroyed in wars, they were recalled in poetry.
- A strong reminder of the Mesopotamians' pride in their cities is found in the **Epic of Gilgamesh**, written on 12 **tablets**[5]. Gilgamesh, the hero of the epic, is believed to have ruled the city of Uruk.
- He was a great hero who conquered people from distant lands but was shocked by the death of his close friend.
- After his friend's death, Gilgamesh embarked on a journey to discover the secret of immortality. Despite his efforts, Gilgamesh failed to obtain immortality and returned to Uruk.

Traditions in Mesopotamia

- Mesopotamian society primarily consisted of **nuclear families**[6]. The father was the head of the family.
- Marriage proposals were made through declarations, followed by consent from the bride's parents and the exchange of gifts between families.
- After marriage, the bride received a share of her father's **inheritance**[7], while sons inherited father's house, herds and fields.
- Mesopotamian society and culture welcomed different people and cultures.

5 Tablets A flat piece of stone, clay or wood that has writing on it.

6 Nuclear Family A composite family including husband, wife and their children.

7 Inheritance It includes money, property or objects that someone gives you when they die.

- Nomadic groups from the Western desert migrated to the prosperous agricultural regions, where they arrived as herders, farm workers, or soldiers. Many of them eventually settled down and prospered.
- Some nomadic groups, like the **Akkadians, Amorites, Assyrians** and **Aramaeans**, gained power and established their own rule.
- The kings of Mari, who were Amorites, respected Mesopotamian gods and even built a temple for Dagan, the God of the steppe.
- Herders from various tribes who were allowed to move within the kingdom, were closely watched.
- The intermixture of different cultures contributed to the strength and resilience of Mesopotamian civilisation.

Quick Test 3

1. What does the irregular shape of house plots in Ur indicate?
2. What did people of Ur do with their household refuse?
3. How did light enter the rooms in houses of Ur?
4. How did Mesopotamians remember their cities after they were destroyed in war?
5. Who is said to have ruled the city of Uruk?

1.4 The Development of Writing

- Writing is a way of communicating ideas using symbols that represent spoken words.
- The earliest Mesopotamian tablets, dating back to around 3200 BCE, contained picture-like signs and numbers.
- These tablets recorded lists of goods, such as oxen, fish and bread loaves, that were brought into or distributed from the temples of Uruk, a city in Southern Mesopotamia.
- Writing started because people needed to keep track of things they bought and sold.
- Mesopotamians wrote on tablets made of clay. A tablet is a flat slab of stone, clay, or wood used for inscription.
- A scribe is someone who wrote down things. He would make the clay wet and shape it into a good size. Then, they would press little triangle-shaped signs (called cuneiform) into the wet clay.

▲ *A Clay Tablet Written on both Sides in Cuneiform*

- These tablets were dried in the Sun, making them hard and indestructible. Once a written record became outdated, the tablets were often destroyed.
- Every minor transaction was recorded on a new tablet, resulting in the discovery of hundreds of tablets in Mesopotamian sites. These tablets have provided valuable insights into Mesopotamian society and history, surpassing the knowledge available about India.

The System of Writing

- Cuneiform[8] signs represented syllables (like "-put-," "-la-," or "-in-") rather than individual consonants or vowels (like "b" or "a" in English).
- This syllabic system made writing a complex skill, requiring scribes to learn hundreds of signs and work quickly with wet clay before it dried. It was a big achievement to figure out how to use pictures to show the sounds of a particular language.

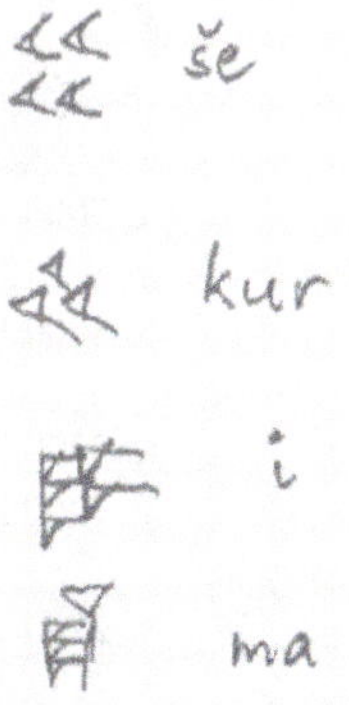

▲ *Cuneiform Syllabic Signs*

8 **Cuneiform** It is derived from the latin words *cuneus* meaning wedge and *forma* meaning shape.

Literacy in Mesopotamia

- Despite the existence of hundreds of cuneiform signs, most Mesopotamians were unable to read or write due to the complexity of the system.
- Kings who could read were proud of their skill and often wrote about it in their inscriptions.

The Uses of Writing in Mesopotamia

- A Sumerian epic poem about Enmerkar, depicts the connection between city life, trade and writing.
- Enmerkar was one of the earliest rulers of Uruk. In Mesopotamian tradition, Uruk was known as **The City**. Enmerkar is associated with the organisation of the first trade of Sumer.
- Writing was used for maintaining records of various activities, including land transactions, legal matters and the deeds of kings.
- Writing was employed to create dictionaries and provide legal validity to land transactions.
- Kings used writing to announce changes made in customary laws.
- Writing served as a means of storing information and sending messages over long distances.
- Writing was considered a symbol of the superiority of Mesopotamian urban culture.

The Legacy of Mesopotamian Writing

- Mesopotamian tablets from around 1800 BCE included multiplication, division, square and square root tables, as well as tables of compound interest.
- Students learned about area, volume and time divisions, which have been adopted and used throughout history, from the successors of Alexander to medieval Europe.
- Mesopotamians recorded **solar** and **lunar eclipses**, along with the positions of stars and constellations in the night sky.
- Without writing and urban institutions like schools, where students could read, copy and learn from earlier written tablets, the significant achievements of Mesopotamia might not have been preserved.

Quick Test 4

1. What did Mesopotamian tablet contain?
2. What do you mean by cuneiform?
3. Who was the ruler of the city of Uruk?
4. Writing was used for which activities?

TIMELINE

c. 7000-6000 BCE	Beginning of agriculture in the Northern Mesopotamian plains.	c. 2000 BCE	Spread of Cuneiform writing to Syria, Turkey and Egypt; Mari and Babylon emerge as important urban centres.
c. 5000 BCE	Earliest temples in Southern Mesopotamia built.	c. 1800 BCE	Mathematical texts composed; Sumerian no longer spoken.
c. 3200 BCE	First writing in Mesopotamia.	c. 1100 BCE	Establishment of the Assyrian kingdom.
c. 3000 BCE	Uruk develops into a huge city, increasing use of bronze tools.	c. 1000 BCE	Use of Iron.
c. 2700-2500 BCE	Early kings, including, possibly the legendary ruler Gilgamesh.	720-610 BCE	Assyrian empire.
c. 2600 BCE	Development of the Cuneiform script.	668-627 BCE	Rule of Assurbanipal.
c. 2400 BCE	Replacement of Sumerian by Akkadian.	331 BCE	Alexander conquers Babylon.
2370 BCE	Sargon, king of Akkad.	c. 1st century CE	Akkadian and cuneiform remain in use.
		1850s	Decipherment of the Cuneiform script.

Mind Map

WRITING AND CITY LIFE

1 Mesopotamia and its Geography

- Mesopotamia region includes the present region of Iraq.
- Silt deposition by rivers of Eupherats and Tigris mountain supported agriculture in Southern mesopotamia.

2 Urbanism in Mesopotamia

- People changed their livelihood from food production to economic activities.
- People in urban areas were not self dependent for their needs.

3 Movement of Goods into Cities

- Mesopotamia followed Barter system with Iran and Turkey for their raw material needs.
- Rivers were used as a medium of transportation.

4 Urbanisation in Southern Mesopotamia; Temple & Kings

Natural Hazards & Agriculture

- Villages of Mesopotamian city were prone to floods, drought and river course changes.

Role of Temple in Urbanisaiton

- Some of the early city developed gradually around temples. Uruk was the famous temple town.
- Temples were dedicated to gods like the Moon god of Ur and Inanna.
- Temples were also the sites of grain grinding, weaving and oil pressing.

5 Life in the City

Structure & Belief in Society

- Nuclear family system with patriarchy was the social norm.
- Ruling elites had significant wealth as seen in royal graves at 'Ur'.
- Marriage involved declaration, consent, gifts and temple offerings.

Excavation at UR

- UR had narrow streets, unreachable for wheeled carts.
- Houses structure shows poor town planning.
- Roofs were sloped towards inner courtyard and river water was channelised to inner courtyard with the help of drains and clay pipes.

6 Mari: Trading Town in a Pastoral Zone

- Royal capital of Mari flourished after 2000 BCE.
- Some nomadic herders become prosperous and establish their rules, e.g., Akkadian, Amorites, Assyrians and Aramaeans.

7 Development of Writing

- First Mesopotamian clay tablet written around 3200 BCE and contained picture like sign and numbers.
- Writing become cuneiform by 2600 BCE in Sumerian language.
- Summerian language get replaced by Akkadian language in 2400 BCE.

8 The System of Writing

- Scribes had to learn hundreds of signs.
- Cunieform was a significant intellectual achievement representing the system of sound of a particular language in virtual form.
- Writing was seen as a symbol of kingship and urban life.
- Enmerker (ruler of uruk) created first clay tablet.

9 Literacy and Oral Tradition in Mesopotamia

- Due to complexity of sign and writing, only few people could read and write.
- Official letters were read aloud to kings for understanding.

10 The Legacy of Writing

- Mesopotamian made progress in Science and Mathematics, as they wrote about division of time and year into clay tablets.
- Intellectuals were appointed for record keeping purpose.

NCERT Folder

Intext Questions

1. Many societies have myths about floods. These are often ways of preserving and expressing memories about important changes in history. Find out more about these, noting how life before and after the flood is represented. (Pg. 10)

Ans. Life before and after the flood as represented in different myths such as

- As per Bible, God was angry with humanity's misdeeds and thus flood was a reversal of creation. He asked a man named Noah to build ark (boat) to save some species so that life continued after the flood. Before flood, animals and humans coexisted in peace but after flood, God gave mankind control of animals so that they can now eat animals by removing blood.
- Another mythical story among indigenous inhabitants of Andaman Islands tells how Puluga the creator, stopped visiting the people when they stopped following commands given to them at the creation. Without warning, he sent a devastating flood and only four people survive. When they landed they found that they had lost their life and all living things had died. Puluga then created the animals and plants but did not return fire to the survivors.

2. Discuss whether city life would have been possible without the use of metals. (Pg. 12)

Ans. City life would not have been possible without the use of metals.

Use of metals was one of the main causes for the development of city life. It helped in inventing new metal tools and increasing the efficiency of human work in various fields. Following are different metals that made city life possible

- Iron metal without which manufacturing industry and agricultural industry would not have been developed.
- Copper and aluminium metal is important in electrical industry.
- Gold, platinum, silver which are precious metals were used as currency exchange and wealth generation.
- Construction of roads, houses, offices, airplanes, ships, rockets, etc, all of which are important components of city life would not have been possible without use of metals.

3. Why do you think Assurbanipal and Nabonidus cherished early Mesopotamian traditions? (Pg. 27)

Ans. Assurbanipal and Nabonidus cherished the Mesopotamian traditions because of the following reasons

- **Legitimacy of Rule** By honouring ancient traditions, both kings strengthened their authority by connecting their reigns to the greatness of earlier rulers.
- **Cultural Continuity** They preserved ancient knowledge and traditions to ensure the rich heritage of Mesopotamia continued through their rule.
- **Religious Respect** Both kings believed that following ancient religious practices would bring divine favour and help secure their kingdoms.
- **Historical Awareness** They valued Mesopotamia's long history and saw themselves as protectors of its culture, preserving the wisdom and achievements of the past.

Answer in Brief

1. Why do we say that it was not natural fertility and high levels of food production that were the causes of early urbanisation?

Ans. It is often said that natural fertility and high levels of food production were not the only causes of early urbanisation. There were other causes also which are as follows

- Increase in trade, manufacturing and services.
- Division of labour and interdependence on one another.
- Increasing need for mineral resources, metals, stones which increased trade and commerce result in urbanisation.
- Rulers encouraged settlement of villagers close to themselves which emerged as urban areas.

2. Which of the following were necessary conditions and which the causes of early urbanisation and which would you say were the outcome of the growth of cities?

(i) Highly productive agriculture
(ii) Water transport
(iii) The lack of metal and stone
(iv) The division of labour
(v) The use of seals
(vi) The military power of kings that made labour compulsory.

Ans. The following were necessary conditions for urbanisation

- Highly productive agriculture
- The division of labour

- Water transport

Causes of early urbanisation are

- The use of metal like Bronze and stone
- The military power of kings that made labour compulsory.

Outcome of the growth of cities are

- Development of urban institutions like schools.
- Transfer of knowledge from one region to other. For example, time divisions and mathematics from Mesopotamia transmitted to other parts of world.
- Multiculturalism i.e. people of different cultures living together.

3. Why were mobile animal herders not necessarily a threat to town life?

Ans. Mobile animal herders were dependent on towns for exchanging young animals, leather and meat in return for grains, metal tools, etc, so they were not a threat to town life.

4. Why would the early temple have been much like a house?

Ans. Early temple which was a small shrine made of unbaked bricks have been much like a house because they also had an open courtyard around which rooms were constructed like houses. Temple was also a house of a god and people also use to sit in temples and process their produce like pressing, grain grinding, spinning and weaving.

Answer in a Short Essay

1. Of the new institutions that came into being, once city life had begun, which would have depended on the initiative of the king?

Ans. There were several institutions which came into being once city life had begun. These were temples, trade centres, tablet writers, permanent army, craftmen, builders, sculptors, etc.

Of these, the new institutions which were depended on the initiative of the king were trade centres, temples, seal making, sculpture and the art of writing.

2. What do ancient stories tell us about the civilisation of Mesopotamia?

Ans. Ancient stories tell us following things about civilisation of Mesopotamia

- Mesopotamians had most productive agriculture compared to all other ancient systems including Roman Empire.
- Mesopotamians had developed language and art of writing. They used tablets to record information. They took pride as they knew how to read and write.
- There were different classes of people like kings, queens, lords, servants in Mesopotamia. While kings, queens, lords had huge wealth, others had little share of wealth.
- Mesopotamians built temples for various Gods like Moon God of Ur and Inanna, the Goddess of Love and War.
- Nuclear family was the norm of Mesopotamian society.
- There was no town planning in Mesopotamia. There were no street, drains. Cleanliness was not maintained on the streets, as it was evident that waste from the house was thrown on streets.
- Mesopotamians were also superstitious about houses.
- Mesopotamian society and culture was open to different people and cultures.

Exam Pattern Questions

Objective Type Questions

Multiple Choice Questions (MCQs)

1. The term used for Southern region of Mesopotamia was

(a) Babylonia (b) Assyrian
(c) Mesopotamian (d) None of these

2. Which one among the following is the main cause for the development of urbanisation in the Mesopotamia? **CBSE Diksha**

(a) Slave trade
(b) Employment generation
(c) Expansion of trade
(d) Decline of agricultural production

3. **What are the different kind of cities that emerged in Southern Mesopotamia?**
(a) Cities that developed around temples.
(b) Cities that developed as centres of trade.
(b) Imperial cities
(d) All of the above

4. **Name two gods for whom temples were built.**
(a) Moon God of Ur
(b) Inanna, the Goddess of Love and War
(c) Apollo
(d) Both (a) and (b)

5. **Name any famous epic of Mesopotamians.**
(a) Gilgamesh
(b) Nabopolassar
(c) Wars of Babylon
(d) None of the above

6. **Who established their rule in Mari?**
(a) Akkadians (b) Amorites
(c) Assyrians and Aramaeans (d) All of these

7. **Mesopotamians people wrote on tablets made of** **CBSE Diksha**
(a) wood (b) clay
(c) paper (d) cloth

8. **In Mesopotamia, writing was used for**
(a) keeping records, making dictionaries.
(b) giving legal validity to land transfer.
(c) narrating the deeds and reforms of the king.
(d) All of the above

9. **Arrange in sequence.**
(i) Use of iron
(ii) Establishment of the Assyrian King
(iii) Assyrian empire
(iv) Rule of Assurbanipal

Codes
(a) (ii), (i), (iii), (iv) (b) (i), (ii), (iv), (iii)
(c) (iv), (iii), (ii), (i) (d) (i), (iii), (iv), (ii)

10. **Identify the ruler or historical figure with the help of the following information.**
- He was a king of Mari and hosted royal dignitaries.
- His palace had 260 rooms, including a room with awe-inspiring wall paintings.
- He is associated with courtyard 106, where the king's table was lavishly served.

Options
(a) Assurbanipal (b) Zimrilim
(c) Nabonidus (d) Hammurabi

11. **Consider the following statements and choose the incorrect option.**
I. In Mesopotamian society, the joint family is the norm.
II. Married son and his family resided with his parents.
III. The father was the head of the family.

Codes
(a) Only I (b) Only II
(c) Both II and III (d) Both I and II

12. **Identify the name of the site from the information given below.**
(i) It was one of the earliest temple towns in which depictions of armed heroes and their victims were found.
(ii) The site was continuously occupied from about 4200 BCE to about 400 CE.
(iii) The site came to have a defensive wall at a very early date.
(iv) By about 2800 BCE it had expanded to 400 hectares.

Options
(a) Mari (b) Uruk
(c) Mohenjodaro (d) None of these

13. **Identify the term through the features.**
(i) Scribe wrote this type of different signs on to the smoothened surface of the tablet.
(ii) It is derived from the latin word means 'wedge' and 'shape'.
(a) Sameria (b) Akkadian
(c) Cuneiform (d) None of these

14. **Identify the name of the kingdom from the information given below.**
(i) Most of its territory was used for pasturing sheep and goats.
(ii) Amorites were the kings of this kingdom.
(iii) Amorites raised a temple at this kingdom for Dagan, God of the steppe.
(iv) It is a good example of an urban centre prospering on trade.

Options
(a) Mari (b) Uruk
(c) Babylon (d) None of these

15. **Complete the following with the correct option regarding the role of leaders in the history of their empires.**

Zimrilim: Mari :: Assurbanipal: ....
(a) Egypt (b) Babylon
(c) Nineveh (d) Ur

16. **Complete the following with the correct option regarding the association of deities with ancient Mesopotamian cities:**

The Moon God: Ur :: .... : the Goddess of Love.

(a) Inanna (b) Mari
(c) Warka (d) Uruk

Assertion-Reason

17. **Assertion** (A) The city of Babylon remained a major center of culture and trade even after its conquest by the Achaemenids in 539 BCE.

Reason (R) Babylon was known for its triple walls, large palaces, temples and extensive trading networks.

Codes

(a) Both A and R are true and R is the correct explanation of A
(b) Both A and R are true, but R is not the correct explanation of A
(c) A is true, but R is false
(d) A is false, but R is true

18. **Assertion** (A) Food resources of Mesopotamia were rich and its mineral resources were few.

Reason (R) Mesopotamia traded their abundant textiles and agricultural produce for wood, copper, tin, silver, gold, shell, etc.

Codes

(a) Both A and R are true and R is the correct explanation of A
(b) Both A and R are true, but R is not the correct explanation of A
(c) A is true, but R is false
(d) A is false, but R is true

19. **Assertion** (A) Assurbanipal collected a vast library at Nineveh, gathering texts from Babylonia.

Reason (R) Babylonia was known for its educational centers where ancient texts were preserved and scribes were trained to read and write.

Codes

(a) Both A and R are true and R is the correct explanation of A
(b) Both A and R are true, but R is not the correct explanation of A
(c) A is true, but R is false
(d) A is false, but R is true

20. **Assertion** (A) Sumerian language ceased to be spoken after 1800 BCE but continued to be taught in schools.

Reason (R) The Assyrian kings saw the Sumerian language as a means to unify their empire.

Codes

(a) Both A and R are true and R is the correct explanation of A
(b) Both A and R are true, but R is not the correct explanation of A
(c) A is true, but R is false
(d) A is false, but R is true

21. **Assertion** (A) Many tablets were found in Mesopotamia which was in Sumerian language and letters were in cuneiform.

Reason (R) Sumerian was the earliest language known to the people of Mesopotamia.

Codes

(a) Both A and R are true and R is the correct explanation of A
(b) Both A and R are true, but R is not the correct explanation of A
(c) A is true, but R is false
(d) A is false, but R is true

Match the Following

22.

List I		List II	
A.	Uruk	1.	Trading town
B.	Mari	2.	River
C.	Euphrates	3.	Temple town
D	Inanna	4.	Goddess of Love and War

Codes

	A	B	C	D		A	B	C	D
(a)	3	1	2	4	(b)	2	1	4	3
(c)	3	1	4	2	(d)	4	2	1	3

23.

List I		List II	
A.	Cuneiform	1.	Ruler of Uruk
B.	Alashiya	2.	A system of writing
C.	Gilgamesh	3.	Stone slabs with inscription or carving
D	Steles	4.	Islands of Cyprus

Codes

	A	B	C	D
(a)	3	1	2	4
(b)	2	4	1	3
(c)	3	1	4	2
(d)	4	2	1	3

24.

List I (Historical Figures)		List II (Achievements/ Contributions)	
A.	Assurbanipal	1.	Freed Babylonia from Assyrian domination
B.	Nabonidus	2.	Legendary ruler of Akkad around 2370 BCE
C.	Nabopolassar	3.	Revived the office of the High Priestess in Ur
D	Sargon of Akkad	4.	Collected a vast library at Nineveh

Codes

	A	B	C	D		A	B	C	D
(a)	1	2	3	4	(b)	4	3	1	2
(c)	3	4	2	1	(d)	2	4	1	3

Picture Based Questions

25. What is the world famous sculpture given below known as?

(a) Mother Goddess
(b) Inanna
(c) Warka Head
(d) Gilgamesh

26. The image below depicts a temple structure which dates back to which of the following era?

(a) 6000 BCE (b) 5000 BCE
(c) 800 BCE (d) 3000 BCE

27. The image below shows a basalt stele from around 3200 BCE. It depicts a bearded man attacking a lion in 2 scenes. What weapon does the hero use to kill the lion in the final scene?

(a) Sword (b) Bow and Arrow
(c) Spear (d) Dagger

28. Study this image of clay tablet excavated from Mesopotamia.

The cuneiform sign written on this tablet was/were
(a) represented as syllables.
(b) represented as constant or vowel.
(c) had not been deciphered yet.
(d) All of the above

29. Study this image of temple excavated from Mesopotamian.

What can be inferred based on the given image about the state of temple building in Mesopotamia?
(a) Temples were constructed by Kings and wealthy traders in Mesopotamia.
(b) Some of the cities were developed around temples.
(c) They were constructed on grandeur scale which accommodated large population for prayers and ritual activities.
(d) All of the above

Answers

1. (a) Babylonia
2. (c) Expansion of trade
3. (d) All of the above
4. (d) Both (a) and (b)
5. (a) Gilgamesh
6. (d) All of these
7. (b) clay
8. (d) All of the above
9. (a) (ii), (i), (iii), (iv)
10. (b) Zimrilim
11. (a) Only I
12. (b) Uruk
13. (c) Cuneiform
14. (a) Mari
15. (c) Nineveh
16. (a) Inanna
17. (a) Both A and R are true and R is the correct explanation of A
18. (b) Both A and R are true, but R is not the correct explanation of A
19. (a) Both A and R are true and R is the correct explanation of A
20. (c) A is true, but R is false
21. (a) Both A and R are true and R is the correct explanation of A
22. (a)
23. (b)
24. (b)
25. (c) Warka Head
26. (d) 3000 BCE
27. (c) Spear
28. (a) represented as syllables.
29. (d) All of the above

Subjective Questions

Short Answer Type Questions

1. What was the direction of archaeological research of Mesopotamia after 1960s?

Ans. Archaeological research in Mesopotamia developed in the nineteenth century. It can be explained in the following ways

- Archaeology in Mesopotamia began in the 1840s. Mesopotamia was important to Europeans because of references to it in the first part of the Bible Old Testament.
- Travellers and scholars of Europe looked on Mesopotamia as a kind of ancestral land and there was an attempt to prove the literal truth of the Old Testament through archaeological work.
- By 1960s, it was understood that the stories of the Old Testament were not literally true. Even archaeological techniques became more sophisticated and refined.
- Attention was given to different questions, including reconstruction of life of ordinary people. Establishing the literal truth of Biblical narratives moved back into the background.

2. What were the significant changes due to urbanism?

Ans. The significant changes due to urbanism were

- **Change in Trade** Apart from food production, other activities like trade, manufacturing and services also become prominent.
- **Division of Labour** City people ceased to be self-sufficient and depend on other people for products or services. For example, a stone seal maker requires bronze tools from a bronze tool maker because he himself cannot make the tools. Similarly, a bronze tool maker will get his raw materials from a merchant. Thus, division of labour became another significant change due to urbanism.

3. What is the need for a social organisation in urban cities?

Ans. The need for a social organisation on urban cities is due to following reasons

- Fuel, metals, various stones, wood, etc. come from many different places for city manufacturers. Thus, organised trade and storage is needed.

- Deliveries of grain and other food items from the village to the city, and food supplies need to be stored and distributed.
- Many activities need to be coordinated and a system is needed where some people command and others obey.

4. Explain the features of the seal, an urban artefact in context of Mesopotamia.

Ans. A number of seals have been excavated from Mesopotamia. Some of the important features of the seal are as follows

- These were made of stone and were cylindrical in shape.
- These seals were fitted with a stick and then rolled over wet clay so that a continuous picture got engraved over it. This work was done by skilled craftsmen.
- The name of the owner, his God, his official, ranks, etc were also engraved on seals.
- Seals were used by merchants to send their goods form one place to another.
- Goods were first packed and a seal was put at the head of the pack to ensure its authenticity.

5. Discuss the importance of efficient transport in urban development.

Ans. The efficient transport system was important for urban development as

- It takes too much time or too much animal feed, to carry grain, charcoal or other goods into cities on back of animals or bullock carts without an efficient transport system.
- The problems in animal transport were that perishable goods like vegetables and fruits become inedible if it takes too much time.
- Very less quantity of goods can be transported and feeding animals for transport was costly and increases the prices of goods.
- Thus, the cheapest mode of transportation i.e. over water was used. Boats loaded with sacks of grain, goods are propelled by the current of the river and wind, without any fuel which makes transportation efficient and thus helping in the urban development.

6. What were the steps taken by the Mesopotamian king to increase his influence and control?

Ans. Following steps were taken by Mesopotamian king to increase his influence and control

- The king himself paid attention towards the well-being of his people.
- To increase his influence, he paid special attention towards the community temple and offer preciously booty to the gods.
- He patronised the settlement of new villages close to his empire.
- Local people were not forced to do the work of temple and begar for the king.
- For the beautification of the temples, king sent men in various directions to collect precious metals and stones. These metals and stones were used by the king to beautify the temples.

All of these king's efforts show that he was very kind towards the need of his people. This helped him to increase his influence and control.

7. Mention some superstitions in which people of Ur believed.

Ans. People of Ur were superstitious about houses. These were recorded in Omen tablets. Some surperstitions were

- They believed that raised threshold i.e. a strip of wood or stone forming the bottom of a doorway brought wealth.
- They believed that a front door that did not open towards another house was lucky.
- They believed that if the main wooden door of house opened outwards, the wife would be a torment to her husband.

8. Discuss the procedure of marriage in the city of Ur.

Ans. The procedure of marriage in the city of Ur was as follows

- A declaration was first made about the willingness to marry by groom's (boy) family.
- Then, the bride's parents give their consent to the marriage.
- Now, a gift was given by the groom's family to the bride's family.
- When the wedding took place, gifts were exchanged by both the families, who ate together and made offerings in a temple.
- Then, mother-in-law would come to bride's house to fetch her. Here, bride was given her share of the inheritance by her father and then, she goes to groom's family.

9. Explain about the communities in the kingdom of Mari. Why were there clashes between the animal herders and farmers of Mari?

Ans. Some communities in the kingdom of Mari had both farmers and pastoralists, but most of its territory was used for pasturing sheep and goats. Herders need to exchange young animals, cheese, leather and meat in return for grain, metal tools, etc., and the manure of a penned flock is also of great use to a farmer.

Animal herders and farmers of Mari were both important to each other, yet there were clashes between them because

- A shepherd may take his flock to water across a sown field, to the ruin of the crop.
- Herdsmen being mobile can raid agricultural villages and seize their stored goods.
- For their part, settled groups may deny pastoralists access to river and canal water along a certain set of paths.

10. Discuss the brief history of Babylonia.

Ans. Babylon was an important city of Mesopotamia. The city was recognised as Babylonia after 2000 BCE and was Southern region of Mesopotmia. A man from the Southern marshes, Nabopolassar released Babylonia from Assyrian domination in 625 BCE. His successors increased their territory and organised building projects at Babylon.

Achaemenids of Iran ruled Babylon afterwards and later in 331 BCE Alexander conquered it. For a long period, Babylon was a leading city of the world with more than 850 hectares area, a triple wall, great palaces, temples, a ziggurat or stepped tower and a pathway for ceremonies leading to the ritual centre.

11. What were the natural man-made problems for agriculture?

Ans. Natural hazards and man-made problems include

- The natural outlet channels of Euphrates would have too much water in an year and this would flood the crops.
- People who live on the upstream stretches of a channel could divert so much water into their fields leaving villages downstream without water.
- People could neglect to clean out the silt from their stretch of their channel, blocking the flow of water further down.

12. 'However rich the food resources of Mesopotamia, its mineral resources were few'. What did Mesopotamians do to overcome this problem? **Competency Based Que**

Ans. Mesopotamia was rich in food resources but its mineral resources were few as

- Most parts of Southern Mesopotamia lacked stones for tools, seals and jewels.
- The wood of the Iraqi date-palm and poplar was not good enough for carts, cart wheels or boats.
- There was no metal for tools, vessels or ornaments.

To solve the problem of mineral resources, ancient Mesopotamians would have traded their abundant textiles and agricultural produce for wood, copper, tin, silver, gold, shell and various stones from Turkey, Iran, or across the Gulf. These regions had mineral resources but much less scope for agriculture.
Thus, both the regions became mutually beneficial to each other.

13. Discuss the system of writing of Mesopotamians and their literacy levels.

Ans. Mesopotamians writing involved cuneiform signs. Cuneiform means wedge-shaped, broad at based and narrow at top. The sound that a cuneiform sign represented was not a consonant or vowel (like s or a in the English alphabets), but syllables (like -put-, or -la-, or -in-). So, the Mesopotamian scribe had to learn hundreds of signs.

The scribe further had to handle a wet tablet and get it written before it dried. This shows system of writing was not only a skilled craft but also a huge intellectual achievement.

As there were hundreds of signs to learn and most of them being complex, very few Mesopotamians could read and write.

14. 'Through Mesopotamian history, nomadic communities of the Western desert filtered into the prosperous agricultural heartland'. Justify the statement and discuss the outcomes of this migration. **Competency Based Que**

Ans. 'Through Mesopotamian history, nomadic communities of the Western desert filtered into the prosperous agricultural heartland'. This statement can be justified in the following ways

- Several nomadic communities from Western desert would come into the rich agricultural region of Mari kingdom. Shepherds would bring their flock into the sown area in the summer. These groups were known as herders, harvest labourers or hired soldiers.
- They occasionally became prosperous and settled down in this region.
- Among them a few gained power to establish their own rule. Some of them are Akkadians, Amorites, Assyrians and Aramaeans.

Thus, one of the important outcomes of this migration was that Mesopotamian society and its culture became open to different people and cultures and thus, strengthening its civilisation with the intermixture.

15. 'Though kingdom of Mari was not militarily strong, it was exceptionally prosperous'. Justify this statement.
Competency Based Que

Ans. The kingdom of Mari was not militarily strong but it was exceptionally prosperous due to its trade related activities which were

- Boats carrying grinding stones, wood, wine and oil jars would stop at Mari on their way to the Southern cities. Officers of this town would inspect the cargo and charge a portion of the value of the goods before allowing boat to continue downstream.
- Barley came in special grain boats. Copper came from 'Alashiya', the islands of Cyprus.
- Bronze which was the main industrial material for tools and weapons was also traded.

Thus, it supports the fact that Mari was not military strong but exceptionally prosperous.

16. List the important findings from the small town at Abu Salabikh.

Ans. Excavations in the small town at Abu Salabikh revealed following interesting facts

- It was about 10 hectares in area in 2500 BCE with population less than 10,000.
- Fossils of different plants and animals were found.
- Partially burnt fish bones were found in the streets.
- Evidences of dung cakes used as fuel and kitchens were identified.
- Living rooms had fewer traces of fossils.
- Pigs roamed freely on streets.
- Some pig bones were found in one house burial and from this we can infer that the dead person might have been given some pork for his nourishment afterlife.
- There were different rooms in a house which were both roofed and also open to sky.

17. Explain how the geographical conditions of Mesopotamian civilisation affect its history.

Ans. The geographical conditions of Mesopotamian civilisation affect its history in the following ways

- Mesopotamia civilisation, flourished on the land lying between the two rivers, the Tigris and Euphrates. This land was very fertile and suitable for agriculture, because water was available in large quantity. Here, the climate was warm and pleasant. Also river had fishes for consumptions.
- In the North of Mesopotamia was a stretch of upland called steppe where animal herding offered people better livelihood.

18. Why is the Mesopotamian civilisation called the 'cradle of civilisation'?

Ans. Mesopotamia is called the cradle of civilisation because it was one of the first regions where cities emerged in around 5000 BCE. Some of the examples of early cities are Uruk and Ur. These cities saw advancements such as the invention of writing, organised governance and structured trade networks.

Mesopotamian societies developed irrigation for agriculture, bronze tools for efficiency and monumental architecture like temples and ziggurats. The division of labour and social organisation enabled the growth of complex societies. These developments set the foundation for future civilisations and contributed to the progress of human culture.

19. How did the development of writing benefit Mesopotamian cities?

Ans. Writing, developed in Mesopotamia around 3200 BCE, played a critical role in urban life. It was initially used to record transactions, such as goods brought into or distributed from temples.

Over time, writing evolved for purposes like legal documentation, communication and preserving stories of kings and gods. It ensured efficient administration in cities, helped maintain trade records, and supported the organisation of resources. The written records also aided in resolving disputes and standardising laws. Writing's intellectual achievements influenced education and cultural continuity for thousands of years.

20. What role did temples play in early Mesopotamian cities?

Ans. Temples in Mesopotamian cities, such as those built around 5000 BCE, were more than places of worship; as they served as administrative and economic hubs. They were seen as the homes of gods and held significant power, controlling agricultural fields, herds and fisheries.

Temples managed food processing, weaving and distribution activities. They employed many people, kept written records and maintained the city's economy. The religious significance of temples also reinforced the authority of city rulers, who offered precious items to gods to gain favour and legitimacy.

21. Why did early Mesopotamian cities rely on trade with distant lands?

Ans. Mesopotamian cities had limited natural resources, with little access to stone, metal, or quality timber. To sustain their economies, they relied on trade to obtain these materials. Agricultural surpluses, especially grains and textiles, were exchanged for copper, tin, gold, silver and precious stones from regions like Turkey, Iran and the Gulf.

This trade supported tool-making, construction, and luxury goods production. Organised trade required efficient transportation systems, such as riverboats and contributed to the development of strong social and administrative systems in cities.

22. How did the invention of the potter's wheel influence Mesopotamian urban life?

Ans. The invention of the potter's wheel around 3000 BCE was a major technological milestone in Mesopotamian urban life. It allowed craftsmen to produce pottery in large quantities and with greater uniformity. Pots were essential for storing and transporting food, water, and other goods, especially in growing cities.

This innovation supported trade and everyday life by meeting the demand for containers. It also demonstrated the increasing specialisation of labour in Mesopotamian cities, as urban economies began to rely on crafts and services alongside agriculture.

Long Answer Type Questions

1. Discuss the geographical features of Mesopotamia. Explain the importance of each region.

Ans. Mesopotamia (present-day Iraq) is a land of diverse environments. The following are its geographical features along with its importance

- In the North-East, there are green, wavy plains which are gradually rising to mountain ranges and are covered with trees, clear streams and wild flowers. This region has enough rainfall to grow crops. Agriculture began between 7000 and 6000 BCE here.
- In the North, there is a stretch of high land called a steppe. This region supports animal herding. After the winter rains, sheep and goats feed on the grasses and low shrubs that grow here.
- To the East, tributaries of the Tigris provide routes of communication into the mountains of Iran.
- In the South, there is a desert. The first cities and writing emerged in this region. The reason for desert supporting growth of cities is because of the presence of rivers Euphrates and Tigris. These rivers carry loads of silt. When water from these rivers is released onto the fields, fertile silt is deposited.
- Euphrates river on entering desert divides into several small channels. These channels were used as irrigation canals. This made Southern Mesopotamian agriculture most productive.
- Apart from agriculture, sheep and goats were also economical in the form of meat, milk and wool in Mesopotamia. Fish was also available in rivers and date palms gave fruit in summer.

2. "Temples evolve into a vital urban institution in Mesopotamian society". How did temples develop in Mesopotamia? What role did temples play in Mesopotamian society? Competency Based Que

Ans. Temples in Mesopotamia developed in the following ways

- Temples have been one of the vital institutions in the civilisation of Mesopotamia. Around 5000 BCE, settlements started developing in Southern Mesopotamia and some of them developed around temples.
- Early settlers began to build and rebuild temples at selected spots in their villages. The earliest known temple was a small shrine made of unbaked bricks.
- Temples were considered as residences of various Gods like Moon (God of Ur) and Inanna (the Goddess of Love and War). These early temples were similar to ordinary houses.
- Over a period of time, these temples which are built using bricks became larger over time. Several rooms were constructed around open courtyards.

The role of temples in Mesopotamian society was as follows

- Temples became more than residences of God after some time.
- Other activities like processing of produce like pressing, grain grinding, spinning and the weaving of woollen cloth was done at temple.
- Temple gradually developed into the main urban institution which is involved in activities like organiser of production, employer of merchants, keeper of written records of distributions and allotments of grain, plough animals, bread, beer, fish, etc.
- Kings started offering precious things to the gods and beautifying the community's temples.
- Kings made temples as centres of welfare institutions. They used to benefit the community by organising and distributing the temple wealth in efficient way.

Thus, the temples evolved from a small house like structures to main urban institution for administration and welfare activities.

3. What was the role of kings in developing cities of Mesopotamia? Explain how kings helped developing temple town Uruk. What were the major achievements made under the guidance of kings?

Ans. Kings have played a major role in developing the cities in Mesopotamia. They encouraged the settlement of villagers close to themselves so that they can get army rapidly.

Kings helped developing temple town Uruk in the following ways

- Kings built a defensive wall around Uruk. War captives and local people were put to work for the temple or directly for the ruler. This was a compulsory condition rather than agricultural tax.
- People who were put to work were paid rations like grain, cloth and oil. It was estimated that one of the temples took 1500 men working 10 hours a day and five years to build.
- Kings used people to effectively build temples. Kings also commanded people to fetch stones, metal ores to make bricks or lay bricks for a temple or send them to long distances to bring suitable materials.
- Kings encouraged many activities and thus there were some technical advances at Uruk around 3000 BCE.

The major achievements under the guidance of kings were

- Architects learnt to construct brick columns as there was no wood to bear the weight of the roof of large halls.
- Hundreds of people were made to work at making and baking clay cones that could be pushed into temple walls, painted in different colours, creating a colourful mosaic.
- Sculpture also had superb achievements. This was done using imported stones. The Warka Head is a classic example in the field of sculpture.
- Another major technological landmark was invention of potter's wheel which enabled mass production.

Thus, king played major role in developing cities of Mesopotamia by achieving major landmarks.

4. What do you know about the town planning of Ur city? Discuss the features of houses, cleanliness and burials in Ur city.

Or **Illustrate the features of town planning in Mesopotamia city of Ur.** **CBSE Diksha**

Ans. **Town Planning in Ur** Ur was one of the earliest cities to have been excavated.

The town planning of the city was done in the following manner

- It had ordinary houses with narrow winding streets. This indicates that even a wheeled cart could not have reached many of the houses.
- Sacks of grain and firewood would have arrived on donkey back to these houses. Narrow winding streets and the irregular shapes of house plots indicate that Ur lacked town planning.
- Ur did not have any street drains like Mohenjodaro. Drains and clay pipes were found in inner courtyards of the Ur houses.
- The house roofs were sloped inwards and rainwater was channelled via the drainpipes into sumps in the inner courtyards. This was done to avoid the unpaved streets from becoming slushy after rainfall.

Houses and Burials in Ur People of Ur were superstitious about houses. They thought that a raised threshold would give them wealth, a front door that did not open towards another house was lucky and if the main wooden door of a house opened outwards, then wife would be a physical and mental torture to husband.

There was a town cemetery at Ur in which the graves of royalty and commoners have been found and some individuals were also buried under the floors of ordinary houses.

Cleanliness in Ur Cleanliness was not well maintained in Ur. People used to sweep all their household waste onto the streets and use to just walk over it. This made streets levels rise over a period of time. In order to keep mud flowing inside the houses after rains, thresholds were also raised. This shows there was lot of patch work in Ur town planning without any future vision.

5. Discuss about following four kings

(i) Gilgamesh **(ii) Zimrilim**
(iii) Assurbanipal **(iv) Nabonidus**

Ans. (i) **Gilgamesh** ruler was mentioned in Gilgamesh epic. He was supposed to have ruled city of Uruk. He was a great hero and expanded his rule far and wide. After a tragic incident in his life i.e. death of his friend, he went to search for secret of immortality across the world but he failed to find one. He returned to city of Uruk and felt comfort in the city which his people had built.

(ii) **Zimrilim** was the king of Mari. The great palace of Mari was the residence of his family, the hub of administration and a place of production especially precious metal ornaments. King used to live a lavish life. It can be inferred from the food list at king's table like flour, bread, meat, fish, fruit, beer and wine which were served in large quantities.

He probably ate in the company of many others. Apart from this, the palace was also very huge with around 260 rooms with an area of 2.4 hectares. There was large courtyards. The king met with foreign dignitaries and his own people in a well decorated huge room.

(iii) **Assurbanipal** was the last Assyrian king who ruled Babylonia during 668-627 BCE. He collected a library at his capital, Nineveh in the North. He made great efforts to gather tablets on history, epics, omen literature, astrology, hymns and poems. He was a great king who preserved the rich literature of knowledge for the future generations.

(iv) **Nabonidus** was the last ruler of independent Babylon. He was a tolerant king and respected Mesopotamian traditions. He consecrates his daughter to office of High Priestess after he was ordered in his dream by the God of Ur. He also repaired the statue of Sargon, king of Akkad which was brought in a broken state to him.

6. "Mesopotamians have made tremendous progress in writing". When and how did writing start in Mesopotamia? Discuss the progress made by the Mesopotamians in field of writing. Competency Based Que

Ans. **Development of Writing in Mesopotamia** It started mostly around 3200 BCE. The first Mesopotamian tablets contained picture-like signs and numbers. These tablets consisted of lists of goods like oxen, fish, bread loaves, etc that were brought into or distributed from the temples of Uruk. This shows that writing began when society needed to keep records of different transactions.

Mesopotamians wrote on tablets of clay. A scribe would wet the clay and mould it into a size, he could hold comfortably in one hand. After carefully smoothening its surfaces, he would then press wedge-shaped signs on to the smoothened surface while it was still moist. This was then dried in the Sun, thus making it hard and indestructible. These hundreds of tablets helped modern historians to discover and reconstruct the Mesopotamian history.

Progress made by Mesopotamians in field of Writing

By 2600 BCE, the letters became cuneiform and the language was Sumerian. Writing was now used not only for keeping records but also for making dictionaries, giving legal validity to land transfers, narrating deeds of kings and announcing the changes a king had made in the customary laws of the land.

After 2400 BCE, Akkadian language replaced Sumerian. Cuneiform writing in the Akkadian language continued to be used until the first century CE. Later from 1400 BCE, Aramic language emerged. This language was similar to Hebrew. It became widely spoken after 1000 BCE. It is still spoken in parts of Iraq.

7. "None of the momentous Mesopotamian achievements would have been possible without writing." Discuss the achievements of Mesopotamians in the field of writing. How did it help the successors and other regions of world? Competency Based Que

Ans. The first Mesopotamian tablets were written around 3200 BCE with picture like signs and numbers.

The various achievements of Mesopotamians in the field of writing were

- Major use of Mesopotamian writing for modern world is that present historians could use these hundreds of written tablets and reconstruct early history.
- They used tablets to keep the record of transactions, make dictionaries, give legal validity to land transfers, narrate the deed of kings and announcing changes a king has made in the customary laws of the land.
- Other major achievement of Mesopotamians was time divisions and mathematics.
- Writing also helped king to send messages to other kings in far distances, thus developing contacts.

Writing helped the successors and others regions of the world in the following ways

- Writing enabled development of science which helped generations of scholars to read and build upon existing knowledge.
- Tablets with multiplication and division tables, square and square-root tables and tables of compound interest helped people to know more about mathematics. They also had information about finding areas and volumes.
- Time divisions developed by Mesopotamians were adopted by the successors of Alexander and then transmitted to the Roman world, then world of Islam and to medieval Europe.
- Mesopotamians also noted and recorded observations on solar and lunar eclipse. They also recorded the observed positions of starts and constellations in the night sky. This later helped people to develop more on astronomy.

- Writing encouraged the establishment of urban institutions like schools where students were shaped into future intellectuals who could build on the work of their predecessors.

8. Give an estimate of the Sumerian Civilisation of Mesopotamia.

Ans. The Sumerian Civilisation was the first to flourish in Mesopotamia. Some of the main features of this civilisation are as follows

- **Political Life** There were many city states. King had to perform many duties; and he ruled with the help of other officials.
- **Economic Life** Their main occupations were agriculture, domestication of animals and trade. They were skilled craftsmen. They cultivated wheat and barley and also invented the wheel.
- **Art** Introduction of columns, vaults and arch; Ornamentation of temples and buildings. Various crafts were found there.
- **Social Life** The Sumerian society was divided into classes. Slavery prevailed there and women occupied high position.
- **Religious Life** They worshiped many Gods. Their building of temples was called Ziggurat. They had belief in life after death. Priests occupied high position in their society.
- **Literature** Their literature consisted of stories, songs, epics, hymns.
- **Science** They had done great progress in mathematics, astronomy, astrology and medicine.

Source Based Questions

Read the sources given below and answer the following questions.

1. The Warka Head

This woman's head was sculpted in white marble at Uruk before 3000 BCE. The eyes and eyebrows would probably have taken lapis lazuli (blue) and shell (white) and bitumen (black) inlays, respectively. There is a groove along the top of the head, perhaps for an ornament. This is a world-famous piece of sculpture, admired for the delicate modelling of the woman's mouth, chin and cheeks. And it was modelled in a hard stone that would have been imported from a distance.

(i) What was the Warka Head? What was it made of?

(ii) List different materials used for eyes and eyebrows of Warka Head. Why was there a groove along the top of the head?

(iii) In which city was Warka Head sculpted? Why was it admired?

Ans. (i) The Warka Head was a world famous piece of sculpture of a woman's head. It was made of white marble.

(ii) Different material like Lapis lazuli, shell and bitumen were used for eyes and eyebrows of Warka Head. The groove along the top of the head was perhaps for an ornament.

(iii) The Warka Head was sculpted in Uruk before 3000 BCE. It was admired for delicate modelling of the woman's mouth, chin and cheeks.

2. The Seal – An Urban Artefact

In India, early stone seals were stamped. In Mesopotamia until the end of the first millennium BCE, cylindrical stone seals, pierced down the centre, were fitted with a stick and rolled over wet clay so that a continuous picture was created.

They were carved by very skilled craftsmen, and sometimes carry writing: the name of the owner, his god, his official position, etc. A seal could be rolled on clay covering the string knot of a cloth package or the mouth of a pot, keeping the contents safe.

When rolled on a letter written on a clay tablet, it became, mark of authenticity. So the seal was the mark of a city dweller's role in public life.

(i) What kind of seals were used in Mesopotamia until the end of first millennium BCE?

(ii) What did seal carry in writing? What was the importance of seal?

(iii) How were contents of seal kept safe?

Ans. (i) Cylindrical stone seals were used in Mesopotamia until the end of first millennium BCE. They were pierced down the centre fitted with a stick so that they were rolled over wet clay and a continuous picture was created.

(ii) The seal carried the name of the owner, his god, his official position, etc. The seal was important as it was the mark of a city dweller's role in public life.

(iii) A seal was rolled on clay covering the string knot of a cloth package or the mouth of a pot, thus keeping the contents safe.

3. The Palace at Mari of King Zimrilim (1810–1760 BCE)

The great palace of Mari was the residence of the royal family, the hub of administration and a place of production, especially of precious metal ornaments. It was so famous in its time that a minor king came from North Syria just to see it, carrying with him a letter of introduction from a royal friend of the king of Mari,

Zimrilim. Daily lists reveal that huge quantities of food were presented each day for the king's table: flour, bread, meat, fish, fruit, beer and wine. He probably ate in the company of many others, in or around courtyard, paved white.

You will notice from the plan that the palace had only one entrance, in the North. The large, open courtyards were beautifully paved. The King would have received foreign dignitaries and his own people in Audience hall, a room with wall paintings that would have awed the visitors. The palace was a sprawling structure, with 260 rooms and covered an area of 2.4 hectares.

(i) **What was great palace of Mari used for? How many entrances does the palace has and in which direction?**

(ii) **What was mainly produced in great palace of Mari?**

(iii) **What were the varieties of food that king had each day? Whom did king receive in Audience hall?**

Ans. (i) It was residence of the royal family, hub of administration and a place of production. Palace had only one entrance, in the North.

(ii) Precious metal ornaments were produced in the great palace of Mari.

(iii) King had on his table a variety of food such as flour, bread, meat, fish, fruit, beer and wine. King received foreign dignitaries and his own people in Audience hall.

4. Excavating Mesopotamian Towns

Today, Mesopotamian excavators have much higher standards of accuracy and care in recording than in the old days, so that few dig huge areas the way Ur was excavated. Moreover, few archaeologists have the funds to employ large teams of excavators. Thus, the mode of obtaining data has changed. Take the small town at Abu Salabikh, about 10 hectares in area in 2500 BCE with a population less than 10000. The outlines of walls were at first traced by scraping surfaces.

This involves scraping off the top few millimetres of the mound with the sharp and wide end of a shovel or other tool. While the soil underneath was still slightly moist, the archaeologist could make out different colours, textures and lines of brick walls or pits or other features. A few houses that were discovered were excavated.

The archaeologists also sieved through tons of earth to recover plant and animal remains, and in the process identified many species of plants and animals and found large quantities of charred fish bones that had been swept out on the streets. Plant seeds and fibre remained after dung cakes had been burned as fuel and thus kitchens were identified. Living rooms were those with fewer traces.

Because they found the teeth of very young pigs on the streets, archaeologists concluded that pigs must have roamed freely here as in any other Mesopotamian town. In fact, one house burial contained some pig bones – the dead person must have been given some pork for his nourishment in the afterlife! The archaeologists also made microscopic studies of room floors to decide which rooms in a house were roofed (with polar logs, palm leaves, straw, etc) and which were open to the sky.

(i) **Name the town discussed in source. Discuss briefly about it.**

(ii) **Give the meaning of the word 'sieve'.**

(iii) **Why did burial contain some pigbones?**

Ans. (i) Abu Salabikh is the name of the town discussed in the source. It is about 10 hectares in area with a population less than 10,000.

(ii) Sieve is a tool with mashes through which finer particles of a mixture of various sizes passed to separate them.

(iii) Pigbones in the burial inferred that the dead person must have been given some pork for his nourishment in the afterlife.

5. An Early Library

In the Iron Age, the Assyrians of the North created an empire, at its height between 720 and 610 BCE, that stretched as far as West as Egypt. The state economy was now a predatory one, extracting labour and tribute in the form of food, animals, metal and craft items from a vast subject population.

The great Assyrian kings, who had been immigrants, acknowledged the Southern region, Babylonia, as the centre of high culture and the last of them, Assurbanipal (668-627 BCE), collected a library at his capital, Nineveh in the North. He made great efforts to gather tablets on history, epics, omen literature, astrology, hymns and poems. He sent his scribes South to find old tablets. Because scribes in the South were trained to read and write in schools where they all had to copy tablets by the dozen, there were towns in Babylonia where huge collections of tablets were created and acquired fame. And although Sumerian ceased to be spoken after about 1800 BCE, it continued to be taught in schools, through vocabulary texts, sign lists, bilingual (Sumerian and Akkadian) tablets, etc.

So even in 650 BCE, cuneiform tablets written as far back as 2000 BCE were intelligible – and Assurbanipal's men knew where to look for early tablets or their copies.

Copies were made of important texts such as the Epic of Gilgamesh, the copier stating his name and writing the date. Some tablets ended with a reference to Assurbanipal:

'I, Assurbanipal, king of the universe, king of Assyria, on whom the gods bestowed vast intelligence, who could acquire the recondite details of scholarly erudition, I write down on tablets the wisdom of the gods... And I checked and collated the tablets. I placed them for the future in the library of the temple of my god, Nabu, at Nineveh, for my life and the well-being of my soul, and to sustain the foundations of my royal throne...'. More important, there was cataloguing: a basket of tablets would have a clay label that read: 'n number of tablets about exorcism, written by X'. Assurbanipal's library had a total of some 1,000 texts, amounting to about 30,000 tablets, grouped according to subject.

(i) Why was state economy predatory one?

(ii) Which region was centre of high culture?

What kind of tablets were gathered by Assurbanipal?

(iii) How was Sumerian taught in schools?

Ans. (i) State economy was predatory one because state extracted labour and tribute in the form of food, animals, metal and craft items from a vast subject population.

(ii) The Southern region Babylonia was centre of high culture.

Tablets on history, epics, omen literature, astrology, hymns and poems were gathered by Assurbanipal. He sent his scribes in the South to collect old tablets.

(iii) Gradually Sumerian language ceased to be spoken after about 1800 BCE, but it continued to be taught in schools. This language was taught through vocabulary texts, sign lists, bilingual tablets (Sumerian and Akkadian language).

6. And, an Early Archaeologist!

A man of the Southern marshes, Nabopolassar, released Babylonia from Assyrian domination in 625 BCE. His successors increased their territory and organised building projects at Babylon. From that time, even after the Achaemenids of Iran conquered Babylon in 539 BCE and until 331 BCE when more than 850 hectares, with a triple wall, great palaces and temples, a ziggurat or stepped tower and a processional way to the ritual centre. Its trading houses had widespread dealings and its mathematicians and astronomers made some new discoveries.

Nabonidus was the last ruler of independent Babylon. He writes that the God of Ur came to him in a dream and ordered him to appoint a priestess to take charge of the cult in that ancient town in the deep south. He writes: 'Because for a very long time the office of High Priestess had been forgotten, her characteristic features nowhere indicated, I bethought myself day after day...' Then, he says, he found the stele of a very early king whom we today date to about 1150 BCE and saw on that stele the carved image of the Priestess. He observe the clothing and the jewellery that was depicted. This is how he was able to dress his daughter for her consecration as Priestess.

On another occasion, Nabonidus's men brought to him a broken statue inscribed with the name of Sargon, King of Akkad.(We know today that later ruled around 2370 BCE.) Nabonidus and indeed many intellectuals, had heard of this great king of remote times. Nabonidus felt he had to repair the statue. 'Because of my reverence for the gods and respect for kingship,', he writes, 'I summoned skilled craftsmen and replaced the head'.

(i) Who released Babylonia from Assyrian domination? Which other group conquered Babylon?

(ii) Describe Babylon city.

(iii) Why did Nabonidus appoint a priestess?

Ans. (i) Nabopolassar, a man from Southern marshes released Babylonia from Assyrian domination. Achaemenids of Iran in 539 BCE conquered Babylon.

(ii) It was a premier city of the world. Its area was more than 850 hectares, with a triple wall, great palaces and temples, a stepped tower and a pathway for ceremonies to the ritual centre.

(iii) Nabonidus appointed a priestess because God of UR came to Nabonidus in a dream and ordered him to appoint a priestess to take charge of the cult in Babylon in the deep South.

Map Based Questions

1. **Identify the following locations marked in the map of West Asia given below.**

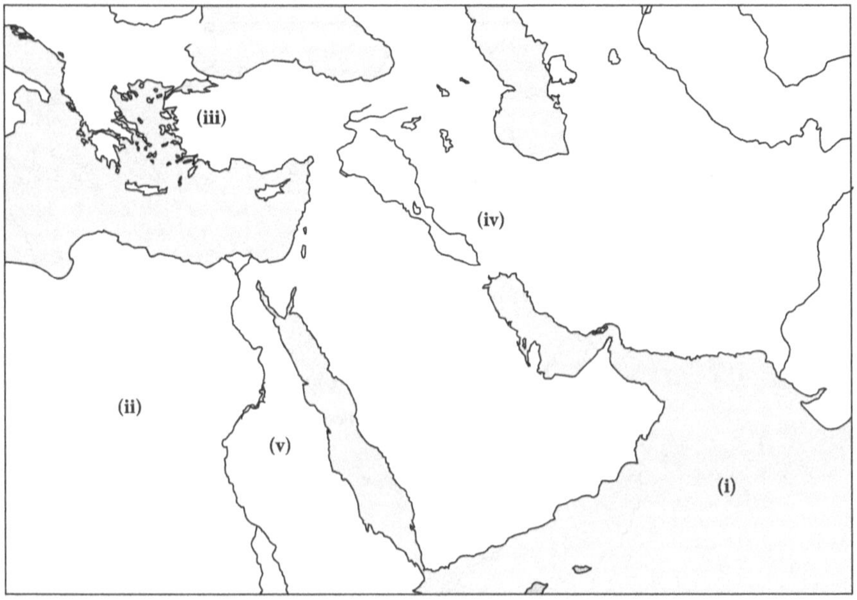

Ans.

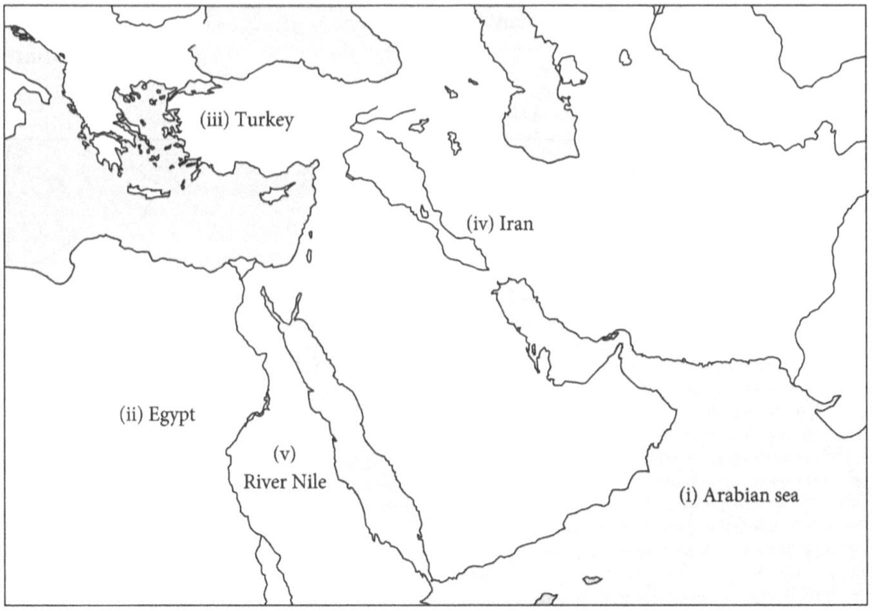

2. Point the following locations on a map of West Asia.

(i) Mediterranean Sea (ii) Black Sea (iii) Caspian Sea (iv) Red Sea
(v) Persian Gulf

Ans.

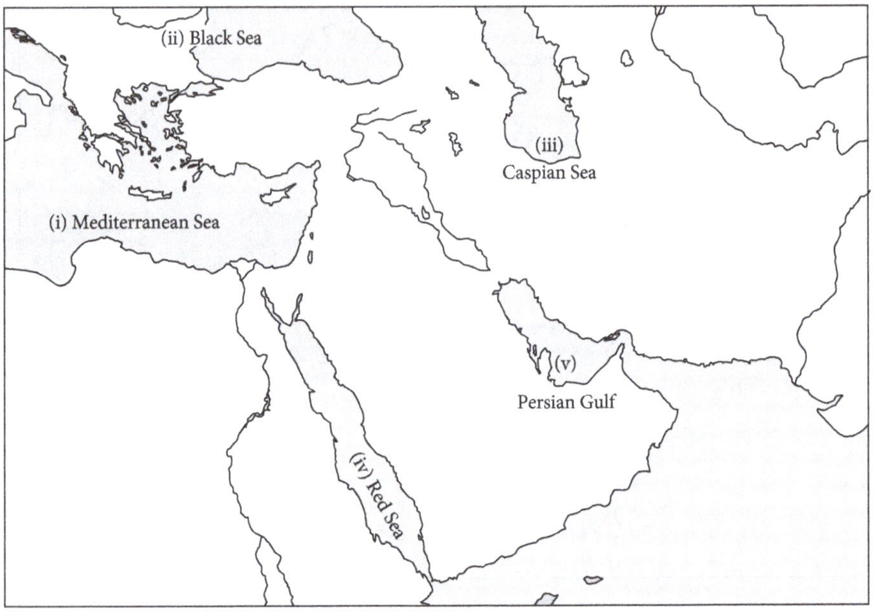

3. Point the following locations on map of Mesopotamia.

(i) Mari (ii) Uruk (iii) Ur (iv) Nimrud
(v) Babylon

Ans.

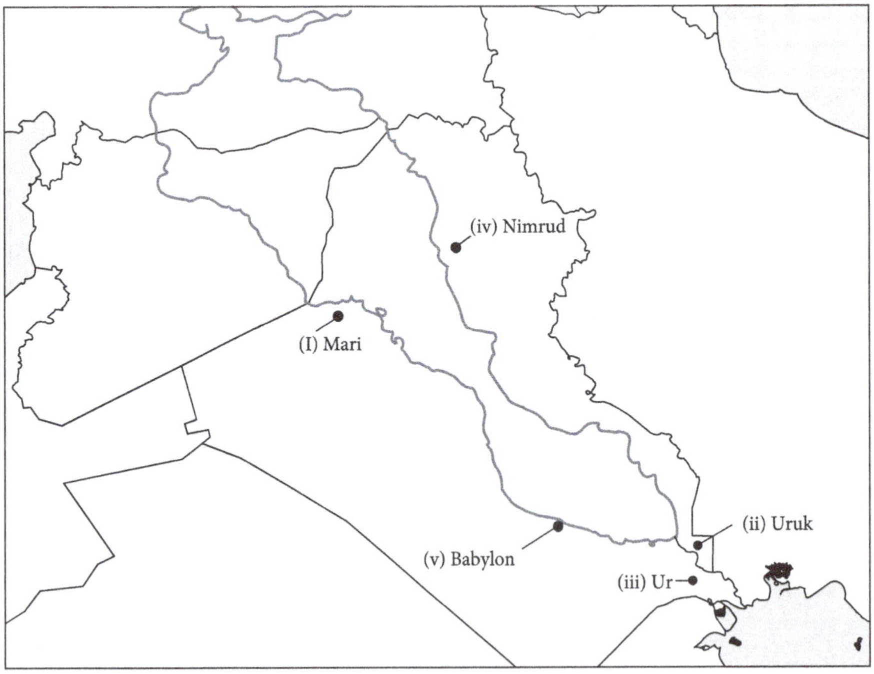

SELF ASSESSMENT TEST

Objective Type Questions

1. Who was the last ruler of Babylon city?
   (a) Nobopolassar (b) Nabonidus (c) Alexander (d) None of these
2. .... was a king of Mesopotamia.
   (a) Enmerker (b) Zimrilim (c) Gilgamesh (d) All of these
3. In Mesopotamia, the .... family was the norm.
   (a) nuclear (b) joint (c) patriarchal (d) None of these
4. What type of communities filtered into Mesopotamia?
   (a) Urban communities (b) Nomadic communities
   (c) Maritime communities (d) Agricultural communities
5. Who were put to work for the temple or the ruler?
   (a) Only local people (b) War captives and local people
   (c) Only skilled artisans (d) Only farmers
6. Match the following.

	List I		List II
A.	First writing in Mesopotamia	1.	2600 BCE
B.	Development of the Cuneiform script	2.	5000 BCE
C.	Earliest temples in Southern Mesopotamia	3.	3200 BCE
D	Alexander conqueres Babylon	4.	331 BCE

Codes

	A	B	C	D
(a)	3	1	2	4
(b)	2	4	1	3
(c)	3	1	4	2
(d)	4	2	1	3

Short Answer Type Questions

7. The division of labour is a mark of urban life in Mesopotamian city. Justify the statement.
8. Discuss the sources available to understand Mesopotamian civilisation.
9. Some of the early temples in Mesopotamia were possibly not unlike the ordinary house. Discuss.
10. Examine how the greatest legacy of Mesopotamia to the world is its scholarly tradition of time reckoning.
11. Examine the features and importance of Mesopotamian seals.

Long Answer Type Questions

12. Mesopotamians valued city life in which people of many communities and cultures lived side by side. Justify the statement.
13. Mesopotamian society and culture were thus open to different people and cultures. Discuss.
14. Although the kingdom of Mari was not militarily strong, it was exceptionally prosperous. Explain.
15. Discuss the features of the houses that were systematically excavated in the 1930s in the town of Ur.
16. Explain the story on the development of Mesopotamian writing.

SECTION B EMPIRES

TIMELINE II (C. 100 BCE to 1300 CE)

This timeline focuses on kingdoms and empires. Some of these such as the Roman empire were very large, spreading across three continents. This was also the time when some of the major religious and cultural traditions developed. It was a time when institutions of intellectual activity emerged. In this period books were written and ideas travelled across the continents. Some things that are now part of our everyday lives, were used for the first time during this period.

2
CHAPTER

This chapter discusses the organisation of the Roman Empire, its political forces and social groups. The Roman Empire covered a vast territory, including most of Europe, the Fertile Crescent and North Africa. The empire declined in the West from the 5th century but remained prosperous in the East.

YOUR STUDY GOALS

2.1 Archaeological Sources of the Roman Empire
2.2 Geography of the Roman Empire
2.3 Phases of the Roman Empire
2.4 Early Roman Society
2.5 Economy of Early Roman Empire
2.6 Late Roman Empire (Late Antiquity)

YOUR PRACTICE GOAL

- Objective Type Questions (25 Qs ; MCQs, A-R, Matching, Picture Based)
- Subjective Questions (23 SAs, 8 LAs)
- Source Based Questions (3 Qs)
- Map Based Questions (4 Qs)

An Empire Across Three Continents

- Two major empires, **Rome** and **Iran** (the Parthians and later the Sasanians), dominated Europe, North Africa, and the Middle East between the birth of Christ and the 7th century.
- These two superpowers were rivals, separated by a narrow strip of land along the Euphrates river.
- The Roman Empire was much more diverse as compared to Iran, which was predominantly Iranian in population.
- Iran controlled the region from South of the Caspian Sea to Eastern Arabia and parts of Afghanistan.
- These superpowers divided most of the world. They were referred to as "Ta Ch'in" (greater Ch'in) by the Chinese.

2.1 Archaeological Sources of the Roman Empire

Roman historians used a rich collection of sources that can be divided into three categories

1. Textual Sources

- These include histories, letters, speeches, sermons and laws.
- **'Annals'** were the histories that were written year-by-year by contemporaries.

▲ *Papyrus Scrolls*

2. Documentary Sources

- These include inscriptions on stone (many survived in Greek and Latin).
- These also include papyri, writing material made from the **papyrus**[1] plant of the Nile river.
- Documents like contracts, accounts, letters, and official records on papyrus have been studied by "papyrologists."

3. Material Sources/Remains

- These include structures like buildings, monuments, pottery, coins, mosaics, and landscapes discovered by archaeologists.

2.2 Geography of the Roman Empire

- The **Mediterranean** Sea was the central region of the Roman Empire. It separates the continents of Europe and Africa.
- The Mediterranean stretches from Spain in the West to Syria in the East. Rome controlled all the regions around the Mediterranean, both to the North and South.
- The **Northern boundary** of the Roman Empire is formed by two major rivers which are **Rhine river** and **Danube river**.
- The **Southern boundaries** of the empire extended to the large **Sahara Desert** in North Africa.

▲ *Roman Empire from North Africa*

2.3 Phases of the Roman Empire

- There were two phases of the Roman Empire
  1. **Early Empire** The whole period of the third century.
  2. **Late Empire** From the third century to the end of the empire.

1 **Papyrus** It was a reed-like plant that grew along the banks of the Nile in the Egypt and was processed to produce a writing material.

The Early Roman Empire

- **Augustus** became the first emperor and established the regime called the "Principate" (early Roman regime) in 27 BCE.
- Though Augustus was the sole ruler, Roman records portrayed him as the "*Princeps*" (leading citizen) and not an absolute ruler.
- The **Senate** controlled Rome earlier when it was a **Republic**[2].

Organisation of the Empire

There were three main bodies in the Roman Empire. The **Emperor** and the **Senate** were at the top, and next to them was the **Army**. The emperor used to work in close association with the Senate.

Senate and Aristocracy

- The **Senate**[3] represented the **aristocracy**[4], including the wealthiest families and later, mainly landowners of Italian descent.
- Most of the Roman histories were written by people from the senatorial class.
- The emperors were criticised when they were hostile (rude) to the Senate.

Role of the Army in Roman Empire

- Unlike the Persian empire's **conscripted**[5] army, the Roman army was professional. It required the soldiers to serve for at least 25 years.
- By the fourth century, the army numbered 600,000 had the power to influence the fate of emperors.
- The soldiers often protested for better wages and service conditions. These protests often resulted in small-scale wars.
- The Senate hated and feared the army because it was a source of violence.
- An emperor's success often depended on his control of the army and when the armies were divided, it led to a **civil war**[6]. In 69 CE, a civil war occurred where four emperors took the throne one after the other.

Succession in Roman Empire

- The succession to the throne was generally based on **family descent**, either natural or through adoption.
- The army was strongly attached to the principle of succession. For example, **Tiberius** (14-37 CE), the second emperor, was adopted by Augustus to ensure a smooth transfer of power although he was not his natural son.

Warfare and Expansion

- External wars were less common during the first two centuries of the Roman Empire because the empire inherited by Tiberius from Augustus was already so large.
- The "**Augustan Age**" was a time of *peace* that came after a long period of wars and conquests.
- The only major attempt to expand the Roman Empire during the early period was made by Emperor **Trajan**. He conquered lands across the Euphrates river from 113 to 117 CE. However, his successors later gave up these lands.

---

2 **Republic** It was the name of the regime in which the real power was with the Senate, a small body of wealthy families who formed the nobility.

3 **Senate** Senate was a council of elders or important citizens who advised rulers and helped make decisions.

4 **Aristocracy** The highest social class in some countries which typically owns land and traditionally have more money and power than the other people in society.

5 **Conscripted** It is an army which is forcibly recruited as military service is mandatory for certain groups of people.

6 **Civil war** It refers to armed struggles for power within the same country, in contrast to conflicts between different countries.

Expansion of Roman Direct Rule

- Rome slowly grew in size by taking control of nearby kingdoms from the Near East[7] and turning them into Roman provinces.
- By the early second century, kingdoms West of the Euphrates were annexed into Roman territory. These kingdoms were extremely wealthy. For example, Herod's kingdom generated 5.4 million *denarii* per year (approximately 1,25,000 kg of gold).
- All territories except Italy were organised into provinces and subjected to taxation.
- In the second century, the Roman Empire became very large. It stretched from **Scotland** in the West to **Armenia** in the East and from **the Sahara** in the South to the **Euphrates** in the North.

Rise and Shift of Power to the Provinces

- The biggest cities of the empire, such as **Carthage, Alexandria** and **Antioch**, became the real base of the imperial system.
- The government collected taxes from the provincial countryside through the cities, which brought a lot of money to the empire.
- The local upper classes helped the Roman state in administration. They administered their own territories and collected taxes from them.
- By the second and third centuries, *provincial* elites supplied much of the administrative and military manpower.
- This new elite (local upper class) became more powerful than the senatorial class, and were supported by the emperors.
- Emperor **Gallienus** excluded senators from serving in the army and commanding military forces, to prevent them from controlling the empire.

▲ *Pont du Gard, near Nimes, France, first century BCE*

- In the late first, second and the third centuries, the Roman army and administration were largely composed of people from the provinces.

Cities of the Roman Empire

- A Roman city was an urban centre with its own magistrates, city council, and a territory containing villages under its jurisdiction.
- No city was within another city's territory.
- Villages could be upgraded to cities and vice versa.
- People living in cities usually had better access to food during shortages and famines compared to those living in rural areas.
- Roman engineers constructed massive infrastructure, including bridges to transport water, such as the **Pont du Gard** in France.
- Other features of urban life included public baths and higher levels of entertainment. For example, *spectacula* (shows) organised for atleast 176 days of the year.

The Third-Century Crisis

- From the 230s, the empire faced multiple threats, both internal and external.

Sasanian Threat

- The new Sasanian dynasty in Iran which emerged in 255 CE, rapidly expanded towards the Euphrates.

7 Near East From the perspective of someone who lived in the Roman Mediterranean, this referred to all the territory East of the Mediterranean,chiefly the Roman provinces of Syria, Palestine and Mesopotamia and in a looser sense the surrounding territories, for example Arabia.

- A famous rock inscription claimed that **Shapur I**, the Sasanian (Iranian) ruler, killed 60,000 Roman soldiers and captured Antioch, the empire's Eastern capital.

Invasions by Tribal Groups

- Tribes such as the **Alamanni,** the **Franks** and the **Goths** attacked the empire's borders along the Rhine and Danube.
- Between 233-280 CE, repeated invasions occurred along the provinces from the Black Sea to the Alps and Southern Germany.
- The Romans had to give up much of the land beyond the Danube river because tribal leaders, whom they called barbarians, fought against them.

Rapid Succession of Emperors

- The third century saw rapid changes in emperors, contributing to instability across the empire.
- Almost 25 emperors in 47 years were changed, due to which there was tension in this period.

Quick Test 1

1. Name three continents in which the Roman Empire was present.
2. Who was the first emperor of the Roman Empire?
3. What was the nature of succession?
4. Name three biggest urban centres of the Roman Empire.
5. Which emperor excluded senators from military command?

2.4 Early Roman Society

- The Roman Empire comprised diverse territories and cultures, unified by a common government.
- **Greek** and **Latin** were the primary administrative languages. Upper class people of the East preferred *Greek* and those from the West preferred *Latin.*
- All subjects within the empire were under the emperor's rule, regardless of language or location.

Family and Marriage

- The **Nuclear Family**[8] was more common in Roman households.
- Adult sons typically did not live with their families, and adult brothers rarely shared households.
- Slaves were considered part of the family unit.
- By the first century BCE, wives retained full rights to their family property even after marriage.
- Men married in their late twenties to early thirties, while women typically married in their late teens to early twenties, creating a gender age gap.
- Marriages were often arranged, leading to male dominance over women.
- **Divorce** was easy through a simple notice from either the husband or wife.
- Fathers had significant legal control over their children. This included the power to decide their fate by leaving unwanted infants to die.

Position of Women

- Women had significant legal rights to own and manage property.
- A woman's dowry was controlled by her husband during marriage, but this did not impact her status as her father's heir.

8 Nuclear Family A small family consisting of a mother, father and their children.

- Upon her father's death, she became an independent property owner.
- A married couple was not considered a single financial entity. The husband and wife remained two separate individuals, with the wife having full legal independence.

Literacy

- The use of reading and writing varied across different parts of the Roman Empire. This is evident from archaeological evidence from **Pompeii**[9], which was buried in a volcanic eruption in 79 CE.
- Walls on main streets often had advertisements. Graffiti (writing or drawings on walls) were found throughout the city.
- In Egypt, formal documents like contracts were typically written by professional scribes. These documents gave information about who could not read or write.
- Literacy was more common in Egypt among soldiers, army officers and estate managers.

Cultural Diversity

The empire was culturally rich, it had following features

- Numerous religious cults and local deities.
- A variety of languages.
- Diverse clothing styles and food.
- Different social organisations (tribal/non-tribal) and settlement patterns.

Language

Dominant languages in the Roman Empire included the following

- Aramaic in the Near East
- Coptic in Egypt
- Punic and Berber in North Africa
- Celtic in Spain and the North-West

Many of these linguistic cultures were mainly oral until a writing system was developed. For example, Armenian began to be written only in the fifth century, while a Coptic translation of the Bible existed by the third century. Additionally, the spread of Latin replaced the written forms of other widely spoken languages, such as Celtic, which stopped being written after the first century.

Social Hierarchies in Early Roman Empire

- Tacitus, a senator and historian of the Roman Empire described the leading social groups of the early empire as follows
  - **Senators (Fathers)** The most prestigious social group.
  - **Equestrian Class (Knights or horsemen)** Leading members of Roman society.
  - **Respectable Citizens** People attached to prominent houses.
  - **Lower Class (Untidy Class)** People addicted to circus and theatrical displays; included slaves.
- By the early 3rd century, half of the senators were from Italian families.
- By the reign of Constantine I in the 4th century, the senators and equestrian class had merged into a unified aristocracy. Half of this new aristocracy were of African or Eastern origin.
- Late Roman aristocracy was wealthy but less powerful than military elites. **Military elites** mostly came from non-aristocratic families.
- The Middle Class consisted of people in imperial service, including bureaucrats, soldiers, merchants, and farmers from Eastern provinces. Tacitus described the middle class as clients of great senatorial houses.
- Middle Class families depended on government service and state support.

9 Pompeii A wine merchant's dining room which had walls decorated with paintings of mythical animals.

- Lower Class (***Humiliores***) included the rural labour force, workers in industrial and mining sectors, migrant workers for harvesting and construction, self-employed artisans, casual labourers in cities, and thousands of slaves, particularly in Western regions.

Income and Corruption of Higher Classes

- The late Roman bureaucracy (both higher and middle ranks) was wealthy, receiving salaries in gold. They invested most of their income in buying land.
- **Olympiodorus**, a 5th-century historian and ambassador, stated that Roman aristocrats had annual incomes of up to 4,000 lbs (1,814 kg) of gold.
- Corruption was widespread, especially in the judicial system and the administration of military supplies.
- Higher bureaucrats and provincial governors often forced people for personal gain.

State and Civil Rights

- The Roman government introduced laws to control corruption.
- Historians and intellectuals actively criticised corrupt practices.
- The Roman state was authoritarian and did not tolerate disagreement and the government usually responded to protests with violence.
- Public **mockery**[10] of emperors was common, particularly in the East, without fear of punishment.
- By the 4th century, a strong tradition of **Roman law** had evolved, allowing some criticism, which limited the power of even the most cruel emperors.
- The law actively protected **civil rights**[11] and bishops like Ambrose openly challenged emperors when they treated civilians too harshly.

Quick Test 2

1. What languages were spoken in Egypt?
2. What did the walls of Pompeii city carry?
3. Who discussed the social groups of the Roman Empire?
4. Name the bishop who confronted powerful emperors.

2.5 Economy of Early Roman Empire

- The Roman Empire had a highly developed economy and advanced technology, contradicting the common belief that it was a backward society.
- Water power was used in many ways across the Mediterranean, and water-powered milling technology improved significantly.
- The empire also used hydraulic mining techniques, especially in Spain's gold and silver mines, with large-scale industrial operations taking place in the first and second centuries.
- There was a well-organised banking and commercial network. There was widespread use of money.

Economic Infrastructure

- The Roman Empire had important economic infrastructure including harbours, mines, quarries, brickyards and olive oil factories.
- Major trade commodities included wheat, wine and olive oil. They mainly came from Spain, Gallic provinces, North Africa, Egypt and Italy.

---

10 **Mockery** Behaviour or speech that makes fun of someone or something in a hurtful way.
11 **Civil rights** Civil rights protect an individual's right to equal social opportunities and equal protection under the law.

- Wine and olive oil were transported in containers called **amphorae.**
- Archaeological remains of over 50 million vessels were found at **Monte Testaccio** in Rome.
- By studying these containers, historians learned about their shapes, what they were used for, and where they were made.
- They examined the composition of the clay in artefacts and matched it with clay from various locations around the Mediterranean. This helped them figure out the origin of the objects.

Olive Oil Economy

- Olive oil production became a large-scale industry, reaching its height around 140-160 AD.
- It was mainly carried in containers called **Dressel 20.**
- Spanish producers took over markets that were once led by Italian olive oil makers.
- The success of Spanish olive growers was later matched by North African producers.
- After 425 AD, regions like Aegean, Southern Asia Minor, Syria and Palestine became major exporters of olive oil and wine.

Regions of Fertility and Wealth

- **Campania (Italy)** was famous for producing some of the finest wines in the empire.
- **Sicily** was known for its significant wheat production, with large quantities exported to Rome.
- **Galilee** was densely cultivated, indicating its rich agricultural output.
- **Byzacium (Tunisia)** was another major wheat-producing region that exported wheat to Rome.
- **Southern Gaul (Gallia Narbonensis)** and **Fayum (Egypt)** were among the most populated or wealthiest parts of the empire.
- **Baetica (Southern Spain)** was famous for producing Spanish olive oil, which came from numerous estates along the banks of the **Guadalquivir river**.

Underdeveloped Regions

- Some region of Roman Empire remained less developed, either due to geography or the socio-economic practices of their inhabitants.
- In Numidia (modern-day Algeria), the area was mostly focused on raising animals. People practised **transhumance**[12], which means they moved their livestock seasonally. These local pastoral communities often travelled with their oven-shaped huts known as *mapalia.*
- After the Roman Empire expanded into North Africa, the movements of pastoralists were limited, and their grazing lands became smaller.
- Even in Spain, the North was less developed and mainly inhabited by **Celtic-speaking peasants** living in hilltop villages called *castella.*

Slavery and Labour

- Slavery was deeply established in the ancient world, including the Mediterranean and the Near East.
- By the reign of **Augustus**, there were about **3 million slaves** in Italy, out of a population of 7.5 million.

12 Transhumance It is the herdsman's regular annual movement between the higher mountain regions and low-lying ground in search of pasture for sheep and other flocks.

- With the decline of warfare and peace in the 1st century, the supply of slaves decreased.
- Slave owners began depending on **slave breeding**[13] or cheaper alternatives like **wage labour**.
- Maintaining slaves became costly as they had to be fed and supported the whole year, unlike hired labourers.
- In the Eastern provinces, the use of slaves in agriculture declined because it became economically unsustainable.
- Freed slaves often ran businesses or served as business managers where large numbers was not required.

Management of Labour

- Roman writers were more interested in management of labour.
- **Columella**, a 1st-century writer from Spain, advised landowners to keep extra stock of tools to maintain continuous production, despite the decline in slave labour.
- Close supervision of slaves and free workers was emphasised to ensure productivity.
- Workers were often grouped into smaller teams (e.g., groups of 10), which made supervision easier.
- **Pliny the Elder**, the author of **Natural History**, criticised the use of slave gangs as an inefficient method of production, where slaves were often chained together by their feet.

Conditions of Labour

- In Alexandrian **frankincense**[14] factories, strict rules were enforced. The aprons of workers were sealed, they had to wear a mask or a tight net on their heads and before leaving, they had to remove all their clothes.
- Many Egyptian peasants left their villages to avoid agricultural labour. A law from 398 mandated that workers be branded for identification if they tried to escape.
- Employers sometimes used **debt contracts** to keep control over workers. The workers also had to give them money.
- Some poor families entered **debt bondage** for survival. In some cases, parents sold their children into bondage for up to 25 years.
- Widespread rural debt was a significant issue. For example, during the **Jewish revolt of 66 CE**, revolutionaries destroyed **moneylenders' bonds** to gain popular support.
- Most of the labourers were not forced to work, for example, **Emperor Anastasius** built the **city of Dara** in less than three weeks by offering high wages, which attracted workers from all over the East.
- By the 6th century, wage labour had become common in the Mediterranean, particularly in the East.

Quick Test 3

1. What are the containers called that carried wine and oil?
2. How many vessels were found at Monte Testaccio in Rome?
3. What is Dressel 20?
4. What are Mapalia?
5. Which emperor built the Eastern frontier city of Dara?

---

13 Slave Breeding The practice of encouraging female slaves and their partners to have more children, who would also be slaves.
14 Frankincense The European name for an aromatic resin used in incense and perfumes.

2.6 Late Roman Empire (Late Antiquity)

▲ *Part of a Colossal Statue of Emperor Constantine*

- Late **Antiquity** refers to the final phase in the evolution and break-up of the Roman Empire between the 4th and 7th centuries.
- Significant cultural and economic changes characterised the 4th century. **Emperor Constantine** made Christianity the official religion, and Islam rose in the 7th century.

Changes in the Structure and Economy of the State

Diocletian's Reforms

- Emperor Diocletian (284-305 CE) initiated significant structural changes.
- He made the empire smaller by giving up land that wasn't very important for strategy or the economy.
- He fortified the empire's boundaries and separated civilians from military functions, granting more autonomy to military commanders (*duces*).

Monetary and Economic Adjustments

- The Spanish silver mines were depleted, leaving the government without enough silver to maintain a stable currency.
- Emperor Constantine responded by introducing a new denomination called the ***solidus***[15]. It was minted in large quantities, which restored monetary stability.
- Constantinople (modern-day Istanbul in Turkey and previously called Byzantium) was created as a new capital. This required a new Senate and increased number of people in government.
- The Roman economy grew due to monetary stability and a growing population. Key areas of investment included
  - **Rural establishments** and **industrial installations** such as oil presses and glass factories.
  - **New technologies** like screw presses and multiple water-mills.
  - Re-establishment of **long-distance trade** with the East.

Outcomes of Changes

- There were advancements in architecture and an increased sense of luxury.
- The ruling elites became wealthier and more powerful.
- Documents like the Egyptian papyri show that money was widely used, and rural estates generated vast incomes in gold.
- Some regions, particularly in the Near East, became more developed and densely populated than that of the 20th century.

Cultural Developments

- Roman and Greek religious traditions were **polytheistic**[16], with numerous gods like Jupiter, Juno, Minerva and Mars, and many of temples across the empire.
- Judaism was another great religious tradition in the empire. Judaism was not a **monolith**[17] as there was a great diversity within the Jewish communities of late antiquity.

---

15 **Solidus** A coin of 4.5 gm of pure gold.

16 **Polytheistic** Believing in or worshipping multiple gods.

17 **Monolith** It was literally a large block of stone, but here it is used to refer to anything (for example a society or culture) that lacks variety and is something which is of the same type.

- The **Christianisation**[18] of the empire occurred gradually during the 4th and 5th centuries.
- Powerful church leaders, called bishops, enforced strict rules and beliefs on their followers. This created differences between different religious groups, which did not exist before.

Division of the Empire: East and West

Eastern Empire

- The Eastern Empire saw prosperity, and its population grew into the 6th century, even though the Mediterranean plague hit in the 540s.
- The reign of **Justinian** (527-565 CE) was marked by imperial ambitions and prosperity. Justinian recaptured Africa from the Vandals in 533 CE and Italy from the Ostrogoths, though this left Italy damaged and made it easier for the Lombards to invade.
- By the 7th century, the Sasanians started a large-scale invasion of the Eastern provinces, including Egypt.
- The Roman Empire, now called **Byzantium**, recovered these provinces in the 620s CE, but later face further challenges from the South-East.

Western Empire

- The West went through political division. Germanic groups like the Goths, the Vandals and the Lombards took control of important regions.
- The Visigoths in Spain were destroyed by the Arabs between 711 and 720 CE.
- The Franks in Gaul (511-687 CE) and the Lombards in Italy (568-774 CE) were notable post-Roman kingdoms that started the beginnings of the medieval world.

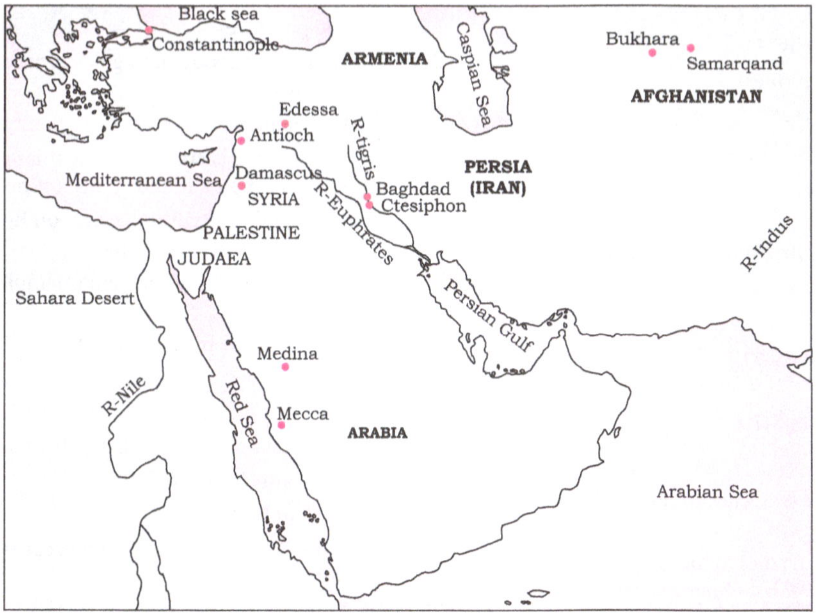

▲ *West Asia*

The Rise of Islam

- One of the most significant political revolutions in the ancient world was the expansion of **Islam**, which began in Arabia.
- By 642 CE, ten years after the death of Prophet Muhammad, large areas of the Eastern Roman Empire and the Sasanian Empire were taken over by the Arabs.

18 **Christianisation** The process by which Christianity spread among different groups of the population and became the dominant religion.

- Islamic conquests expanded into Spain, Sind and Central Asia in the following centuries. The unification of the Arabian peninsula and its various tribes played an important role in this expansion.

Quick Test 4

1. Who made Christianity the official religion?
2. Why did the state not support a stable coin age in silver?
3. What is solidus?
4. Name some Roman/Italian Gods.
5. What is the reign of Justinian known for?

TIMELINE

Time Period	Ruler
27 BCE - 14 CE	Augustus, first Roman emperor
14 - 37 CE	Tiberius
98 - 117 CE	Trajan
117 - 138 CE	Hadrian
193 - 211 CE	Septimius Severus
241 - 72 CE	Shapur I (Sasanian ruler)
253 - 68 CE	Gallienus
284 - 305 CE	Diocletian (Tetrarchy)
309 - 79 CE	Shapur II (Sasanian ruler)
312 - 37 CE	Constantine the Great
354 - 430 CE	Augustine, Bishop of Hippo
408 - 50 CE	Theodosius II
434 - 453 CE	Attila the Hun
493 CE	Ostrogoths established kingdom in Italy
490 - 518 CE	Anastasius
527 - 65 CE	Justinian
531 - 79 CE	Khusro I (Sasanian ruler)
610 - 41 CE	Heraclius
661 - 750 CE	Umayyad dynasty in Syria

Time Period	Event
27 BCE	'Principate' founded by Octavian (later called Augustus)
24 - 79 CE	Life of the Elder Pliny; dies in the eruption of Mount Vesuvius (79 CE), which also buries Pompeii
66 - 70 CE	The great Jewish revolt and capture of Jerusalem by Roman forces
115 CE	Roman Empire reaches its greatest extent under Trajan
212 CE	All free inhabitants of the Roman Empire granted citizenship
224 CE	Founding of the Sasanian Dynasty in Iran by Sasan
250s CE	Persian invasions of Roman territories West of the Euphrates
258 CE	Cyprian bishop of Carthage executed
260s CE	Gallienus reorganises the power of the Roman army
273 CE	Romans destroy the caravan city of Palmyra
297 CE	Diocletian reorganises the Roman Empire into 100 provinces
310 CE	Constantine issues new gold coinage (solidus)
312 CE	Constantine converts to Christianity
324 CE	Constantine becomes the sole ruler of the Roman Empire; founds Constantinople
378 CE	Goths inflict a crushing defeat on Roman armies at the Battle of Adrianople
391 CE	Destruction of the Serapeum (temple of Serapis) at Alexandria
410 CE	Sack of Rome by the Visigoths
428 CE	Vandals capture Africa
533 - 550 CE	Recovery of Africa and Italy under Justinian
541 - 570 CE	Outbreaks of bubonic plague (Justinian Plague)
568 CE	Lombards invade Italy
570 CE	Birth of Muhammad
614-19	Ruler Khusro II invades and occupies Eastern Roman territories
622 CE	Muhammad and companions leave Mecca for Medina
633 - 642 CE	Muslim armies conquer Syria, Palestine, Egypt, Iraq and parts of Iran
698 CE	Arabs capture Carthage
711 CE	Arab invasion of Spain

Mind Map

AN EMPIRE ACROSS THREE CONTINENTS

1 The Early Roman Empire

Beginning of New Empire
- Augustus was the first emperor of Roman empire, who was also known as the 'Principate'.
- Borders of Roman empire stretched from Scotland to Armenia and Sahara to Euphrate.
- Latin and Greek languages were used in administration.

Senate and Army
- Senate was a republican institution before the reign of 'Augustus'.
- Romans had a large standing army, where 25 years of service was mandatory for soldiers.

2 The Third Century Crisis

Emergence of New Kingdom
- Sassanian dynasty emerged around 225 AD in Iran.
- Shapur I (Iranian ruler) defeated Romans and captured Antioch.

3 Early Roman Society

Family and Marriage
- Nuclear family structure with patriarchy.
- Females had legal rights in their natal family.
- Dowry system was prevalent.
- Dissolution of marriage was done through 'divorce'.

Development in Language & Script
- Language like Aramaic, Coptic and Celtic were spoken in different parts of empire.
- Armenian began to be written in 5th century.
- Latin replaced other written languages.
- Celtic was stopped being written after 1st century.
- Bible was translated to Coptic language in middle of 3rd century.

4 Economy of Early Roman Empire

- Pastoral community lost their control on pasture lands due to expansion in Roman territory.
- Wheat, wine and olive oil were traded between different regions.
- Trade monopoly of regions was challenged with the development of newer areas.
- Containers like 'Amphorae' and 'Dressel-20' were used for transportation of liquid.

5 Controlling Workers

Rise of Wage Labour
- High wages attracted labour for large projects.
- Wage labour became more prevalent by the 6th century, especially in the East.

Changes in Slavery and Labour
- Slaves who had been set free by their masters were appointed as 'Business Manager' for the expansion of businesses.
- Both free workers and enslaved were supervised for growth of businesses.

6 Social Hierarchy

- 1st century onwards, silver currency was replaced by Gold currency.
- The social classes in the Roman Empire included senators, equites, middle class, lower class and slaves.
- Middle class included officials, merchants & farmers.
- Lower class included labourers, artisans and slaves.
- Roman law protected civil rights and limited the powers of emperors.

7 Late Roman Empire (Late Antiquity)

Changes in Structure and Economy of the State
- Christanity become official religion of Iran in 4th century and Islam in 7th century.
- Large part of Roman empire was captured by Islamist rulers in mid 7th century AD.
- New Gold coin 'Solidus' was introduced by Shapur II, king of Iran.

Cultural Developments
- The classicial world's traditional religion was polytheism.
- There was great diversity among Jewish communities of late antiquity.
- Christianisation of the empire in 4th and 5th century was a gradual complex process.

NCERT Folder

Intext Questions

1. Who were the three main players in the political history of the Roman Empire? Write one or two lines about each of them. And how did the Roman emperor manage to govern such a vast territory? Whose collaboration was crucial to this?

Ans. The emperor, the aristocracy and the army were the three main players in the political history of the Roman Empire. These are discussed below

(i) **Emperor** It was the highest authority in the empire and all those living in the empire were subjects of a single ruler, the emperor, regardless of where they lived and what language they spoke. The success of individual emperors depended on their control of the army.

(ii) **Aristocracy** The senate was a body representing the aristocracy. They were the wealthiest families of Roman. They hated and feared the army, because it was a source of violence.

(iii) **Army** The army was the largest single organised body in the empire and it had power to determine the fate of the emperors. Soldiers often agitated (worried) for better wages and service conditions.

Roman emperor managed to govern such a vast territory by organising all the territories into provinces, subjected to taxation. Urbanisation helped emperor to govern such a vast territory easily. It was through the cities that government was able to tax the provincial countrysides which generated much of the wealth of the empire.

Collaboration of the provincial upper classes with emperor was crucial to the governance. They supplied most of the cadre that governed the provinces and commanded the armies.

2. How independent were women in the Roman world? Compare the situation of the Roman family with the family in India today.

Ans. Women in Roman world enjoyed more independence than they do in many countries today. After marriage, she was not under husband's authority and retained full rights in the property of her natal family. Women remained primary heir of their father and became an independent property owner on their father's death. Husband and wife were not one financial entity and women enjoyed complete legal independence.

The comparison between the Roman family and the Indian family are as follows

Roman Family	Indian Family (Present)
Prevalence of nuclear family.	More nuclear families but still has significant joint families.
Adult sons did not live with their families and do not share common household.	Adult sons stay with their families till marriage and share common household.
Slaves were included in the family.	There is no concept of slaves in India.
Prevalence of domestic violence.	Domestic violence is a major social problem in India as well.
Father had more legal control over their children.	Both mother and father have legal control over the children.

3. Archaeologists who work on the remains of pottery are a bit like detectives. Can you explain why? Also, what can amphorae tell us about the economic life of the Mediterranean in the Roman period?

Ans. Archaeologists who work on the remains of the pottery are a bit like detectives. Detectives collect evidence, they reconstruct the crime scene, proceed further by connecting the dots and infer through the available evidence. Similarly, archaeologists also excavate evidence through fossils like documents, remains of artefacts, monuments, etc and reconstruct the history and lifestyle of the people and societies. They also infer and assume from collected evidence and build the history with a logical conclusion. Thus, we can say that archaeologists are a bit like detectives.

Amphorae were containers in which liquid wine and olive oil were transported. In a place called Monte Testaccio in Rome, the remains of 50 million vessels (amphorae) were found. This shows that economic life of the Mediterranean in the Roman period was very prosperous and widespread.

4. The text has referred to three writers whose work is used to say something about how the Romans treated their workers. Can you identify them? Re-read the section for yourself and describe any two methods the Romans used to control labour.

Ans. The three writers were Columella, Elder Pliny and Augustine. Their work gave a lot of information about how Romans treated their workers.

The two methods used by the Romans to control labour were

(i) Workers were grouped into gangs or smaller teams.

(ii) A seal was put upon the worker's clothes and they had to wear a mask or a net with a close mesh on their heads and before leaving the factory premises, they had to take off all their clothes.

Answer in Brief

1. If you had lived in the Roman Empire, where would you rather have lived – in the towns or in the countryside? Explain why.

Ans. If I had lived in the Roman Empire, I would like to live in the towns because

- Towns are better provided with food during shortages and famines.
- There is a lot more scope for entertainment in urban centres.
- There is more scope for economic prosperity in towns.

2. Compile a list of some of the towns, cities, rivers, seas and provinces mentioned in this chapter, and then try and find them on the maps. Can you say something about any three of the items in the list you have compiled?

Ans. The compiled list of some of the towns, cities, rivers, seas and provinces are as follows

Towns and Cities	Tangiers, Rome, Naples, Carthage, Spain, Hipponium, Constantinople, Ephesus, Antioch, Damascus, Alexandria and Fayyum.
Rivers	Rhine, Danube, Nile and Guadalquivir.
Seas	Mediterranean sea, Adriatic sea, Aegean sea, Ionian sea, Black sea and Red sea.
Provinces	Gaul, Aquitania, Campania, Macedonia, Egypt, Cyrenaica, Tripolitania, Tunisia, Africa, Proconsularis, Numidia, Morocco, Baetica and Hispania.

Mediterranean Sea

- Rome dominated the sea and all the regions around the sea in both direction, North as well as South.
- The great urban centres of Roman Empire were located on the shores of the Mediterranean.
- Enormous trade activities were carried across the Mediterranean sea.

Spain

- Spain was one of the major towns of Roman Empire.
- Spanish olive oil was traded in huge amounts and circulated very widely. Success of Spanish olive growers encouraged people of other regions.
- Spain had huge gold and silver mines which were used for coinage.

Constantinople

- It was surrounded by sea on three sides.
- Constantine created a second capital at Constantinople (site of modern Istanbul in Turkey).
- Later, Arab empire took control of areas centered on Constantinople.

3. Imagine that you are a Roman housewife preparing a shopping list for household requirements. What would be on the list?

Ans. My shopping list would include

(i) Olive oil, wheat to make bread, wine and other vegetables and meat.

(ii) Containers and vessels needed for storing and cooking food.

(iii) Clothes and ornaments.

(iv) Tickets to spectacula (entertainment shows).

4. Why do you think the Roman government stopped coining in silver? And which metal did it begin to use for the production of coinage?

Ans. The Roman government stopped coining in silver because Spanish silver mines were exhausted and government ran out of sufficient stocks of the metal to support a stable coinage in silver.

Gold metal began to be used for the production of coinage which was started by Constantine and was called solidus.

Answer in a Short Essay

5. Suppose the emperor Trajan had actually managed to conquer India and the Romans had held on to the country for several centuries. In what ways do you think India might be different today?

Ans. Some of changes that might have happened in India if the emperor Trajan had managed to conquer India and the Romans held on to the country are

- **Language** Greek and Latin would have been part of the languages of India and just like we are learning English today, we would have learnt Greek and Latin too.
- **Slavery** It would have been introduced in India.

- **Art and Architecture** Roman style of buildings, monuments and art would have been present in India and must have influenced the local architecture and art.
- **Religion** Christianity and other gods related to Roman culture would have come to India at an early stage.
- **Food Habits** There would be an influence on dietary habits of Romans on Indians.
- **Economics** Our trading activities would have been more diverse.
- **Institutions** Institutions like senate would have influenced present Indian polity.

6. Go through the chapter carefully and pick out some basic features of Roman society and economy which you think make it look quite modern.

Ans. Some of the basic features of Roman society were

- Widespread prevalence of nuclear family.
- Adult sons did not live with the family and it was exceptional for brothers to share a common household.
- Slaves were considered as a part of family.
- Wife was not under husband's authority after marriage. She retained full rights in the property of her natal family. Women enjoyed complete legal independence.
- Marriages were arranged and divorce was a very easy process.
- Roman Empire was diverse with different cults, cultures, gods, languages and tribes.
- There were social hierarchies present. Food habits, residence patterns were dependent on to the class one belonged.
- There were public baths and spectacula (shows) for entertainment.

Basic features of Roman economy were

- Roman economy has got great infrastructure of harbours, mines, quarries, brickyards, olive oil factories, etc.
- Wheat, wine and olive oil were traded and consumed in huge quantities.
- Olive oil industry was one of the prosperous one of Roman economy. There was competition between regions to capture the markets for the goods they produced.
- It also had many regions with exceptional fertility. Wine and olive oil came from these regions.
- It had advanced technologies like water-powered milling technology, use of hydraulic mining techniques, well organised commercial and banking networks and wide spread use of money.

From the above, we can say that nuclear family, multiculturalism, sources for entertainment, women rights, advanced technologies, banking and use of money make Roman Empire look quite modern.

Exam Pattern Questions

Objective Type Questions

Multiple Choice Questions (MCQs)

1. .... was the first emperor, who established the regime in ....

(a) Augustus, 20 BCE (b) Augustus, 27 BCE
(c) Tiberius, 30 BCE (d) None of these

2. The three main players in the Roman Empire were ....

(a) the emperor (b) the aristocracy
(c) the army (d) All of these

3. .... refers to armed struggles for power within the same country, in contrast to conflicts between different countries.

(a) Revolution (b) War
(c) Civil War (d) None of these

4. Carthage, Alexandria and Antioch were the biggest .... of the Roman Empire.

(a) temples (b) Churches
(c) urban centres (d) None of these

5. A conscripted army is

(a) one which is forcibly recruited
(b) militarily service is compulsory for certain groups
(c) Both (a) and (b)
(d) None of the above

6. The Colosseum built in .... where gladiators fought wild beasts.

(a) 79 CE (b) 85 CE
(c) 90 CE (d) 95 CE

7. **Ancient Roman/Italian God(s) was/were**

(a) Jupiter, Juno (b) Minerva
(c) Mars (d) All of these

8. **Constantine converts to Christianity in ....**

(a) 312 CE (b) 322 CE (c) 332 CE (d) 342 CE

9. **Prophet Muhammad died in ....**

(a) 632 CE (b) 642 CE (c) 652 CE (d) 662 CE

10. **Which of the following statement is not true?**

(a) The Roman state was an authoritarian regime.
(b) The Roman law had emerged by the fifth century.
(c) The Roman law was actively used to protect civil rights.
(d) Emperors were not free to do whatever they liked.

11. **Identify the object.**

(i) It was a reed-like plant.
(ii) It grew along the banks of the Nile in Egypt.
(iii) It was processed to produce a writing material.
(iv) It was very widely used in everyday life.

(a) Papyrus (b) Birch (c) Palm (d) Oak

12. **Identify the city.**

(i) It was a city which was buried in a volcanic eruption in 79 CE.
(ii) Walls of the main streets of it often carried advertisements.
(iii) Graffiti were found all over the city.

(a) Carthage (b) Pompeii
(c) Anchoa (d) Alexandria

13. **Identify the term.**

(i) They were the ordinary members of a religious community as opposed to the priests or clergy.
(ii) They have official positions within the community.

(a) Piazza (b) Mapalia (c) Laity (d) Monolith

14. **Identify the saint from the information given below.**

(i) He was the great Catholic bishop.
(ii) He was bishop of the North African city of Hippo from 396 CE.
(iii) His mother was regularly beaten by his father.

(a) Saint Justinian (b) Constantine
(c) Tibarius (d) Saint Augustine

15. **Identify the writer from the information given below.**

(i) He was a first-century writer.
(ii) He came from the South of Spain.
(iii) He recommended that landowners should keep a reserve stock of implements and tools.

(a) Seheca (b) Pliny (c) Columella (d) Lucan

16. **Container to store olive oil : Dressel 20 : : Containers used to transport liquid : ....**

(a) Amphorae (b) Ourries
(b) Harbour (d) Fundi

17. **Silver coins : .... : : Gold coin : Solidus**

(a) Duces (b) Denarius
(b) Aurous (d) Stater

Assertion-Reason

18. **Assertion (A)** From the second century BCE, Rome was a republic.

Reason (R) Government in Rome was based on a complex system of election and gave importance to birth, wealth and slavery.

Codes

(a) Both A and R are true and R is the correct explanation of A
(b) Both A and R are true, but R is not the correct explanation of A
(c) A is true, but R is false
(d) A is false, but R is true

19. **Assertion (A)** Nuclear family was common in Roman society.

Reason (R) Adult sons did not live with their families and it was exceptional for adult brothers to share a common house hold.

Codes

(a) Both A and R are true and R is the correct explanation of A
(b) Both A and R are true, but R is not the correct explanation of A
(c) A is true, but R is false
(d) A is false, but R is true

Match the Following

20.

List I	List II
A. Augustus	1. Built the city of Dara
B. Anastasius	2. First emperor
C. Constantine	3. Separated civilian from military functions
D. Diocletian	4. Introduced new denomination called Solidus

Codes

	A	B	C	D		A	B	C	D
(a)	3	1	2	4	(b)	2	1	3	4
(c)	2	1	4	3	(d)	4	2	1	3

21.

List I	List II
A. Conscripted	1. Forcibly recruited army
B. Mapalia	2. Ordinary members of a religious community
C. Laity	3. Oven-shaped huts

Codes

	A	B	C		A	B	C
(a)	3	1	2	(b)	2	1	3
(c)	2	3	1	(d)	1	3	2

Picture Based Questions

22. Identify the building shown in image below.

(a) Pont du Gard (b) Corinth
(c) Shops in Forum Julium (d) Spectacula

23. What are the objects in the picture called?

(a) Pompeii (b) Frankincense
(c) Mapalla (d) Amphorae

24. Which of the following emperor has been depicted in the image below?

(a) Augustus (b) Constantine
(c) Tiberius (d) Anastasius

25. The below image shows the picture of the colosseum built in the centre of Rome. It belongs to ....

(a) 88 CE (b) 53 CE
(c) 79 CE (d) 98 CE

Answers

1. (b) Augustus, 27 BCE
2. (d) All of these
3. (c) Civil War
4. (c) urban centres
5. (c) Both (a) and (b)
6. (a) 79 CE
7. (d) All of these
8. (a) 312 CE
9. (a) 632 CE
10. (b) The Roman law had emerged by the fifth century.
11. (a) Papyrus
12. (b) Pompeii
13. (c) Laity
14. (d) Saint Augustine
15. (c) Columella
16. (a) Amphorae
17. (b) Denarius
18. (b) Both A and R are true, but R is not the correct explanation of A
19. (a) Both A and R are true and R is the correct explanation of A
20. (c)
21. (d)
22. (a) Pont du Gard
23. (d) Amphorae
24. (b) Constantine
25. (c) 79 CE

Subjective Questions

Short Answer Type Questions

1. Explain about republic in context of Roman Empire. When was it overthrown?

Ans. The republic was the name for a regime in which the reality of power lay with the Senate, a body dominated by a small group of wealthy families who formed the 'nobility'.

- In practice, the Republic represented the government of the nobility, exercised through the body called the Senate.
- The Republic lasted from 509 BC to 27 BC.
- The Republic was overthrown by Octavian in 27 BC. He was the adopted son and heir of Julius Caesar, who later changed his name to Augustus.
- The regime established by Augustus was known as principate. In his reign, the Senate remained as a body representing the aristocracy.

2. Discuss about the boundaries of Roman Empire. Also write the major difference between Roman and Iranian empires?

Ans. **Boundaries of Roman Empire** The Mediterranean sea which stretches from Spain in the West to Syria in the East and separates continents of Europe and Africa was the heart of Roman's Empire. Rome dominated the Mediterranean and all the regions around the sea in both directions, North as well as South. In the North, boundaries are formed by two great rivers, the Rhine and the Danube. In the South, boundaries are formed by huge expanse of the Sahara desert.

Differences between Roman and Iranian Empires
The major difference between the Roman and Iranian empires is that

- The Roman Empire was culturally much more diverse than that of Iran.
- The Parthians and later the Sasanians dynasties that ruler over Iran only ruled over a population that was largely Iranian. Whereas, the Roman Empire, by contrast, was a mosaic of territories and cultures that were chiefly bound together by a common system of government.

3. Why was external warfare less common? Name one major campaign by Roman emperor.

Ans. External warfare was much less common in the first two centuries. This is because

- The empire inherited by Tiberius from Augustus was already so vast that further expansion was felt to be unnecessary.
- The 'Augustan age' was remembered for the peace after a lot of internal strife and centuries of military conquests in the past decades.
- The first two centuries were on the whole free from Civil Wars and thus remained relatively stable.

The only major campaign of expansion in the early empire was Trajan's occupation of territory across the Euphrates which was abandoned by his successors in the years 113-17 CE.

4. Explain about the gradual extension of Roman direct rule.

Ans. The gradual extension of Roman direct rule was accomplished by absorbing a whole series of dependent kingdoms from near East into Roman provincial territory. By early second century, kingdoms which were West of the Euphrates were captured up by the Rome.

These kingdoms were extremely wealthy. For example, Herod's kingdom yielded 5.4 million denarii (a Roman silver coin containing about 4½ gm of pure silver) per year, equal to over 125,000 kg of gold. All the territories of the empire except Italy were organised into provinces and subjected to taxation. During its peak in the second century, the Roman empire stretched from Scotland to the borders of Armenia and from the Sahara to the Euphrates and sometimes beyond.

5. The great urban centres that lined the shores of the Mediterranean were the true bedrock of the imperial system. Discuss **Competency Based Que**

Ans. The great urban centres that lined the shores of the Mediterranean (Carthage, Alexandria, Antioch were the biggest among them) were the true bedrock of the imperial system as

- The cities allowed the government to tax the surrounding countryside, which generated much of the empire's wealth.
- The local upper classes actively collaborated with the Roman state in administering their own territories and raising taxes from them.
- The provincial upper classes provided most of the leaders who governed the provinces and commanded the armies during the second and third centuries. They came to form a new elite of administrators and military commanders who became much more powerful than the senatorial class because they had the support of the emperors.

6. If the first and second centuries were a period of peace, prosperity and economic expansion, the third century brought the first major signs of internal strain. Comment. Competency Based Que

Ans. The third century brought the first major signs of internal strain as

- From the 230s CE, the empire found itself fighting on several fronts simultaneously.
- In Iran, a new and more aggressive Sasanian dynasty emerged in 225 CE and within just 15 years, they were expanding rapidly in the direction of the Euphrates.
- The whole period from 233 to 280 CE saw repeated invasions of a whole line of provinces that stretched from the Black Sea to the Alps and southern Germany.
- The Romans were forced to leave much of the territory beyond the Danube, while the emperors of this period were constantly in the field against what the Romans called 'barbarians'.
- The rapid succession of emperors in the third century shows the challenges the empire was facing in this period

7. Large expanses of Roman territory were in a much less advanced state. Discuss. Competency Based Que

Ans. Large expanses of Roman territory were in a much less advanced state in the following ways

- The herdsman's regular annual movement (transhumance) was widespread in the countryside of Numidia (modern Algeria). These pastoral and semi-nomadic communities were often on the move, carrying their oven-shaped huts (called mapalia) with them.
- As Roman estates expanded in North Africa, the pastures of those communities were drastically reduced and their movements more tightly regulated.
- Even in Spain, the North was much less developed and inhabited largely by a Celtic-speaking peasantry that lived in hilltop villages called castella.

8. Why were public baths not present in Iran? What were the sources of entertainment for Romans?

Ans. Public baths were a striking feature of Roman urban life, but they were not present in Iran. One of the Iranian rulers tried to introduce public baths in Iran but he faced the wrath of the clergy (Church persons) present there. They believed that water was a sacred element and to use it for public bathing was disrespectful to them.

Romans enjoyed a much higher level of entertainment. Amphitheatres were used for military drill and for staging entertainments for the soldiers. For example, one calender tells us that spectacula organised for atleast 176 days of the year.

9. Discuss about the literacy in Roman Empire.

Ans. The rates of casual literacy varied greatly between different parts of the empire. For instance, in Pompeii there was a strong evidence of widespread casual literacy. Walls on the main streets of Pompeii often carried advertisements, and graffiti were found all over the city.

On the other hand in Egypt, the formal documents such as contracts written by professional scribes tell us who can read and write. Here literacy was widespread among certain categories such as soldiers, army officers and estate managers.

10. Who were equites? What change occurred with equites during reign of Constantine I?

Ans. The equites were the knights or horsemen who were traditionally the second most powerful and wealthy group. Originally, they were families whose property qualified them to serve in the cavalry (troops riding horses), hence they got the name. Like senators, most knights were landowners but unlike senators, many of them were also shipowners, traders and bankers i.e they were involved in business activities.

The change occurred with equites during the reign of Constantine I in the early part of fourth century was that the equites and the senators had merged into a unified and expanded aristocracy.

11. Slavery was an institution deeply rooted in the ancient world. Comment. Competency Based Que

Ans. Slavery was an institution deeply rooted in the ancient world both in the Mediterranean and in the Near East. Even though, Christianity emerged and become the state religion, it did not seriously challenge slavery. Bulk of labour work in the Italy during Republican period was performed by slaves.

Under Augustus regime, there were 3 million slaves in a total Italian population of 7.5 million. Slaves were considered as part of investment and some writers advised against their use as it was uneconomical, because they were supposed to be taken care of and fed by owners unlike waged labourers. Slavery declined when warfare declined and much cheaper substitutes such as wage labours came into prominence.

12. What were the reasons for the decline of slavery?

Ans. There were multiple reasons for the decline of slavery in the Roman Empire. They were

- It became uneconomical for landowners to maintain too many slaves by feeding and maintaining them throughout the year.
- As wars declined and peace prevailed, supply of slaves reduced which made people to substitute them with slave breeding and wage labourers.

- Public works in Rome were extensively done by wage labourers, as they were cheaper compared to slaves.
- Most of the slaves were also set free by their masters and made them their business managers to run their businesses.

13. Why was the late Roman bureaucracy comparatively an affluent group? What was the role of corruption in Roman Empire? How did government intervene?

Ans. The late Roman bureaucracy, both the higher and middle ranks was comparatively an affluent group. The reason was that they drew bulk of their salary in gold and invested much of this in buying up assets like land.

There was a great deal of corruption in Roman empire, especially in the judicial system and in the administration of military supplies. The extortion of the higher bureaucracy and the greed of the provincial governors were well known across the empire.

Government intervened repeatedly to curb different forms of corruption by bringing in different laws. Even historians and intelligentsia criticised corrupt practices which acted as detriment to bureaucracy and others.

14. Explain the following terms

(i) Monolith **(ii) Christianisation**

(iii) Laity

Ans. (i) **Monolith** It means literally a large block of stone, but it can also be used to refer to anything such as a society or culture that lacks variety and is all of the same type.

(ii) **Christianisation** It is the process by which Christianity spread among different groups of the population and became the dominant religion.

(iii) **Laity** It refers to the ordinary members of a religious community as opposed to the priests or clergy who have official positions within the community.

15. How did Roman cities treat the countryside?

Ans. The Roman cities treated the countryside or villages in the following ways

- Villages were converted to cities as a mark of imperial favour and cities to villages as a mark of punishment. This shows villages were considered subordinate to cities.
- During famines, city people were provided with enough food supplies and the countryside was totally neglected.
- The city dwellers as a part of their custom used to collect and store enough grain for the whole of the next year immediately after the harvest. They would carry away all the wheat, barley, beans and lentils from the peasants in countryside. They used to leave peasants different kinds of pulses after taking a large proportion of these to the city. This shows cities discriminated and exploited the countryside during the Roman rule.

16. There were important changes in the structure of the state beginning with the Emperor Diocletian. Justify the statement. Competency Based Que

Ans. Steps taken by Diocletian in changing the structure of the state of Roman empire were

- Over-expansion of empire had led Diocletian to cut back by abandoning some territories with little strategic or economic value.
- He also fortified the boundaries, reorganised provincial boundaries and separated civilian from military functions by granting greater autonomy to the military commanders.

Steps taken by Constantine in changing the structure of the state of Roman empire were

- He introduced a new denomination called the solidus. It is a coin of 4.5 gm of pure gold. These coins were minted on large scale and their circulation ran into millions.
- He created a second capital at Constantinople (at the site of modern Istanbul in Turkey) surrounded by sea on the three sides.

17. Discuss about the Western and Eastern parts of the empire during late antiquity.

Ans. In the West, empire was fragmented politically as Germanic groups like Goths, Vandals, Lombards, etc from North took over all the major provinces and established kingdoms. The most important among these were Visigoths in Spain, Franks in Gaul and Lombards in Italy. These kingdoms indicated the beginnings of medieval world.

In the East, empire remained united and reign of Justinian was considered high watermark of prosperity and imperial ambition. He recaptured Africa and Italy. In third century, Sasanians of Iran launched a wholesale invasion on all the major Eastern provinces. All these provinces were recovered in 620s CE by Roman empire.

18. Discuss about the Christianisation in the Roman empire.

Ans. Christianity was declared as the official religion by the emperor Constantine in fourth century. Thus, the process of Christianisation began after this. Christianisation of the empire was a gradual and complex process. Polytheism already existed in the empire. In Western provinces, Christian bishops waged a running battle against beliefs and practices of polytheism and other religious practices.

On the other hand, there was not much criticism from ordinary members of Christianity. Due to this, the boundaries between different religious communities became rigid. Now the religious leaders of Church also enforced a more rigid set of beliefs and practices in which they also had no faith in to control their followers.

19. The expansion of Islam has been called the greatest political revolution in history. Comment.

Ans. The expansion of Islam from its beginning in Arabia has been called as the greatest political revolution that has occurred in the history of the ancient world. By 642 CE i.e. ten years after the death of the Prophet Muhammad, large parts of both the Eastern Roman and Sasanian empires had fallen to the Arabs in a series of wars. These conquests were further extended as far as Spain, Sind and Central Asia.

All this happened first by the defeat of Arab tribes by the emerging Islamic state within Arabia and then in the Syrian desert and on the borders of Iraq. The unification of the Arabian peninsula and its numerous tribes was the factor behind the territorial expansion of Islam.

20. "Cultural diversity of the Roman empire was reflected in many ways and at many levels". Justify this statement. Competency Based Que

Ans. Cultural diversity of the Roman Empire was explained in the following ways

- Roman empire has vast diversity of religious cults and local deities.
- There was plurality of languages that were spoken.
- The styles of dress and costume, the food people ate were different.
- The forms of social organisation like tribal and non-tribal, even their patterns of settlement were different.
- Aramaic was the dominant language group of the Near East, Coptic was spoken in Egypt, Punic and Berber in North Africa, Celtic in Spain and the North-West.
- Greek and Latin were used for the administration and official purposes.

21. Supervision was paramount for both workers and slaves. Discuss. Competency Based Que

Ans. In Roman Empire the general assumption among employers in empire was that without supervision no work would ever get done. The supervision techniques in Roman Empire were as follows

- Supervision was done for both slaves and free workers. The workers were grouped into gangs or smaller teams.
- Columella, a first century writer recommended the group size to be ten, as it will be easier to tell who was putting in effort and who was not working. He recommended that landowners should keep a reserve stock of implements and tools, twice as many as they needed, so that production could be continuous.
- Pliny the Elder, condemned the use of slave gangs as the worst method of organising production, mainly because slaves who worked in gangs were usually chained together by their feet.

The workers were strictly supervised. Pliny said that in the Frankincense factories of Alexandria workers had to wear a mask or a net with a close mesh on their heads and a seal was put upon their aprons. Even before they were allowed to leave the premisis, they had to take off all their clothes.

22. Discuss briefly the shift in market dominance in Roman Empire in trading activities. What was the reason behind it?

Ans. The shift in market dominance in Roman Empire in trading activities can be explained in the following ways

- Different regions of Roman Empire competed with each other for control of the main markets for the goods they produced.
- Archaeologists are able to show that Spanish producers succeeded in capturing markets for olive oil from their Italian counterparts.
- The success of the Spanish olive growers was repeated by North African producers.
- Later after 425 AD, North African dominance was broken by the East.
- In the later fifth and sixth centuries the Aegean, Southern Asia Minor (Turkey), Syria and Palestine became major exporters of wine and olive oil, and containers from Africa show a reduced presence in Mediterranean markets.

The reason behind the rise and fall of prosperity of these regions was depended on how effectively they could organise the production and transport of particular goods and the quality of those goods.

23. What were the different social groups in social structure of Roman Empire?

Ans. Tacitus described the leading social groups of the early empire as follows

- Senators
- Leading members of the equestrian class.
- The respectable section of the people, those who attached to the great houses.
- The lower class who were addicted to circus and theatrical displays.
- Slaves

The first two groups had merged into a unified and expanded aristocracy. The middle class consisted of the considerable mass of persons connected with bureaucracy and army. Below them the vast mass of lower classes were known as humiliores. They comprised of rural as well as industrial labour force, migrant workers, self-employed artisans, casual labourers etc. Thousands of slaves were found in the Western part of the Roman Empire.

Long Answer Type Questions

1. "Roman historians have a rich collection of sources to use for reconstruction of the history". Justify this statement by listing different sources. **Competency Based Que**

Ans. The rich collection of sources that Roman historians used for reconstruction of history can be broadly divided into three groups. They are

Textual Sources It includes histories of the period written by contemporaries which are usually called 'Annals' because the narrative is constructed year-by-year basis. Letters, speeches, sermons, laws and others are part of textual sources that historians used.

Documentary Sources It includes mainly inscriptions and papyri. Inscriptions were usually cut on stone, so a large number of them survived in both Greek and Latin.

The papyrus was a reed-like plant which is processed to produce a writing material that was very widely used in everyday life. Thousands of contracts, accounts, letters and official documents survive 'on papyrus' and have been published by scholars who are called 'papyrologists'.

Material Sources/Remains It includes a very wide collection of items that mainly archaeologists discover by excavation and field survey, buildings, monuments and other kinds of structures, pottery, coins, mosaics and even entire landscapes using aerial photography.

2. "The emperor, the aristocracy and the army were the three main players of the political history of the Roman empire". Justify this statement by discussing each group. **Competency Based Que**

Ans. The emperor, aristocracy and the army were the three main players in the political history of the Roman Empire. They are discussed as follows

- **Emperor** All the subjects lived in the empire were subjects of a single ruler, the emperor, regardless of where they lived and what language they spoke. This explains that emperor was at the top of political hierarchy. Augustus, the first emperor established the regime called the Principate overthrowing the Republic. Though, he was the sole ruler and the only real source of authority, the fiction was kept alive that he was actually only the 'leading citizen', not the absolute ruler. This was done to respect the Senate which was present from earlier.
- **Aristocracy** Senate was the body representing the aristocracy i.e the wealthiest families of Roman and, later, Italian descent, mainly landowners. Most of the Roman histories that survive in Greek and Latin were written by people from senatorial background. Thus, any emperor who was hostile to the senatorial class was judged as worst.
  Army After the emperor and Senate, the other key institution of imperial rule was the army. Romans had a professional army where soldiers had to put in a minimum of 25 years of service. It was the single largest organised body and had power to determine the fate of the emperors. The Senate hated and feared the army, because it was source of unpredictable violence. The success of individual emperors depended on their control of the army and when armies were divided it resulted in civil war.

3. How was it possible for the emperor to cope with the control and administration of a vast and diverse set of territories with a population of 60 million in the mid-second century? What was the role of new provincial upper classes in administration of empire?

Ans. **Control and Administration of Territories**

It was possible for the emperor to cope with the control and administration of a vast and diverse set of territories through the urbanisation of the Roman Empire. The great urban centres were present along the shores of Mediterranean sea. Carthage, Alexandria and Antioch were biggest among them.

These urban centres acted as the true bedrock of the imperial system. It was through the cities that government was able to tax the provincial countrysides which generated much of the wealth of the empire and in turn this wealth was used to run the Empire.

Role of New Provincial Upper Classes in Administration of Empire

- In the process of taxation the local upper classes actively collaborated with the Rome state in administering their own territories and raising taxes for them, thus leading to a dramatic shift of power between Italy and the provinces.
- Throughout the second and third centuries, it was the provincial upper classes who supplied most of the cadre that governed provinces and commanded the armies.
- They formed elite of administrators and military commanders, and became more powerful than the senatorial class with the backing of emperors. After third century, senators of provincial origin became majority. There was a general decline of elites in the political and economic spheres from Italy and increased importance of provincial upper classes in administration of empire.

4. "The rapid succession of emperors in the third century is an obvious symptom of the strains faced by the empire in this period". Look at the statement and discuss about the crisis that occurred in the third-century. Competency Based Que

Ans. In the first and second centuries there was peace, prosperity and economic expansion. But the third century was the starting point for the internal strains in the empire. From the 230s AD, the empire was fighting on several fronts simultaneously.

In Iran, a new and more aggressive dynasty called Sasanians emerged in 225 AD. Within 15 years of rule they had started expanding rapidly in the direction of the Euphrates. On the other hand, Germanic tribes or tribal confederacies like the Alamanni, the Franks and the Goths who were considered barbarians by Romans started to move against the Rhine and Danube frontiers. Thus, the whole period between 233 and 280 AD saw repeated invasions of a whole line of provinces that stretched from the Black Sea to the Alps and Southern Germany. While emperors were constantly in the field against the tribes, the Romans were forced to abandon much of the territory beyond the Danube. This period also saw 25 emperors in 47 years.

Thus, the rapid succession of emperors in the third century represents the strains faced by the empire in this period.

5. Discuss the position of women in the Roman Empire.

Ans. Women enjoyed relatively better position in Roman Empire. After marriage wife was not transferred to husband's authority but she retained full rights in the property of her natal family. Though, woman's dowry went to husband for the duration of the marriage, she still remained primary heir of her father and becomes an independent property owner after her father's death. Thus, Roman women enjoyed considerable rights in owning and managing property. This shows that as per the law, married couple was not one financial entity but two, and the wife enjoyed complete legal independence.

Divorce was also relatively easy. A notice of intent to dissolve the marriage either by husband or wife is enough for divorce. Males married in twenties or early thirties, and women married in the late teens or early twenties, so there was an age gap between husband and wife, and this would have encouraged a certain inequality. As marriages were generally arranged, women were subjected to domination by their husbands.

For example, Augustine, the great catholic bishop form North Africa tells about how his mother was regularly beaten by his father and it was same with other women too.

Thus, we can see that on one hand women enjoyed great deal of independence but on the other, they also faced violence.

6. Discuss the social hierarchy of the early Roman empire as described by a Roman historian Tacitus. CBSE Diksha

Ans. Social hierarchy is how individuals and groups are arranged in a society. It is a society's categorisation of people into socio-economic strata, based upon their occupation and income, wealth and social status or derived power from social or political means.

Tacitus, a senator and an historian of the Roman Empire described the leading social groups of the early empire as follows

(i) Senators
(ii) Leading members of the equestrian class
(iii) The respectable section of the people or middle class
(iv) The untidy lower class
(v) Slaves

- **Senatorial and Equestrian Class** In the early third century, most of the members of the Senate came from Italian families. By the late empire i.e. early part of fourth century, senators and equestrian class merged into a unified and expanded aristocracy, and more than half of the families were of African or Eastern origin. This late Roman aristocracy was very wealthy but not as powerful as military elites who came from non-aristocratic families.
- **Middle Class** It consisted of considerable mass of persons connected with imperial service. Bureaucracy, army, more prosperous merchants and farmers from Eastern provinces were all part of this class. Tacitus described them as respectable middle class who are clients of the great senatorial houses. This class was mainly dependent on the state for their sustenance.
- **Lower Class and Slaves** Below the middle class there were huge mass of the lower classes known as humiliores. They are comprised of a rural labour force, labour employed in large estates, workers in industrial and mining establishments, migrant workers, self-employed artisans, casual labourers in big cities and slaves.

  Many slaves were found all over the Western empire. In Rome, unlike hired workers, slaves had to be fed and maintained throughout the year which increased the cost of holding this kind of labour.

7. What is meant by late Antiquity? Describe the main Political and Economic development of the period. CBSE Diksha

Ans. Late Antiquity refers to the period from the fourth to seventh centuries CE, marking the transition from the Roman Empire to the early medieval period.

This time was characterised by cultural, political and economic changes as the Roman Empire evolved and fragmented. The period saw the rise of Christianity as the state religion, starting with Emperor Constantine, and the eventual emergence of Islam in the seventh century.

Main Political Developments of the Period

- **Reorganisation by Diocletian (284-305 CE)**
  - Diocletian reorganised the empire, reducing its size by abandoning territories with less economic or strategic value.
  - He fortified borders, and separated civilian from military functions, granting more autonomy to military commanders.
- **Establishment of a New Capital**
  - Emperor Constantine (324 CE) founded Constantinople (modern-day Istanbul) as the new capital, surrounded by sea on three sides for protection.
- **Political Fragmentation**
  - In the West, the empire faced invasions from Germanic tribes like the Goths, Vandals and Lombards, leading to the collapse of Roman rule and the formation of smaller kingdoms.
  - In the East, the Roman Empire (Byzantium) remained united and prosperous, particularly under Justinian, who reconquered parts of Africa and Italy but left Italy vulnerable to later invasions.
- **Rise of Islam**
  - By 642 CE, the Arab conquests began to take over major territories of the Roman and Sasanian empires, marking the beginning of a new political and religious order.

Main Economic Developments

- **Monetary Stability and Reforms**
  - The silver currency system collapsed due to exhaustion of silver mines, leading Constantine to introduce a new gold coin, the solidus, which stabilised the economy.
- **Urban Prosperity**
  - Despite challenges, there was strong economic growth, especially in the Eastern Roman Empire. Wealthy elites accumulated vast incomes, and rural estates in Egypt and other regions generated substantial wealth.
- **Expansion of Trade**
  - The period saw the revival of long-distance trade, with economic activities such as investment in oil presses, glass factories, and advanced technologies like water mills.
  - Trade routes flourished, particularly in regions like the Eastern Mediterranean, enhancing urban development and economic strength.
- **Shift in Agricultural and Industrial Production**
  - There was investment in rural estates and industrial installations, leading to higher production and wealth generation in regions like Egypt, Syria and Palestine.

8. "All this looks draconian". Look at the statement and discuss about the conditions of workers in Roman Empire. Were the conditions of labour uniform across the empire or were there any exceptions? Discuss if any. **Competency Based Que**

Ans. The condition of workers in the Roman Empire was bad. Some of the industrial establishments in the Roman Empire enforced tighter controls on the workers. For example, in the Frankincense factories of Alexandria, there was very high degree of supervision on workers which could be considered cruel and inhuman. A seal was put upon the workmen's clothes and they had to wear a mask or a net with a close mesh on their heads. Before they left the premises, they had to take off all their clothes.

Even agricultural labour was so tiring and disliked. Peasants of Egypt were deserting villages to avoid agricultural work. This was same for most of the factories and workshops. A law of 398 was used to brand workers so that they could be recognised if and when they run away and try to hide. Many private employers cast their agreements with workers in the form of debt contracts. This helped them to claim that their employees were in debt to them and thus, ensuring tighter control over them. Thousands of workers surrendered themselves to work in bondage. A lot of the poorer families went into debt bondage in order to survive. Parents used to sell their children into bondage for period of 25 years.

From the above conditions, it can be concluded that the condition of workers was not good in Roman Empire. However, the conditions of all labour were not uniform across the empire. For example, the late fifth century emperor Anastasius built the Eastern frontier city Dara in less than three weeks by attracting labour from all over the East by offering high wages. Evidence from papyri also shows how wage labour was widespread in parts of Mediterranean in the East.

Source Based Questions

Read the sources given below and answer the following questions.

1. Doctor Galen on how Roman Cities Treated the Countryside

'The famine prevalent for many successive years in many provinces has clearly displayed for men of any understanding the effect of malnutrition in generating illness. The city-dwellers, as it was their custom to collect and store enough grain for the whole of the next year immediately after the harvest, carried off all the wheat, barley, beans and lentils, and left to the peasants various kinds of pulse – after taking quite a large proportion of these to the city. After consuming what was left in the course of the winter, the country people had to resort to unhealthy foods in the spring; they ate twigs and shoots of trees and bushes and bulbs and roots of inedible plants...'

(i) What did city dwellers do as part of their custom and what did they leave to peasants?

(ii) What kind of unhealthy foods did country people eat and Why?

(iii) What do you infer from the passage about the treatment of countryside by Roman cities?

Ans. (i) City dwellers would collect and store enough grain for the whole of the next year immediately after the harvest.

They would carry off all the wheat, barley, beans and lentils and left various kinds of pulses to the peasants.

(ii) The country people ate twigs and shoots of trees and bushed and bulbs and roots of inedible plants. They did so because city dwellers left very little for them.

(iii) We can infer from the passage that countryside was neglected and city dwellers took all the resources. The people in countryside suffered immensely due to shortage of the food.

2. On the Treatment of Slaves

'Soon afterwards the City Prefect, Lucius Pedanius Secundus, was murdered by one of his slaves. After the murder, ancient custom required that every slave residing under the same roof must be executed. But a crowd gathered, eager to save so many innocent lives; and rioting began. The senate-house was besieged. Inside, there was feeling against excessive severity, but the majority opposed any change (....) [The senators] favouring execution prevailed. However, great crowds ready with stones and torches prevented the order from being carried out. Nero rebuked the population by edict, and lined with troops the whole route along which those condemned were taken for execution.'

(i) Who was murdered by a slave? What was the ancient custom if a slave committed murder?

(ii) Why did crowd gather? What did they do?

(iii) Who was the emperor at that time? What did the emperor do to execute the decision?

Ans. (i) Lucius Pedanius Secundus was murdered by one of his slaves. If a slave committed murder then as per ancient custom every slave residing under the same roof was to be executed.

(ii) Crowd gathered to save the innocent lives of slaves. They were ready with stones and torches to prevent the order from being carried out.

(iii) Nero was the emperor at that time. He ordered the troops to be present along the whole route, and execute anyone who condemned the decision.

3. Incomes of the Roman Aristocracy, Early Fifth Century

'Each of the great houses of Rome contained within itself everything which a medium-sized city could hold, a hippodrome, fora, temples, fountains and different kinds of baths...

Many of the Roman households received an income of four thousand pounds of gold per year from their properties, not including grain, wine and other produce which, if sold, would have amounted to one-third of the income in gold. The income of the households at Rome of the second class was one thousand or fifteen hundred pounds of gold.'

(i) What was a hippodrome?

(ii) How do we know that Roman households were rich and what amounted to one-third of their income?

(iii) Write about the income of the Roman household.

Ans. (i) Hippodrome was an ancient stadium for horse racing and chariot racing. Each of the great houses of Rome had a hippodrome.

(ii) Roman households received an income of four hundred thousand pounds of gold per year from their properties. From this, we can infer that Roman households were rich. Grain, wine and other produce that were sold, amounted to one-third of the income.

(iii) Many of the Roman households had an income of four thousand pounds of gold per year from their properties. These did not include grain, wine and other produce. The second class of the Roman households had income of one thousand or fifteen hundred pounds of gold.

Map Based Questions

1. Mark the following locations on the map of Europe and North Africa.

(i) Mediterranean Sea (ii) Sahara Desert (iii) Tangiers

(iv) Carthage (v) River Guadalquivir

Ans.

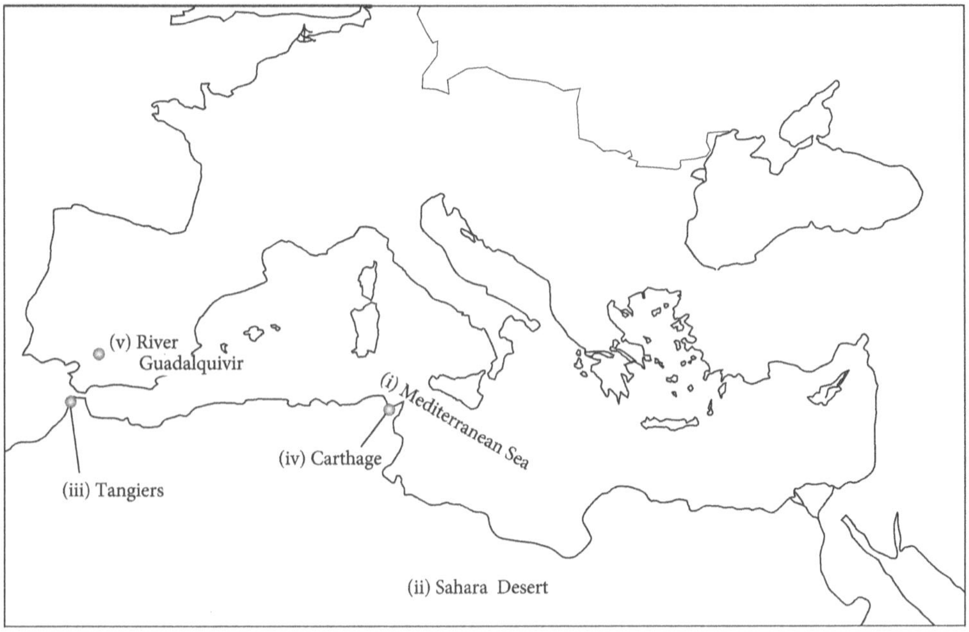

2. Identify the following locations marked on the map of Europe and North Africa given below.

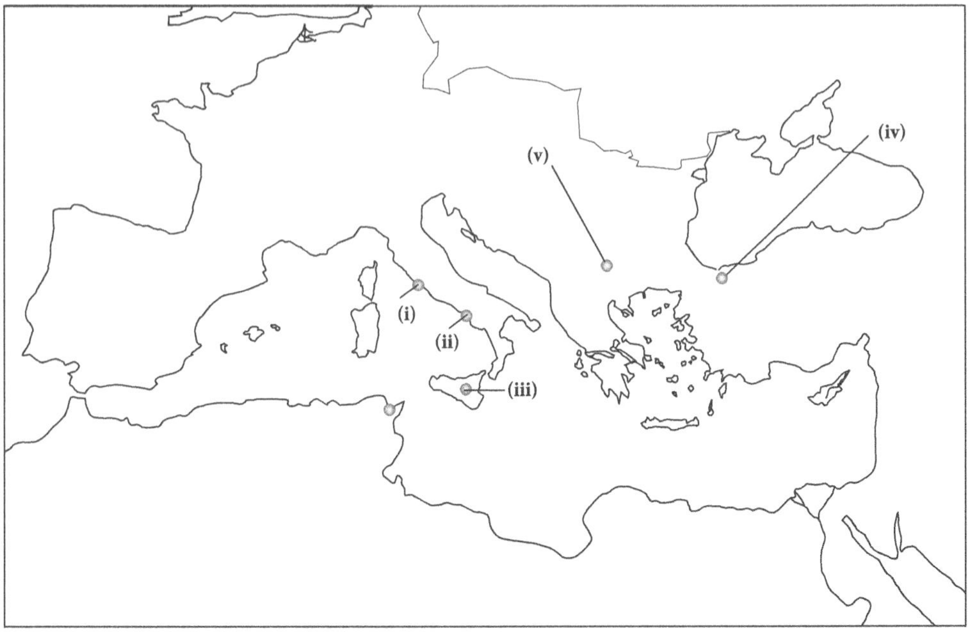

Ans.

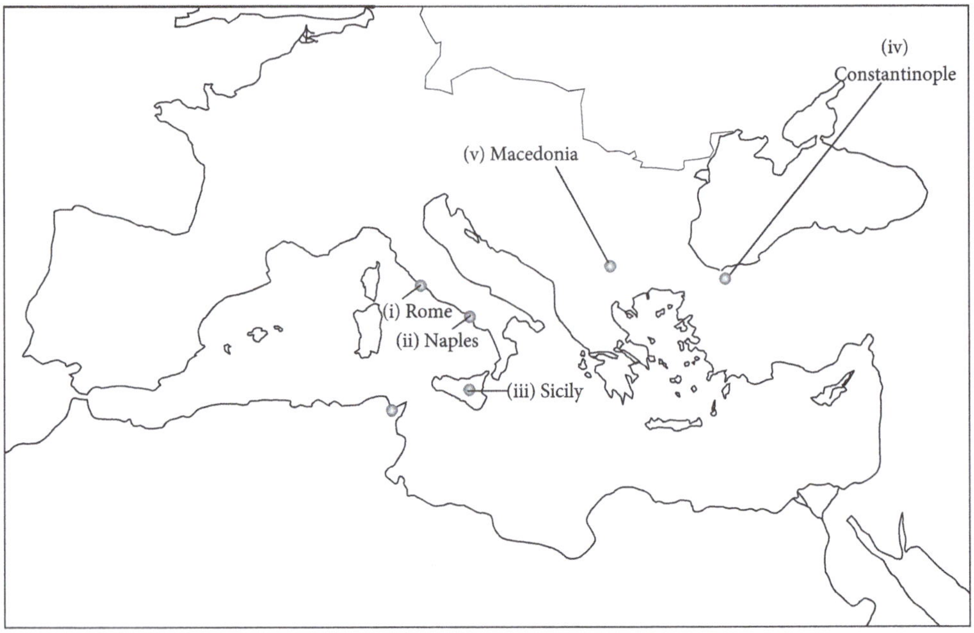

3. Mark the following locations on the map of West Asia.

(i) Damascus (ii) Antioch (iii) Baghdad
(iv) Ctesiphon (v) Medina

Ans.

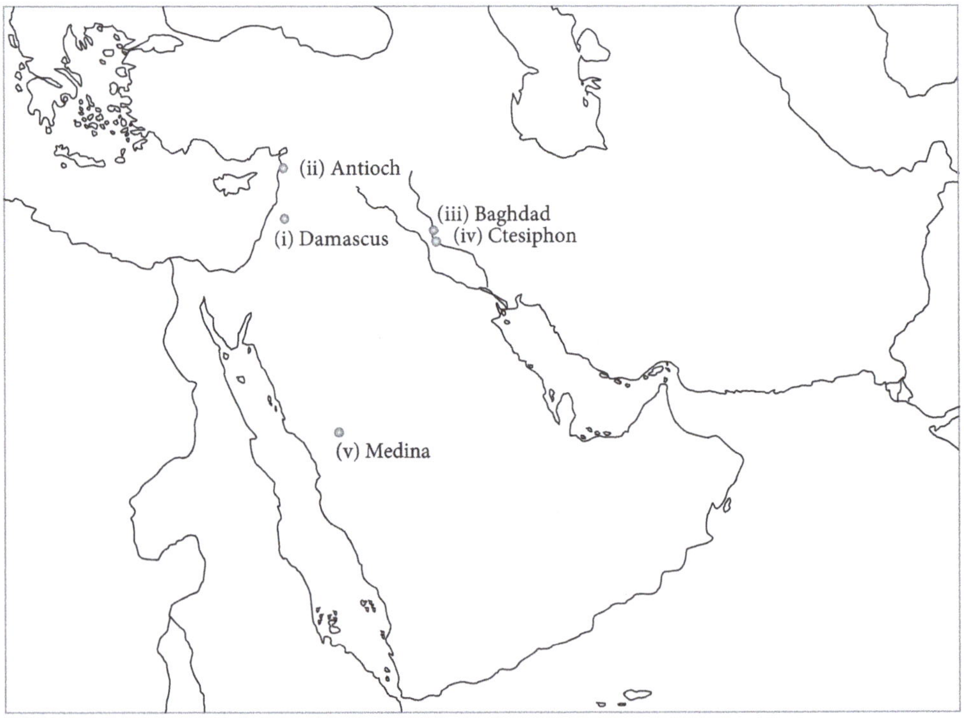

4. **Identify the following locations marked on the map of West Asia given below.**

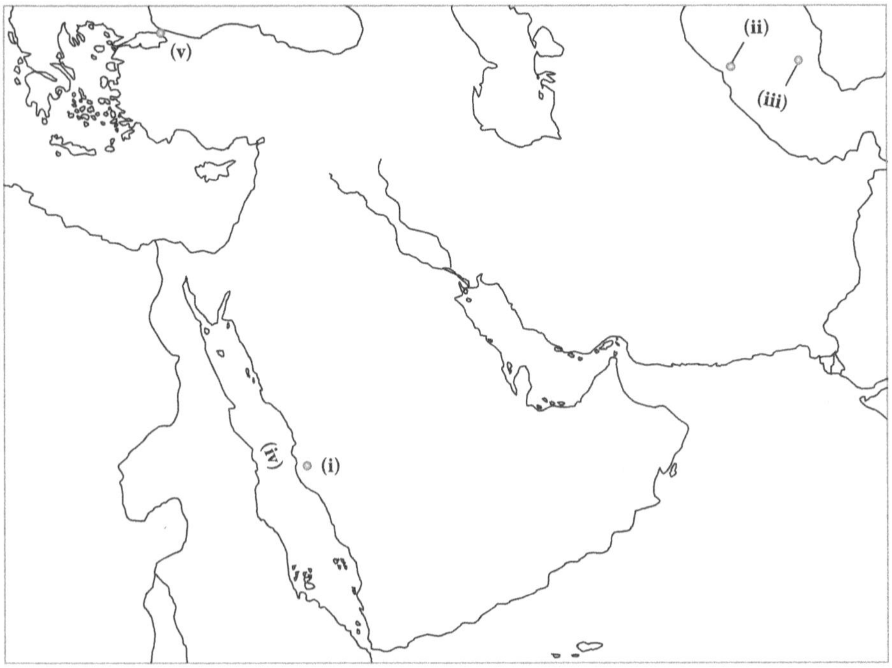

Ans.

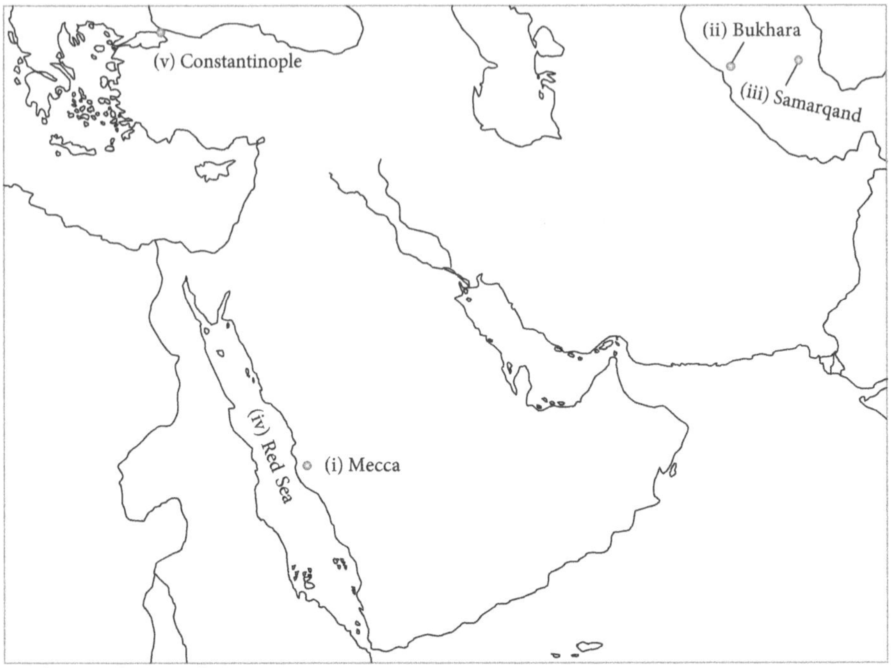

SELF ASSESSMENT TEST

Objective Type Questions

1. Caravan city of Palmyra was destroyed by the Romans in ....
   (a) 260 CE (b) 275 CE (c) 273 CE (d) 300 CE
2. The great Jewish revolt and capture of Jerusalem by Roman forces happened in
   (a) 50-60 CE (b) 66-70 CE (c) 70-80 CE (d) 85-96 CE
3. Jewish war was ....
   (a) a rebellion in Judaea (b) against Roman domination
   (c) ruthlessly suppressed by the Romans (d) All of these
4. Match the following.

	List I		List II
A.	Alexandria	1.	Roman silver coin
B.	Denarii	2.	Urban centres
C.	Celtic	3.	Lower class families
D.	Humiliores	4.	Language spoken in Spain

Codes

	A	B	C	D
(a)	3	1	2	4
(b)	2	1	3	4
(c)	2	1	4	3
(d)	4	2	1	3

Short Answer Type Questions

5. The Roman Empire was a mosaic of territories and cultures that were bound together by a common system of government. Discuss.
6. How can we find cultural diversity in the Roman Empire? Discuss with examples.
7. Name the ancient empire which was expanded across three continents. Why was the empire known so?
8. Explain the impact of the crisis of the third century on the early Roman Empire.
9. Nuclear family was one of the key features of Roman society. Comment.
10. Who was Saint Augustine? Why is he famous in the history of the Roman civilisation?

Long Answer Type Questions

11. Explain why Christianisation of the Roman empire was a complex process.
12. Explain the changes in the structure of the state introduced by emperor Diocletian.
13. What do the social hierarchies tell us about ancient Rome society? Discuss the role of the knights in the empire.
14. 'Slavery was an institution deeply rooted in ancient Roman world.' Explain.
15. Discuss about the corruption in the judicial system and in the administration of military supplies.

3

CHAPTER

This chapter explores how the Mongols, under Genghis Khan, adapted their traditional customs to build a powerful military and effective governance. Ruling a vast empire with diverse peoples and systems required innovation and compromise. This created a nomadic empire that significantly shaped Eurasian history and transformed its own society.

YOUR STUDY GOALS

YOUR PRACTICE GOAL

- Objective Type Questions (37 Qs ; MCQs, A-R, Matching, Picture Based)
- Subjective Questions (15 SAs, 6 LAs)
- Source Based Questions (4 Qs)
- Map Based Questions (2 Qs)

Nomadic Empires

3.1 Sources of History about the Mongols

- Nomads of the **steppes**[1] did not produce their own literature. So, most information about them comes from chronicles, travelogues, and documents by city-based writers.
- These writers often give biased views and depict nomads as barbaric and primitive.
- The success of the Mongols attracted scholars from different backgrounds (Buddhist, Confucian, Christian, Turkish and Muslim), who produced more sympathetic accounts of the Mongols.
- Historians of **sedentary**[2] societies often portrayed nomads as "primitive **barbarians**[3]".

Various Researches on Mongols

Research by Russian Scholars on the Mongols

- Russian scholars in the 18th and 19th centuries produced significant research on Mongols when the Tsarist regime controlled Central Asia.
- This research was primarily based on colonial surveys from travellers, soldiers, merchants and antiquarian scholars.

---

1 **Steppe** A large, flat area of land with grass and very few trees especially in Eastern Europe and Asia.

2 **Sedentary** It means living in groups, permanently in one place.

3 **Barbarian** The term 'barbarian' is derived from the Greek *barbaros* which meant a non- Greek, someone whose language sounded like a random noise: 'barbar'.

Marxist Historiography about Mongols

- In the 20th century, Marxist historians argued that the Mongol Empire was transitioning from a tribal to a feudal society.
- In a tribal society, everyone was considered equal, regardless of their wealth. However, in a feudal society, there were big differences between the lords who owned the land and the peasants who worked on it.

Research by Other Scholars

- Scholars like **Boris Yakovlevich Vladimirtsov** and **Vasily Vladimirovich Bartold** produced valuable research on Mongol society, culture and languages.
- Bartold admired Genghis Khan, but the Stalin government did not. It limited the circulation of the scholar's work. It wasn't until the 1960's during and after Khrushchev's liberal era that his writings were published.

Problems with Multiple Sources

- The sources of Mongol history are in different languages like Chinese, Mongolian, Persian, Arabic, Italian, Latin, French and Russian, creating challenges for historians.
- The Mongolian and Chinese versions of the earliest narrative on Genghis Khan, *The Secret History of the Mongols*, are quite different. The Mongols produced little literature themselves and were mostly written about by foreign scholars.
- The work of scholars like Igor de Rachewiltz on '*The Secret History of the Mongols*' and Gerhard Doerfer on Mongol and Turkic terms in Persian highlights the challenges of studying the history of the Central Asian nomads.

3.2 Mongols

- The Mongols were a diverse group, linked to the Tatars by language, Khitan and Manchus in the East, and the Turkic tribes in the West. Some Mongols were pastoralists, while others were hunter-gatherers.

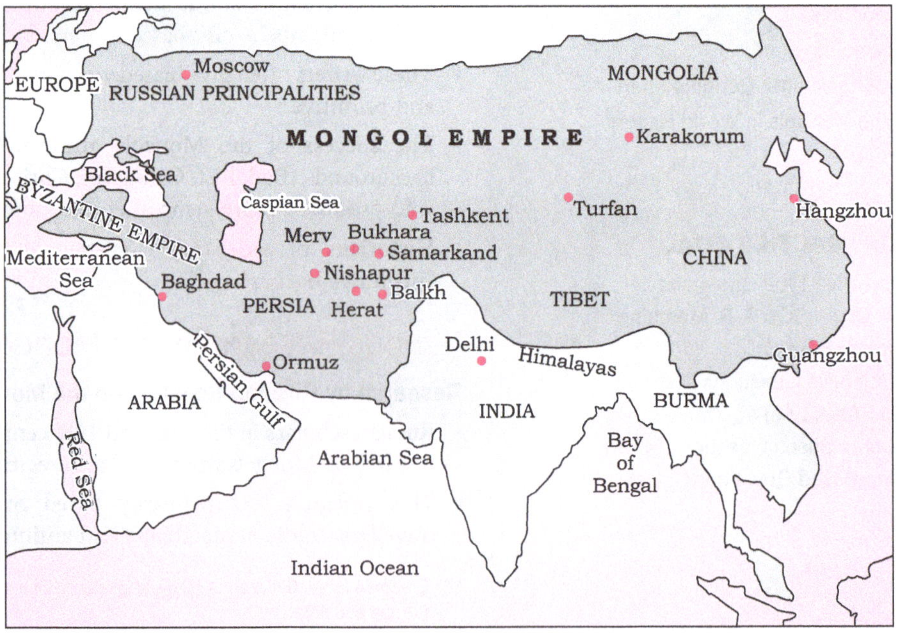

▲ *The Mongol Empire*

Pastoralists Mongols

- Pastoralists domesticated horses, sheep, cattle, goats and camels. They lived a nomadic life in the steppes of Central Asia, in present-day Mongolia.
- This region was characterised by majestic landscapes, surrounded by the Altai mountains in the West and the Gobi desert in the South, and drained by rivers like the Onon and Selenga.

Hunter-Gatherers Mongols

- Hunter-gatherers lived North of the pastoralists in the Siberian forests and were considered lower-ranked than pastoralists.
- They survived by trading furs of animals that were trapped in the summer months.
- The region had extreme weather conditions with harsh winters and dry summers, limiting agricultural potential.
- The nomadic people (both hunter-gatherers and pastorals) who lived in this region didn't have big cities because they couldn't support many people.
- They lived in tents, *gers* (Portable round tents) and moved around with their animals to find food.

Mongol Society

- Mongol society was united by ethnic and linguistic ties but divided by **patrilineal lineage**[4] due to scarce resources. Wealthier families with more animals and pastures had political influence.
- Natural calamities like harsh winters and droughts led to food and fodder shortages, causing conflicts over resources and raids.
- Occasionally, Mongol families would form alliances (**confederacy**[5]) for offensive or defensive purposes. But these groups were small and usually didn't last long.
- Genghis Khan's political system was durable and stable similar to Attila's group, unlike earlier confederacies. It could fight bigger armies with better weapons in China, Iran and Eastern Europe.
- There were other big groups of nomads in Central Asia, like the Juan-juan, Epthalite Huns, Khitan, Hsiung-nu, T'u-chueh, and Uighurs. These groups had a big influence on the history of nomadic people.

Relations between Nomads and Settled Societies

- Despite their differences, nomadic and agrarian societies were not very different from each other.
- The limited resources of the grasslands forced Mongols and other Central Asian nomads to engage in trade with settled communities in China.
- This trade was beneficial for both sides, as agricultural products and iron utensils from China were exchanged for horses, furs, and animals from the grassland. However, trade was not always smooth. Nomadic groups often used military pressure to gain better terms.
- Mongols could force Chinese neighbours to offer more favourable conditions of trade. However, when the Mongols were divided, Chinese influence in the steppe increased leading to boundary wars.
- These wars were more problematic for settled communities, as Chinese people destroyed agriculture and looted cities.

▲ *The Great Wall of China*

4 Patrilineal Lineage It is a kinship system that traces a person's lineage through their father's male descendants.
5 Confederacy It is an alliance for mutual support or common action.

- China had a long history of dealing with nomadic interference. As early as the 8th century BCE, China suffered from nomadic raids.
- To protect themselves, the Chinese built a huge wall for self-defence and to keep the nomads out. This wall is now called the **Great Wall of China**.

Quick Test 1

1. Name two famous Russian scholars who worked on Mongols history.
2. What is the term used for the association formed by the Mongols with the rich and the powerful?
3. Mention any one feature about Mongolia.
4. In Mongol society which families had more animals and pasture land?
5. Which defensive structure was built by the Chinese to save themselves from nomadic intrusion?

3.3 Genghis Khan

- Genghis Khan was born around 1162 CE near the Onon river in the North of present-day Mongolia. His original name was **Temujin**.
- Genghis Khan's father **Yesugei** was killed at an early age. His mother, **Oelun-eke**, raised Temujin, and his brothers and step-brothers.
- Genghis Khan was once captured and enslaved. His wife, **Borte**, was also kidnapped. He had to fight to get her back. During this difficult time, he made some important friends like Boghurchu and Jamuqa who was his blood-brother (*anda*[6]).
- He also made peace with the ruler of the **Kereyits**, **Tughril/Ong Khan**, who was his father's old blood- brother.

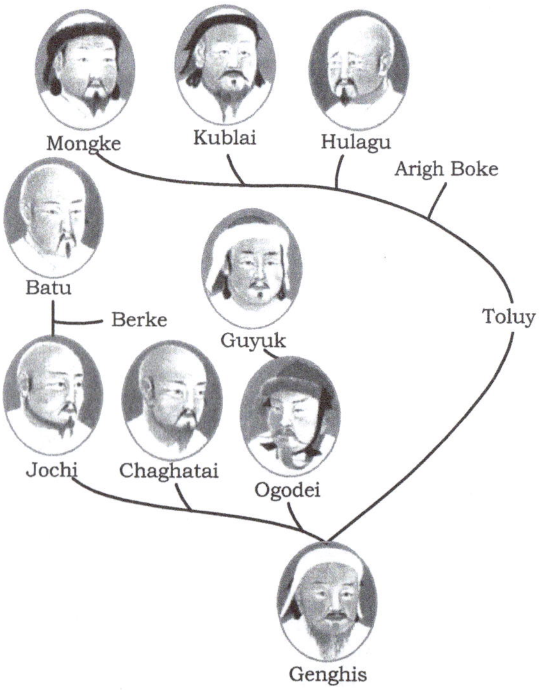

▲ *The Mongol Dynasty*

Temujin to Genghis Khan

- Genghis Khan was friends (ally) with Ong Khan for many years (between 1180s and 1190s). He used these alliances to defeat his enemies.
- Genghis Khan defeated his old friend Jamuqa and became more powerful. He then fought against other tribes, including the Tatars, the Kereyits and Ong Khan in 1203 CE.
- In 1206, Genghis Khan defeated the Naiman people and the powerful Jamuqa, and became the most important leader in the region.
- Before ***quriltai*** in 1206, Genghis Khan changed the Mongol army to be better organised and more powerful. Yasa, the code of law was promulgated by him.
- In *quriltai*, Genghis was named the **Great Khan of the Mongols** and was given the title Genghis Khan, **Oceanic Khan** or **Universal Ruler**. This means he was the most powerful ruler of all the Mongols.

Campaigns of Genghis Khan

- Genghis Khan initially focused on conquering China, which was then divided into three kingdoms
  (i) The **Hsi Hsia** people of Tibetan origin in the North-West provinces

6 Anda It refers to blood-brothers.

(ii) The **Jurchen** of the **Chin dynasty** that ruled North China from Peking.

(iii) The **Sung dynasty** who controlled South China

- Genghis Khan's conquests included defeating the Hsi Hsia in 1209 CE, forcefully crossing over the Great Wall of China in 1213 CE, and getting into Peking in 1215 CE.
- Mongol rule expanded westward, reaching the Amu Darya river, the states of Transoxiana and Khwarazm. Many cities, including Otrar, Bukhara, Samarqand, Balkh, Gurganj, Merv, Nishapur and Herat, either surrendered or were destroyed by Mongol forces.
- The Mongols searched for Sultan Muhammad of Khwarazm into Azerbaijan and defeated Russian forces in Crimea. Another branch of Mongol forces followed Sultan's son Jalaluddin into Afghanistan and the Sindh province.

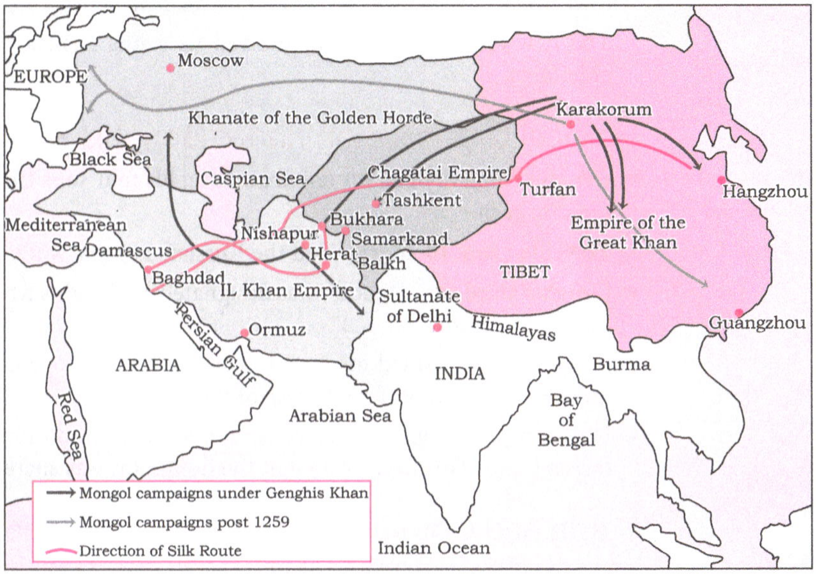

▲ *The Mongol Campaigns*

Strategies and Skills of Genghis Khan

- Genghis Khan spent most of his life in fighting wars. He was a very successful military leader. He was able to come up with new and better ways to fight, which made his army very strong.
- Mongols and Turks were very good at riding horses. This provided speed and mobility to the army. They were also very good at shooting arrows while on horseback. They learned how to do this by practising while hunting.
- The steppe cavalry was always fast moving. They learned how to travel in very cold weather and even cross frozen rivers to attack their enemies.
- Nomads had trouble attacking forts. Genghis Khan solved this problem by learning how to use siege machines (wall-breaking devices) and naphtha bombardment (fire weapons). His engineers made machines that were easy to move and could destroy enemy forts quickly .

Military Organisation under Genghis Khan

- In Mongol and other nomadic societies, all grown-up men who were healthy had to join the army when needed.
- As more tribes joined Genghis Khan, the army became more diverse. It included people who wanted to join, like the **Uighurs**, and people who were defeated, like the **Kereyits**.
- Genghis Khan reorganised his army into divisions of 10s, 100s, 1000s, and 10,000 soldiers.
- Soldiers from different tribes were put together in the same army groups to make them feel more like a team and less loyal to their own tribe. This helped Genghis Khan unite his army.
- His sons and captains, known as ***noyan***[7], led these military units.
- If someone tried to leave their group without permission, they were punished. This changed the old way of life on the steppe and made the different clans feel like they were part of one big group led by Genghis Khan.

7 *Noyan* It refers to the specially chosen captains of an army units.

Rewards to Followers

- Genghis Khan publicly honored some individuals as his blood-brothers (*anda*) and gave others, lower-ranking freemen, the title of bondsmen (*naukar*) to show their close relationship with him.
- The new Mongol aristocracy derived its status from loyalty to the Great Khan, not traditional clan chieftains.

Political Organisation under Genghis Khan's Sons

- Genghis Khan divided his empire among his four sons (Jochi, Chaghatai, Ogodei and Toluy), giving an ***ulus***[8] to each.
- The eldest son, **Jochi**, received the Russian steppes, while **Chaghatai** ruled the Transoxianian steppe.
- Genghis' third son, **Ogodei**, was designated as Genghis Khan's successor, and **Toluy** was given ancestral Mongolian lands.
- Genghis Khan wanted his sons to rule the empire together. So, he put soldiers from each of his sons' groups (***tama***[9]) in different parts of the empire.
- Decisions on campaigns, succession, and distribution of resources were made collectively at *quriltais* (assemblies). This made sure that the dominion was shared by all the members of the family.

Trade and Communication Systems under Genghis Khan

- Genghis Khan established a rapid courier system (*yam*) with fresh horses and riders at regular outposts.
- Nomads contributed a tenth of their herds for maintaining this system, which proved highly efficient. This was called ***qubcur tax***[10] which was paid by the nomads willingly for its multiple benefits.
- After Genghis Khan died, the mail system was made even better. It was very fast and reliable, which surprised people. This helped the Great Khans to know what was happening in all parts of their empire.
- After the wars stopped, Europe and China were connected to Mongolia. Trade along the Silk Road became very strong under the Mongols. The trade routes didn't end in China; they went North into Mongolia to Karakorum.
- Communication and ease of travel was important for the Mongols to keep their empire peaceful. Travellers were given a special pass called a "***paiza***[11]" or "*gerege*" to travel safely.
- Traders had to pay a tax called ***baj tax***[12] for safe travel. This showed that they respected the authority of the Mongol Khan.

Quick Test 2

1. When and where was Genghis Khan born?
2. Which city was destroyed as a revenge by Genghis Khan?
3. Name any two sons of Genghis Khan.
4. What is quriltai?
5. What is *qubcur* tax?

---

8 *Ulus* It is a conquered but not fixed territory.
9 *Tama* It refers to military contingents.
10 *Qubcur tax* A tax imposed on nomads for communication facility provided to them.
11 Paiza A pass or permit to move from one place to another.
12 Baj tax A tax for allowing traders a safe travel.

3.4 Mongols after Genghis Khan

- Genghis Khan died in 1227 CE. By the mid-13th century, the concept of collective rule shared by all brothers was replaced by individual dynasties.
- Succession struggles among Genghis Khan's descendants led to the establishment of separate *ulus* (now it meant territorial dominions).

Following were the dynasties formed by the sons of Genghis Khan

- **Yuan and Il-Khanid dynasties** established in China and Iran by descendants of Toluy.
- **Golden Horde** formed by descendants of Jochi and ruled the Russian steppes.
- **Chaghatai's successors** ruled the steppes of Transoxiana and Turkistan.

Peace Between Nomadic and Settled Communities

- The fighting between nomadic and settled people in the Mongol empire became less in the 13th century.
- In the 1230s, when the Mongols defeated the Chin dynasty in North China, some Mongols wanted to kill all the peasants and turn their land into places for animals to graze.
- By 1270s, when the Mongols conquered South China, **Qubilai Khan**, who was Genghis Khan's grandson, became a protector of peasants and cities.
- In the 1290s, **Ghazan Khan**, who was a Mongol ruler in Iran and a descendant of Toluy, asked people not to treat peasants badly, for the kingdom to be stable and wealthy.

Expansion of Territory After Genghis Khan

- Mongol expansion after the death of Genghis Khan can be divided into two phases
  1. **The First Phase** (1236-42 CE). It signifies the success of Mongols in the Russian steppes, Bulghar, Kiev, Poland and Hungary.
  2. **The Second Phase** (1255-1300 CE) It led to the conquest of all of China (1279), Iran, Iraq and Syria.

First Phase of Expansion

- **Mongke**, Genghis Khan's grandson, warned the French ruler **Louis IX**, reflecting the influence of Genghis Khan's ideas.
- In the 1236-41 campaigns, **Batu** (Genghis Khan's another grandson) destroyed Russian territories, seized Poland and Hungary, and reached Vienna.
- In the 13th century, many people in China, the Middle East, and Europe thought that the Mongols' conquests were the **Wrath of God** and the beginning of Judgment Day.

Second Phase of Expansion

- After the 1260s, the Mongols lost interest in wars in the West. They had the potential to conquer Vienna, Western Europe, and Egypt, but they did not. They were defeated by the Egyptians and ceased their military campaigns in Hungary.
- The main reasons for the decline in Western expansion were as follows
  1. **Internal succession politics** Struggles between Jochi, Ogodei, and Toluyid descendants distracted them from campaigns in Europe.
  2. **Increased focus on China** Toluyid interests in conquering China diverted resources from Western expansion.

Civil Administration Under the Mongols

- Genghis Khan and his successors recruited civil administrators from conquered societies, integrating diverse regions. They were sent to different places, just like Chinese officials were sent to Iran and Persians were sent to China.
- These administrators helped connect the different parts of the empire. They had knowledge and skills that were useful in stopping nomads from attacking settled people.
- The Mongol Khans trusted them as long as they made money for the empire. Sometimes, these officials had a lot of power.

Legal Code of Law: Yasa

- *Yasa* was the legal code of the law introduced by Genghis Khan at the *quriltai* in 1206 to reorganise Mongol society.
- Initially, the term was written as *yasaq*, meaning law, order or decree, which included administrative regulations on hunting, the army and postal systems.
- By the mid-13th century, *yasa* became a symbol of Mongol identity and unity, helping the Mongol people maintain their distinctiveness in a vast empire.
- The *yasa* was a set of rules that helped to unite the Mongol people. It was very important for creating a Mongol empire that included many different people.

3.5 The Mongols in World History

- Many people who lived in cities in China, Iran and Eastern Europe in the 13th century were afraid of and disliked the steppe people. However, for the Mongols, Genghis Khan was the best leader ever.
- Genghis Khan united the Mongol people and stopped them from fighting wih each other. He freed them from the control of the Chinese and made them prosperous. He created a big empire that stretched across many continents.
- He also reopened trade routes and markets, which attracted travellers from far away places, like **Marco Polo**.
- The Mongol Empire embraced the diverse body of people and faiths. The Mongol Khans themselves had different religions, like Shamanism, Buddhism, Christianity and Islam. However, they didn't let their own beliefs affect their rule.
- The Mongol rulers hired people from all different groups and religions to work in the government and army.
- The Mongol empire was made up of people from many different ethnic groups, spoke many different languages, and had many different religions. The Mongols did not feel scared because they had so many different kinds of people.

Genghis Khan as a Source of Inspiration

- Genghis Khan was known as a unifier and empire-builder who continued to inspire future leaders.
- His ability to unite divided groups and create a vast empire was a significant source of inspiration.
- In modern Mongolia, Genghis Khan is regarded as a national hero and an iconic figure shaping national identity.
- After years of Soviet influence, Mongolia is now working to define its identity as an independent country.
- A major part of this is celebrating Genghis Khan as a national hero. His accomplishments are respected and remembered with pride.

Quick Test 3

1. When did Genghis Khan die?
2. In which year did Mongols defend the Chin dynasty of China?
3. Name the territories where Mongols were gained in their first phase expansion.
4. What was *yasa*?
5. Why were the Mongols defeated by the Egyptians?

TIMELINE

Year	Event
c. 1167 CE	Birth of Temujin
1160s-70s CE	Years spent in slavery and struggle
1180s-90s CE	Period of alliance formation
1203-27 CE	Expansion and triumph
1206 CE	Temujin proclaimed Genghis Khan, 'Universal Ruler' of the Mongols
1227 CE	Death of Genghis Khan
1227-60 CE	Rule of the three Great Khans and continued Mongol unity
1227-41 CE	Ogodei, son of Genghis Khan
1246-49 CE	Guyuk, son of Ogodei
1251-60 CE	Mongke, son of Genghis Khan's youngest son, Toluy
1236-42 CE	Campaigns in Russia, Hungary, Poland and Austria under Batu, son of Jochi, Genghis Khan's eldest son
1253-55 CE	Beginning of fresh campaigns in Iran and China under Mongke
1258 CE	Capture of Baghdad and the end of the Abbasid caliphate. Establishment of the Il-Khanid State of Iran under Hulegu, younger brother of Mongke. Beginning of conflict between the Jochids and the Il-Khans.
1260 CE	Accession of Qubilai Khan as Grand Khan in Peking; conflict among descendants of Genghis Khan; fragmentation of Mongol realm into independent lineages – Toluy, Chaghatai and Jochi. (Ogodei's lineage defeated and absorbed into the Toluyid) Toluyids: Yuan dynasty in China and Il-Khanid state in Iran; Chaghataids in steppes North of Transoxiana and 'Turkistan'; Jochid lineages in the Russian steppes, described as the 'Golden Horde' by observers.
1257-67 CE	Reign of Berke, son of Batu; reorientation of the Golden Horde from Nestorian Christianity towards Islam; alliance between the Golden Horde and Egypt against the Il-Khans.
1295-1304 CE	Reign of Il-Khanid ruler Ghazan Khan in Iran; conversion from Buddhism to Islam by Il-Khanid chieftains.
1368 CE	End of the Yuan dynasty in China.
1370-1405 CE	Rule of Timur, a Barlas Turk who claimed Genghis Khanid descent through the lineage of Chaghatai. Establishes a steppe empire that assimilates part of the dominions of Toluy (excluding China), Chaghatai and Jochi. Proclaims himself 'Guregen' - 'royal son-in- law' - and marries a princess of the Genghis Khanid lineage.
1495-1530 CE	Zahiruddin Babur, descendant of Timur and Genghis Khan, succeeds to Timurid territory of Ferghana and Samarqand, is expelled, captures Kabul and in 1526 seizes Delhi and Agra; founds the Mughal empire in India.
1500 CE	Capture of Transoxiana by Shaybani Khan, descendant of Jochi's youngest son, Shiban. Consolidates Shaybani power (Shaybanids also described as Uzbeg, from whom Uzbekistan, today, gets its name) in Transoxiana and expels Babur and other Timurids from the region.
1759 CE	Manchus of China conquer Mongolia
1921 CE	Republic of Mongolia

Mind Map

NOMADIC EMPIRES

1 Rise of the Mongol Empire

- Genghis Khan united all Mongol tribes and connected his reign to the divine elements.

2 Mongols

Mongol Society

- Mongols were pastoralists and cattle herders who earned through trade and cattle herding.
- Mongol society was patrilineal, and rich class possessed more animals and pasture.
- Genghis Khan's political system was durable and countered larger armies.

Relations between Nomads and Settled Societies

- Mongol and Central Asian tribes traded for agro-products and iron utensils in exchange of horses, fur, etc.
- Chinese rulers fortified borders with wall around 8th century BCE to deal with invasions. These fortifications started to be integrated into a common defersive outwork known as the 'Great Wall of China'.

3 Genghis Khan

- Genghis Khan was born around 1162 near the Orion river region and died in 1227.
- After victorious battles in 1206, he called himself as Great Khan of Mongols.
- Genghis Khan used seige engine and naptha bombardment technique against fortified encampments.
- Genghis Khan began military campaign in winters by using frozen rivers as highways.
- Rapid shooting arches with good horseriding skills was the backbone of Mongol army.

4 Social, Political & Military Organisation

Trade and Communication Systems Under Genghis Khan

- Yam was the rapid postal and communication system and 'Qubcur tax' was collected from Mongol nomads willingly.
- Traders paid 'Baj' tax and traveller paid 'Paiza or Gerege' tax for safe passage.

Military and Political Organisation

- Genghis Khan used decimal system and Noyan army unit system into army.
- Genghis Khan assigned newly conquered regions under four 'ulus'.
- Quriltai was an assembly of Mongol chieftains and members of the ruling family, where decision related to state and family was taken collectively.
- Civil servants were recruited from different areas.
- Genghis Khan appointed 'Ogodei' as his successor, who changed the capital of empire to Karakorum.
- Yasaq were codified laws promulgated by Genghis Khan in 1206.

5 Mongols After Genghis Khan

- Genghis Khan died in 1227 CE after which collective rule was replaced by individual dynasties.
- In 1230s, Mongols defeated the Chin dynasty in North China.
- After 1260s, Mongols lost interest in wars in the West.

6 The Mongols in World History

- Mongols restored trade route which attracted travellers like 'Marco Polo'.
- Timur rose to power around the end of the 14th century.
- Timur declared independent sovereignty after getting married to Genghis Khan's family.

NCERT Folder

Intext Questions

1. Assume that Juwaini's account of the capture of Bukhara is accurate. Imagine yourself as a resident of Bukhara and Khurasan who heard the speeches. What impact would they have had on you?

Ans If I were the resident of Bukhara and Khurasan, after hearing to the speeches I would have felt scared and considered Mongols as most cruel. It would have made me sad that I have to give away my wealth to some plunderers. Thereafter, I would have lived in fear thinking about Mongols.

2. Why was there a conflict of interests between pastoralists and peasants? Would Genghis Khan have expressed sentiments of this(Ghazan Khan's speech) nature in a speech to his nomad commanders?

Ans. There was a conflict of interest between pastoralists and peasants because

- Mongols were both pastoralists and hunter-gatherers. During natural calamities, they would run out of the resources and trespass into the other lands leading to conflicts.
- Mongols pastoral economy and limited resources was not enough to sustain them, so they used to ride the neighbouring settled cities and villages.
- They would plunder the peasants and loot the wealth for their sustenance.
- They used to dislocate agriculture and loot the cities which was devastating for peasants, whereas pastoralists had minimal damage.

Genghis Khan would not have expressed same sentiments like that of the Ghazan Khan's speech to his nomad commanders. Genghis Khan has plundered the towns and both elites and peasants suffered from his anger. He did not differentiate anyone. But Ghazan Khan was more sympathetic to peasantry who were not rebels.

3. Did the meaning of *yasa* alter over the four centuries separating Genghis Khan from Abdullah Khan? Why did Hafiz-i Tanish make a reference to Genghis Khan's *yasa* in connection with Abdullah Khan's prayer at the Muslim festival ground?

Ans. Yes, meaning of *yasa* altered over the four centuries separating Genghis Khan from Abdullah Khan. In its earliest form *yasa* meant law, decree or order.

But mid of 13th century, Mongols used *yasa* in a more general sense to mean the legal code of Genghis Khan.

Hafiz-i Tanish made a reference to *yasa* in connection with Abdullah Khan's prayer at the Muslim festival ground to justify Abdullah Khan's actions which were in contradiction with Genghis Khan's actions. He wanted to tell that he was doing it according to *yasa* of Genghis Khan so as to not give an impression that Abdullah Khan was insulting Genghis Khan.

Answer in Brief

1. Why was trade so significant to the Mongols?

Ans. Trade was significant to the Mongols because of the following reasons

- Mongols were dependent on pastoralism and some of them were dependent on hunting and gathering. Both these occupations could not sustain Mongol's dense population. Hence they relied on trade for their livelihood.
- The steppe lands where Mongols used to live, also had very little resources. Cultivation of food was not possible there.

Thus, due to these conditions, Mongols and other Central Asian nomads had to trade and barter with their settled neighbours in China. This was mutually beneficial to both the groups.

2. Why did Genghis Khan feel the need to fragment the Mongol tribes into new social and military groupings?

Ans. Genghis Khan felt the need of fragmentation of the Mongol tribes into new social and military groupings due to the following reasons

- Mongols had their own separate identities and were the inhabitant of the steppe region. Genghis Khan wanted to bring them in contact with other tribals through social groupings.
- Mongols were very brave. Genghis Khan used their bravery to organise them into military groups and built a powerful empire.
- Childhood experiences of Genghis Khan were also responsible for the fragmentation of Mongol tribes. Genghis Khan himself had to suffer a lot during his childhood.

3. How do later Mongol reflections on the yasa bring out the uneasy relationship they had with the memory of Genghis Khan?

Ans. *Yasa* meant a law, decree or an order. It was concerned with organisation of hunt, the army and postal system.

By 13th century, Mongols used it as the legal code of Genghis Khan. Initially, Genghis Khan was very harsh towards his conquered subjects.

For example, he punished people of Bukhara brutally according to *yasa*. He plundered (looted) peasants and converted agricultural lands into pastoral lands.
But later, Mongol rulers wanted to be looked as more good for all the sections of society. They themselves have

adopted settled life. Some of the rulers openly became protectors of peasants. Later, rulers like Abdullah Khan went to Bukhara for performing holiday prayers.

These kind of later Mongol actions using *yasa* brings out uneasy relationship they had with the memory of Genghis Khan.

4. 'If history relies upon written records produced by city-based literati, nomadic societies will always receive a hostile representation'. Would you agree with this statement? Does it explain the reason why Persian chronicles produced such inflated figures of casualties resulting from Mongol campaigns?

Ans. Yes, I agree with the statement as it is mostly true about the city based scholars work on nomadic societies.

For example, Mongols have not written much about themselves, most of the chronicles available were written by city based scholars who are biased against nomadic societies often referring them with derogatory terms like barbarians.

They looked at nomadic societies through their cultural lens. This is the reason why Persian chronicles have increased number of deaths regarding Mongol campaigns. Persian chronicles produced during 13th century in Il-Khanid Iran were greatly exaggerated. For example, when Genghis Khan captured Bukhara, as per the eyewitness, there were 400 soldiers who defended citadel. Persian chronicle inflated the number to 30,000 soldiers.

Answer in a Short Essay

5. Keeping the nomadic element of the Mongol and Bedouin societies in mind, how in your opinion, did their respective historical experiences differ? What explanations would you suggest account for these differences?

Ans. The difference between Mongol and Bedouin societies were

Mongol Society	Bedouin Society
Mongols were nomads from Central Asian steppes.	Bedouins were nomadic arab tribes living in desert area.
Mongols were pastoralists and hunter- gatherers.	Bedouins used to move from dry to green areas of the desert in search of food and fodder for camels.
Genghis Khan became a dominant personality which was recognised by an assembly of Mongol chieftains.	Bedouins joined Prophet Muhammad by converting to Islam impressed by his achievements.
Mongols were tolerant to other religions, cultures and did not impose their personal beliefs on public.	In Bedouin societies, they were converted to Islam and their personal beliefs were imposed on public.
Mongols expanded their empire mainly on military discipline and strategies.	In Bedouins society, religion was main motivating force for expansion of empire.
Mongols campaigns were very destructive, they devastated the cities, they raided and plundered the wealth.	It was not the same in case of Bedouin societies.

The differences in both the societies were due to different geographical, social, political and economical reasons. The difference in political reasons like after death of Muhammad, there was no established law of succession which led to many civil wars but Genghis Khan had clearly made succession rules and this led to stability after his death.

6. How does the following account enlarge upon the character of the Pax Mongolica created by the Mongols by the middle of the 13th century?

The Franciscan monk, William of Rubruck, was sent by Louis IX of France on an embassy to the great Khan Mongke's court. He reached Karakorum, the capital of Mongke, in 1254 and came across a woman from Lorraine (in France) called Paquette, who had been brought from Hungary and was in the service of one of the prince's wives who was a Nestorian Christian. At the court, he came across a Parisian goldsmith named Guillaume Boucher, 'whose brother dwelt on the Grand Pont in Paris'. This man was first employed by the Queen Sorghaqtani and then by Mongke's younger brother. Rubruck found that at the great court festivals, the Nestorian priests were admitted first, with their regalia, to bless the Grand Khan's cup, and were followed by the Muslim clergy and Buddhist and Taoist monks.

Ans. The above account depicts the character of the Pax Mongolica by the middle of the 13th century as

- Visit of William of Rubruck to embassy of Great Khan shows that Mongols had established relationships with neighbouring empires and did not live in isolation.
- The presence of woman from Lorraine shows that Mongols recruited people from different regions of the world without any discrimination.
- Presence of Parisian goldsmith shows that Mongols encouraged artisans from different countries and without hesitation put them under highest positioned people like queen in Mongol empire.
- Presence of Nestorian priests, Muslim clergy, Buddhist and Taoist monks shows that Mongols never put their personal beliefs in public policy.
- Their regime was pluralistic, multi-cultural, multi-ethnic, multi-lingual and multi-religious. This shows that Mongols had a great vision for building a great empire.

Mongols were successful in creating such an empire called Pax Mongolica, and its character was enhanced and enlarged due to the pluralistic Constitution of Mongol regime both in letter and spirit.

Exam Pattern Questions

Objective Type Questions

Multiple Choice Questions

1. The Mongols were **CBSE Diksha**
(a) intimidating (b) terrible
(c) nomadic (d) crazy

2. **Among the following, which group built the largest empire in the world by the early 14th century**
(a) The Huns (b) The Ottomans **CBSE Diksha**
(c) The Saljuq Turks (d) The Mongols

3. **The Mongols travelled with their herds to pastures land and lived in tents called** **CBSE Diksha**
(a) *anda* (b) *gers* (c) *noyan* (d) *yasa*

4. **Mongol rulers were more interested in ....**
(a) India (b) Russia (c) Japan (d) China

5. **The childhood name of Genghis Khan was** **CBSE Diksha**
(a) Morin Khurr (b) Nominjin
(c) Yamujin (d) Temujin

6. **Who was responsible for introducing the Yasa during the quriltai of 1206?**
(a) Sons of Genghis Khan (b) Genghis Khan
(c) Mongol Generals (d) Tribal Chiefs

7. **The Assembly of chieftains where all decisions relating to the family or the state was** **CBSE Diksha**
(a) Tajen (b) *Quriltai*
(c) *Qucbur* (d) *Yasa*

8. **China was divided into ....**
(a) the Hsi Hsia people of Tibetan origin in the North-Western provinces.
(b) the Jurchen whose Chin dynasty ruled North China from Peking and the Sung dynasty who controlled South China.
(c) Uighurs and Sung dynasty
(d) Both (a) and (b)

9. **During Genghis Khan's attempt to conquer China, North China was ruled by** **CBSE Diksha**
(a) His Hsia (b) Jurchen
(c) Sung dynasty (d) Ogodei

10. **Name the great cities that were surrendered to the Mongol forces.**
(a) Otrar, Bukhara, Samarqand, Balkh
(b) Gurganj, Merv
(c) Nishapur and Herat
(d) All of the above

11. **Name two groups outside Mongol tribes who were accommodated in the confederacy.**
(a) Turkic Uighurs and Kereyits
(b) Kiyat and Borjigid
(c) Kiyat and Kereyits
(d) None of the above

12. **Genghis divided his army into new military units which were required to serve under his ..... .**
(a) four sons (b) brothers
(c) son-in laws (d) None of these

13. **Genghis Khan modified the old steppe system by**
(a) dividing the old tribal groupings.
(b) distributing their members into new military units.
(c) Both (a) and (b)
(d) None of the above

14. **Genghis Khan was considered a cruel conqueror because he**
(a) forced people to become Muslim
(b) gave cities a chance to surrender
(c) brought Southern China into the empire
(d) caused many people to be slaughtered

15. **What was known as the *yam*?** **CBSE Diksha**
(a) Administration system (b) Courier system
(c) Army system (d) Calvary system

16. **Genghis Khan died in ....**
(a) 1230 (b) 1227
(c) 1225 (d) 1220

17. **Who was Mongke?** **CBSE Diksha**
(a) Trader (b) Priest
(c) Grandson of Genghis Khan (d) Monk

18. **Who controlled the office of Great Khan in the first two generations?**
(a) The descendants of the Jochi
(b) The Ogodei allied
(c) The descendants of Chaghatai
(d) Both (a) and (b)

19. **Mongol Khan belonged to which of the following faiths?**
(a) Shaman, Buddhist (b) Christian and Islam
(c) Both (a) and (b) (d) None of these

20. **What is one of Genghis Khan's achievements?** CBSE Diksha

(a) Unified Mongols
(b) Migrated to Africa
(c) He attacked the Brazilian Empire
(d) He attacked the Roman Empire

21. **Consider the following statements and choose the correct option.**

(i) The hunter-gatherers lived to the North of the pastoralists in the Siberian forests.
(ii) Early from 9th Century BCE, China suffered much from nomad intrusion and other regimes.
(iii) The Jurchen of China dynasty ruled South China from Peking.
(iv) Ogodei was the second son of Genghis Khan.

Codes

(a) Only (i)
(b) Only (ii)
(c) Both (i) and (ii)
(d) Both (iii) and (iv)

22. **Consider the following statements and choose the correct option.**

(i) Genghis Khan was born around 1262 CE.
(ii) Hsi Hsia people were of Tibetan origin in South-West provinces.
(iii) Some Mongols were pastoralists while others were hunter-gatherers.
(iv) The hunting skills of Mongols and Turks provide speed and mobility to the army.

Codes

(a) Only (i) (b) Only (iii)
(c) Both (i) and (ii) (d) Both (iii) and (iv)

23. **Arrange in sequence.**

(i) Temujin remained an ally of Ong Khan.
(ii) Temujin proclaimed Genghis Khan.
(iii) Rule of three Great Khans and continued Mongol unity.

Codes

(a) (iii), (ii), (i) (b) (i), (ii), (iii)
(c) (ii), (i), (iii) (d) (ii), (iii), (i)

24. **Arrange in sequence.**

(i) Establishment of the Republic of Mongolia
(ii) Babur found the Mughal empire
(iii) Manchus of China conquer Mongolia

Codes

(a) (ii), (iii), (i)
(b) (iii), (ii), (i)
(c) (iii), (i), (ii)
(d) (i), (ii), (iii)

25. **Identify the name of the ruler from the information given below.**

(i) He was born sometime around 1162 near the Onon river in the North of present-day Mongolia.
(ii) He was the son of Yesugei, the chieftain of the Kiyat.
(iv) The young Boghurchu was his first ally.
(v) He died in 1227.

Codes

(a) Batu Khan (b) Genghis Khan
(c) Chaghatai Khan (d) Arghun

26. **Identify the name of the ruler from the information given below.**

(i) He ascended to the throne in 1295.
(ii) He was the first Il-Khanid ruler to convert to Islam.
(iii) He ruled Iran till 1304.
(iv) He was a descendant of Genghis Khan's youngest son Toluy.

(a) Berke
(b) Uskhal
(c) Mubarak Shah
(d) Ghazan Khan

27. **Anda: Blood-brother : : Naukar: ....**

(a) Follower (b) Bondsmcn
(c) Soldier (d) Tax collector

28. **Qubcur: Tax :: *Yasa*: ....**

(a) Military (b) Communication
(c) Law (d) Religion

29. **Yam: Communication : : Tama: ....**

(a) Army (b) Territory
(c) Tax (d) Trade

Assertion-Reason

30. **Assertion (A)** From Genghis Khan's reign the Mongols had recruited civil administration from the conquered societies.

Reason (R) Chinese secretaries deployed in Iran and Persians in China.

Codes

(a) Both A and R are true and R is the correct explanation of A
(b) Both A and R are true, but R is not the correct explanation of A
(c) A is true, but R is false
(d) A is false, but R is true

31. **Assertion (A)** The hunters-gatherers lived to the North of the pastoralists in the Siberian forests.

Reason (R) They were lower ranked people than pastoralists.

Codes

(a) Both A and R are true and R is the correct explanation of A
(b) Both A and R are true, but R is not the correct explanation of A
(c) A is true, but R is false
(d) A is false, but R is true

32. **Assertion (A)** Genghis Khan's reign was full of conquests and expanding territory where boundaries changed frequently.

Reason (R) Genghis Khan's youngest son, Toluy, received the ancestral lands of Mongolia.

Codes

(a) Both A and R are true and R is the correct explanation of A
(b) Both A and R are true, but R is not the correct explanation of A
(c) A is true, but R is false
(d) A is false, but R is true

Match the Following

33.

List I	List II
A. Temujin	1. Mother of Genghis Khan
B. Yesugei	2. Childhood name of Genghis Khan
C. Oelun-eke	3. Father of Genghis Khan
D. Boghurchu	4. Friend of Genghis Khan

Codes

	A	B	C	D		A	B	C	D
(a)	3	1	2	4	(b)	2	3	1	4
(c)	2	1	4	3	(d)	4	2	1	3

34.

List I	List II
A. Jochi	1. Received Transoxianian steppe
B. Chaghatai	2. Received Russian steppes
C. Ogodei	3. Received areas near Karakorum
D. Toluy	4. Received the ancestral land of Mongolia

Codes

	A	B	C	D
(a)	3	1	2	4
(b)	2	4	1	3
(c)	2	1	3	4
(d)	2	1	4	3

Picture Based Questions

35. **Which of the following rivers of Monglian has been depicted in the below image?**

(a) Turel river (b) Selenge river
(c) Ider river (d) Onon river

36. **The given image shows the 'The Great Wall of China' which was built as a series of fortification to save the peasants of Northern China from the raids of**

(a) Nomadic herdsmen from the Eurasian steppe
(b) Military of the Roman Empire
(c) Iqtadars of the Arabian Empire
(d) None of the above

37. **The given image depicts the capture of Baghdad by the Mongols, it marked the end of which of the following empires?**

(a) Sassanid dynasty (b) Umayyad Caliphate
(c) Abbasid caliphate (d) None of these

Answers

1. (c) nomadic
2. (d) The Mongols
3. (b) *gers*
4. (d) China
5. (d) Temujin
6. (b) Genghis Khan
7. (b) *Quriltai*
8. (d) Both (a) and (b)
9. (b) Jurchen
10. (d) All of the above
11. (a) Turkic Uighurs and Kereyits
12. (a) four sons
13. (c) Both (a) and (b)
14. (d) caused many people to be slaughtered
15. (b) Courier system
16. (b) 1227
17. (c) Grandson of Genghis Khan
18. (d) Both (a) and (b)
19. (c) Both (a) and (b)
20. (a) Unified Mongols
21. (a) Only (i)
22. (b) Only (iii)
23. (b) (i), (ii), (iii)
24. (a) (ii), (iii), (i)
25. (b) Genghis Khan
26. (d) Ghazan Khan
27. (b) Bondsmen
28. (c) Law
29. (a) Army
30. (b) Both A and R are true, but R is not the correct explanation of A
31. (a) Both A and R are true and R is the correct explanation of A
32. (b) Both A and R are true, but R is not the correct explanation of A
33. (b)
34. (c)
35. (d) Onon river
36. (a) Nomadic herdsmen from the Eurasian steppe
37. (c) Abbasid caliphate

Subjective Questions

Short Answer Type Questions

1. What does the term barbarian mean?

Ans. The term barbarian is derived from the Greek word *'barbaros'* which meant a non-Greek, someone whose language sounded like a random noise 'bar-bar'.

In Greek texts, barbarians were depicted like children, unable to speak properly, cowardly, not manly, luxurious, cruel, slothful, greedy and politically unable to govern themselves. The stereotype used the term barbarian for the Germanic tribes, the Gauls and the Huns.

2. Discuss the historiography produced by Marxist scholars.

Ans. Marxist historiography argued that the mode of production in that period was the reason for the nature of social relations. According to it, Genghis Khan and the emerging Mongol empire was witnessing a transition from tribal to a feudal mode of production i.e. from a classless society to one where there are differences between lords who are owners of land and the peasant. Though, it was a deterministic history by Marxists, it produced excellent research work on Mongol empire.

3. What were the problems with sources of history in different languages?

Ans. Problems with sources of history in different languages were as follows

- The transcontinental span of the Mongol empire also meant that the sources available to scholars are written in a vast number of languages.
- The same text was produced in two languages with different contents which created disparities.

  For example, the Mongolian and Chinese versions of the earliest reports on Genghis Khan were quite different. The Latin and Italian versions of Marco Polo's travels to the Mongol court do not match.
- Historians also had problem of inferring the meanings of the words in different languages and apply it to Mongols context.

4. Discuss the geographical features of the Mongols residence areas.

Ans. Mongols led nomadic life in the steppes of Central Asia in a tract of land in the area of the modern state of Mongolia. Following were the geographical features of the Mongols residence

A majestic landscape with wide horizons, wavy plains, surrounded by the snow-capped Altai mountains to the West, the dry Gobi desert in the South and drained by the Onon and Selenga rivers.

- Onon and Selenga rivers and numerous springs from the melting snows of the hills in the North and the West.
- Luxuriant and plenty of grasses for pasture and animals for hunting were available.
- Mongols who were hunter-gatherers resided in the Siberian forests.
- These areas had extreme climatic conditions with harsh, long winters followed by brief, dry summers.

5. Discuss about Mongols briefly.

Ans. The Mongols were a diverse body of people linked by similarities of language to the Tatars, Khitan and Manchus to the East, and the Turkic tribes to the West. While some of them were pastoralists, others were hunter-gatherers.

Pastoralists lived in the steppes of Central Asia in a tract of land in the area of the modern state of Mongolia. The hunter-gatherers resided to the North of the pastoralists in the Siberian forests. Hunter-gatherers were humbler body of people than pastoralists, making a living from trade in furs of animals.

6. Discuss the relations between nomadic and agrarian societies.

Ans. The social and political organisations of the nomadic and agrarian societies were very different, but the two societies were hardly foreign to each other.

The scant resources of the steppe lands forced Mongols and other Central Asian nomads to trade and barter with their settled neighbours in China. This was mutually beneficial to each other, as agricultural produce and iron utensils from China were exchanged for horses, furs and animals hunted in the steppe. There was also tension between both the groups, especially when both of them applied military pressure to increase the profit.

7. Discuss how Temujin emerged as a dominant personality in the politics of steppe lands.

Ans. Temujin emerged as a dominant personality in the politics of steppe lands in the following ways

- During 1180s and 1190s, Temujin remained an ally of Ong Khan and used the alliance to defeat powerful enemies like Jamuqa, his old friend who had become a hostile enemy.
- After defeating Jamuqa, Temujin felt confident and moved against other tribes like the powerful Tatars who killed his father, the Kereyits and Ong Khan himself in 1203.
- The final defeat of the Naiman people and the powerful Jamuqa in 1206 made Temujin as the dominant personality on the politics of the steppe lands. He further defeated Hsi Hsia people by 1209, breached the Great Wall of China in 1213 and devastated Peking in 1215.

8. Why did Chinese build Great Wall of China?

Ans. Chinese built Great Wall of China to protect their population. Throughout its history, China suffered extensively from nomad intrusion and different regimes right from as early as 8th century BCE. They built fortifications to protect their population. Starting from the 3rd century BCE, these fortifications started to be integrated into a common defensive structure known today as the Great Wall of China. This shows the amount of disturbance and fear created by nomadic raids on the agrarian societies of North China and that resulted in building the Great Wall of China.

9. Discuss some military skills that proved to be effective for Mongols success.

Ans. Some military skills that proved to be effective for Mongols success were

- The horse riding skills of the Mongols and Turks provided speed and mobility to their army.
- Mongol's ability to shoot arrows rapidly from horseback, perfected during regular hunting expeditions. The steppe army fighting on horses had always travelled light and moved quickly.
- Nomads were weak against fortified camps, Genghis Khan overcame this problem by learning the importance of artillery and fire based weapons. His engineers prepared light portable equipment and this was used against opponents with devastating effect.

10. How did Genghis Khan assign the responsibility of governing the newly conquered people to his four sons?

Ans. Genghis Khan assigned the responsibilities to his sons in following ways

- **Eldest son, Jochi** He was given the Russian steppes which extended as far West as his horses could roam.
- **Second son, Chaghatai** He was given Transoxianian steppe and lands North of the Pamir mountains adjacent to those of his brother.
- **Third son, Ogodei** Genghis Khan decided that Ogodei would succeed him as the Great Khan.
- **Fourth son, Toluy** He was given the ancestral lands of Mongolia.

11. Genghis Khan had designed a rapid courier system that connected the distant areas of his regime. Explain. **Competency Based Que**

Ans. Genghis Khan had designed a rapid courier system that connected the distant areas of his regime in the following ways

- Fresh horses and despatch riders were placed in outposts at regularly spaced distances.
- For the maintenance of this communication system, the Mongol nomads contributed a tenth of their herd i.e. either horses or livestock as provisions. This was called the *qubcur* tax which was paid by nomads willingly for the multiple benefits that it brought to them.
- The courier system (yam) was further refined after Genghis Khan's death and its speed and reliability surprised travellers.

- It enabled the Great Khans to keep a check on developments at the farthest end of their regime across the continental landmass.

12. Discuss the Mongke's warning to French ruler. Were these empty warnings effective?

Ans. After Genghis Khan's death in 1227 CE, his successors also went in the same spirit like him. Genghis Khan's grandson Mongke gave the following warnings to the French ruler

- He warned French ruler Louis IX that there should only one lord in the world that is Genghis Khan.
- He warned about the consequences of bringing any army against them.
- These warnings were effective because another grandson of Genghis Khan, Batu in his campaigns destroyed Russian lands up to Moscow, seized Poland and Hungary, and camped outside Vienna.

13. Why did conquered people did not have affirmity towards Mongol rulers?

Ans. Conquered people did not have affirmity towards Mongol rulers because during the campaigns in the first half of the 13th century, cities were destroyed, agricultural lands were laid to waste, and trade and handicraft production got disrupted.

Tens of thousands of people were killed, even more were enslaved. All class of people from the elites to peasants suffered.

Due to such instability, the underground canals, *qantas* in the arid Iranian plateau did not get regular maintenance and were destroyed which led to desertification of lands. Thus, such outcomes due to campaigns by Mongols created a fear and hatred in minds of conquered people.

14. 'The army of Genghis Khan was a mixture of diverse people'. Comment. **Competency Based Que**

Ans. It is true that the army of Genghis Khan was a mixture of diverse people. Among the Mongols and other nomadic societies, all adult males of the tribe who were fit, became part of armed forces when the occasion demanded.

The unification of different Mongol tribes and subsequent campaigns against diverse people introduced new members into Genghis Khan's army complicating the composition. The army had become heterogeneous from a small, undifferentiated body.

It included groups like the Turkic Uighurs who had accepted Genghis Khan's authority willingly and defeated people like the Kereyits who were also accommodated in the confederacy despite their earlier warfare.

15. Enumerate various causes for the success of Genghis Khan. **CBSE Diksha**

Ans. Genghis Khan's military success come from his ability to innovate and adapt steppe arrangements into effective strategies.

Following were the causes for the success of Genghis Khan

- The horse riding and hunting skills of Mongols and Turks provided speed and mobility to the army.
- Their abilities as rapid shooting archery from horseback were further perfected during regular hunting expeditions which doubled the chance of victory over the enemies.
- They carried out campaigns in the depths of winter by using frozen rivers as highways to enemy cities and camps.
- They brought their knowledge of moving light in terrain as an effective military strategy.
- He understood the importance of artillery and fire-based weapons.
- His engineers built light portable equipment which he used against his opponents.

Long Answer Type Questions

1. In pre-industrial age of poor technological communications, what skills were deployed by the Mongols to administer and control such a vast empire and handle diverse social and religious groups?

Ans. Genghis Khan initiated some changes in Mongol people with a vision to establish a great empire and administer, and control it. These changes were

- Genghis Khan worked to systematically erase the old tribal identities of the different groups who joined his confederacy. He changed the old steppe order and divided old tribal groupings and distributed their members into new military units. So now a military contingent had people from different groups and this integrated them into a single group with an identity derived from Genghis Khan.
- Genghis Khan rewarded the people who were loyal to him. He publicly honoured some of them as his blood-brothers (*anda*). Some others were given special ranking as his bondsmen (*naukar*), a title that marked close relationship with the master. The old rankings were removed and new aristocracy derived its status from a close relationship with the Great Khan of the Mongols.
- The new military contingents were kept under the control of his four sons. He also assigned the responsibility of governing newly conquered people to his four sons. This decentralised the power and also provided a sense among all the family members that everyone is sharing the power in the empire. This

feeling was further strengthened by *quriltais* i.e. assembly of chieftains where all decisions were collectively taken. He also declared that which son was going to access the throne after him, which made it easy for avoiding future rebellions.

- Genghis Khan also developed rapid courier system that connected distant areas of his regime. This was further refined and developed by later Great Khans to keep a check on developments at the farthest end of their regime across the continental landmass.
- Mongol Khans themselves belonged to multiple faiths like Shaman, Buddhist, Christian and Islam, but they never imposed their personal beliefs on public policy. They recruited administrators and armed contingents from people of all ethnic groups and religions. Thus, their empire was multi-ethnic, multi-lingual and multi-religious.
- Genghis Khan has laid foundation and given a direction to his descendants which helped Mongols to administer and control such a vast empire. Their tolerance to all religions and ethnicities also helped them to keep the empire intact.

2. "Genghis Khan has spent most of his life in military combat. His military achievements were astounding". Justify the statement and discuss his various conquests. Competency Based Que

Ans. It is justified that Genghis Khan spent most of his life in military combat. His military achievements were

- Genghis Khan remained an ally of Ong Khan and used the alliance to defeat powerful enemies like Jamuqa. Then he defeated other tribes like powerful Tatars, the Kereyits and Ong Khan. He defeated the Naiman people and became a dominant personality in Mongol politics.
- In 1209, he defeated Hsi Hsia in the North-Western provinces of China. In 1213 CE, he breached the Great Wall of China and raided Peking in 1215 CE. Genghis Khan was satisfied with the progress of his campaigns and returned to Mongolian homeland in 1216 CE and left the military affairs of the region to his subordinates.
- In 1218 CE, Genghis Khan defeated Qara Khita who controlled the Tien Shan mountains in North-West of China and Mongol rule had reached the Amu Darya, and the states of Transoxiana and Khwarazm.
- Between 1219 and 1221 CE, the great cities like Otrar, Bukhara, Samaqand, Balkh, Gurganj, Merv, Nishapur and Herat surrendered to Mongol forces.
- Mongol forces in pursuit of Sultan Muhammad pushed into Azerbaijan, defeated Russian forces at the Crimea and encircled the Caspian sea.

Genghis Khan died in 1227 CE. We can see that he spent his entire life in military combat and laid the foundation for the biggest empire world has ever seen i.e. Mongol empire.

3. Discuss the expansion of Mongol's empire after the death of Genghis Khan. What differences arose among the family members of Genghis Khan after his death?

Ans. Expansion of Mongol Empire Mongol expansion after Genghis Khan's death was divided into two distinctive phases. The first was during 1236-42 CE and second was during 1255-1300 CE.

In the first phase of expansion, Mongols gained majorly the Russian steppes, Bulghar, Kiev, Poland and Hungary. In the second phase, the whole of China, Iran, Iraq and Syria were conquered. After this campaign boundaries of empire were established. Though Vienna, Western Europe, as well as Egypt was within the grasp of Mongol forces, their retreat from Hungarian steppes and defeat at hands of the Egyptian forces signalled the emergence of new political trends.

Differences among the Family Members

After the death of Genghis Khan, the internal politics of succession within the Mongol family started. This argument can be supported through following points

- The descendants of Jochi and Ogodei allied to control the office of Great Khan in the first two generations. These interests became more important than the campaigns in Europe.
- Later, Toluyid branch of Genghis Khanid descendants marginalised Jochi and Ogodei lineages.
- When Mongke, a descendant of Toluy, accessed the throne, the campaigns were pursued in Iran during 1250s. But in 1960s, Toluyid interests were in the conquest of China, so forces and supplies were diverted to heartlands of Mongol dominion.
- As a result, the Mongols fielded a small, understaffed force against the Egyptian military. Thus, their defeat with Egyptians and the increased preoccupation with China of the Toluyid family marked the end of Western expansion of Mongols.
- Conflict between Jochid and Toluyid descendants along the Russian-Iranian boundary diverted Jochids away from further European expansion. The internal conflicts between members of ruling family had mixed results. Mongol expansion was suspended in the West but their campaigns reunited China under the Mongols.

4. Discuss the evolution of '*yasa*'. How did it help Mongols to unite and create a universal empire?

Or **'Yasa played an important role in uniting Mongols.' Justify the statement.** CBSE Diksha

Ans. Evolution of Yasa

As per the research of David Ayalon, *yasa* was the code of law that Genghis Khan had promulgated at the *quriltai* in 1206. It had elaborated on the complex ways in which the memory of the Great Khan was shaped by his successors.

In its earliest formulation, the term was written as *yasaq* which meant law, decree or order. *Yasaq* was concerned about administrative regulations like the organisation of the hunt, the army and the postal system. By the middle of 13th century, Mongols started using the term *yasa* in a more general sense to mean the 'legal code of Genghis Khan'.

Significance of *Yasa* in uniting Mongols and creating a Universal Empire

By the mid of 13th century, Mongols had emerged as a unified people and created the largest empire, the world had ever seen. They ruled over sophisticated urban societies with their respective histories, cultures and laws. The one way in which they could protect their identity and distinctiveness was through a claim to a sacred law given to them by their ancestor. The *yasa* gave them this identity and distinctiveness.

The *yasa* was a compilation of all the customary traditions of Mongol tribes, but they referred it as Genghis Khan's code of law to give it a status equivalent to that of laws given by Moses and Solomon. Thus, this authoritative code could be imposed on their subjects.

The *yasa* served to unite the Mongol people around a body of shared beliefs and acknowledged the love towards Genghis Khan and his descendants. Though, they absorbed different aspects of settled lifestyle, *yasa* gave them confidence to retain their ethnic identity and impose their 'law' on their defeated subjects.

Thus, the powerful ideology which was inspired by the vision of Genghis Khan became important in the construction of a Mongol universal empire.

5. Discuss the communication and trade system under Mongols. CBSE Diksha

Ans. The Mongol empire, especially under Genghis Khan, developed sophisticated systems of communication and trade, which played a crucial role in the administration and expansion of their vast empire. Here's an outline of these systems

Communication System under the Mongols

- Genghis Khan created the *Yam*, a courier system to ensure swift communication across the vast empire.
- Relay stations were established at regular intervals, with fresh horses and riders, allowing for quick transmission of messages.
- Nomadic Mongols contributed *qubcur* tax (a portion of their herds) to maintain the system.
- This courier system allowed the Great Khans to keep a close eye on distant regions, ensuring the efficient flow of information.
- The Mongol empire issued *paiza* (passports) to facilitate safe passage for merchants, diplomats, and travellers, promoting ease of movement.
- The *baj* tax was levied on traders for using Mongol-protected routes, which acknowledged the Khan's authority and ensured safe trade.
- The communication network was enhanced even after Genghis Khan's death, becoming highly efficient and reliable.

Trade System under the Mongols

- The Mongol empire revived and protected the Silk Road, facilitating commerce between Europe, the Middle East, and China.
- The Mongol Empire linked the economies of the East and West, leading to flourishing markets across the continent.
- Mongol territories became central points for trade, extending beyond China to their capital, Karakorum and other regions.
- Along with goods, ideas, technology, and culture also moved freely. This trade network facilitated the exchange of knowledge, including innovations in medicine, astronomy and military strategies.
- The Mongols encouraged foreign merchants and scholars to travel across the empire, contributing to a rich cultural and intellectual exchange.

Thus, the Mongols under Genghis Khan created one of the most efficient communication and trade networks of their time, bridging vast distances across Eurasia. Their systems not only supported administrative control but also revitalised long-distance trade, shaping the economic and cultural landscape of the medieval world.

6. Elaborate social, political and military organisation under Mongols. CBSE Diksha

Ans. Following were the aspects with respect to social, political and military organisation under Mongols

Social Organisation

- Among the Mongols all the able-bodied, adult males of the tribe carried arms: they constituted the armed forces when the occasion demanded.
- The unification of the different Mongol tribes and subsequent campaigns against diverse people introduced new members into Genghis Khan's army. It included groups like the Turks, Chinese and Arabs who had accepted his authority willingly.
- The society included groups like the Turkic Uighurs, the defeated people like - the Kereyits. It was a body composed of diverse population.

Political Organisation

- Genghis Khan assigned the responsibility of governing the newly- conquered people to his four sons. These comprised the four *ulus*. Military contingents of the individual princes were placed in each *ulus*.
- The sense of a dominion shared by the members of the family was underlined at the assembly of chieftains, *quriltai*, where all decisions relating to the family or the state for the forthcoming season campaigns, distribution of plunder, pasture lands and succession were collectively taken.

Military Organisation

- Genghis Khan worked to systematically erase the old tribal identities of the different groups who joined his confederacy.
- His army was organised according to the old steppe system of decimal units. Any individual who tried to move from his allotted group without permission received harsh punishment.
- He divided the army into four units and they were required to serve under his four sons and specially chosen captains of his army units called *noyan*.
- The soldiers who had served Genghis Khan loyally through different challenges for many years were publicly honoured, some of these individuals as his 'blood-brothers' and others were given special ranking as his bondsmen, a title that marked their close relationship with their master.

Source Based Questions

Read the sources given below and answer the following questions.

1. The Capture of Bukhara

Juwaini, a late 13th century Persian chronicler of the Mongol rulers of Iran, carried an account of the capture of Bukhara in 1220. After the conquest of the city, Juwaini reported, Genghis Khan went to the festival ground where the rich residents of the city were and addressed them: 'O people know that you have committed great sins, and that the great ones among you have committed these sins. If you ask me what proof I have for these words, I say it is because I am the punishment of God. If you had not committed great sins, God would not have sent a punishment like me upon you'... Now one man had escaped from Bukhara after its capture and had come to Khurasan. He was questioned about the fate of the city and replied: 'They came, they [mined the walls], they burnt, they slew, they plundered and they departed.'

(i) **Who was Juwaini?**

(ii) **How did Genghis Khan justify the sins of Bukhara city residents?**

(iii) **Which city was captured in the passage? What did the survivor tell about the destruction of city?**

Ans. (i) Juwaini was a late 13th century Persian chronicler of the Mongol rulers of Iran. He carried an account of the capture of Bukhara in 1220.

(ii) Genghis Khan called himself the punishment sent by God, and said that if they were not sinners, God would not have sent him to punish them. In this way, he justified the sins of Bukhara city residents.

(iii) Bukhara city was captured in 1220 by Genghis Khan. The survivor told that Mongols came and brought down walls, burnt city, murdered people, looted the wealth and then went away.

2. Estimated Extent of Mongol Destruction

All reports of Genghis Khan's campaigns agree at the vast number of people killed following the capture of cities that defied his authority. The numbers are staggering: at the capture of Nishapur in 1220; 1,747,000 people were massacared while the toll at Herat in 1222 was 1,600,000 people and at Baghdad in 1258 - 800,000. Smaller towns suffered proportionately: Nasa, 70,000 dead; Baihaq district, 70,000; and at Tun in the Kuhistan province, 12,000 individuals were executed.

How did medieval chroniclers arrive at such figure? Juwaini, the Persian chronicler of the Ilkhans stated that 1,300,000 people were killed in Merv. He reached the figure because it took thirteen days to count the dead and each day they counted 100,000 corpses.

(i) **Which cities were generally destroyed more by Genghis Khan's campaigns? Name four cities where lakhs of people were killed.**

(ii) **Name two smaller towns which saw the wrath of Genghis Khan.**

(iii) **Who stated the number of people killed at Merv? How did they reach to the figure about number of people killed in Merv?**

Ans. (i) The cities which were destroyed more by Genghis Khan's campaigns were those which ignored his authority. Nishapur, Herat, Baghdad and Merv were the cities where lakhs of people were killed.

(ii) The smaller towns which saw the wrath of Genghis Khan were Nasa where 70,000 were dead and Tun in the Kuhistan province where 12,000 people were killed.

(iii) Juwaini, the Persian chronicler of the Ilkhans stated that 13,00,000 people were killed in Merv.

After counting 100,000 corpses per day for thirteen days, the figure of 13,00,000 people killed in Merv was arrived.

3. Ghazan Khan's Speech

Ghazan Khan (1295-1304 CE) was the first Il-Khanid ruler to convert to Islam. He gave the following speech to the Mongol-Turkish nomad commanders, a speech that was probably drafted by his Persian *wazir* Rashiduddin and included in the minister's letters:

'I am not on the side of the Persian peasantry. If there is a purpose in pillaging them all, there is no one with more power to do this than I. Let us rob them together. But if you wish to be certain of collecting grain and food for your tables in the future, I must be harsh with you. You must be taught reason. If you insult the peasantry, take their oxen and seed and trample their crops into the ground, what will you do in the future? ... The obedient peasantry must be distinguished from the peasantry who are rebels...'

(i) To whom Ghazan Khan gave his speech and who drafted his speech?

(ii) "There is no one with more power to do this than I". What was he referring to do? Who is I?

(iii) What was Ghazan Khan trying to teach his nomad commanders?

Ans. (i) Ghazan Khan gave his speech to the Mongol-Turkish nomad commanders, and his speech was probably drafted by Persian *wazir* Rashiduddin.

(ii) Here 'I' is Ghazan Khan. He was telling if there is a purpose to destroy peasants, he is the most powerful one to do it.

(iii) Ghazan Khan is trying to teach his commanders that if peasantry, oxen and crops were destroyed, they would not have food and grains in future. The obedient peasantry must be distinguished from the peasantry who were rebels.

4. Yasa

In 1221 CE, after the conquest of Bukhara, Genghis Khan had assembled the rich Muslim residents at the festival ground and had admonished them. He called them sinners and warned them to compensate for their sins by parting with their hidden wealth. The episode was dramatic enough to be painted and for a long time afterwards people still remembered the incident. In the late 16th century, 'Abdullah Khan, a distant descendant of Jochi, Genghis Khan's eldest son, went to the same festival ground in Bukhara. Unlike, Genghis Khan, however, 'Abdullah Khan went to perform his holiday prayers there. His chronicler, Hafiz- Tanish, reported this performance of Muslim piety by his master and included the surprising comment: 'this was according to the *yasa* of Genghis Khan'.

(i) How did Genghis Khan want to compensate rich people's sins?

(ii) Who was Abdullah Khan? Why did Abdullah Khan go to festival ground in Bukhara?

(iii) Why did Hafiz-i Tanish report that piety was in accordance with *yasa* of Genghis Khan?

Ans. (i) Genghis Khan warned rich residents of Bukhara to compensate their sins by giving away their hidden wealth.

(ii) Abdullah Khan was a distant descendant of Jochi who is Genghis Khan's eldest son. He went to festival ground to perform his holiday prayers.

(iii) Hafiz-i Tanish reported that piety was in accordance with *yasa* of Genghis Khan because he wanted to justify the actions of Abdullah Khan by referring to *yasa* of Genghis Khan, so that one should not think that he is disrespecting Genghis Khan who was his ancestor.

Map Based Questions

1. Mark the following locations on the map of the Central Asia.

(i) Karakorum **(ii) Turfan**
(iii) Delhi **(iv) Samarqand**
(v) Nishapur

Ans.

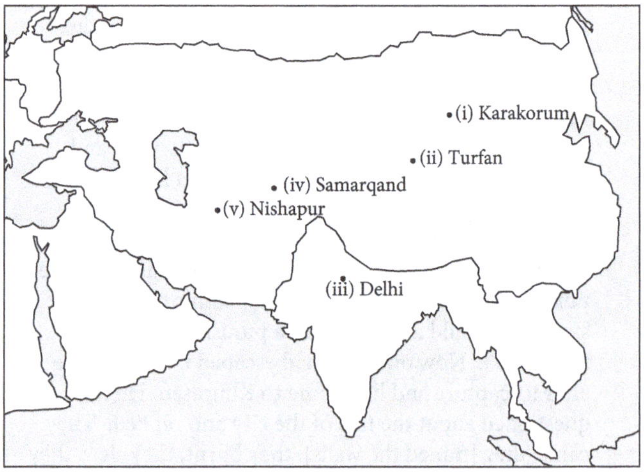

2. **Identify the following locations marked on the map of the Central Asia given below.**

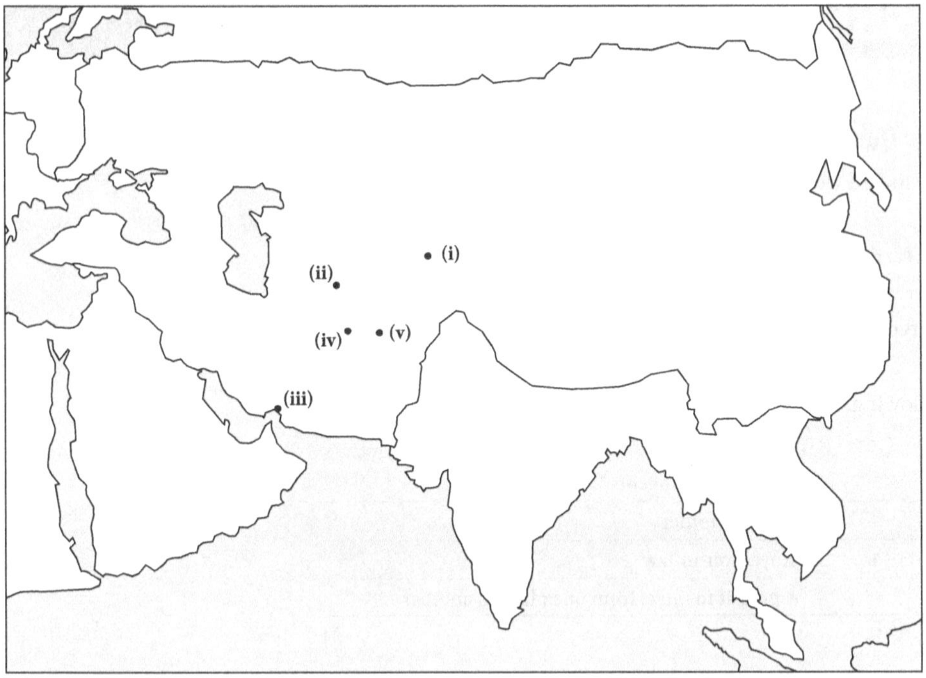

Ans.

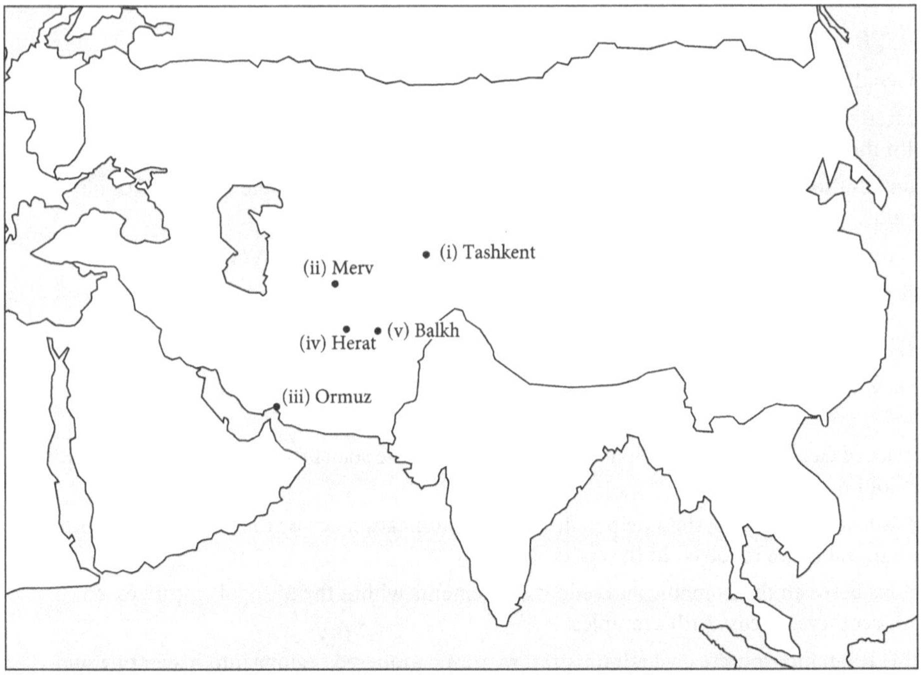

SELF ASSESSMENT TEST

Objective Type Questions

1. Mongols were linked with the .... in the East.
   (a) Tatars (b) Khitans (c) Manchus (d) All of these
2. .... was earlier name of Genghis Khan.
   (a) Mongke (b) Temujin (c) Ogodei (d) Guyuk
3. *Qubcur* was a type of
   (a) tax (b) province (c) animal (d) None of these
4. Match the Following.

List I	List II
A. *Anda*	1. Military contingents
B. *Tama*	2. Blood- brother
C. *Paiza*	3. Royal son-in-law
D. *Guregen*	4. A permit to move from one place to another

Codes

	A	B	C	D
(a)	3	1	2	4
(b)	2	1	4	3
(c)	2	1	3	4
(d)	4	2	1	3

Short Answer Type Questions

5. Unlike Attila, Genghis Khan's political system was far more durable. Discuss.
6. How did the scarce resources of the steppe lands influence the Mongols and other central Asian nomads relationship with their sedentary neighbours in China?
7. Examine the contribution of Genghis Khan's reorganisation of the Mongol people to success of his military campaigns.
8. What were the consequences of Sultan Muhammad's execution of Mongol envoys in 1218?
9. Analyse the role of Genghis Khan's use of Mongol cavalry in his military success?

Long Answer Type Questions

10. What were the key factors leading to the decline of Mongol military expansion in the West after the 1260s?
11. Discuss the impact of Genghis Khan's military reorganisation on the social structure and tribal identities within the Mongol Empire.
12. How did Genghis Khan's courier system help maintain communication across the vast Mongol Empire and what were the challenges involved in the system?
13. The contradictions between the nomadic and sedentary elements within the Mongol empire eased through the 13th century. Discuss with examples.
14. How did Genghis Khan incorporate civil administrators from conquered regions into his empire and what role did they play in governance?

SECTION C
CHANGING TRADITIONS

TIMELINE III (C. 1300 CE to 1700 CE)

The period under consideration witnessed several major developments in Europe, including changes in agriculture and the lives of peasants. It was also marked by a range of cultural developments. This timeline draws attention to contacts between the continents, stimulated in many instances by the growth of trade. The impact of these contacts was varied. While ideas, inventions and goods were shared across continents, there was also constant warfare between kingdoms to control land, resources and access to trade routes. As a result, men and women were often displaced and enslaved, if not exterminated. In many ways, the lives of people were transformed beyond recognition.

4

CHAPTER

Between the 9th and 16th centuries, socio-economic and political changes occurred in Western Europe. The Church became a powerful force in European politics.
The relationship between Christian priests, landowning nobles and peasants is important for understanding European history.

YOUR STUDY GOALS

YOUR PRACTICE GOAL

- Objective Type Questions (35 Qs ; MCQs, A-R, Matching, Picture Based)
- Subjective Questions (19 SAs, 9 LAs)
- Source Based Questions (5 Qs)
- Map Based Questions (2 Qs)

The Three Orders

4.1 Sources of Medieval European Society

- European historians have conducted extensive research on regional and local history. This detailed work has been possible due to the abundance of historical materials like documents on land ownership, prices and legal cases.
- Churches maintained records of births, marriages and deaths, helping in family and population studies.
- Inscriptions and songs provided insights into trade and community activities.
- These sources help historians to understand economic life, population growth and peasant revolts.

1 **Feudalism** A social system that existed in Europe during the Medieval Era in which people worked and fought for nobles who gave them protection and the use of land in return.

2. **Medieval Era** It refers to the period in European history between the fifth and the fifteenth centuries.

4.2 An Introduction to Feudalism

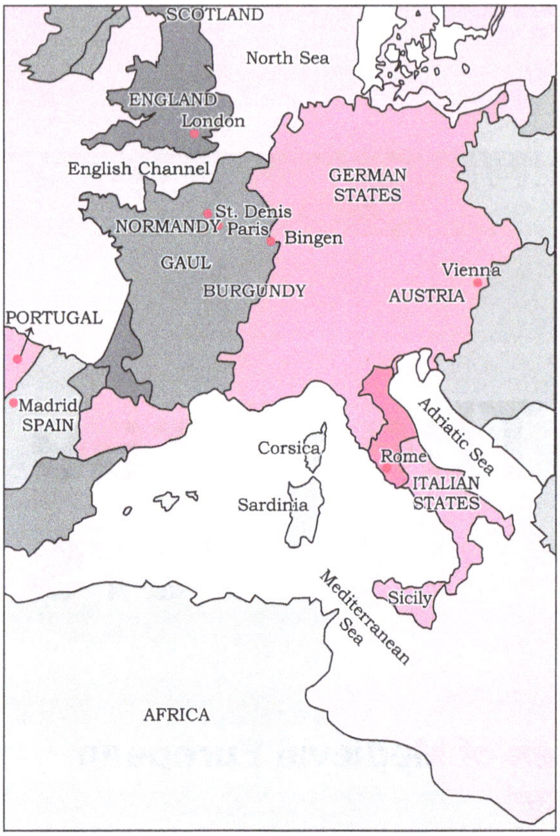

▲ *Western Europe*

- Historians use the term "**feudalism**[1]" to describe the economic, legal, political and social relationships that existed during the **medieval**[2] era, roughly between the 5th and 15th centuries.
- The word 'Feudalism' has been derived from the German word "**feud**," meaning a piece of land.
- This system primarily developed in medieval France and later spread to England and Southern Italy.
- In an economic sense, Feudalism refers to a kind of **agricultural production** based on the relationship between lords and peasants. Their relationship involved economic, social and political factors.
- Peasants provided labour services to lords in exchange for military protection. Lords also exercised judicial control over their peasants.
- The origin of feudalism can be traced to the Roman Empire and the reign of **Frankish King Charlemagne** (742-814 CE). However, it became the main social structure in much of Europe by the late 11th century.

'Marc Bloch: Earliest Scholar on 'Feudalism'

- **Marc Bloch** was a French historian who made significant contributions to the study of feudalism. He challenged the traditional focus on political history and emphasised the importance of international relations, the lives of ordinary people, geography and collective behaviour.
- Bloch's work, **Feudal Society**, provides a detailed analysis of French society between 900 and 1300 CE. The book describes the medieval socio-economic, legal, political and social relationships.
- Bloch's career was cut short when the Nazis shot him during World War II.

Feudalism in France and England

France

- The Franks, a Germanic tribe, gave their name to Gaul, which became **France**.
- **Gaul**, a province of the Roman Empire, had diverse landscapes, including coastlines, mountains, rivers, forests and plains suitable for agriculture.
- The Christian French kings ruled the kingdom from the 6th century.
- In 800 CE, **King Charlemagne** was crowned **Holy Roman Emperor** by the Pope. This strengthened the relationship between the French monarchy and the Church.

England

- In the 11th century, a **Duke from Normandy** conquered the island of England-Scotland which was separated from France by a narrow channel.
- Feudalism developed in England after Norman's conquest.
- The Angles and Saxons had settled in England in the 6th century. **William**, the Duke of Normandy, defeated the Saxon King of England in the 11th century.
- There were disputes between England and France over territory and trade. **William I** mapped and distributed land to 180 Norman noble.

- Lords became chief tenants of the king and provided military service in the form of knights. The Lords gifted land to knights in exchange for service. Private warfare was not allowed for knights.
- Anglo-Saxon peasants became tenants of various landholders.

Quick Test 1

1. What does Feud mean?
2. Who was Marc Bloch?
3. Which king was given the title of 'Holy Roman Emperor' by the Pope?
4. Which king defeated the Saxon king of England?

4.3 The Three Orders

Society was categorised into three orders: clergy, nobility and peasantry depending on their work.

The First Order: The Clergy

- **Bishops** and **clerics**, members of the Christian clergy, constituted the first order and guided Christians throughout Europe.
- Most villages had their own churches, where people gathered every Sunday for sermons and to pray together.
- **Serfs**[3] and physically challenged people were banned from becoming priests. Women also could not become priests. Men who became priests could not marry.
- Bishops were considered the religious nobility. They owned large estates, lived in luxurious palaces and held significant wealth.
- The Catholic Church was a powerful institution that did not rely on the king for its authority.
- The Church had its own laws, owned significant amounts of land granted by rulers and could levy taxes.
- The Pope was the head of the Western Church and lived in Rome.
- The Church had the right to collect a **tithe**[4]. The Church also received money through **endowments**[5], donations made by wealthy individuals for their own benefit or for the well-being of their dead relatives for their afterlife.

The Church and Feudalism

- The Church adopted some important ceremonies from feudal customs.
- The act of kneeling in prayer with folded hands and a bowed head was inspired by how knights pledged loyalty to their lords.
- In feudal culture the term '**lord**' was used to refer to God. It reflects the overlap between religious and secular practices.

The Church and Society

- Even after adopting Christianity, Europeans kept some of their old magical beliefs.
- **Christmas** and **Easter** became important religious holidays around the 4th century.
- Christmas originated from a pre-Roman festival that followed the solar calendar, while Easter replaced a festival associated with the arrival of spring, which was based on the lunar calendar.
- On Easter, people would tour their village lands. With the arrival of Christianity, villages came to be known as **parishes**[6], led by a priest.

---

3 Serfs A person who is forced to live and work on land that belongs to a landowner whom they have to obey.
4 Tithe A kind of tax collected by the Church from the peasants in France. It was 1/10th of the total produce.
5 Endowments A sum of money or property donated to a person or organisation, to be used for a specific person.
6 Parish It is the area under the supervision of one priest.

- Although religious holidays were mainly for prayer, people often celebrated with festivities and feasts.
- Pilgrimage involving long journeys to shrines of martyrs or large churches was an important aspect of Christian life.

Monks and Monasteries

- Monks were highly committed Christians who lived in isolated communities called **abbeys**[7] or **monasteries**[8]. It was different from clerics who lived among people.

▲ *St. Michael's Benedictine Abbey in Farnborough, England.*

- Monasteries were often situated far from human habitation.
- **St. Benedict** founded a famous monastery in Italy in 529 CE, followed by **Cluny** in Burgundy in 910 CE.
- Monks took a vow to remain in their monastery for life and dedicated themselves to prayer, study and manual labour like farming.
- Both men and women could join monastic life. Women were called **nuns**[9]. Monks and nuns were required to remain unmarried throughout their lives.
- Most abbeys were single-sex communities, with separate monasteries for both men and women.
- Monasteries often grew into large communities with extensive buildings, landholdings, schools or colleges and hospitals.
- **Abbess Hildegard** developed the practice of community singing of prayers in Churches.
- In the 13th century, some groups of monks known as **friars**[10] chose to travel and preach to people. They depended on the charity they received for their livelihood.
- By the 14th century, the value and purpose of monasticism were increasingly criticised.
- Langland's poem '*Piers Plowman*' (1360-1370 CE) criticised the luxurious lifestyles of some monks and compared them with the simple faith of ordinary people.
- **Geoffrey Chaucer's "*Canterbury Tales*"** included funny portrayals of a nun, a monk and a friar, making fun of certain parts of monastic life.

The Second Order: The Nobility

- The nobles or landowners were placed in the second order. Nobles had a central role in social processes due to their control over land. This control came from the system of **vassalage**.
- Vassalage was a feudal system where a person pledged loyalty and service to a superior in exchange for protection and land.
- Kings and their subjects, as well as nobles and peasants, were linked by vassalage. Nobles were loyal to the king, while peasants were loyal to their landowners or nobles.
- A nobleman was loyal to a superior, known as a ***seigneur***, in a formal ceremony involving oaths and rituals performed in a church.
- Both *seigneur* and vassal made a mutual promise that seigneur would protect the vassal who would be loyal to him.
- In the ceremony, the vassal receives a written charter or a staff (stick like) or even a piece of Earth as a symbol of the land that was being given to the vassal by his master.

---

7 **Abbey** It is derived from the Syriac abba, meaning father. An abbey was governed by an abbot or an abbess.
8 **Monastery** It is derived from the Greek word 'monos' meaning someone who lives alone.
9 **Nuns** Women monks are called nuns.
10 **Friars** A group of monks who moved from place to place, preaching to the people and living on charity.

Privileges of Nobles

- A noble had absolute control over his property.
- He also had power to raise troops called **feudal levies**, conduct his own courts of justice and print his own money.
- He was the lord of all the people settled on his land. His vast lands included his own house, private fields, pastures and the homes and fields of his tenant-peasants. His house was called a **manor**.
- Peasants farmed the nobleman's private lands. They were also required to fight as soldiers when necessary.

The Manorial Estate

- The lord lived in a manor house and controlled villages.
- Manorial estates varied in size, with smaller ones having twelve families and larger ones having up to sixty families.
- The estates produced most necessities for daily life, including grain, tools, weapons, building materials, textiles and wine.
- Women spun and wove the fabric and children worked in the wine-presses of the lords.
- Estates often included woodlands for hunting, pastures for livestock, a church and a castle for defence.
- The manors could not be self-sufficient because it required goods like salt, millstones and metalware from outside sources.
- Lords who desired a luxurious lifestyle imported items such as furnishings, musical instruments and ornaments from other places, as they were not produced locally.

The Knights

- The localised wars became common in Europe from the 9th century, this created a demand for skilled horsemen, as untrained peasants were insufficient.
- A new class of warriors, known as **knights**, emerged to meet this demand. They were linked to lords just like lords were linked to kings.
- Lords gave knights fiefs, which were pieces of land that could be inherited and expanded.
- A fief typically included a house for the knight and his family, a church, buildings for dependents and agricultural facilities like a watermill and wine-press.
- Peasants cultivated the land of the fief and in return, knights paid a fee to their lord and promised to fight for them in wars.
- Knights practised **fencing**[11] and combat tactics daily to maintain their skills.
- Knights could serve many lords, but their main loyalty was to their first lord.

Minstrels

- From the 12th century, **minstrels** (a medieval period singer) travelled from manor to manor, to entertain nobles with songs about brave kings and knights.
- Many manors had a narrow balcony above the main hall, known as the **minstrel's gallery**. The minstrels entertain the nobles with their songs from the gallery as they enjoy their meals in the hall.

The Third Order: Peasants, Free and Unfree

- The majority of population, who supported the first two orders were cultivators. They were either free peasants or serfs.
- Free peasants and serfs were tenants who cultivated the land owned by the lords.

11 Fencing The art or practice of attacks and defence with a sword.

Free Peasants

- Male peasants were required to provide military service for at least forty days per year.
- Peasant families were required to work on the lord's land or estate for at least three days. The result of this labour was called labour-rent.
- Peasants also performed unpaid tasks such as digging ditches, gathering firewood, building fences, and repairing roads and buildings.
- Women and children contributed to the household expenditure by spinning thread, weaving cloth, making candles and pressing grapes for the lord's wine.
- A direct tax called the **taille**[12] was sometimes imposed exclusively on peasants, while clergy and nobles were exempted.

Serfs

- Serfs cultivated plots of land that belonged to the lord. They were required to work on the lord's land without wages and could not leave the estate without permission.
- Serfs were dependent on the lord's mill, oven and wine presses for their essential needs.
- The lord had the authority to decide who a serf could marry. A fee was required for the lord to give his blessing to a serf's chosen partner.

Quick Test 2

1. Name the three orders present in feudal society.
2. What were Canterbury Tales about?
3. Who were the singers who travelled from manor to manor, singing songs which told stories about brave kings and knights?
4. What was a fief?
5. Who were the minstrels?

4.4 Social and Economic Relations between People of Three Orders

Initially, the first two orders believed that the social system was stable. However, changes were gradually transforming this system.

Following were the changes that took place

Environmental Changes

- From the 5th to the 10th centuries, most of Europe was covered with large forests. This limited the amount of land available for farming.
- Peasants often hid in forests to escape oppression.
- A cold climatic period led to long winters and reduced agricultural yields.
- From the 11th century, a warmer climate made farming better. There were longer growing seasons and it was easier to plough the fields because there was less frost.
- As forests decreased, more land was available for farming.

12 **Taille** The taille was a direct land tax levied on the French peasantry and non-nobles during the Old Regime. It was a household tax based on land ownership and was paid directly to the state.

Land Use

- Early farming technology was basic. Peasants used wooden ploughs pulled by oxen, which could only dig into the top layer of soil.
- Fields needed to be dug by hand every four years, making agriculture a labour-intensive process.
- A simple crop rotation[13] system was used, where one field was cultivated with winter wheat and the other was left fallow. This led to soil deterioration and frequent famines.
- Poor nutrition and frequent famines made life difficult for the common people.
- Lords, wanted to maximise their income, since they could not increase land output, peasants had to cultivate all the land on the estate. They spent more time doing this than they were legally required to.
- Since they couldn't openly protest, peasants used passive resistance instead. They spent more time cultivating their own fields and avoided performing unpaid extra services for the lord.
- Disputes arose between peasants and lords over pasture and forest lands. Peasants wanted to share the use of resources, but lords insisted that those resources were their private property.

Changes in Land Use

- A significant agricultural advancement was the transition from a two-field to a three-field system.
- Farmers divided their land into three fields, planting winter wheat or rye in one, spring crops like peas, beans, lentils for human use and oats and barley for the horses in another and leaving the third fallow. This rotation ensured continuous cultivation without exhausting the soil.
- The three-field system led to a substantial increase in food production per unit of land.
- The cultivation of legumes like peas and beans provided a valuable source of vegetable protein for the average European diet and better fodder for animals.
- The increased efficiency of the three-field system allowed peasants to cultivate smaller farms (20-30 acres by the 13th century) while producing more food. This required less labour and gave peasants time for other activities.

New Agricultural Technologies

- By the 11th century, cultivators started using **heavy iron-tipped ploughs** and mould-boards[14]. These ploughs could dig deeper and the mould-boards turned the topsoil properly. Thus, nutrients from the soil were better utilised.
- Instead of earlier neck-harness, the shoulder harnesses were used for animals which could now help in putting greater power.
- Horses were now fitted with iron horseshoes which prevented foot decay.
- Wind and water energy were used for agriculture.
- Water-powered and wind-powered mills were set up all over Europe for the purposes like milling corn and pressing grapes.

Economic Impact of Technological Changes

- The financial burden of implementing technological advancements like watermills and windmills was too high for most peasants, so lords took the initiative to establish them.
- Peasants played an active role in agricultural advancements by expanding cultivable land, adopting the three-field system and establishing blacksmith workshops for tool production and repair.

---

13 Crop-rotation It is the practice of planting different crops sequentially on the same plot of land to improve soil health, optimise nutrients in the soil.

14 Mould-boards It is a curved blade of a plough which was used to turn the Earth over.

- The increasing use of money weakened the personal bonds that formed the foundation of feudalism. Lords began demanding cash rent instead of services.
- Cultivators sold their crops to traders for money, which were then sold in towns.
- The increased use of money led to higher prices, especially during times of poor harvests. Agricultural prices doubled between the 1270s and the 1320s.

The Fourth Order

- The Fourth Order comprised of New Towns and Towns People.
- The expansion of agriculture led to population growth and improved lifespan (an average European lived 10 years longer in the 13th century compared to the 8th). Women and girls had shorter lifespans in comparison to men, as men ate better food.
- Deserted and ruined towns from the Roman era started to revive as agriculture improved and supported bigger populations.
- Periodic fairs and small marketing centres emerged to facilitate the sale of surplus grains by peasants. Over time, these centres grew into towns featuring town squares, churches, roads filled with shops and homes and administrative offices.
- Other towns developed around castles, bishops' estates or large churches.
- Some of these larger towns had populations reaching 30,000, potentially forming a fourth social order.

New Towns

- In towns, people paid taxes to the lord (who owned the land) instead of providing them services.
- Towns offered the freedom of choosing paid work, attracting many serfs who escaped their lord's control.
- A serf could gain freedom if they managed to remain in a town for a year and a day without being found by their lord.
- Free peasants and escaped serfs often formed a significant part of the unskilled labour force in towns.
- Shopkeepers and merchants became numerous due to increased economic activity.
- The growing complexity of urban life created a demand for individuals with specialised skills, such as bankers and lawyers.

Guilds

- Guilds, or associations, were the fundamental units of economic organisation in medieval towns.
- Each skill or industry had its own guild, which regulated the quality, price and sale of products.
- A **guild-hall**[15] was a prominent feature of every town. It served as a venue for ceremonial functions and formal meetings of guild leaders.

Trade and Commerce

- By the 11th century, new trade routes with West Asia were established.
- **Scandinavian**[16] merchants traded furs and hunting-hawks for cloth from the South, while English traders exported tin.
- In France, commerce and crafts began to expand in the 12th century. Craftsmen settled in specific locations to produce and trade goods, rather than travelling from manor to manor.
- The growth of towns and trade led to the rise of wealthy and powerful merchant classes who opposed the power of the nobility.

---

15 **Guild-hall** A place in every town where ceremonial functions and meetings of the guild take place.

16 **Scandinavian** Scandinavian means belonging or relating to a group of Northern European countries that includes Denmark, Norway and Sweden, or to the people, languages, or culture of those countries.

Cathedral Towns and their Design

- Wealthy merchants contributed to the construction of large churches, known as cathedrals, through donations.
- Cathedrals were built through the collective efforts of various groups, including monasteries and individuals who contributed labour, materials and funds.
- Cathedrals were stone structures that took many years to complete. As construction progressed, the surrounding areas became more populated.
- Cathedrals often became centres of pilgrimage, leading to the development of small towns.
- Cathedrals were designed in such a way that
  - The Priest's voice could be heard clearly within the hall where large numbers of people gathered
  - The singing by monks could sound beautiful.
  - The melodious ringing of bells calling people to prayer could be heard over a long distance.
  - Stained glass was used for windows. By day, sunlight made them shine *inside* the Cathedral and by night, candle light made them visible outside.
  - These stained glass windows depicted biblical stories, making them understandable to illiterate people.

▲ *Salisbury Cathedral, England*

Quick Test 3

1. Name any two new agricultural technologies emerged by the 11th century.
2. Name three changes that affected the social and economic relations.
3. What was the most revolutionary change in land use?
4. At which place were the ceremonial functions and formal meetings of heads of the guilds took place?
5. What do you mean by cathedrals?

4.5 The Crisis of the 14th Century

Europe's economic expansion slowed down by the early 14th century due to three factors

- Climatic Changes
- Shortage of Metal Money
- Bubonic Plague (Black Death)

Changes in Climatic Conditions

- The warm summers of the previous 300 years in Northern Europe were replaced by bitterly cold summers by the end of the 13th century. This resulted in a shorter growing season and made it more difficult to cultivate crops on higher ground.
- Storms and oceanic flooding destroyed numerous farms, leading to decreased tax revenue for governments.
- Deforestation, large-scale cultivation and intensive ploughing depleted the soil, despite the use of the three-field rotation system.

- The combination of population growth, excessive resource consumption and deforestation led to a shortage of pastureland and subsequent declines in cattle numbers. The convergence of these factors resulted in severe famines across Europe between 1315 and 1317, followed by significant cattle deaths in the 1320s.

Shortage of Metal Money

- The shortage of metal money, primarily due to decreased silver production in Austria and Serbia, negatively impacted trade.
- To address this shortage governments were forced to reduce the silver content of their currency and mix it with less valuable metals.

Deadly Bubonic Plague (Black Death)

- The growth of trade in the 13th and 14th centuries brought an increase in the number of ships arriving in European ports with goods from foreign lands.
- These ships also brought rats, which were infected with the deadly bubonic plague, also known as the **Black Death.**
- The Black Death caused a deadly epidemic, killing an estimated 20-40% of Europe's population. Trade centres and cities were particularly affected by the plague, leading to significant economic disruption.
- Infants, the young and the elderly were more affected by the plague. The overall population of Europe declined from 73 million in 1300 CE to 45 million in 1400 CE.
- The plague caused significant loss of life, leading to labour shortages. This created imbalances between agriculture and manufacturing.
- The decreased demand for agricultural goods led to lower prices.
- The shortage of labour, especially in agriculture, led to a significant increase in their demand for wages.
- Surviving workers were able to demand higher wages due to the limited labour supply.

Social Unrest

- The decline in agricultural prices and the rise in wages significantly reduced the income of lords.
- Lords tried to disregard their money-contracts with peasants and revive labour services. This led to violent resistance from peasants, particularly those who were better educated and more prosperous.
- Peasant revolts occurred in Flanders (1323 CE), France (1358 CE) and England (1381 CE). These rebellions were severely defeated, but the most violent rebellions took place in regions with the highest economic prosperity.
- Even though lords made strong efforts to stop the peasant revolts, they couldn't restore the old feudal system. The shift to a money-based economy, instead of peasants working directly for the lords, had become too important to reverse.

Political Changes

- The 15th and 16th centuries witnessed significant developments in both political and social spheres in Europe.
- European kings strengthened their military and financial power, leading to the creation of powerful new states. These kings are often referred to as **new monarchs** by historians.
- **Louis XI** in France, **Maximilian** in Austria, **Henry VII** in England and **Isabella** and **Ferdinand** in Spain were authoritarian rulers who established standing armies, permanent bureaucracies and national taxation systems.
- Spain and Portugal also began exploring and expanding overseas during this period.

Rise of New Monarchies

- European kings were able to increase their power because of changes in society that happened during the 12th and 13th centuries.
- The decline of the feudal system, including lordship and vassalage, along with slow economic growth, created opportunities for kings to strengthen their power over both powerful and less powerful individuals.
- Kings stopped using armies of knights and instead created professional armies with guns and cannons. This made kings stronger than the nobles.
- Kings needed more money to have bigger armies. Hence, they raised taxes to get this money. This helped them protect their land, make their kingdoms bigger and stop people from rebelling against them.
- Centralisation and taxation were opposed by the aristocracy.
- In England, rebellions against royal authority were crushed in 1497 CE, 1536 CE, 1547 CE, 1549 CE and 1553 CE.
- In France, Louis XI (1461-1483) faced a long struggle against powerful dukes and princes.
- The smaller nobles, often part of local areas, resisted the king's take over of their powers.
- In France, there were wars about religion in the 1500s. These wars were between the king and the people who wanted more power for their own areas.

▲ *Nemours Castle, France, Fifteenth Century*

- The nobility quickly adapted to the new political landscape, becoming loyal supporters of the new regimes.
- Royal absolutism was seen as a modified form of feudalism because the same social class that had ruled as lords continued to hold power.
- Many members of the nobility were appointed to permanent positions within the administrative service.

Changes in the New Regime

- The king in the new regimes was not at the top of a hierarchical system based on personal loyalty and trust. He was now the central figure in a society, based on patron-client relationships.
- Both strong or weak monarchies, needed the support of powerful people. To get this support, they often used money or rewards.
- Money became a powerful tool for non-aristocratic individuals, such as merchants and bankers, to gain access to the court. By lending money to kings, they were able to increase their influence within the state system.
- This marked a break from the traditional feudal system, as rulers began to include non-feudal elements in the state structure.

4.6 The Evolution of French and English Governments

France

- In 1614 CE, during the reign of the young King Louis XIII, a meeting of the Estates-General of France was held. It was a French Assembly with three groups representing clergy, nobility and the common people.
- The Estates-General was not called again until 1789, as kings were reluctant to share power with these three orders.

England

- Before the Norman conquest, the Anglo-Saxons had a Great Council, which the king was required to consult before imposing taxes.
- This council eventually evolved into Parliament, consisting of the House of Lords (representing lords and clergy) and the House of Commons (representing towns and rural areas).

Conflict and Change

- **King Charles I** ruled for 11 years (1629-1640 CE) without calling Parliament. However, when he needed funds, he was forced to call the Parliament.
- A section of Parliament waged war against King Charles I, leading to his execution and the establishment of a short-lived republic.
- The republic gave way to a monarchy again, but with the condition that Parliament would be called regularly.

Modern Governments

- Currently, France has a republican form of government and England has a monarchy.
- The historical events that happened in these countries after the 17th century shaped their modern governmental structures.

Quick Test 4

1. Which natural disasters contributed to reduced farm income?
2. When did severe famines strike Europe?
3. Which group of the population was most affected by the plague?
4. What did rulers replace the feudal levy system with?
5. What became a key tool for monarchs to gain the cooperation of powerful individuals?

TIMELINE

Year	Event
481 CE	Clovis becomes king of the Franks.
486 CE	Clovis and the Franks begin the conquest of Northern Gaul.
496 CE	Clovis and the Franks convert to Christianity.
714 CE	Charles Martel becomes mayor of the palace.
751 CE	Martel's son, Pepin, deposes the Frankish ruler, becomes king and establishes a dynasty. Wars of conquest double the size of his kingdom.
768 CE	Pepin succeeded by his son Charlemagne (Charles the Great).
800 CE	Pope Leo III crowned Charlemagne as Holy Roman Emperor.
840 CE onwards	Raids by Vikings from Norway.
1066 CE	Normans defeated Anglo-Saxons and conquered England.
1100 CE onwards	Cathedrals being built in France.
1315-17 CE	Great famine in Europe.
1347-50 CE	Black Death.
1338-1461 CE	Hundred Years War between England and France.
1381 CE	Peasants' revolts.
1461-1559 CE	New monarchs in France.
1474-1556 CE	New monarchs in Spain.
1485-1547 CE	New monarchs in England.

Mind Map

THE THREE ORDERS

1 An Introduction to Feudalism

- It is an agricultural system involving lords and peasants.
- Lords provided protection to peasants and peasants performed labour services for them.

2 Feudalism in France and England

- Frank was 'Germanic tribe' which emerged as a dominated group in gaul and called it France.
- Pope gave title of 'Holy Emperor' to King Charle-Magne to ensure his support.
- Angels and Saxon tribes get settled in England in the 6th century.
- Fedualism was developed in England after 11th century.

3 The First Order: The Clergy

- Pope was the head of Western church in Rome.
- Bishops were the religious nobility class.
- Monks were religious communities who lived in abbeys or monasteries.
- Uncertainity grew against monasticism (religious way of life, living isolated from other people and self-disciplined life) in 14th century.

4 The Second Order: The Nobility

- The big landlords were vassals of kings while peasants were vassals of the land owners.
- Knight was the new class of warriors which provided good cavalry support to lords in exchange of gief (a piece of land).

5 The Third Order: Peasants, Free and Unfree

- Peasants had dual roles of cultivators and foot soldiers.
- Free peasants held their farm as tenants of the lord and had to render military service for atleast 40 days.
- Serf were unfree peasants who cultivated plots of landlords.

6 Social and Economic Relations between People of Three Orders

- From the 5th Century, Europe had vast forests limiting farmland.
- Warmer climate later improved farming and expanded cultivation areas.
- Iron tipped plough, shoulder harness technique let to immense growth in agriculture sector.
- Peasants switched from two field system to three field system, which enhanced agricultural production.

7 The Fourth Order: New Towns and Towns People

- From 11th century onwards, towns began to grow due to growth in agricultural production.
- Periodic market and fairs were organised in cities for selling agro-products.

8 The Crisis of the 14th Century

- Cold climate reduced crops, leading to famine and starvation.
- Soil exhaustion and cattle deaths worsened food shortages.
- Labour shortages raised wages, agriculture and trade suffered imbalance.

9 Social Unrest

- Peasants revolted against lords trying to revive feudal labour.
- Rebellions ended feudal privileges despite being violently crushed.

10 Political Changes

- Kings gained power through standing armies, taxes and centralisation.
- Nobles resisted but eventually became loyal to monarchs for survival.
- England's Parliament shaped politics, while France avoided shared power.

NCERT Folder

Intext Questions

1. Discuss social hierarchies based on different criteria: occupation, language, wealth, education. Compare medieval France with Mesopotamia and the Roman Empire.

Ans. Social hierarchies based on different criteria such as occupation, language, wealth and education compare to medieval France with Mesopotamia and the Roman Empire were

- In medieval France, king was at the top of hierarchy, then came priests/clergy, nobility, knights, merchants, bankers, other professions and last came the peasants and serfs.
- In Mesopotamia, king was at the top of hierarchy, then nobility, the priests, the upper class, the lower class and the slaves.
- In Roman Empire, king was at the top of hierarchy, then senators, equestrian class, middle class, lower class and finally slaves. Greek and Latin speaking and writing people were meant to be superior than others.

2. Discuss examples of expected patterns of behaviour between people of different social levels, in a medieval manor, a palace and in a place of worship.

Ans. Expected patterns of behaviour between people of different social levels were

At Medieval Manor A lord's house was called manor. Troops, peasants, tenants and other craftsmen used to live in the land owned by lord. Lord used to live a luxurious life with rich food and wealth, whereas peasants used to live on very little income and poor diet. Lord used to dominate others and peasants behaved inferior to lords.

At the Palace King lived at the palace. He had lot of servants and soldiers stationed at his service. King led a luxurious life and did not work. He gave lands to lords and in turn collected taxes. Nobles supplied army to king at the time of wars. Most of the times, king was not in touch with common man.

At Place of Worship Churches, monasteries and cathedrals were main places of worship. Pope was the head of all churches. Bishops and priests were next in hierarchy. People had to kneel down and bow before god to pray. Monks and nuns lived in isolated places compared to priests. They used to help in developing arts.

3. Look carefully at this map and the drawing of a town. What would you notice as special features of medieval European towns? How were they different from towns in other places and other periods of time?

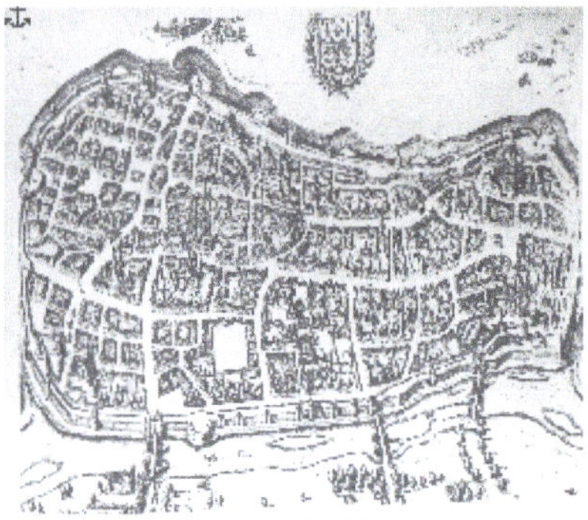

Rouen, French cathedral town, seventeenth-century map.

Ans. The special features of medieval European towns were

- Roads were wide and well connected
- Entire town was divided into blocks
- There was a boundary wall at the perimeter as protection,
- Town was built on the banks of the river
- Bridges built across the river

They were different from the towns in other places and other periods of time in the way they were designed. The kind of town planning with broad roads and marketplace, shops were missing in the towns in other places and other periods of time.

4. Read through the events and processes listed with dates and connect them into a narrative account.

	11th to 14th Centuries
1066 CE	Normans defeat Anglo-Saxons and conquer England
1100 CE onwards	Cathedrals being built in France
1315-17 CE	Great famine in Europe
1347-50 CE	Black Death
1338-1461 CE	Hundred Years War between England and France
1381 CE	Peasant's revolts

Ans. In 1066 CE, Normans crossed English channel, defeated Anglo- Saxons and conquered England. From then, French ruled England and king distributed his lands to nobles and others. By the year of 1100 CE and onwards, the rich people in France started donating money to Churches and with this money large Churches called cathedrals were being built in France.

All these riches suddenly reversed when climatic changes occurred and resulted in Great Famine which affected Europe very badly in 1315-17 CE. On top of this in 1347-50 CE, severe epidemic in the form of plague infection came to Europe through the trading ships.

Most of the population died due to this infection which was called the Black Death. There after, due to economic and other crisis conflicts arose, wars happened between England and France were known as hundred years war from 1338 to 1461 CE.

Meanwhile peasants revolted against the lords in 1381 CE, who tried to impose feudal rules again. Lords wanted to impose feudal levies and get back the privileges but peasants successfully revolted and made sure that feudal privileges are not reimposed.

Answer in Brief

1. Describe two features of early feudal society in France.

Ans. The two features of early feudal society were

(i) The agricultural production was based on the relationship between lords and peasants. The peasants cultivated their own land as well as that of the lord.

(ii) The peasants performed labour services for the lords, who in exchange provide military protection to them. Lords had extensive judicial control over the peasants.

2. How did long-term changes in population levels affect economy and society in Europe?

Ans. The long-term changes in population levels affected economy and society in Europe in following ways

- Clearance of forests and expansion of cultivation in these lands.
- Invention of new agricultural technologies and increase in the production of food grains to sustain large number of people.
- The discarded towns of Roman empire were revived again. Towns developed and more economic activities were carried which in turn created wealth for the people.

3. Why did knights become a distinct group and when did they decline?

Ans. Frequent local wars in Europe in the 9th century created knights as a distinct group. Peasant soldiers were not enough to fight in these wars and it was realised that skilled cavalry was essential. This created rise in the importance of knights who were connected to lords and the lords to the king. In exchange for protection, a lord would give a knight a piece of land known as a 'fief'.

Later in 12th and 13th century, feudal system of lordship and vassalage was ended. King started building a professional army equipped with guns which crushed the aristocracies. Thus, knights identity declined in later periods.

4. What was the function of medieval monasteries?

Ans. The functions of the medieval monasteries were

- To inspire the people to donate.
- To inspire the people to serve the sick.
- To encourage to develop art and architecture.
- To inspire the people to lead a simple life.

Answer in a Short Essay

5. Imagine and describe a day in the life of a craftsman in a medieval French town.

Ans. In medieval French town, there was a feudal system. So people living on the lord's land had to provide services to the lord. A craftsman used to work for the lords, making and repairing their weapons and equipment. They go from one manor to another to sell their goods.

In later times, instead of services to lord, they paid taxes and sold their goods in market at one place instead of roaming from one place to another. They used to trade their goods for food. When guilds were formed, craftsmen worked under the supervision of guilds. This controlled the quality of the product, its price and its sale.

6. Compare the conditions of life for a French serf and a Roman slave.

Ans. The conditions of life for a French serf were

- They used to cultivate the land of lord. Much of their produce was given to the lord.
- They also had to work on the land which belonged exclusively to the lord. They received no wages and could not leave without the lord's permission.
- Serfs could use only their lord's mill to grind flour, his oven to bake their bread and his wine presses to make wine and beer.
- Lord also decided whom should a serf marry.
- Serfs life was exploited by lords and because of these problems, they used to run away to other towns to escape from the lord.

The conditions of life for a Roman slave were

- Slaves were considered as a part of the family in Roman empire. They were bought by masters and were supposed to be fed and maintained by the masters.
- They did not have any rights in Roman empire. If one slave murdered anyone, then all the slaves living under one roof alongwith the accused were executed.
- There were inhuman practices like slave breeding i.e. slaves were encouraged to have more children because they also will become slaves.
- Slaves who worked in groups were often chained together by their feet.
- In later period, slaves were freed by their masters.

Exam Pattern Questions

Objective Type Questions

Multiple Choice Questions

1. Which group was included in the three orders of European Society?
(a) The Clergy (b) The Nobility
(c) The Peasantry (d) All of these

2. Identify the correct order of the three orders of the European society. **CBSE Diksha**
(a) The nobility, the peasantry and the clergy
(b) The clergy, the peasantry and the nobility
(c) The clergy, the nobility and the peasantry
(d) The nobility, the clergy and the peasantry

3. The base is of classification among the three orders was **CBSE Diksha**
(a) education (b) wealth
(c) nature of work (d) race

4. The term feudalism is derived from the German word **CBSE Diksha**
(a) Chapel (b) Feud
(c) Friar (d) Manor

5. The .... , a Germanic tribe gave their name to Gaul, making it France.
(a) Clovis (b) Franks
(c) Pepin (d) None of these

6. Gaul province of the Roman empire became **CBSE Diksha**
(a) Italy (b) France
(c) England (d) None of these

7. The king who was declared the Holy Roman emperor was **CBSE Diksha**
(a) Charlemagne (b) Louis I
(c) Louis IX (d) Gaul

8. The noble or lord gave the knight a piece of land called ....
(a) Fief (b) Manor
(c) Clod (d) None of these

9. The word 'monastery' is derived from the Greek word 'monos' which means
(a) someone who lives alone
(b) someone who is a saint
(c) someone who is a believer of Christianity
(d) None of the above

10. 'Abbey' is derived from the Syriac abba which means
(a) Lord (b) Master
(c) Father (d) None of these

11. Christ's birth celebrated on 25th December replaced an old **CBSE Diksha**
(a) pre-Jewish festival
(b) pre-Roman festival
(c) pre-Norman festival
(d) pre-Danes festival

12. Who was the author of 'Canterbury Tales'? **CBSE Diksha**
(a) Langland (b) Chaucer
(c) Keats (d) Charles

13. Noble could raise troops known as **CBSE Diksha**
(a) Manor (b) Vassalage
(c) Peasant (d) Feudal levies

14. The most revolutionary change in the land use was the switch from a two-field system to **CBSE Diksha**
(a) one field system (b) four field system
(c) three field system (d) five field system

15. By the eleventh century instead of the basic wooden ploughs, cultivators began using **CBSE Diksha**
(a) heavy copper tipped ploughs
(b) heavy iron tipped ploughs
(c) heavy bronze tipped ploughs
(d) heavy brass tipped ploughs

16. The main factors that affected the social and economic relations in European society was/ were ....
(a) The environmental changes
(b) Land use
(c) New agricultural technology
(d) All of the above

17. From the 12th century, large churches or.............. were being built in France. **CBSE Diksha**
(a) Fief (b) Monasteries
(c) Cathedrals (d) Parish

18. House of Lords and House of Commons are a part of the Parliament of which country? **CBSE Diksha**
(a) France (b) England
(c) Germany (d) Italy

19. **Consider the following statements and choose the correct option.**

I. Marc Bloch was one of the earliest scholars from France who worked on feudalism.

II. **Feudalism was developed in England from 13th century.**

III. The Catholic Church was not a powerful institution and didn't depend on the king.

IV. Serfs, physically challenged and women could become priests.

Codes

(a) Only I (b) Only II
(c) Both I and II (d) Both III and IV

20. **Consider the following statements and choose the incorrect option.**

I. Europeans became Christian but they still believed in some of their old magic traditions.

II. From 4th century, Christmas and Easter became important.

III. Nobles had no absolute control over their property.

IV. The kings of France and people were linked by vassalage.

Codes

(a) Only I (b) Both I and II
(c) Only III (d) Only IV

21. **Arrange in sequence.**

(i) Peasants revolts (ii) Black Death

(iii) Hundred years of war between England and France

Codes

(a) i, ii, iii (b) ii, iii, i (c) iii, ii, i (d) ii, i, iii

22. **Identify the name of the person from the information given below**

(i) He was the Duke of Normandy.

(ii) In the eleventh century, he crossed the English Channel with an army and defeated the Saxon King of England.

(iii) He distributed the land in sections to 180 Norman nobles who had migrated with him.

Options

(a) Henry VII (b) Louis XI
(c) William I (d) Ferdinand

23. **Identify the name of the plague infection spread in the Europe from the information given below.**

(i) It was the deadly bubonic plague infection.

(ii) It was caused by rats which came along with ships from distant countries in European ports.

(iii) 20 per cent of the people of the whole of Europe died due to this plague.

Options

(a) The White Death (b) The Black Death
(c) The Yellow Death (d) The Wild Death

24. **Vassalage: Loyalty :: Fief: ....**

(a) Land (b) Money
(c) Service (d) Power

25. **Lord: Landowner :: Vassal: ....**

(a) Priest (b) Farmer
(c) Noble (d) Peasant

26. **Feudalism: Social System :: Manor: ....**

(a) Religious building (b) Land unit
(c) Military group (d) Trade

Assertion-Reason

27. **Assertion (A)** Monks took vows to remain in the abbey for the rest of their lives.

Reason (R) All Abbeys were single sex communities, i.e. separate Abbeys for men and women.

Codes

(a) Both A and R are true and R is the correct explanation of A
(b) Both A and R are true, but R is not the correct explanation of A
(c) A is true, but R is false
(d) A is false, but R is true

28. **Assertion (A)** In France from the twelfth century minstrels travelled from manor to manor, singing songs, which told stories.

Reason (R) These travelling bards were very popular as many people could not read and manuscripts were few.

Codes

(a) Both A and R are true and R is the correct explanation of A
(b) Both A and R are true, but R is not the correct explanation of A
(c) A is true, but R is false
(d) A is false, but R is true

Match the Following

29.

List I	List II
A. Clergy	1. Religious communities
B. Abbeys	2. Religious leaders
C. Nobles	3. Agricultural labourers
D. Serf	4. Control over land

Codes

	A	B	C	D		A	B	C	D
(a)	3	1	2	4	(b)	2	1	4	3
(c)	2	1	3	4	(d)	4	2	1	3

30.

List I	List II
A. Manor	1. Kind of tax collected by the Church from the peasants.
B. Fief	2. Area under the supervision of one priest.
C. Parish	3. Land given by the Lord to the Knights.
D. Tithe	4. House of the Lord.

Codes

	A	B	C	D		A	B	C	D
(a)	3	1	2	4	(b)	2	4	1	3
(c)	3	1	4	2	(d)	4	3	2	1

Picture Based Questions

31. Identify the building from the following options.

(a) St. Peter's Basilica
(b) Milan Cathedral
(c) St. Andrews Cathedral
(d) Saint Michael's Benedictine Abbey

32. Identify the building from the following options.

(a) Ballybunion Castle
(b) Hever Castle
(c) Buda Castle
(d) Dunseverick Castle

33. Why were the glass of window of Chartres Cathedral stained with pictures of stories from Bible?

(a) To educate the illiterate
(b) To increase the beauty of the cathedral
(c) For preaching lessons to children.
(d) None of the above

34. Identify the building from the following options.

(a) Chartres Cathedral
(b) Notre-Damede
(c) Salisbury Cathedral
(d) Metz Cathedral

35. Study this sketch of an English ploughmen, carefully and answer the following question by choosing the correct option.

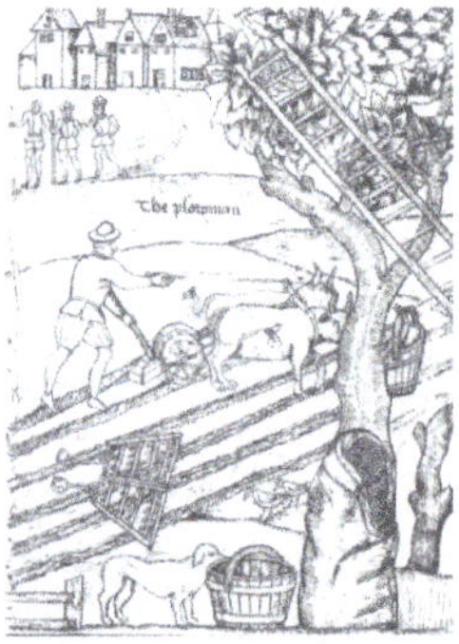

What can be inferred from this sketch about the agricultural operation in Europe in sixteenth century?

(a) It was primitive in nature.
(b) It utilised modern technologies and industrial machinery for cultivation.
(c) Both (a) and (b)
(d) None of the above

Answers

1. (d) All of these
2. (c) The clergy, the nobility and the peasantry
3. (c) nature of work
4. (b) Feud
5. (b) Franks
6. (b) France
7. (a) Charlemagne
8. (a) Fief
9. (a) someone who lives alone
10. (c) Father
11. (b) pre-Roman festival
12. (b) Chaucer
13. (d) Feudal levies
14. (c) three field system
15. (b) heavy iron tipped ploughs
16. (d) All of the above
17. (c) Cathedrals
18. (b) England
19. (a) Only I
20. (c) Only III
21. (c) iii, ii, i
22. (c) William I
23. (b) The Black Death
24. (a) Land
25. (c) Noble
26. (b) Land unit
27. (c) A is true, but R is false
28. (a) Both A and R are true and R is the correct explanation of A
29. (b)
30. (d)
31. (d) Saint Michael's Benedictine Abbey
32. (b) Hever Castle
33. (a) To educate the illiterate
34. (c) Salisbury Cathedral
35. (a) It was primitive in nature.

Subjective Questions

Short Answer Type Questions

1. Write a short note on Marc Bloch.

Ans. Marc Bloch was one of the earliest scholars from France who worked on feudalism. He argued that history consisted much more than just political history, international relations and the lives of great people. He stressed on the importance of geography in shaping human history and the need to understand the collective behaviour or attitudes of groups of people.

Bloch's book '*Feudal Society*' was about social relations, hierarchies, land management and the popular culture of French society between 900 and 1300 CE. He was shot dead by the Nazis in the Second World War.

2. Where can we trace the roots of the feudalism? What kind of political and social aspects were covered by feudalism?

Ans. The roots of the feudalism can be traced to practices that existed in the Roman empire and during the age of the French king Charlemagne. But feudalism as an established way of life in large parts of Europe was believed to have emerged in the 11th century.

In feudal system, peasants cultivated their own land as well as that of the lord. The peasants performed labour services for the lords, who in exchange provided military protection. Lords also had extensive judicial control over peasants. Thus, feudalism not only included economic aspects but also social and political aspects of life too.

3. How did feudalism develop in England?

Ans. Feudalism developed in England in 11th century in the following ways:

- In the 11th century, William, the Duke of Normandy crossed the English channel that separated France and England with his army and defeated the Saxon King of England.
- After this, William I mapped the land and distributed it in blocks to 180 Norman nobles who had migrated with him. The lords became the chief tenants of the king, and were expected to give him military help.
- They were supposed to supply a certain number of knights to the king. These lords supplied some of their own lands to knights who would serve them in return.
- Lords, however could not use their knights for private warfare, which was forbidden in England. Anglo-Saxon peasants became tenants to different landholders.

Thus, system of feudalism was introduced and institutionalised by the William I in England.

4. "Religious and lay worlds of feudalism shared many customs and symbols". Discuss. Competency Based Que

Ans. Religious and lay worlds of feudalism shared many customs and symbols in the following ways

- The important ceremonies conducted by the Church were copied from formal customs of the feudal elite. The act of kneeling while praying, with hands enfolded and head bowed, was an exact copy of the way in which a knight conducted himself while taking oaths of loyalty to his lord.

- Similarly, the use of the term lord for god was another example of feudal culture that found its way into the practices of the Church.

Thus, the religious and the lay worlds of feudalism shared many customs and symbols.

5. What changes did Christianity bring in the practices and life of European society?

Ans. Some of the changes Christianity brought in the European society were

- An old pre-Roman festival, the slate of which was determined by the Solar calendar was replaced with Christ's birth celebration on 25th December.
- Traditionally, people of each village used to make a tour of their village lands and with the coming of Christianity they continued with this practice but they called the village the *'Parish'* i.e. the area under the supervision of one priest.
- Pilgrimage became an important part of a Christian's life and many people went on long journeys to shrines of martyrs or to big Churches.

6. Discuss who were Monks and how they used to live their lives.

Ans. Monks were deeply religious people who chose to live isolated lives. They lived in religious communities called abbeys or monasteries which were far from human habitations. They took oath to remain in monastery for the rest of their lives and to spend their time in prayer, study and manual labour.

Both men and women could become monks and nuns, respectively. They did not marry. They developed the practice of community singing of prayers in Church. Some group of monks called *friars* used to move from one place to another preaching to the people and living on charity.

7. Enlist any four rules that were followed by Monks as mentioned in the manuscript of Benedictine monasteries.

Ans. The four rules that were followed by Monks as mentioned in the manuscript of Benedictine monasteries were

(i) Permission to speak should rarely be granted to monks.

(ii) Humility means obedience and no monk should own private property.

(iii) Idleness is the enemy of the soul, so friars and sisters should be occupied at certain times in manual labour, and at fixed hours in sacred reading.

(iv) The monastery should be laid out in such a way that all necessities be found within its bounds i.e. water, mill, garden, workshops.

8. Discuss the vassalage system. How the kings of France were linked to the people by vassalage?

Ans. Vassalage was a system in which a mutual relationship of loyalty and service was established between a lord and his vassal. In society, priests were put in the first order and nobles in the second order. The nobility enjoyed privileges in the social process. They had complete contol over the land. This control was the outcome of the 'vassalage' practice.

The kings of France were linked to the people by vassalage or slavery. The big landowners, the nobles were vassals of the king and peasants were vassals slave of the landowners. A nobleman accepted the king as his senior. They made a mutual promise that lord would protect the vassal, who would be loyal to him.

This relationship involved elaborate rituals and exchange of in a Church. At this ceremony, the vassal received a written charter or a staff or even a piece of Earth. It symbolises the land that was being given to him by his master.

9. Discuss the lords' economic aspects. Was a manor self-sufficient.

Ans. A lord owned large tracts of land which contained his own houses, his private fields and pastures and the homes and fields of his tenant-peasants. His house was called a manor. His private lands were cultivated by peasants. He had blacksmiths, carpenters, stonemasons, women weaving fabric, children pressing wine in his estate.

Manor was not completely self-sufficient because salt, millstones and metalware had to be obtained from outside sources.

Lords who lived a luxurious life bought rich furnishings, musical instruments and ornaments from other places.

10. Discuss the minstrels and the life of Serfs.

Ans. A minstrel was a musical entertainer in the medieval era. In France, from the 12th century, minstrels travelled from manor to manor, singing songs which told stories about brave kings and knights.

Serfs belonged to the word 'to serve'. They cultivated plots of land which belonged to lord. Most of the produce they cultivated was given to lord. They could not leave estate without lord's permission. The lord could decide whom a serf should marry, or might give his blessing to the serf's choice on payment of a fee. Thus, we can see that life of Serfs was totally under the control of lords.

11. "Peasants did not bow quietly to oppression". Look at the statement and discuss how did peasants react to lord's oppression. Competency Based Que

Ans. Peasants did not bow quietly to oppression of the lords. The lords wanted to maximise their incomes. As it was not possible to increase output from the land, the peasants were forced to bring under cultivation all the land in the manorial estate, and spend more time in doing this, than they were legally bound to do.

As peasants could not protest openly, they followed passive resistance in the following ways :

- They spent more time in cultivating their own fields, and kept much of the product of that labour for themselves.
- They also avoided performing unpaid extra services.

The lords treated forest and pasture lands as their private property and peasants opposed and came into conflict with them. For peasants, these lands were like resources to be used by whole community.

12. The basis of economic organisation was guild. Discuss. Competency Based Que

Ans. Guild was the basis of economic organisation. Each craft or industry was organised into a guild, an association which controlled the quality of the product, its price and its sale.

Some of the importance key funcions of a guild were

- **Quality Control** Ensures product consistency.
- **Price Regulation** Sets pricing limits.
- **Apprenticeship** Trains new members.
- **Market Control** Manages trade and competition.
- **Guiild Halls** Hosts meetings and decisions.
- **Social Infuence** Impacts local politics.

13. New trade routes with West Asia were developing. Discuss its outcomes. Competency Based Que

Ans. By the 11th century, new trade routes with West Asia were developing. It had the following outcomes

- Scandinavian merchants sailed South from the North Sea to trade furs and hunting hawks for cloth.
- English traders arrived to sell tin.
- By the 12th century, commerce and crafts began to grow in France.
- Craftsmen, who once travelled from manor to manor, started settling in towns for easier production and trade.
- As towns grew and trade expanded, town merchants became wealthy and powerful.
- Town merchants began to rival the power of nobility.

14. Discuss the features of newly designed cathedrals.

Ans. The following were the important features of the newly designed cathedrals

- Priest's voice could be heard clearly within the hall and the singing of monks could sound beautiful and the melodious ringing bells calling people to prayer could be heard over a long distance.
- Stained glass would look radiant for people inside the cathedral during the day's sunlight and after sunset, the light of candles would make them visible to people outside.
- The stained glass windows narrated the stories in the Bible through pictures which helped illiterate people to read and understand.

15. How did change in the environmental conditions help Europeans?

Ans. The change in environmental conditions helped Europeans in the following ways

- The land availability for agriculture was limited as Europe was covered with forests from 5th to the 10th centuries. Europe was experiencing cold climatic environment in this period. But from the 11th century, Europe entered a warm phase.
- Average temperatures increased and thus growing season for crops increased and soil was now less subjected to frost.
- Lands were more easily ploughed. There was a significant reduction in the forest line in many parts of Europe and this made expansion of the area under the cultivation possible.

Overall due to the change in environmental conditions, Europe's agriculture had taken a great uplift.

16. Discuss the primitive methods used in farming by European people initially.

Ans. Agricultural technology was very primitive initially in Europe.

Primitive methods used in farming by European people were

- Peasants used wooden plough, drawn by oxen. This plough could only scratch the surface of the Earth and affect the productivity of the soil.
- Agriculture became labour intensive. For example, fields had to be dug by hand, often once in four years.
- Ineffective method of crop rotation was in use. The land was divided in half, one field was planted in autumn with winter wheat, while the other field was left empty.
- Rye was planted on the piece of empty land in the next year while other half was put to empty. This system deteriorated the soil slowly.

17. **What were the reasons that led to the emergence of monarchies?**

Ans. The reasons for the emergence of monarchies were

- The social changes that took place in twelfth and thirteenth centuries led to the emergence of monarchies.
- The end of feudal system of lordship and vassalage and slow rate of economic growth gave kings opportunity to increase their control on people.
- The system of feudal levies for the armies was dispensed by the rulers. Instead they introduced professionally trained infantry equipped with guns and siege artillery directly under their control. Taxes were increased to support larger armies and thus used by them to defend and expand their empire.

18. **Explain the three orders that existed in the Medieval period in Europe.** CBSE Diksha

Or **Mention the classes in European society under the feudal system that had developed in the later years of the middle ages**

Ans. The three orders which existed in the Medieval period in Europe were

(i) **The Clergy** The Church was a powerful institution. The Pope, the head of the Catholic Church, lived in Rome. Bishops were religious nobility. The Church played a major role in influencing Medieval European society. They collected the tithe, a tax from the peasants.

(ii) **Nobility** It had a privileged role in the social process with absolute control over his land. People belonging to the nobility were appointed to higher posts in administration, army and the Church. They were also exempted from paying certain taxes.

(iii) **The peasantry** It had two sections: Free peasants and serfs.

The free peasants had their own lands but worked as tenants of the land. They had to give military service for at least forty days in a year. They had to work on the lord's fields for three days generally in a week in the form of labour-rent.

The serfs tilled the land of lord. Most part of the produce was submitted to the lord. They had to work on the lands of the lord without wages. They were not allowed to leave the estate without prior permission from the lord.

Or The classes in European society under the feudal system that had developed in the later years of the middle ages were

(i) **Feudal Classes** The king stood at the top. He bestowed lands to a number of lords. These lords distributed lands to lesser lords called barons.

(ii) **Dukes and Earls** The Dukes and Earls were king's Vassals. They showed loyalty to the king. In the time of war, the king could demand military help from his Vassals. The feudal lords kept soldiers. They levied taxes.

(iii) **The Peasants** They formed the lowest class. Their number was largest in society. The peasants were divided into many classes especially in freeholders and serfs. A new class emerged which was the middle class. Reasons for its development were the coming of new inventions and development of trade and industries.

19. **How did England shape its power structure during 17th century?**

Ans. In England before Norman conquest, the Anglo-Saxons had a great council. King had to consult it before imposing taxes. This was later developed into Parliament which consisted the 'House of Lords', where lords and the clergy were members, the other was 'House of Commons' representing towns and rural areas.

After the execution of King Charles I, Parliament established a republic. This system of republic did not last long giving way to monarchy but on a condition that Parliament would be called regularly.

Thus, by all this efforts and historical events England had shaped its power structure during 17th century.

Long Answer Type Questions

1. **Mention various features of feudalism in Europe.** CBSE Diksha

Ans. Following were the features of feudalism in Europe

- **Land-based Economy** Land was the main source of wealth, with lords owning the land and peasants working on it.
- **Hierarchy** Society was divided into three main classes: the clergy (religious leaders), nobility (landowners/warriors) and peasants (farmers).
- **Vassalage System** Lords granted land to vassals (nobles) in exchange for military service. Vassals, in turn, could have their own vassals, such as knights.
- **Mutual Obligations** Lords provided protection and land, while vassals and peasants offered military service and labour.
- **Peasants' Role** Peasants, especially **serfs**, were bound to the land and provided labour in exchange for protection. Free peasants had more rights but also worked for lords.
- **Decentralised Power** Local lords had significant autonomy, often controlling their own courts, minting currency and holding political power, sometimes surpassing that of kings.

- **Knights and Warfare** Knights provided military protection and followed a code of chivalry. They were granted land (fiefs) by their lords in exchange for service.
- **Self-sufficiency** Most manors were self-sufficient, producing food, clothing and tools, with limited external trade for luxuries.
- **Judicial and Political Authority** Lords acted as local judges and held political influence, often rivalling the authority of the king.
- **Catholic Church's Role** The Church owned significant land, collected taxes (tithe) and mirrored feudal structures, with bishops acting like feudal lords.

Feudalism in Europe developed as a way to organise society, land ownership and labour, particularly after the fall of the Roman Empire and into the Middle Ages. It shaped political, social and economic life for centuries.

2. 'A small manorial estate could sustain a dozen families while larger estate might include fifty or sixty'. Look at the statement and discuss the features of a manorial estate. **Competency Based Que**

Ans. In manorial estate, a lord had his own manor-house and he also controlled villages. The features of manorial estate were

- Some lords controlled hundreds of villages where peasants lived. A small manorial estate could contain a dozen families.
- Almost everything needed for daily life was found on the estate like grain was grown in the fields, blacksmiths and carpenters maintained the lord's implements and repaired his weapons, while stonemasons looked after his buildings.
- Women spun and wove fabric and children worked in the lord's wine-presses.
- The estate had extensive woodlands and forests where the lords hunted. They contained pastures where his cattle and his horses grazed.
- There was a church on the estate and a castle for defence. From the 13th century, some castles were made bigger for use as a residence for a knight's family.
- In fact, in England castles were practically unknown before the Norman Conquest and developed as centres of political administration and military power under the feudal system.
- The manor could not be completely self-sufficient because salt, millstones and metal-ware had to be obtained from outside sources.
- Those lords who wanted a luxurious lifestyle and were keen to buy rich furnishings, musical instruments and ornaments not locally produced, had to get these from other places.

3. Discuss in detail about the third order. Explain the life of peasants and serfs in the third order.

Ans. The third order consisted mainly of cultivators. They were of two kinds which were peasants and serfs.

Life of the peasants in third order was

- They held their farms as tenants of the lord. They also rendered their military service to the lord.
- Peasants set aside certain days of the week, to work in lord's estate which was called labour rent.
- They also did some unpaid labour services like gathering, firewood, building fences and repairing roads and buildings.
- Women and children used to help in the fields, spun thread, wove cloth, made candles and pressed grapes to make wine.
- They also used to pay tax called 'taille' which was imposed by lord.

Life of the serfs in third order was

- Serfs cultivated land belong to the lord and most of the produce was given to him. Serfs also worked on lord's exclusive lands without any wages.
- They were under the control of lord and could not leave the estate without his permission.
- They had to use only lord's mill to grind the flour, his oven to bake bread and his wine presses to make wine and beer.
- They had to marry only the one that was chosen by lord.

4. "By the 11th century, there is evidence of several technological changes". Look at the statement and discuss in detail about the technological changes happened in agriculture and how did they help European society? **Competency Based Que**

Or **Illustrate the technological changes that affected agriculture during the eleventh century.** **CBSE Diksha**

Ans. New Technologies introduced in Agriculture

There were many new technologies that were introduced in agriculture. They were

- New heavy iron-tipped ploughs which could dig deeper and mould-boards that turn the topsoil properly were introduced.
- Instead of neck harness, the shoulder harness came into use. This helped animals to exert greater power.
- Horses were fitted with iron horse shoes and this helped in preventing foot decay.
- Water powered and wind powered mills were setup in Europe for purposes like milling corn and pressing grapes.
- There was shift from two-field to a three-field system which increased the production of grains.

Benefits of New Technology to European Society

- All these improvements in agricultural technology had double the food availability.
- There was a greater use of plants like peas and beans which gave proteins to average European. This also increased the lifespan of European people.
- Efficiency of agriculture increased, average land holdings reduced and correspondingly use of labour was also reduced.
- With increased agricultural production and increased incomes, there was revival of towns and gradual development of town like features such as town square, Church, roads, etc.

Thus, with new technologies agriculture improved and in turn it had positive effects on different fields of society and increasing prosperity of the people.

5. By the early fourteenth century, 'Europe's economic expansion slowed down.' In context to the statement, enumerate various crises of the fourteenth century. CBSE Diksha

Ans. By the early fourteenth century, Europe's economic expansion slowed down due to following reasons

Climate Change

- Colder temperatures and shorter growing seasons made agriculture difficult.
- Reduced crop yields led to widespread famine, particularly from 1315-1317 CE.

Soil Degradation

- Intensive farming and lack of soil conservation led to the exhaustion of arable land.
- As a result, agricultural productivity decreased further.

Famine and Population Decline

- Repeated famines reduced the population significantly.
- The worst affected group was the peasants, leading to malnutrition and further reducing agricultural output.

Shortage of Metal Currency

- A decline in silver mining caused a shortage of metal coins, disrupting trade and commerce.
- Governments resorted to debasing currency by mixing it with cheaper metals.

Black Death (Bubonic Plague)

- The plague struck Europe from 1347 to 1350 CE, killing approximately 20-40% of the population.
- Trade routes facilitated the spread of the plague, affecting cities the most.

Social and Economic Imbalance

- Labour shortages caused by the plague led to rising wages and a decline in agricultural production.
- The nobility lost income and the peasantry revolted due to increased demands for labour and services.

Peasant Revolts

- Economic hardships led to widespread peasant revolts, notably in France (1358 CE) and England (1381 CE).

6. With increase in agriculture from the 11th century, towns began to grow again in Europe. Discuss. Competency Based Que

Ans. From 11th century, as agriculture increased, towns began to grow again with increased population.

Surplus grains and other goods led to the growth of periodic fairs and small marketing centres which slowly developed into town like features. In other places, towns grew around large castles, bishop's estates or large Churches.

Towns offered the prospect of paid work and freedom from the lord's control for young people of peasant families. The free peasants or escaped serfs were provided as unskilled labours in town. There was also increase in shopkeepers and merchants. Need for individuals with specialised skills made bankers and lawyers emerge.

Each craft or industry was organised into a guild which controlled the quality of the product, its price and sale. The guild-hall was a feature of every town. Guards protected the town walls and musicians were called to play at feasts and in civic processions, and hotelkeepers looked after travellers. With new trade routes, trade, commerce and crafts began to grow. Craftsmen settle in one place in towns and sold their goods for food. As number of towns grew and trade continued to expand, town merchants became rich and powerful, and rivalled the power of the nobility.

7. Discuss about the crisis created by the change in climatic conditions and shortage of metals in the Europe during 14th century.

Ans. The problems created by the change in climatic conditions and shortage of metals were

- In Northern Europe, at the end of 13th century, climatic conditions changed drastically. The earlier warm summers of previous 300 years were replaced by bitterly cold summers. This reduced the time for growing crops by a month.
- Storms and oceanic floods destroyed many farmlands. This resulted in less income to governments as the taxes collected were less.
- Intensive ploughing also exhausted the soil despite the practice of the three field-rotation of crops, because soil was not properly conserved.
- The shortage of grass and fodder reduced the number of cattles. Population growth was high and resources were less. This resulted in famine and followed by huge cattle deaths.

- Trade was hit by a huge shortage of metal money because output of silver mines in Austria and Serbia reduced. This forced the government to reduce the silver content of the currency and to mix it with cheaper metals.

8. Discuss about the plague epidemic in Europe during 14th century? How did this crisis affect the economy and social conditions in Europe?

Ans. Plague Epidemic in Europe

One of the major catastrophes that happened in Europe was plague epidemic in 14th century. The effects of this epidemic were huge in changing the social and economic conditions of Europe. The trade expanded in the 13th and 14th centuries and ships started arriving at European ports from different countries.

Alongwith the ships, the rats carrying the deadly bubonic plague infection also came. This was referred to as the Black Death.

Effects of Plague Epidemic

- The estimate of deaths increased due to this epidemic which is 20 per cent of the people of the whole Europe, and in some places it was 40 per cent of the population.
- Trade centres and cities were the hardest hit. In enclosed communities like monasteries and convents, even if one individual contracted the plague, it took no time spreading to all others and no one was survived at the end.
- The plague was deadly among infants, youngs and the elderly. The population of Europe from 73 million in 1300 CE got reduced to 45 million in 1400 CE.
- Plague not only killed people but it also had post effects on social and economic conditions. It caused huge social dislocation.
- Depopulation resulted in shortage of labour and this created imbalances in agriculture and manufacture.
- Prices of agricultural products dropped as there were few people to buy. Wage rates increased because demand for labour increased, who now demanded twice of their earlier wages.

9. "The resistance of the aristocracies crumbled in the face of the firepower of the kings". Look at the statement and discuss about the political changes in 15th and 16th centuries in Europe. Competency Based Que

Ans. The following were the changes that took place in 15th and 16th centuries in Europe

- European kings strengthened their military and financial power. They created new powerful states that were very important to Europe.
- Louis XI in France, Maximilian in Austria, Henry VII in England and Isabelle and Ferdinand in Spain were absolutist rulers who organised standing armies, a permanent bureaucracy and national taxation. In Spain and Portugal, these kings played a role in Europe's expansion overseas.
- In 12th and 13th centuries, feudal system was ended. Lordship and vassalage became words of past. Due to slow economic growth, kings got an opportunity to increase their control on powerful and also the weaker section of people.
- Kings introduced new armies who were professionally trained and were equipped with guns and siege artillery. They were under the direct control of the king.
- There was centralisation of power unlike earlier times and there was royal absolutism.
- In France, Louis XI waged a long struggle against dukes and princes. In the 16th century, the religious wars in France were a contrast between royal privileges and regional liberties.
- Both weak and powerful monarchies, needed the cooperation of those who could command authority. Patronage became the means of ensuring cooperation. It could also be obtained by means of money.

Source Based Questions

1. Read the sources given below and answer the following questions.

In the 12th century, Abbess Hildegard of Bingen wrote: 'Who would think of herding his entire cattle in one stable – cows, donkeys, sheep, goats, without difference? Therefore it is necessary to establish difference among human beings, so that they do not destroy each other... God makes distinctions among his flock, in heaven as on Earth. All are loved by him, yet there is no equality among them.'

(i) Who is the author of the source? What is the author trying to convey through the source?

(ii) Why is it necessary to establish difference?

(iii) What analogy did author use to justify inequality?

Ans. (i) Abbess Hildegard of Bingen is the author of the source.

The author is trying to justify the social differences and the inequality present among the human beings.

(ii) It is necessary to maintain differences so that humans do not destroy each other. God had also made distinctions among his flock in heaven as on Earth. He loved all of them but there is no equality among them.

(iii) Author says just like entire cattle consisting of cows, donkeys, sheep and goats cannot be kept in one stable, similarly all humans cannot be grouped into one without any differences.

2. In Benedictine monasteries, there was a manuscript with 73 chapters of rules which were followed by monks for many centuries. Here are some of the rules they had to follow:

Chapter 6: Permission to speak should rarely be granted to monks.

Chapter 7: Humility means obedience.

Chapter 33: No monk should own private property

Chapter 47: Idleness is the enemy of the soul, so friars and sisters should be occupied at certain times in manual labour and at fixed hours in sacred reading.

Chapter 48: The monastery should be laid out in such a way that all necessities be found within its bounds: water, mill, garden, workshops.

(i) What is the source describing about? What is the enemy of the soul?

(ii) Mention two rules that monks should follow.

(iii) How monastery should be built?

Ans. (i) The source is describing about the rules that monks were supposed to follow. Idleness is the enemy of the soul. So, monks were supposed to be occupied with work everytime.

(ii) The two rules that monks should follow were that they should not own private property and they should have all the humility in order to be obedient.

(iii) Monastery should be built in such a way that all the necessities are available within its boundary like water, mills, garden and workshops.

3. 'When in April the sweet showers fall
And pierce the drought of March to the root
And the small birds are making melody
That sleep away the night with open eye...
(So Nature pricks them and their heart engages);
Then people long to go on pilgrimages,
And palmers long to seek the foreign shrines
Of far-off saints, revered in various lands.
And especially from every shire
Of England, to Canterbury they make their journey.'

(i) What does the first two lines of source mean?

(ii) What are small birds doing and where the people are going?

(iii) Who are palmers?

Ans. (i) The first two lines meant that when the rain showers fall in April, they ended the drought of March and the water reached to the roots of the plants.

(ii) Small birds are singing and chirping and the people are going to pilgrimages to visit far-off saints in holylands.

(iii) Palmer is a person wearing two crossed palm leaves as a sign of a pilgrimage made to the holyland.

4. 'Because of the inadequacy which we often felt on feast days, for the narrowness of the place forced the women to run towards the altar upon the heads of the men with much anguish and noisy confusion, [we decided] to enlarge and amplify the noble church...

We also caused to be painted, by the exquisite hands of many masters from different regions, a splendid variety of new windows...Because these windows are very valuable on account of their wonderful execution and the profuse expenditure of painted glass and saphire glass, we appointed an official master craftsman for their protection, and also a goldsmith...who would receive their allowances, namely, coins from the altar and flour from the common storehouse of the brethren, and who would never neglect their duty, to look after these [works of art].'

(i) Why was noble Church being enlarged?

(ii) What kind of glass were windows made up of? Who were appointed for the protection of windows?

(iii) How did Church ensure that appointed people did not neglect their duty?

Ans. (i) The narrowness of place during feast days forcing women to go towards altar with anger and noisy confusion was the reason for the Church being enlarged.

(ii) Painted and sapphire glass were used to make windows. An official master craftsman and a goldsmith were appointed for the protection of windows.

(iii) The appointees for protection of windows were given allowances like coins from the altar and flour from the common store house, so that they would never neglect their duty.

5. 'How many valiant men, how many fair ladies, (had) breakfast with their kinfolk and the same night supped with their ancestors in the next world! The condition of the people was pitiable to behold. They sickened by the thousands daily, and died unattended and without help.

Many died in the open street, others dying in their houses, made it known by the stench of their rotting bodies. Consecrated churchyards did not suffice for the burial of the vast multitude of bodies, which were heaped by the hundreds in vast trenches, like goods in a ships hold and covered with a little earth.'

(i) What was author referring to in the source?

(ii) Why was condition of the people pitiable?

(iii) What does the line "consecrated churchyards did not suffice for the burial of the vast multitude of bodies" in the source mean?

Ans. (i) In the source, author was referring to epidemic that was killing several thousands of people and the havoc it is creating.

(ii) The condition of people was pitiable because thousands of people were getting sick everyday and dying unattended.

(iii) The line "consecrated churchyards did not suffice for the burial of the vast multitude of body" means that many people died during the plague and the burial ground in churchyard was not sufficient to bury huge number of bodies which were in hundreds.

Map Based Questions

1. Mark the following locations on the map of Western Europe.

(i) London **(ii) Madrid**
(iii) Paris **(iv) St. Denis**
(v) Vienna

Ans.

2. Identify the following locations marked on the map of Western Europe given below.

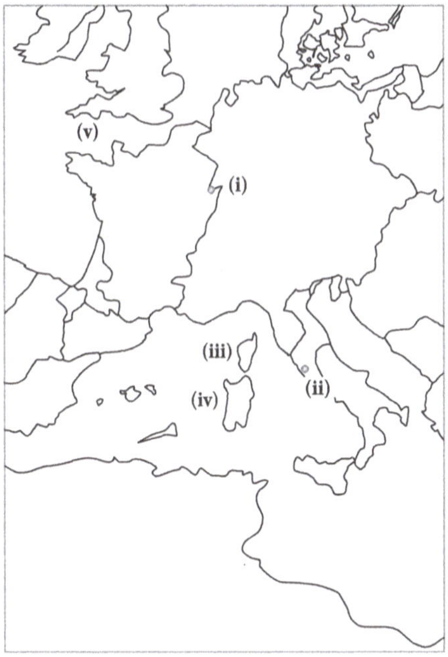

Ans.

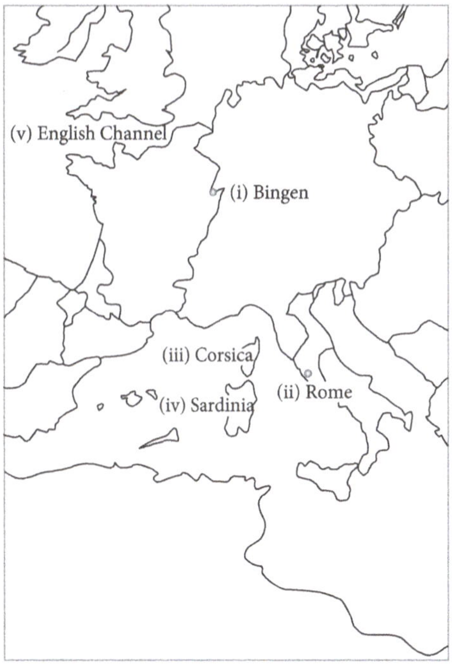

SELF ASSESSMENT TEST

Objective Type Questions

1. The term palmer means
   (a) a monk who travels to distant shrines.
   (b) a knight who works for his lord.
   (c) a farmer who cultivates for the knight.
   (d) None of these
2. The direct tax imposed on peasants by the king was known as ....
   (a) Tithe
   (b) Manor
   (c) Taille
   (d) None of these
3. The .... who moved from place to place preaching to the people were known as Friars.
   (a) Monks
   (b) Priests
   (c) Social reformers
   (d) None of these
4. Match the Following.

List I	List II
A. Abbes Hildegard	1. Compared life of monks with ploughmen.
B. Langland	2. Monk who travels to distant shrines.
C. Chaucer	3. Develop the practice of community singing of prayers in church.
D. Palmers	4. Canterbury tales

Codes

	A	B	C	D		A	B	C	D
(a)	3	1	4	2	(b)	2	1	4	3
(c)	2	1	3	4	(d)	4	2	1	3

Short Answer Type Questions

5. How did frequent local wars in Europe contribute to the rise of knights?
6. Examine how the Church was a powerful institution in Europe.
7. Analyse the warm phase in which Europe entered from the 11th century.
8. Though Europeans become Christians, they still held on to some of their old beliefs in magic and folk traditions. Comment.
9. What were the key technological advancement in agriculture during the 11th century?
10. How did improvements in food production affect life expectancy in Medieval Europe?

Long Answer Type Questions

11. Discuss in detail about nobility as the second order which had a central role in social processes.
12. Examine the various obligations that free peasants had to fulfill for their landlords and how did this shape their lives?
13. Changes in agricultural technology and land use were more dramatic in the transformation of the social system. Discuss.
14. By the early 14th century, Europe's economic expansion slowed down. Justify the statement.
15. Examine how the nobility adapt to the rise of royal absolutism in Medieval Europe.

5

CHAPTER

This chapter discusses the rise of a distinct urban culture and the evolving sense of history in Europe. It also highlights how people began to contrast their 'modern' world with the ancient civilisations of Greece and Rome.

YOUR STUDY GOALS

YOUR PRACTICE GOAL

- Objective Type Questions (39 Qs ; MCQs, A-R, Matching, Picture Based)
- Subjective Questions (15 SAs, 7 LAs)
- Source Based Questions (6 Qs)
- Map Based Questions (2 Qs)

Changing Cultural Traditions

5.1 Sources of History about Changes Occurred in Europe

- The 14th century onwards witnessed a significant increase in historical materials, including documents, printed books, paintings, sculptures, buildings and textiles.
- Much of this material is carefully preserved in archives, art galleries and museums across Europe and America.
- From the 19th century, historians used the term 'Renaissance' (rebirth) to describe the cultural changes of this period. The Swiss scholar Jacob Burckhardt (1818-1897 CE) was particularly influential in highlighting these changes.
- Burckhardt believed that politics was not the only significant aspect of history; culture was equally important.
- In 1860, he published *The Civilisation of the* ***Renaissance***[1] *in Italy*, explaining the emergence of a humanist culture in Italian towns from the 14th to 17th centuries.
- He described the modern individual as capable of making independent decisions and developing skills, contrasting with the medieval individual, whose thoughts were controlled by the church.

1 **Renaissance** It is the period of European history between the 14th and 17th centuries when there was a new interest in science and in ancient art and literature, especially in Italy.

5.2 The Revival of Italian Cities

- After the fall of Western Roman Empire, many towns in Italy that were once active political and cultural centres, lost their significance.

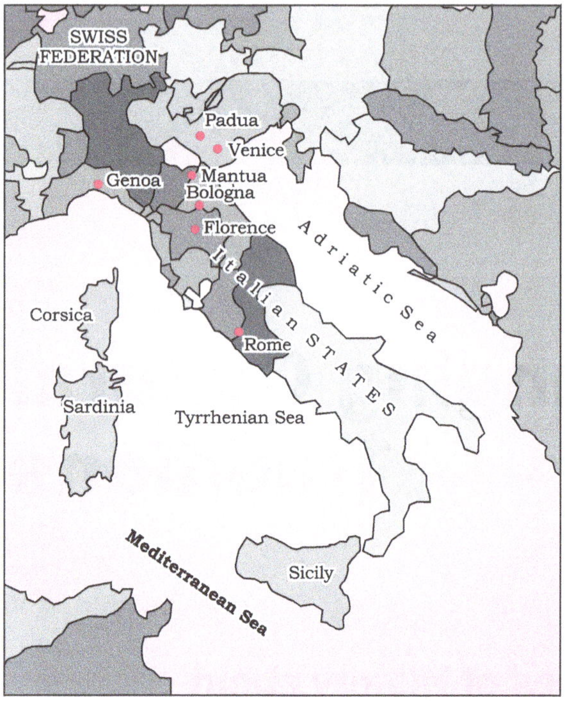

▲ *The Italian States*

- The cities became weaker because there was no one strong leader to rule them and the Pope in Rome was not very powerful.
- While Western Europe was changing because of feudalism and the Catholic Church, Eastern Europe was influenced by the **Byzantine Empire** and **Islam** was growing in power in the West.
- These developments indirectly contributed to the revival of Italian culture.

Growth of Italian Towns

- The expansion of trade between the Byzantine Empire and Islamic countries led to the revival of ports along the Italian coast.
- When trade with China started along the Silk Route[2] in the 12th century and trade with Western European countries grew, Italian cities became even more important.
- Italian towns no longer viewed themselves as part of a powerful empire but rather as independent city-states. While **Florence** and **Venice** were republics, many other cities were ruled by princes.
- **Venice** and **Genoa** were particularly vibrant cities, differing from other parts of Europe in several ways. In these cities, the priests and nobles did not have much power. Instead, wealthy merchants and bankers helped in governing the cities. This made the people who lived there, feel proud to be citizens.

Quick Test 1

1. In 1860, who wrote the book 'The Civilisation of the Renaissance in Italy'?
2. Eastern Europe was under which empire?
3. What was the cause of the revival of ports on the Italian coast?
4. In Italy, which two city-states were republics?

5.3 Universities and Humanism

Universities

- Some of the earliest universities in Europe were established in Italian towns, with **Padua** and **Bologna** becoming **centres of legal studies** as early as the 11th century. Universities became more important and people started studying law more.
- As trade became more important in Italian cities, there was a need for more lawyers and notaries[3] who knew how to write and understand laws.
- People wanted to study law because it was useful for doing business. They often learned about law by studying the old Roman laws.

2 Silk Route It was an ancient network of trade routes that were for centuries connecting the Asian continent with East and West.

3 Notaries A notary is a person who is allowed to perform specific legal tasks, such as creating or certifying contracts, deeds and other documents that can be used in different places.

Humanism

- **Francesco Petrarch** (1304-1378 CE) emphasised the importance of studying ancient Greek and Roman texts to gain a better understanding of their civilisation. This approach, known as **humanism**[4], highlighted the value of learning from the past and questioned the dependence on religious teachings alone.
- In the early 15th century, the term "humanist" was used to describe teachers of grammar, rhetoric, poetry, history and moral philosophy.
- The word "**humanities**" itself derived from the Latin word "*humanitas,*" meaning culture.
- The Roman lawyer and essayist **Cicero** (106-43 BCE), a contemporary of **Julius Caesar**, used the term "humanities" to refer to subjects that were not connected to religion. These subjects were acquired through individual development, discussion and debate.
- The revolutionary ideas of humanism gained attention in many universities, particularly in Petrarch's home-town of Florence.
- By the end of the 13th century, Florence had become a renowned centre of intellectual and artistic creativity.
- **Dante Alighieri** (1265-1321 CE), a layman who wrote on religious themes and **Giotto** (1267-1337 CE), an artist known for his realistic portraits, were influential figures in Florence's cultural development.

▲ *Giotto's Painting of the child Jesus, Assisi, Italy.*

- Individuals with diverse interests and skills, such as scholars, diplomats, theologians, and artists, were often referred to as **Renaissance Man**[5].

The Humanist View of History

- Humanists believed that a **dark age** began after the collapse of the Roman Empire.
- The time after the Roman Empire ended was called the **Middle Ages** or **medieval period**[6]. This lasted for about 1,000 years.
- During this time, it was believed that the Church had complete control over people's minds and had destroyed the knowledge of the Greeks and Romans.
- Humanists used the term '**modern**' to describe the period beginning in the 15th century. This marked a shift from the medieval era, which they viewed as a period of intellectual and cultural decline.

Periodisation used by humanists and by later scholars

5th-14th century	The Middle Ages
5th-9th century	The Dark Ages
9th-11th century	The Early Middle Ages
11th-14th century	The Late Middle Ages
15th century onwards	The Modern Age

4 **Humanism** A system of values and beliefs that is based on the idea that people can solve the problem using reason instead of religion.
5 **Renaissance Man** A person with many interests and skills.
6 **Medieval period** It was a time in European history that began with the fall of the Roman Empire in 476 CE and lasted until the Renaissance in the 14th, 15th, or 16th century.

5.4 The Arab's Contribution to Science and Philosophy

- During the Middle Ages, monks and clergymen did not share the writings of the Greeks and Romans with many people. Arab translators played a crucial role in preserving and translating ancient manuscripts.
- In the 14th century, many scholars began to study these translated works of Greek writers like Plato and Aristotle.
- Some European scholars learned Greek through Arabic translations, while others studied translated works of Arabic and Persian scholars. These translations covered fields such as natural science, mathematics, astronomy, medicine and chemistry.
- **Ptolemy's *Almagest***, a significant work on astronomy written in Greek before 140 CE, was translated into Arabic. It carries the Arabic definite article 'al' which brings out the Arabic connection.
- Some Muslim writers were regarded as men of wisdom in the Italian world. They were **Ibn Sina** (Avicenna in Latin 980-1037 CE), an Arab Physician and philosopher of Bukhara in Central Asia, and **al-Razi** (Rhazes), author of a medical encyclopaedia.
- **Ibn Rushd** (Averroes in Latin, 1126-98 CE), a philosopher of Spain, wanted to find a link between philosophy and religion. Christian thinkers later followed his approach.
- Humanists sought to expand educational opportunities beyond traditional subjects like law, medicine, and theology. Humanist subjects were gradually introduced into schools in Italy and other European countries.

Artists and Realism

- Humanists used various forms of expression such as art, architecture and books, to effectively spread their ideas.
- Artists were influenced by studying the remains of Roman culture, which they found in the ruins of ancient Roman cities.
- Italian sculptors sought to revive the Roman tradition of creating perfectly proportioned human figures. **Donatello's** (1386-1466 CE) life-like statues, created in 1416, marked a significant achievement in this revival.

Artists and Science

- Artists visited medical school laboratories to study bone structures.
- **Andreas Vesalius** (1514-1564 CE), a Belgian professor of medicine at the University of Padua, was the first to dissect human bodies and started the study of modern physiology.

Painters and Techniques

- Painters did not have older works to reference as models, yet they focused on creating realistic art.
- Understanding geometry helped the painters to create perspective and by observing how light changes, their paintings gained a three-dimensional effect.
- The use of oil as a painting medium enriched the colours and textures of artworks.
- Chinese and Persian art, introduced by the Mongols, influenced the colours and designs of costumes in many paintings.

▲ *Leonardo da Vinci*

Leonardo da Vinci

- Leonardo da Vinci (1452-1519 CE) was a renowned artist with diverse interests, including: botany, anatomy, mathematics and art.
- His famous works include ***Mona Lisa*** and ***The Last Supper*** and he designed a **flying machine**, inspired by his dream of flight.
- He signed his work as "Leonardo da Vinci, disciple of Experiment."

5.5. Architecture: Paintings, Sculptors, Relief

- Rome saw an amazing revival in the 15th century, following a period of political weakness caused by the election of two rival popes in 1378 CE.
- The revival of the pope's power led to a new interest in Rome's history. Archaeological excavations of Roman ruins inspired a new architectural style, a revival of the imperial Roman style, now known as **classical**.
- Popes, wealthy merchants and aristocrats employed architects, artists and sculptors to decorate buildings with paintings, sculptures and reliefs.
- Artists came to be known individually by name, not as members of a group or a guild like earlier times.

▲ *Italian architecture in the sixteenth century*

Notable Architects

Michelangelo Buonarroti (1475-1564 CE)

- He is renowned for painting the ceiling for the Pope in the Sistine Chapel in Rome.
- He also created the sculpture **The Pieta** and designed the dome of **St. Peter's Church**.

Filippo Brunelleschi (1337-1446 CE)

- He is known for designing the **Duomo of Florence**.
- He initially started his career as a sculptor.

▲ *The Pieta by Michelangelo*

Quick Test 2

1. Who was the contemporary of Julius Caesar?
2. Who was 'Renaissance Man'?
3. Name a book on astronomy which was written in Greek.
4. Which style of architecture is known as classical style?
5. Who designed the spectacular Duomo of Florence?

5.6 The First Printed Books in Europe

- The invention of printing in the 16th century revolutionised the spread of knowledge, allowing Italian written works to reach other countries.
- Europeans owe the printing technology to the Chinese and Mongol rulers, as European traders and diplomats learned about it during visits to their courts.
- Other innovations, such as firearms, the compass and the abacus, also came from similar exchanges.

Advantages of Printing Technology

- Previously, texts existed only in a few hand-written copies. In 1455 CE, 150 copies of the **Bible** were printed in **Johannes Gutenberg's** (1400-1458 CE) workshop, a German inventor who created the first printing press. Earlier, a monk would have taken the same amount of time to write just one copy.
- By 1500 CE, many classical Latin texts were printed in Italy, enabling students to buy printed books instead of relying solely on lecture notes. This facilitated the rapid spread of ideas, opinions and information.
- A printed book promoting new ideas could reach many readers. This accessibility led to a growing reading habit among the public.
- Printed books helped spread humanist ideas from Italy to other parts of Europe by the end of the 15th century. This was different from earlier ideas, which were usually limited to particular places.

5.7 A New Concept of Human Beings

- Humanist ideas helped people to think for themselves and be less controlled by religion. This led many Italians to focus on becoming rich, powerful and famous, but they were still religious.
- **Francesco Barbaro** (1390-1454 CE), a humanist from Venice, advocated for wealth acquisition as a virtue.
- **Lorenzo Valla** (1406-1457 CE), believed that studying history could inspire people to be better. He also criticised the Christian rules against enjoying life in his book '***On Pleasure***'.
- During this time, there was also a focus on good manners, including polite speech, appropriate dressing and cultural skills.
- Humanism suggested that individuals could shape their lives through means beyond power and wealth. This idea contrasted with the feudal belief in three separate social orders.

Views of Niccolo Machiavelli on Humans

- One of the scholars named Niccolo Machiavelli wrote about human nature in the 15th chapter of his book 'The Prince'.
- He believed that 'all men are bad and always ready to show their bad nature partly because of the fact that human desires are never ending.' He also believed that self-interest is the powerful motive behind every human action.

The Position of Women in Europe

- The new ideals of individuality and citizenship excluded women. Men from wealthy families dominated public life and were decision makers in their houses.
- Educated sons were trained for business or public roles, while women had little influence over how their husbands ran their businesses. Younger sons were sent to join the Church.

▲ *Isabella d' Este*

- Marriages were often arranged to help businesses grow. If a family couldn't afford a big dowry, their daughters were sent to live in a convent or monastery.
- Women's roles were mostly limited to household management, with few opportunities in public life.
- In merchant families, women's positions differed. Wives often assisted in running shops and managed businesses when their husbands were away.
- The early death of a merchant could lead to a widow taking a more significant public role, as highlighted by the Marchesa of Mantua, **Isabella d 'Este** (1474-1539 CE), who ruled Mantua while her husband was absent.

Aspirations of Women

- Some women were intellectually creative and recognised the importance of a humanist education.
- **Venetian Cassandra Fedele** (1465-1558 CE) believed that all women should learn to read and write, even if it didn't make them famous or successful.
- Fedele, who was proficient in Greek and Latin, was invited to give lectures at the University of Padua. Her writings highlights the importance of education during that time.
- Fedele believed that women should be treated equally to men. She criticised the idea that freedom only meant something for men. The women also wanted to be economically powerful, own property and get an education.

Debates within Christianity

- Italian towns connected with the world through trade, travel, military conquests and diplomatic relations.
- Only educated and rich people could enjoy and follow the new cultural trends. Most people, who could not read or write, did not know much about these changes.

- Many scholars in Northern European universities were interested in humanist ideas in the 15th and early 16th centuries. They studied classical Greek and Roman texts, along with Christian holy books.
- In Italy, professional scholars led the humanist movement. They wanted to study ancient texts and simplify religion. Some Church members also supported this idea. These people believed that humans are free to make their own choices and think for themselves.
- Later scholars suggested that a distant God created man but he allowed complete freedom for individuals to pursue happiness in this world.

Criticism of the Church

- Christian humanists like **Thomas More** (1478-1535 CE) in England and **Erasmus** (1466-1536 CE) in Holland criticised the Church as greedy, exploiting ordinary people.
- Clergy members sold **indulgences**[7], saying that people could pay money to be forgiven for their sins.
- As people began reading the Bible in their own language, they saw that it was different from what religion was teaching them. This led to peasant rebellions against Church-imposed taxes and frustration among princes over the Church's interference in governance.
- Humanists showed that the clergy's claim to have special powers to judge people and collect taxes was not true. They found out that a document called the '**Donation of Constantine**' was fake.

Reformers in Christianity

- In 1517 CE, **Martin Luther** (1483-1546 CE) led a movement against the Church, advocating for complete faith in God as the path to a righteous life and entry to heaven. This movement became known as the **Protestant Reformation.**
- Churches in Germany and Switzerland broke ties with the Pope and the Catholic Church.
- Luther's ideas spread in Switzerland through **Ulrich Zwingli** (1484-1531 CE) and **Jean Calvin** (1509-1564 CE).
- Reformers, who were often supported by merchants, were more powerful in towns. The Catholic Church still had a lot of influence in rural areas.
- More **radical**[8] German reformers, like the **Anabaptists**, combined salvation with social equality, rejecting taxes and advocating for choosing priests. Peasants who were treated badly by the feudal system were interested in these new ideas. Luther did not support radical movements and instead supported the suppression of peasant rebellions in 1525 CE.
- Protestants facing oppression by Catholic rulers claimed the right to remove unjust leaders and select leaders of their choice in France.

Reformation

- Over time, the Catholic Church allowed Protestants to worship freely. In England, the monarch became the head of the Church, breaking ties with the Pope.
- The Catholic Church was also affected by Protestant ideas and began reforming from within. In Spain and Italy, church leaders emphasised the importance of living simply and serving the poor.
- **Ignatius Loyola** established the **Society of Jesus** in 1540 CE in Spain, to counter Protestantism. His followers, known as Jesuits, focused on serving the poor and expanding knowledge of other cultures.

---

7 **Indulgences** Documents sold by Church and supposed to free the buyer from the burden of sins he had committed.

8 **Radical** A person who favours extreme changes in existing views, habits, conditions, or institutions

Quick Test 3

1 How many copies of the Bible were printed in 1455 CE?
2 Who believed that the study of history leads man to strive for a life of perfection?
3 What was the view of Thomas More on Church?
4 What was the movement led by Martin Luther called?
5 A Society of Jesus was set by whom in 1540 CE?

5.8 The Copernican Revolution

▲ *Self-portrait by Copernicus*

- Scientists challenged the Christian belief that humanity was naturally sinful and that the Earth was the centre of the universe.
- **Copernicus** (1473-1543 CE), a contemporary of Martin Luther, argued that planets, including Earth, revolve around the Sun. He shared his writings, ***De revolutionibus*** (The Rotation), only when he was dying.
- A half-century later, astronomers like **Johannes Kepler** (1571-1630 CE) and **Galileo Galilei** (1564-1642 CE) further explained the differences between Earth and heaven.
- **Galileo's work, *The Motion*** and **Kepler's *Cosmographical Mystery*** demonstrated that Earth is part of a Sun-centred system, with planets orbiting in elliptical paths rather than circular ones.
- Galileo asserted that the Bible, while guiding spiritual matters, does not explain celestial mechanics.
- The scientific revolution was culminated with **Isaac Newton's Gravitational Theory**.
- These thinkers showed that knowledge relies on observation and experimentation rather than mere belief.

Scientific Revolution

- The introduction of experimentation boosted the development of fields such as Physics, Chemistry and Biology, marking the Scientific Revolution.
- New scientific groups helped people learn about science and understand the world in a new way. This made some people stop believing in God and instead believe in the power of nature. Even believers began to view God as distant, not directly involved in earthly affairs.
- Scientific societies like the **Paris Academy** (established in 1670 CE) and the **Royal Society in London** (founded in 1662 CE) spreaded these ideas by conducting public lectures and experiments.

5.9 European Renaissance in the Fourteenth Century

- Some historians, like **Peter Burke**, argue that Burckhardt overemphasised the differences between the 14th century and the past by coining the term Renaissance, suggesting a rebirth of Greek and Roman civilisation.
- Scholars and artists replaced the pre-Christian worldview with a Christian one.
- It is simple to say the Renaissance was a time of energy and creativity, while the Middle Ages were just dark and undeveloped.
- Many features of the Renaissance in Italy can be linked to the 12th and 13th centuries. Some historians suggest that a similar cultural growth happened in France in the 9th century.

Other Factors for Changes in Europe

- The technologies and skills developed in Asia were often more advanced than those of the Greeks and Romans.
- Trade and the sharing of knowledge grew stronger between Europe, Asia and North Africa when Islam spread and the Mongols conquered new lands.
- Europeans learned not only from Greeks and Romans but also from India, Arabia, Iran, Central Asia and China.

New Developments

- One significant change during renaissance period was the separation of public and private spheres.
- The public sphere included government and formal religion, while the private sphere involved family and personal beliefs.
- Individuals had both public and private roles, leading to an emphasis on individuality.
- Different regions of Europe started to have separate sense of identity based on their language.

Quick Test 4

1. Name any two astronomers of the 17th century.
2. Who proposed the theory of Gravitation?
3. In which year, the Paris Academy was established?
4. Mention an important development in the 18th century.

TIMELINE

Year	Event
1300 CE	Humanism taught at Padua University in Italy.
1341CE	Petrarch was given the title of 'Poet Laureate' in Rome.
1349 CE	University established in Florence.
1390 CE	Geoffrey Chaucer's *Canterbury Tales* published.
1436 CE	Brunelleschi designed the Duomo in Florence.
1453 CE	Ottoman Turks defeated the Byzantine ruler of Constantinople.
1454 CE	Gutenberg prints the Bible with movable type.
1484 CE	Portuguese mathematicians calculate latitude by observing the Sun.
1492 CE	Columbus reaches America.
1495 CE	Leonardo da Vinci paints *The Last Supper*.
1512 CE	Michelangelo paints the Sistine Chapel ceiling.
1516 CE	Thomas More's *Utopia* published.
1517 CE	Martin Luther wrote the Ninety-Five Theses.
1522 CE	Luther translated the Bible into German.
1525 CE	Peasant uprising in Germany.
1543 CE	Andreas Vesalius writes *On Anatomy*.
1559 CE	Anglican Church established in England, with the king/queen as its head.
1569 CE	Gerhardus Mercator prepares a cylindrical map of the Earth.
1582 CE	Gregorian calendar introduced by Pope Gregory XIII.
1628 CE	William Harvey linked the heart with blood circulation.
1673 CE	Academy of Sciences set up in Paris.
1687 CE	Isaac Newton's *Principia Mathematica* published.

Mind Map

CHANGING CULTURAL TRADITIONS

1 The Revival of Italian Cities

- After the fall of Western Roman empire, political and cultural centres in Italy lost their identity.
- Western Europe was controlled by feudal lords and Latin church.
- Eastern Europe was under Byzantine empire.
- Some powerful independent cities like Venice and Horence were republic.

2 Universities and Humanism

- Earliest universities of Europe were setup in Italian towns.
- Law emerged as a popular subject due to growth in economic activities.
- Subjects like humanities began to be taught in some universities.
- The term 'Humanist' was used for masters who taught grammar, rhetoric, poetry and moral science, etc.

3 The Humanist View of History

- Humanist believed that they were restoring true civilisation after centuries of dark age, which was prevalent since collapse of Roman empire.

4 The Arab Contribution to Science and Philosophy

- Arab Scholars preserved and translated Greek and Roman writings.
- Some European scholars began reading Greek translated works of Arabic and Persian scholars.

5 Artist and Realism

- Art, architecture and books were effective medium of transmitting humanist ideas.
- Andreas Vesalius was first to dissect the human body.

6 Architecture: Paintings, Sculpture, Relief

- Rome revived in the fifteenth century with stronger Popes.
- Classical Roman style inspired architecture, art and sculpture in Rome.

7 The First Printed Books

- Johannes Gutenberg invented the first printing press and printed 150 Bibles in 1455.
- By 1500, many classical texts written in Latin had been printed in Italy.

8 A New Concept of Human Being

- Religious values were diverted towards materialism.
- Francesco Barbaro and Lorenzo Valla raised their voice in favour of pleasure through materialism.

9 Aspiration of Women

- Men from aristocratic families dominated public life and decision making.
- Daughters were sent to live the 'life of a nun' in case of inadequate arrangement of dowies.
- Women have active role in some businesses in case of unavailability of their husbands.

10 Debates within Christianity

- New culture developed due to trade operation in Italy.
- Unnecessary rituals of Christianism were condemned by the scholars.
- Martin Luther (a German monk) started a movement called 'Protestant Reformation' against church in 1517.

11 The Copernican Revolution

- Religious restrictions were challenged by the new scientific discoveries of Copernicus, Keppler, etc.
- These scientists challenged the ideas of church about planets, their movement, etc.
- Thinkers taught that knowledge should be based upon observations and experiments rather than on beliefs.

12 European Renaissance in the 14th Century

- Renaissance was a period of cultural, artistic, scientific and intellectual revival that began in Italy in early 14th century.
- Many historians like Peter Burke has critically analysed the term Renaissance, firstly used by Jacob Burckhardt.

NCERT Folder

Intext Questions

1. Describe the different scientific elements in the work of 16th century Italian artists.

Ans The different scientific elements in the work of 16th century Italian artists were

- Artists went to laboratories of medical schools to learn about bone structures and maintain same accuracy in their work.
- Painters used knowledge of geometry to understand the perspective.

They used the changing quality of light to acquire a three dimensional effects.

Thus, artists used anatomy, geometry, physics, etc to enhance their art.

2. Compare the aspirations for women expressed by a woman (Fedele) and by a man (Castiglione). Did they have only women of a particular class in mind?

Ans Aspirations for women expressed by Fedele were

- She wanted women to study even if it does not promise them rewards or dignity.
- She questioned the idea that women were incapable of achieving the qualities of a humanist scholar.
- She criticised the republic for creating a highly limited definition of freedom that favoured the desires of men over those to women.

Aspirations of women expressed by Castiglione were

- Women should not resemble men in their ways, manners, words, gestures and behaviour.
- He wanted women to have soft and delicate tenderness and feminine sweetness in every movement.
- Women have to perform well and gracefully to the sports suitable for them.

No, they did not have only women of a particular class in mind. While Fedele might be talking about women in general, Castiglione might possibly be talking about women from upper classes.

3. What were the issues on which the Protestants criticised the Catholic Church?

Ans The issues on which Protestants criticised the Catholic Church were

- A person did not need priests to establish contact with God. The faith in God alone can guide people to the right life and entry into heaven.
- The Protestants wanted to practise religion in a simple way instead of unnecessary rituals.
- Church had become an institution of greed, extorting money from poor.
- They were against the clergy who were selling indulgences, the documents which will free the buyer from their sins.
- They proved the clergy's claim to judicial and fiscal powers to be false.

Answer in Brief

1. Which elements of Greek and Roman culture were revived in the 14th and 15th centuries?

Ans The elements of Greek and Roman culture that were revived in the 14th and 15th centuries were

- Law was now studied in the context of earlier Roman culture. There was an emphasis on the study of ancient Greeks and Romans from a closer point of view. Many scholars translated works of Greek writers like Plato, Aristotle and Ptolemy.
- Artists were inspired by the works of past. They admired the figures of perfectly proportioned men and women sculpted so many centuries ago and wanted to continue same tradition.
- Painters also took inspiration from the Greek and Roman culture. There was a revival of imperial Roman style in the architecture.
- All the classical texts which were in Latin were printed in Italy and made them available to common people.
- In religious sphere, the religious practices according to ancient texts were encouraged instead of unnecessary rituals that were added in later times.

2. Compare details of Italian architecture of this period with Islamic architecture.

Ans The comparison between Italian architecture period and Islamic architecture is as follows

Italian Architecture	Islamic Architecture
This architecture was inspired as a new style of architecture in Italy when the ruins in Rome were carefully excavated. This was actually a revival of the imperial Roman style.	Mosques, shrines and tombs represented mainly the Islamic architecture.
Artists and sculptors decorated buildings with paintings, sculptures and reliefs.	Arches, domes, minarets and open courtyards were the main architectural features of Islamic architecture.
This architecture depicted human beings in sculptures. It also depicted Mary and Jesus in human forms in their sculptures.	There was a rejection of representing living beings in the religious art of Islam. So, calligraphy and arabesque art forms became prominent in Islamic architecture.

3. Why were Italian towns the first to experience the ideas of humanism?

Ans The Italian towns were the first to experience humanism because

- The subject Humanism was first began to teach in Italian schools, colleges and universities.
- The earliest universities in Europe were setup in Italian towns. The universities of Padua and Bologna had been centres of legal studies.
- Grammar, rhetoric, poetry, history and moral philosophy were taught in Italian universities.
- Number of classical books were written and composed by both Roman and Greek scholars.
- Great scholars, artists were present in Italian towns who propagated ideas of humanism.

4. Compare the Venetian idea of good government with those in contemporary France.

Ans The comparison between Venetian idea of good government and government of contemporary France is as follows

Venetian Idea of Good Government	Government of Contemporary France
Clergy should not be politically dominant and there should be no powerful feudal lords.	Kings became powerful and there was increase in centralisation.
Active participation from different sections of people in governing the city should be there.	Old feudal lords became new nobility in the kings courts and administration.
There should be a sense of citizenship among the people and it should not be weaken even during the rule of cruel military rulers.	Autocracy was the general form of government in France and it was highly centralised monarchy. The king regarded himself as the representative of God on the Earth.

Answer in a Short Essay

5. What were the features of humanist thought?

Ans The features of humanist thought were

- Skills should be developed by individuals through discussion and debate.
- Not just religion but other subjects like grammar, rhetoric, poetry, history and moral philosophy were also given importance.
- Humanists were multi-skilled people. They were scholar-diplomat-theologian-artist combined in one.
- Not only formal education but also art, architecture and books were used to transmit humanist ideas. Artists focused on realism and perfection in their art. Paintings were also made as realistically as possible.
- Individuals were capable of shaping their own lives through means other than the mere pursuit of power and money.

Finally, the foundation to renaissance was laid by the humanist thought.

6. Write a careful account of how the world appeared different to 17th century Europeans.

Ans The world appeared different to 17th century Europeans in the following ways

- Renaissance encouraged different views to emerge in Europe. It gave rise to rationality and logical thinking in the people.
- Scientists questioned the established practices and notions of different institutions like Church. The turning point was the work of Copernicus which stated that Sun is the center of the universe and Earth and other planets rotate around it.
- Later, writings of astronomers like Johannes Kepler and Galileo Galilei filled the gap between heaven and Earth.
- The revolution of science reached its peak with Newton's Theory of Gravitation.
- There was also shift in the beliefs towards God. People now believed that nature is source of creation and God does not directly regulate the act of living in the material world.
- The scientific societies were established to promote scientific ideas and establish a new scientific culture in the public domain.
  The Paris Academy was established in 1670 CE and the Royal Society of London in 1662 CE. They held lectures and conducted experiments for public viewing.
- Europe started a little late than other parts of the world like India, Arabia, Iran, Central Asia and China in technological advancement but it slowly picked up the pace and other parts of the world stagnated in technological advancements.

Thus, Europe had become more scientifically advanced in 17th century compared to the other parts of world.

Exam Pattern Questions

Objective Type Questions

Multiple Choice Questions (MCQs)

1. The Renaissance originated in
(a) Italy (b) France
(c) Germany (d) Britain

2. The Italian city .... was/were a republic(s).
(a) Florence (b) Bologna
(c) Venice (d) Both (a) and (c)

3. The Mongols opened up trade with China through .... **CBSE Diksha**
(a) Silk Route (b) Mecca
(c) Sri Lanka (d) Venice

4. One of the most vibrant Italian city was **CBSE Diksha**
(a) Venice (b) Rome
(c) Florence (d) All of these

5. Arab philosopher of Spain whose method was adopted by Christian thinkers **CBSE Diksha**
(a) Ibn Sina (b) Al Razi
(c) Ibn Rushd (d) Dante

6. The term 'Renaissance Man' means **CBSE Diksha**
(a) a person who is very strong
(b) a person who is very clever
(c) a person who is very bold
(d) a person with many interests and skills.

7. Name the author of the medical Encyclopedia during Renaissance **CBSE Diksha**
(a) Ptolemy (b) Petrarch
(c) Al-Razi (d) Dante

8. The Muslim writer who was regarded as a man of wisdom in the Italian world **CBSE Diksha**
(a) Ibn Sina (b) Aristotle
(c) Ptolemy (d) Petrarch

9. Who was the first one to dissect human body? **CBSE Diksha**
(a) Andreas Vesalius (b) Ibn Sina
(c) Aristotle (d) Francesco Barbaro

10. Name the sculpture of 'The Pieta'. **CBSE Diksha**
(a) Lorenzo Valla (b) Machiavelli
(c) Leonardo da Vinci (d) Michelangelo

11. Which architect designed the spectacular duomo of Florence? **CBSE Diksha**
(a) Fillipo Brunelleschi (b) Lorenzo Valla
(c) Machiavelli (d) Michelangelo

12. Who made the first printing press? **CBSE Diksha**
(a) Lorenzo Valla (b) Machiavelli
(c) Johannes Gutenberg (d) Michelangelo

13. By 1500, many classical texts printed in Italy were in language **CBSE Diksha**
(a) Latin (b) English
(c) German (d) Spanish

14. By the .... century, sale and purchase of books began in Europe.
(a) 15th (b) 16th
(c) 17th (d) 18th

15. Humanist from Venice was **CBSE Diksha**
(a) Francesco Barbaro (b) Lorenzo Valla
(c) Niccolo Machiavelli (d) None of these

16. 'Even though the study of letters promises and offers no reward for women and no dignity' was the statement quoted by **CBSE Diksha**
(a) Isabella d'este (b) Cassandra Fedele
(c) Balthasar Castiglione (d) None of these

17. Luther's ideas popularised in Switzerland by
(a) Ulrich Zwingli (b) Copernicus
(c) Thomas More (d) None of these

18. Society of Jesus was set up by **CBSE Diksha**
(a) Erasmus (b) William Harvey
(c) Ignatius Loyola (d) Francesco Barbaro

19. The theory "that the planets including the Earth rotate around the Sun" was given by **CBSE Diksha**
(a) Copernicus (b) Kepler
(c) Galileo (d) Newton

20. The theory of the Earth as part of Sun centered system was made popular by **CBSE Diksha**
(a) Copernicus (b) Kepler
(c) Galileo (d) Newton

21. The term celestial means
(a) Divine quality (b) Heavenly quality
(c) Worldly quality (d) Both (a) and (b)

22. Who formulated the theory of Gravitation? **CBSE Diksha**
(a) Copernicus
(b) Isaac Newton
(c) Johannes Kepler
(d) Galileo Galilei

23. The Royal Society in London was formed in ....
(a) 1662 (b) 1682 (c) 1690 (d) 1700

24. In which year Gregorian calendar was introduced by Pope Gregory XIII?
(a) 1682 (b) 1582 (c) 1685 (d) 1575

25. Consider the following statements and choose the incorrect option.
I. Persons with many interests and skills were referred as Renaissance Man.
II. Duomo of Florence was designed by Michelangelo Buonarroti.

Codes
(a) Only I (b) Only II
(c) Both I and II (d) None of these

26. Consider the following statements and choose the correct option.
I. Jacob Burckhardt was a German scholar.
II. German historian Leopold von Ranke was the teacher of scholar Jacob Burckhardt.

Codes
(a) Only I (b) Only II
(c) Both I and II (d) None of these

27. Arrange in sequence
(i) Martin Luther writes the Ninety-Five Theses.
(ii) Thomas More's Utopia published.
(iii) Peasants uprising in Germany.

Codes
(a) (ii), (i), (iii) (b) (i), (ii), (iii)
(c) (ii), (iii), (i) (d) (iii), (i), (ii)

28. Identify the name of the person from the information given below.
(i) He was born in 106 BCE.
(ii) He was a Roman lawyer and essayist.
(iii) He was a contemporary of Julius Caesar.
(a) Dante (b) Giotto
(c) Plato (d) Ciero

29. Identify the name of the scholar from the information given below.
(i) She was born in 1465 CE.
(ii) She questioned the idea that women were incapable of achieving the qualities of a humanist scholar.
(iii) She was known for her proficiency in Greek and Latin.
(iv) She was invited to give lectures at the University of Padua.
(a) Cassandra Fedele (b) Castiglione
(c) Fulvia (d) Cornelia

30. Al-Khwarizmi : Algebra : : Ibn Sina: ....
(a) Philosophy (b) Medicine
(c) Astronomy (d) Chemistry

31. Aristotle : Greece : : Averroes: ....
(a) India (b) Spain
(c) Persia (d) Egypt

Assertion-Reason

32. Assertion (A) Martin Luther supported Radicalism.
Reason (R) Martin Luther launched a campaign against the Catholic Church.

Codes
(a) Both A and R are true and R is the correct explanation of A
(b) Both A and R are true, but R is not the correct explanation of A
(c) A is true, but R is false
(d) A is false, but R is true

33. Assertion (A) Christians had believed that the Earth was a sinful place and the heavy burden of sin made it immobile.
Reason (R) Copernicus suggested that the Earth stood at the center of the universe around which moved the celestial planets.

Codes
(a) Both A and R are true and R is the correct explanation of A
(b) Both A and R are true, but R is not the correct explanation of A
(c) A is true, but R is false
(d) A is false, but R is true

Picture Based Questions

34. Which of the following Italian city has been depicted in the picture below?

(a) Florence (b) Milan
(c) Venice (d) Genoa

35. Who among the following is associated with the below image?

(a) Leonardo da Vinci
(b) Michelangelo
(c) Donatello
(d) Andreas Vesalius

36. Identify the building given below.

(a) Dome of the Florence
(b) Duomo di Milano
(c) Pantheon
(d) Duomo di Orvieto

37. Which scientist is shown in the image below?

(a) Copernicus (b) Johannes Kepler
(c) Isaac Newton (d) None of these

Match the Following

38.

List I	List II
A. Andreas Vesalius	1. The Pieta
B. Michelangelo Buonarroti	2. Duomo of Florence
C. Filippo Brunelleschi	3. First to dissect the human body
D. Leonardo da Vinci	4. Mona Lisa

Codes

	A	B	C	D		A	B	C	D
(a)	3	1	2	4	(b)	2	3	1	4
(c)	2	1	4	3	(d)	4	2	1	3

39.

List I	List II
A. Francesco Barbaro	1. Society of Jesus
B. Lorenzo Valla	2. Defended the acquisition of wealth as a virtue
C. Niccolo Machiavelli	3. Criticised the Christian commandment against pleasure
D. Ignatius Loyola	4. The Prince

Codes

	A	B	C	D		A	B	C	D
(a)	3	1	2	4	(b)	2	4	1	3
(c)	2	3	4	1	(d)	2	1	4	3

Answers

1. (a) Italy
2. (d) Both (a) and (c)
3. (*a*) Silk Route
4. (a) Venice
5. (c) Ibn Rushd
6. (d) a person with many interests and skills.
7. (c) Al-Razi
8. (a) Ibn Sina
9. (a) Andreas Vesalius
10. (d) Michelangelo
11. (a) Fillipo Brunelleschi
12. (c) Johannes Gutenberg
13. (a) Latin
14. (a) 15th
15. (a) Francesco Barbaro
16. (b) Cassandra Fedele
17. (a) Ulrich Zwingli
18. (c) Ignatius Loyola
19. (a) Copernicus
20. (c) Galileo
21. (d) Both (a) and (b)
22. (b) Isaac Newton
23. (a) 1662
24. (b) 1582
25. (b) Only II
26. (b) Only II
27. (a) (ii), (i), (iii)
28. (d) Ciero
29. (a) Cassandra Fedele
30. (a) Philosophy
31. (b) Spain
32. (d) A is false, but R is true
33. (c) A is true, but R is false
34. (c) Venice
35. (b) Michelangelo
36. (a) Dome of the Florence
37. (a) Copernicus
38. (a)
39. (c)

Subjective Questions

Short Answer Type Questions

1. Discuss the views of historian Jacob Burckhardt on politics and culture.

Ans. Jacob Burckhardt was a Swiss scholar from University of Basle in Switzerland. He was a student of the German historian Leopold von Ranke. Ranke had taught him that the primary concern of the historian was to write about states and politics using papers and files of government departments.

Burckhardt was dissatisfied with these limited goals that his master had set out for him. To him, politics was not the only concerned subject in writing history. History for him was concerned with culture as well as politics.

2. Discuss the humanist culture that Jacob Burckhardt spoke about in his book.

Ans. In 1860 CE, Jacob Burckhardt wrote a book called 'The Civilisation of the Renaissance' in Italy. He wanted readers to emphasise on literature, architecture and painting to tell the story of how a new humanist culture had emerged in Italian towns from the 14th to the 17th century.

This culture was characterised by a new belief that man as an individual was capable of making his own decisions and developing his skills. He was also modern compared to medieval man and his mind was not controlled by the Church.

3. List some new developments that happened during renaissance period.

Ans. Some of the new developments that happened during renaissance period were as follows

- Private and the public spheres of life began to be separated.
- Individuals had private as well as public role. For example, an artist was not only a member of a guild but also he was known for himself as an individual.
- There was increased belief that all individuals had equal political rights.
- Different regions of Europe started to have their separate sense of identity based on language.

4. How did humanist scholars divide the history of Europe from their perspective?

Ans. Humanist scholars divided the history of Europe from their perspective in the following ways

- Humanist scholars assumed that a new age had begun in Europe from the 14th century.
- The term middle ages in medieval period was used for the millennium after the fall of Rome.
- In the middle age, the humanist scholars argued that the Church had complete control over men's minds and due to this, all the learning of the Greeks and Romans had been wiped out.
- The humanists used the word modern for the period from the 15th century.

5. Discuss briefly the humanist culture and its effect on people in Europe.

Ans. Humanist culture loosened the control of religion over human life. Italians were now attracted to material wealth, power and glory. That did not mean that they were irreligious.

Effects of human culture on people in Europe were as follows

- Francesco Barbaro (1390-1454 CE), a humanist from Venice, defended the acquisition of wealth as a good moral quality.
- Lorenzo Valla (1406-1457 CE) believed that study of history leads man to aim for a life of perfection. In his book 'On Pleasure', he criticised the Christian commandment against pleasure.
- During this period, there was lot of focus on good manners, that how one should speak politely, dress correctly and what skills a person of culture should learn.

6. How did painting enrich during renaissance period?

Ans. Painting enriched during renaissance period in the following ways

- Painters started to paint as realistically as possible although they did not have older works to use as model.
- They found that knowledge of geometry helped them to understand the depth and distance and by changing the quality of light their pictures acquired a three dimensional effects.
- Oil as a medium for painting also gave a greater richness of colour to paintings than before.
- Chinese and Persian art provided by Mongols influenced the colours and designs of costumes in many paintings.

7. What were the advantages of printing technology in Europe?

Ans. The advantages of printing technology in Europe were:

- In earlier times, texts existed in a few hand-written copies. With printing technology, in 1455 CE, 150 copies of the Bible were printed in the workshop of Johannes Gutenberg (1400-1458 CE) whereas press/monk would have taken same time to write one copy of Bible.

- Many classical texts which were in Latin had been printed in Italy by 1500 CE. Students could now buy the printed books and were not dependent only on lecture notes.
- Ideas, opinions and information spread rapidly. A printed book promoting new ideas could now reach hundreds of readers within no time. This also developed reading habit among people.
- Due to circulation of the printed books, the humanist culture of Italy spread rapidly across the Alps from the end of 15th century.

8. What was the position of women in merchant families in Europe?

Ans. Position of women in merchant families was as follows

- Shopkeepers were often assisted by their wives in running the shop.
- Wives looked after business when their men were away on work.
- The early death of a merchant forced his widow to perform a larger public role. For example, Isabella d'Este (1474-1539 CE) was a famous woman, who ruled the state when her husband was not present.

9. Discuss the different reasons for the revival of Italian cities.

OR **Enumerate various factors that led to the revival of Italian cities.** CBSE Diksha

Ans. The Italian cities started reviving because of the following reasons

- Effect of Latin Church in the Western Europe and effect of Byzantine empire and Islam in Eastern Europe helped in the revival of Italian culture.
- There was an expansion of trade between the Byzantine empire and the Islamic countries which resulted in the revival of ports on the Italian coast.
- Mongols opened up trade with China via the Silk route. There was an increase in trade with Western European countries. This result in revival of Italian towns during this period as they played a central role in trade.

10. State the significance of the growth in Trade and Towns in the period of Renaissance.

Ans. The significance of the growth in Trade and Towns in the period of Renaissance is stated below

- The growth in trade led to the emergence of a new class in the society i.e. the middle class. This class had become quite rich due to the growth of trade and commerce.
- Without the middle class whole hearted support, no ruler could ever think of freeing himself from either the Church or the Feudal Lords.
- The liberty to the people of the newly developed towns was helpful in bringing the modern age.

11. Enumerate the evil practices of the Catholic Church in Medieval Period that led to the movement against them. Competency Based Que

Ans. The evil practices of the Catholic Church in Medieval Period that led to the movement against them were

- The Catholic remained closely associated with King and power for many centuries.
- The Catholics preferred to live in luxury and away from the common man.
- The Catholics were empowered to collect taxes and fines so they became the representatives of the Kings than the representative of the God. Such exploitative and unquestioned powers made them immoral, corrupt and undignified.

12. What reforms did Catholic Church initiate due to the impact of Protestantism?

Ans. The reforms initiated by Catholic Church due to the impact of protestantism were

- Catholic Church allowed Protestants to worship as they chose. In England, rulers ended the connection with pope and king/queen started being head of the Church.
- In Spain and Italy, Churchmen encouraged a simple life and service to the poor.
- In Spain, Ignatius Loyola, in an attempt to combat Protestantism, set up the Society of Jesus and his followers were called Jesuits. Their mission was to serve the poor and to widen their knowledge of other cultures.

13. Discuss briefly the life of Copernicus.

Ans. Copernicus (1473-1543 CE) was a great scientist and a contemporary of Martin Luther. According to Christians, the Earth was a sinful place and this weight of sin made it unchanging. The Earth is at the centre of the universe and the celestial planet moved around it. But, Copernicus opposed this view as he asserted that the planets, including the earth rotate around the Sun.

He was a sincere Christian and was afraid of the possible reaction to his theory by conservative clergymen. Due to this reason, he did not want his book, *'De revolutionibus'* to be printed. He gave his writings when he was on deathbed, to his follower, Joachim Rheticus.

14. **State the main factors that helped in the growth of nation-states in Europe.**

Ans. The main factors that helped in the growth of nation-states in Europe were as follows

- The decline of feudalism reduced the power of the feudal lords. It enabled the strong rulers to consolidate the absolute power in their hands.
- The middle class traders and merchants supported their rulers who would protect their trade interest.
- The growth of national language and the vast literature also helped in the growth of nation-states.
- The Reformation Movement deprived the Pope and the clergy of their privileges. As a result, the national churches which were established in many countries also helped in the establishment of the nation-states.

15. **How were scholars from North Europe similar and different from their Italian counterparts?**

Ans. Scholars from North Europe were similar and different from their Italian counterparts in the following ways

- In the 15th and 16th centuries, many scholars in North Europe were attracted to humanist ideas. They too like Italians focussed on classical Greek and Roman texts along with the holy book of the Christians.
- In Italy, humanist movement was dominated by professional scholars but in North Europe, humanism attracted many members of the Church.
- The European scholars asked Christians to practise religion same as it was laid down in ancient texts and stop doing unnecessary rituals. They saw humans as free and rational agents.

Long Answer Type Questions

1. **What kind of changes humanist ideas had brought in the religious sphere?**

Ans. Humanist ideas had brought in many changes in religious sphere, which were as follows

- Inspired by humanist ideas, many scholars asked Christians to practise the religion in the way it is laid down in the ancient texts and stop doing unnecessary rituals.
- Humanists like Thomas More and Erasmus felt that Church had become an institution of greed, collecting money forcefully from the ordinary people.
- The Bible was printed in local languages and this enlightened Christians and they came to realise that the religion did not permit many practices as suggested by the clergy.
- Peasants began to revolt against the taxes imposed by the Church. Common man resented the extortions of churchmen and princes did not like their interference in state administration.
- Humanists proved that the clergy's claims to judicial and fiscal powers originated from a document called the 'Donation of Constantine' issued by Constantine. Humanist scholars were successful in proving that this was not genuine but forged.
- The protestant reformation began as a movement that encouraged people to have complete faith in God, believing that faith alone could lead them to live the right life and gain entry into heaven. There was a campaign against Catholic Church which stated that a person did not need priests to establish contact with God.
- Church started reforming itself. It encouraged a simple life and service to the poor.

2. **Discuss the realistic art of Italians. Describe the revival of architecture in Europe and give some examples of great works in Europe.**

Ans. **Realistic Art of Italians**

Art and architecture had become very famous in Europe during renaissance period. Artists were inspired by the works of past and Italian sculptors continued the realistic tradition of ancient Roman art. For example in 1416 CE, Donatello created a new record with his life-like statues. Artists were so concerned about the realism that they went to medical laboratories to learn about the bone structure.

Although painters did not have old works to refer, they still tried to paint as realistically as possible. They used tricks of geometry and light to make their paintings look more realistic. For example, Leonardo da Vinci, one of the greatest artists and his world famous paintings Mona Lisa and The Last Supper belonged to this period. In the colours and designs of costumes in many paintings, there is evidence of the influence of Chinese and Persian art which was made available to Europeans by Mongols.

Revival of Architecture in Europe

The ruins in Rome were carefully excavated by archaeologists and this inspired new style in architecture which was actually a revival of the imperial Roman style called classical.

Examples of Great Works in Europe

Some of the impressive examples are the painting of the ceiling on Sistine Chapel, a sculpture called The Pieta, dome of St Peter's Church all by Michelangelo Buonarroti and spectacular Duomo of Florence by Filippo Brunelleschi.

3. "Europeans are indebted not to their own scholars but to Arab translators". Look at the statement and discuss in detail about the contribution of the Arabs in development of Science and Philosophy.
Competency Based Que

Ans. Contribution of Arabs in the Development of Science and Philosophy were as follows

(i) **Preservation of Greek and Roman Knowledge**
- Arab scholars preserved and translated the works of Greek philosophers like **Plato** and **Aristotle**, which were largely inaccessible to Europeans during the Middle Ages.

(ii) **Translation Movement**
- The House of Wisdom in Baghdad became a major center for translation, where Arab scholars translated Greek, Persian and Indian texts into Arabic, making knowledge available for future generations.

(iii) **Mathematics**
- Arabs made significant contributions to algebra (derived from the Arabic word "al-jabr") and introduced the decimal number system to Europe, which was originally from India.
- Scholars like Al-Khwarizmi (whose name is the origin of the word "algorithm") played a key role in this mathematical advancement.

(iv) **Astronomy**
- Arab scientists improved upon Ptolemaic models of astronomy and made important contributions to astronomical tables and observations.
- Ibn al-Haytham (Alhazen) made significant achievements in the understanding of optics and celestial mechanics.

(v) **Medicine**
- Arab physicians such as Ibn Sina (Avicenna) and Al-Razi (Rhazes) wrote comprehensive medical encyclopaedias, advancing knowledge in medicine, surgery and pharmacology.
- Avicenna's "The Canon of Medicine" was a key medical text in Europe for centuries.

(vi) **Philosophy**
- **Ibn Rushd** (Averroes) played a vital role in appeasing **Aristotelian philosophy** with Islamic thought, influencing both **Christian** and **Jewish philosophers** in Europe.
- Arab philosophers wanted to restore logical thought by mixing **Greek philosophy** with the **Islamic** teachings.

(vii) **Chemistry and Alchemy**
- Arab scholars advanced the field of alchemy, laying the groundwork for modern chemistry. They introduced methods of distillation, sublimation and purification of substances.

(viii) **Transmission to Europe**
- These translations were later transmitted to Europe through Spain and Italy, particularly during the time of the Reconquista and Crusades, leading to a revival of classical knowledge in Europe.

(ix) **Scientific Method**
- Arab scholars emphasised empirical observation and experimentation, which contributed to the development of the **scientific method** that became foundational to European scientific inquiry.

4. "Men from aristocratic families dominated public life and were decision-makers in their families. They educated their sons to take their place in business or in public life. "What was the position of women during the renaissance period? **Competency Based Que**

Ans. Position of women during the renaissance period was as follows

- **Limited Public Role** Women were mostly confined to domestic roles, with men dominating public and political life.
- **Arranged Marriages** Marriages were arranged for alliances and dowries were crucial. Without dowries, women were often sent to convents.
- **Education** Formal education was rare for women, though a few elite women like Cassandra Fedele advocated for women's education.
- **Role in Business** Merchant women sometimes managed businesses when their husbands were away or deceased.
- **Cultural Contribution** Some women were patrons of the arts or writers, though their recognition was limited.
- **Social Expectations** Women were expected to be modest, obedient and focus on family duties.
- **Narrow Expectations of Women's Roles** Humanist scholars, like Castiglione, emphasised that women should have feminine virtues like grace and modesty but should not try to match men in intellectual or public pursuits. This reinforced the traditional roles of women as obedient, modest and primarily focused on family.

Despite these limitations, a few women like **Isabella d'Este** gained prominence in politics and culture, but such cases were rare.

5. Discuss different scientific developments that happened in Europe during Renaissance period. Mention the main characteristics of Renaissance. CBSE Diksha

Ans. Scientists of Europe developed and questioned many existing beliefs and brought out new theories during renaissance period which were as follows

- Scientists of renaissance period questioned the Christian belief of man as a sinner.
- Copernicus asserted that planets including the Earth rotate around the Sun which was against the existing belief that Earth stood at the center of the universe.
- The difference between heaven and Earth was bridged through the writings of astronomers like Johannes Kepler and Galileo Galilei.
- The theory that Earth is part of Sun centered system was made popular by Kepler's Cosmographical Mystery. This also proved that planets move around the Sun not in circles but in ellipses.
- Galileo confirmed the notion of the dynamic world in his work 'The Motion'.
- The revolution in science reached its peak with Issac Newton's theory of Gravitation.
- Scientists now used experiments and investigations to prove something. This approach expanded the subjects like physics, chemistry and biology.
- Many societies like Paris Academy, Royal Society were started to deliver lectures and conduct experiments for public viewing.

The main characteristics of Renaissance include

- Focus on classical texts and the potential of human beings, emphasising education, individuality, and rational thought.
- Renewed interest in Ancient Greek and Roman culture, shifting focus from religious beliefs to reason and creativity.
- Artistic innovation, with artists like Leonardo da Vinci, Michelangelo etc., developing realistic techniques such as perspective and anatomy.
- Advancement in scientific inquiry through empirical mehods, observation and experimentation, laying the foundation for modern science.
- Emphasis on individualism, encouraging personal achievement, self-expression and creativity.
- Growth of secularism, with a focus on worldly influencing art, politics and culture.
- Patronage from wealthy families and institutions, enabling artists and scholars to flourish.
- Invention of the printing press, making books more accessible and spreading knowledge widely across Europe.

6. What were the different views on European renaissance by different scholars? How was Europe indebted to other regions of the world?

Ans. Different Views on European Renaissance

Renaissance was considered as the rebirth of ideas from Greek and Roman traditions. The views by different scholars on European renaissance were:

- Scholars like Burckhardt argued that there was a new humanist culture emerging in Italian towns and the man from this period i.e. 14th to 17th century was considered modern as he was capable of making his own decisions and developing his skills. He was regarded as modern in contrast to medieval man whose thinking was controlled by the church.
- Scholars like Peter Burke of England opposed the view that there was a sharp difference between the renaissance period and the previous one.
- Some scholars viewed that renaissance as a period of dynamism and artistic creativity and the middle ages as a period of gloom and lack of development, was over-simplification.
- Some historians suggest that in the 9th century in France, there was a similar literary and artistic emergence like that of renaissance period.

Indebtedness of Europe to other Regions of the World

- Cultural changes in Europe were not shaped only by the classical civilisation of Greece and Rome. During this time, technologies and skills in Asia had moved far ahead of Greeks and Romans.
- The Europeans learned not just from the Greeks and Romans, but from India, Arabia, Iran, Central Asia and China. They were indebted to the knowledge they got from all these regions. But this was not acknowledged because historians saw this period from the Euro-centric view.

7. How did the cities of Venice and Genoa differ from other parts of Europe? CBSE Diksha

Ans. Venice and Genoa differ from other parts of Europe in the following ways

(i) **Political Independence**

- Unlike many other parts of Europe, which were dominated by feudal lords and the clergy, Venice and Genoa were independent city-states.
- They were republics, governed by rich merchants and bankers rather than by kings or feudal rulers.

(ii) **Absence of Feudalism**

- Feudal lords and clergy were not politically dominant in Venice and Genoa. In contrast, much of Europe was under feudal control, where land ownership and vassalage played central roles in society.

(iii) **Merchant Control**

- The cities were controlled by wealthy merchants and traders, who also played a significant role in governance. Their power came from trade, rather than land ownership, which was the basis of power in feudal Europe.

(iv) **Focus on Trade**

- Venice and Genoa were major maritime powers and their economies were built on trade and commerce. They had vast trading networks across the Mediterranean and beyond, making them wealthier and more commercially oriented than other European regions.

(v) **Citizen Participation**

- In these cities, the idea of **citizenship** was well-established, with active participation from different sections of society in the governance of the city.
- This sense of citizenship was strong, even under harsh military rulers.

(vi) **Strong Urban Identity**

- The people of Venice and Genoa had a strong sense of urban pride and identity, unlike in rural Europe where society was organised around manors and villages.

Source Based Questions

1. Read the sources given below and answer the following questions.

Cardinal Gasparo Contarini (1483-1542) writes about the democratic government of his city-state in The Commonwealth and Government of Venice (1534).

'...to come to the institution of our Venetian commonwealth, the whole authority of the city... is in that council, into which all the gentlemen of the city being once past the age of 25 years are admitted...

Now first I am to yield you a reckoning how and with what wisdom it was ordained by our ancestors, that the common people should not be admitted into this company of citizens, in whose authority [lies] the whole power of commonwealth... Because many troubles and popular tumults arise in those cities, whose government is swayed by the common people...many were of contrary opinion, deeming that it would do well, if this manner of governing the commonwealth should rather be defined by ability and abundance of riches. Contrariwise the honest citizens, and those that are liberally brought up, oftentimes fall to poverty... Therefore our wise and prudent ancestors... ordered that this definition of the public rule should go rather by the nobility of lineage, than by the estimation of wealth: yet with that temperature [proviso], that men of chief and supreme nobility should not have this rule alone (for that would rather have been the power of a few than a commonwealth) but also every other citizen whosoever not ignobly born: so that all which were noble by birth, or ennobled by virtue, did...obtain this right of government.'

(i) What was the minimum age limit for the council? Why were common people not allowed in the council?

(ii) Who is the author of the source? What is he talking about?

(iii) Which citizens according to the author fall to poverty? Who has right of government?

Ans. (i) In Venetian Commonwealth Council, the minimum age limit to enter the council was 25 years old. The common people were not allowed in the council because many troubles and disorders arise in the cities in which common people hold power.

(ii) Cardinal Gasparo Contarini is the author and he is writing about the democratic government of the city-state i.e. the Commonwealth and Government of Venice.

(iii) The honest citizens and those that are liberally brought up, falls to poverty. Any citizen who is noble by birth or became noble by virtue had right of government.

2. Giovanni Pico Della Mirandola (1463-94), a humanist of Florence, wrote on the importance of debate in On the Dignity of Man (1486).

'For [Plato and Aristotle] it was certain that, for the attainment of the knowledge of truth they were always seeking for themselves, nothing is better than to attend as often as possible the exercise of debate. For just as bodily energy is strengthened by gymnastic exercise, so beyond doubt in this wrestling-place of letters, as it were, energy of mind becomes far stronger and more vigorous'.

(i) Who is the author of the source? What did the author write about?

(ii) What did GP Della Mirandola say about the importance of debate in 'On the Dignity of Man'?

(iii) What is the analogy used by the author to describe the importance of debate?

Ans. (i) Giovanni Pico Della Mirandola is the author of the source.
The author, a humanist from Florence, wrote on the importance of debate in 'On the Dignity of Man'.

(ii) He discussed the importance of debate in 'On the Dignity of Man'. For Plato and Aristotle, it was certain that for the attainment of the knowledge of truth they were always seeking for themselves. According to them, nothing is better than to attend as often as possible the excercise of debate.

(iii) The author says that bodily energy can be strengthened by doing gymnastic exercise in the same way participating in the debate will strengthen mind and it become stronger and more vigourous.

3. "Art" is embedded in nature; he who can extract it, has it...Moreover, you may demonstrate much of your work by geometry. The more closely your work abides by life in its form, so much the better will it appear...No man shall ever be able to make a beautiful figure out of his own imagination unless he has well stored his mind by much copying from life.' - Albrecht Durer (1471-1528)

The sketch by Durer (Praying Hands) gives us a sense of Italian culture in the 16th century, when people were deeply religious, but also had a sense of confidence in man's ability to achieve near perfection and to unravel the mysteries of the world and universe.

(i) What is the name of the artist mentioned in the source? What are the views of this artist on art?

(ii) When can a man make a beautiful figure?

(iii) What does Praying Hands sketch describe?

Ans. (i) The name of the artist is Albrecht Durer.
Durer says, art is a part of nature and one who can extract it can only become a good artist.

(ii) A man can make a beautiful figure not out of his own imagination but when he stored his imagination in his mind by copying much things from the life.

(iii) Praying Hands shows the two side of Italian people. On one side, they are deeply religious and on the other, they also have the confidence to achieve near perfection to solve the mysteries of world and universe.

4. Nicolo Machiavelli wrote about human nature in the 15th chapter of his book, The Prince (1513).

'So, leaving aside imaginary things, and referring only to those which truly exist, I say that whenever men are discussed (and especially princes, who are more exposed to view), they are noted for various qualities which earn them either praise or condemnation.
Some, for example, are held to be generous, and others miserly. **Some, are held to be benefactors, others are called grasping, some cruel, some compassionate, one man faithless, another faithful, one man effeminate and cowardly, another fierce and courageous, one man courteous, another proud, one man lascivious, another pure, one guileless, another crafty, one stubborn,** another flexible, one grave, another frivolous, one religious, another special, and so forth.

Machiavelli believed that 'all men are bad and ever ready to display their vicious nature partly because of the fact that human desires are insatiable'.

The most powerful motive Machiavelli saw as the incentive for every human action is self-interest.

(i) Who is the author of the source? What is his book's name?

(ii) What is the source about?

(iii) What did Machiavelli believe about men? What is the reason behind men displaying their vicious nature?

Ans. (i) Nicolo Machiavelli is the author of this source. He wrote a book named 'The Prince'.

(ii) The author has written about human nature in his book. 'The Prince' in 1513 and the same is being said in the above source.
In his book he described the political problems of that period which Italy had to face.

(iii) Machiavelli believed that all men are bad and always ready to show their bad nature.
Men displayed their vicious nature because human desires are never ending. The most powerful motive for human actions is self-interest.

5. Balthasar Castiglione, author and diplomat, wrote in his book The Courtier (1528):

'I hold that a woman should in no way resemble a man as regards her ways, manners, words, gestures and bearing. Thus, just as it is very fitting that a man should display a certain robust and sturdy manliness, so it is well for a woman to have a certain soft and delicate tenderness, with an air of feminine sweetness in her every movement, which, in her going and staying and whatsoever she does, always makes her appear a woman, without any resemblance to a man. If this precept be added to the rules that these gentlemen have taught the courtier, then I think that she ought to be able to make use of many of them, and adorn herself with the finest accomplishments...For I consider that many virtues of the mind are as necessary to a woman as to a man, as it is to be of good family, to shun affectation: to be naturally graceful; to be well mannered, clever and prudent; to be neither proud, envious or evil-tongued, nor vain...to perform well and gracefully the sports suitable for women'.

(i) **Who was Balthasar Castiglione? According to him, in what way woman should not resemble a man?**

(ii) **What kind of stereotype did author make about women?**

(iii) **What are the virtues that both men and women should have?**

Ans. (i) Balthasar Castiglione was an author and diplomat who wrote a book called 'The Courtier'.

According to him, a woman should not resemble a man in her ways, manners, words, gestures and behaviour.

(ii) The author made stereotype about women that they should be soft and delicate and there should be feminine sweetness in her every movement i.e. in her going and staying and whatsoever she does, should always makes her appear a woman, without any resemblance to a man.

(iii) According to author, many virtues of the mind are necessary to both men and women. They should be well mannered, clever and judicious in spending. They should also not be proud, envious or evil tongued.

6. William Tyndale (1494-1536), an English Lutheran who translated the Bible into English in 1506, defended Protestantism thus:

'In this they be all agreed, to drive you from the knowledge of the scripture, and that ye shall not have the text thereof in the mother-tongue, and to keep the world still in darkness, to the intent they might sit in the consciences of the people, through vain superstition and false doctrine, to satisfy their proud ambition, and insatiable covetousness and to exalt their own honour above king and emperor, yea, and above God himself. Which thing only moved me to translate the New Testament. Because I had perceived by experience, how that it was impossible to establish the lay-people in any truth, except the scripture were plainly laid before their eyes in their mother-tongue that they might see the process, order, and meaning of the text.

(i) **Who was William Tyndale?**

(ii) **What were the objectives of William Tyndale to translate the Bible into English?**

(iii) **Why did William Tyndale want to translate the New Testament?**

Ans. (i) William Tyndale was an English Lutheran who translated the Bible into English in 1506 CE and defended Protestantism.

(ii) The objectives of William Tyndale to translate the Bible into English were

- To make available the copies of the Bible to the layman.
- To expose the malpractices indulge by the Church on the name of the text written in it (Bible).

(iii) William Tyndale want to translate the New Testament because common people will know the real truth and meaning of the scripture only when the scripture is translated in their mother tongue.

Map Based Questions

1. Mark the following locations on the map of Italy.

(i) Padua (ii) Venice (iii) Genoa (iv) Adriatic Sea (v) Sardinia

Ans.

2. Identify the following locations marked on the map of Italy.

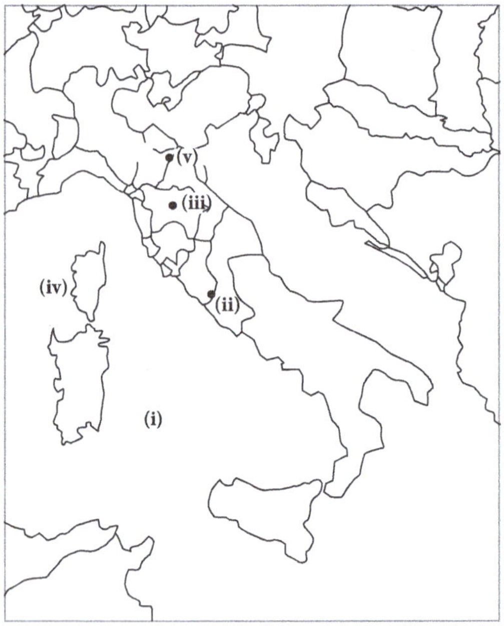

Ans.

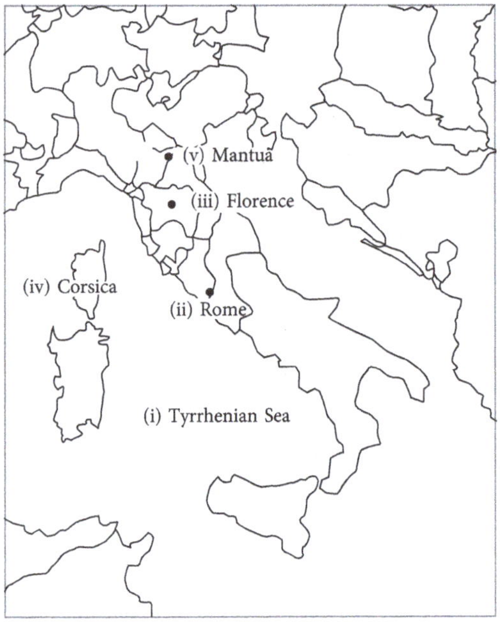

SELF ASSESSMENT TEST

Objective Answer Type Questions

1. What significant development helped revive Italian culture?
   (a) The rise of local kings
   (b) The expansion of trade
   (c) The decline of the Latin Church
   (d) The establishment of new political centers
2. Which universities were centers of legal studies from the 11th century?
   (a) Oxford and Cambridge
   (b) Padua and Bologna
   (c) Paris and Salamanca
   (d) Florence and Venice
3. The earliest universities in Europe had been set up in .... town.
   (a) Italian (b) Spanish (c) British (d) None of these
4. Roman lawyer and essayist Cicero was a contemporary of ....
   (a) Alexander (b) Julius Caesar (c) Aristotle (d) None of these
5. Who were primarily responsible for translating ancient manuscripts into Arabic?
   (a) European scholars
   (b) Arab translators
   (c) Greek philosophers
   (d) Jewish scholars
6. Match the Following.

List I	List II
A. Establishment of Anglican church	1. 1492
B. Introduction of Gregorian calendar	2. 1673
C. Academy of Sciences set up in Paris	3. 1582
D. Columbus reaches the America	4. 1559

Codes

	A	B	D	D		A	B	C	D
(a)	3	1	4	2	(b)	4	3	2	1
(c)	2	1	4	3	(d)	4	2	1	3

Short Answer Type Questions

7. Discuss the new concept of human beings.
8. How the Italian cities were revived?
9. What were the contribution of Arab towards Science and Philosophy?

Long Answer Type Questions

10. Examine how the position of women in the families of merchants was different.
11. Humanists reached out to people in a variety of ways. Justify the statement.
12. Describe about the Copernican Revolution. Was there a European renaissance in the 14th century? Comment.
13. Describe about the changes with Christianity during the period of renaissance.
14. How the aspiration of women was changing during the early modern age?

Allinone

SECTION D
PATHS TO MODERNISATION

TIMELINE IV (C. 1700 CE to 2000 CE)

This timeline give an idea of what was happening in different parts of the world in the last three centuries, and how people in different countries contributed to the making of our modern world. It will tell about the slave trade in Africa and the establishment of the Apartheid regime in South Africa, about social movements in Europe and the formation of nation states, about the expansion of imperial powers and the process of colonisation, and about democratic and anticolonial movements that swept through the world in the last century. It will also refer to some of the inventions and technological developments that are associated with modernity.

6
CHAPTER

From the 18th century, European immigrants settled in various regions, including South America, Central America, North America, South Africa, Australia and New Zealand. This led to the displacement of native[1] populations.
European settlements came to be known as colonies. When they gained independence, they became states or countries.

▼ **YOUR STUDY GOALS**

- 6.1 History of American and Australian Natives
- 6.2 European Imperialism
- 6.3 North America
- 6.4 Australia
- 6.5 Winds of Change

▼ **YOUR PRACTICE GOAL**

- Objective Type Questions (37 Qs ; MCQs, A-R, Matching, Picture Based)
- Subjective Questions (11 SAs, 6 LAs)
- Source Based Questions (5 Qs)
- Map Based Questions (2 Qs)

Displacing Indigenous Peoples

6.1 History of American and Australian Natives

- Until the mid-20th century, American and Australian history textbooks primarily focused on European exploration and colonisation of the Americas and Australia. The indigenous populations were often portrayed as hostile and marginalised.
- Anthropologists in America began studying native American cultures in the 1840s.
- Since the 1960s, native Americans and Australians have been encouraged to write or dictate their own histories. The historical works and fiction written by indigenous people are now widely available.
- Museums in these countries often feature galleries dedicated to native American and Australian art and culture, showcasing their unique way of life. Indigenous communities have also taken the initiative to establish their own museums, such as the National Museum of the **American Indian**[2] in the USA.

1 Native A person born in the place he/she lives in. Till the early 20th century, the term was used by Europeans to describe the inhabitants of countries they had colonised.

2. American Indian American Indian/Amerind/Amerindian Native peoples of North and South America and the Caribbean.

6.2 European Imperialism

- Spain and Portugal did not significantly expand their American empires after the 17th century. On the other hand, European powers, such as France, Holland and England, actively expanded their trading activities and established colonies in America, Africa and Asia.
- Ireland, was not formally a colony, but it was indirectly under English control due to the dominance of English landowners.

Establishment of Colonies

Following are the various motivations and methods of European colonisation

- **Profit-Driven Colonisation** The prospect of profit was a primary cause of European colonisation in the 18th century.
- **Trading Companies as Colonial Powers** Trading companies, such as the East India Company, gained significant political power in South Asia. They defeated local rulers, took control of territories, and adopted existing administrative systems to collect taxes from landowners. They also invested in infrastructure, such as mines, plantations and railways, to facilitate trade.
- **African Colonisation** European involvement in trade in Africa was primarily coastal in the early period. Entry into the interior of Africa occurred in the late 19th century, followed by the infamous "Scramble for Africa," where European powers divided and distributed the continent among themselves.
- **Settler Colonies** In regions like South Africa, Ireland, New Zealand and Australia, European settlers formed the majority of the population. English became the official language in these colonies, except for Canada, where both English and French were official languages.

Names Given by Europeans

Some of the names given by Europeans to countries of New World were

- **America** First used after the publication of the travels of Amerigo Vespucci (1451-1512).
- **Canada** Derived from ***kanata*** which means village in the language of the Huron-Iroquois and was heard by the explorer Jacques Cartier in 1535.
- **Australia** 16th century name for land in the Great Southern Ocean. ***Austral*** in Latin means South.
- **New Zealand** Name given by Tasman of Holland, who was the first to locate these islands in 1642. *Zee* in Dutch means sea.

Quick Test 1

1. Anthropologists began studying which culture in 1840s?
2. Which countries did not expand their empires after the 17th century?
3. Name the countries which were colonised by Dutch and British.
4. Who was the first to discover New Zealand in 1642?

6.3 North America

- The North American continent stretches from the Arctic Circle to the Tropic of Cancer, and from the Pacific Ocean to the Atlantic Ocean.
- It features diverse landscapes, including the deserts of Arizona and Nevada to the West of the Rocky Mountains. The Sierra Nevada mountains, the Great Plains, the Great Lakes, the valleys of the Mississippi and Ohio rivers and the Appalachian mountains are in the East. Mexico is located to the South, while Canada is covered by approximately 40% of forests.
- North America is rich in natural resources, including oil, gas and minerals, which have supported the development of numerous industries in both the United States and Canada.
- Agriculture is also a significant industry, with wheat, corn and fruit being widely grown. Fishing is a major industry in Canada.

- Over the past 200 years, immigrants from Europe, Africa and China have contributed to the development of mining, industry and large-scale agriculture in North America.
- **Indigenous peoples**[3] have inhabited North America for thousands of years before European contact.

The Native Peoples of North America

- The first inhabitants of North America arrived from Asia over 30,000 years ago *via* a land-bridge across the Bering Straits. During the last Ice Age (10,000 years ago), they migrated further South.
- Natives lived in villages along river valleys, cultivated vegetables and maize, and relied on fish and meat.
- They hunted bison and wild buffalo, utilised horses obtained from Spanish settlers for easier travel.
- They practised sustainable hunting, killing only what they needed for food.
- Natives did not engage in extensive agriculture, leading to no surplus production, kingdoms or empires.
- There were some territorial disputes, but land ownership wasn't a big problem.

▲ *Wampum Belts, made of Coloured Shells Sewn together*

- They were satisfied with the food and shelter the land provided without feeling the need to own it.
- Making alliances and exchanging gifts was an important cultural tradition of natives.
- Various unwritten languages were spoken, and historical knowledge was passed orally through generations.
- Natives were skilled craftsmen and good at understanding their region's climates and landscapes.

Entry of European Traders in North America

- The European traders reached the North coast of North America in the 17th century after a two-month voyage.
- These traders came to North America with the intention of trading in fish and furs, which was facilitated by the expertise of the native people in hunting.
- In the Southern areas along the Mississippi river, the French saw that the natives gathered regularly to trade crafts and food that were unique to their tribes or regions.
- The Europeans offered blankets, iron vessels, guns (which replaced bows and arrows for hunting animals), and alcohol in exchange for local products.
- The natives became addicted to alcohol, which gave the Europeans an advantage in dictating the terms of trade. Even the Europeans themselves became addicted to tobacco, which originated from the native Americans.

Terms used for the Native People

- The term ***aborigine*** is specifically used to refer to the indigenous people of Australia. It comes from the Latin words 'ab' (from) and 'origine' (origin).
- The terms **American Indian**, **Amerind** and **Amerindian** are used to describe the indigenous peoples of North and South America, including the Caribbean.
- In Canada, the term **First Nations peoples** is used to refer to the organised native groups recognised by the Canadian government. The term **bands** was used in the Indian Act of 1876, but since the 1980s, 'nations' has been the preferred term.
- The term **indigenous people** is a general term that refers to people who are native to a particular place.
- **Native American** is the most commonly used term for the indigenous peoples of the Americas.
- The term **Red Indian** is derived from the brown-complexion of these people, as Columbus mistakenly believed he had landed in India.

▲ *A woman of the Winnebago tribe of Wisconsin*

3 **Indigenous People** People belonging naturally to a place.

Mutual Perceptions between European Traders and Natives

- The Western Europeans of the 18th century defined civilised people based on their literacy, adherence to an organised religion, and urban lifestyle. In contrast, the native Americans were seen as uncivilised by the Europeans.
- The French philosopher Jean-Jacques Rousseau admired the native Americans, viewing them as untouched by the corruptions of civilisation and referring to them as 'noble savages.'
- William Wordsworth described native Americans as people living close to nature with limited imaginative and emotional capacities.

Exchange of Commodities between Natives and Europeans

- The native Americans believed that the goods they exchanged with Europeans were gifts given in friendship. However, for the Europeans, these goods were *commodities* that could be sold for profit in Europe, serving as a means to become wealthy.
- The native Americans struggled to understand the concept of supply and demand in the European market. They were often confused when European traders offered them a large quantity of goods in exchange for their own, sometimes even giving them excessive amounts.
- The greed of the Europeans, particularly their killing of hundreds of beavers for their fur, caused great distress among the native Americans. Native Americans feared that the animals would seek revenge for this destruction.

Europeans Settling in America

- The first European traders arrived in America in the 17th century. Later, groups of Europeans who were being tortured for their religious beliefs left Europe to seek a new life in America.
- Initially, there was plenty of empty land, but as time passed, Europeans began to move inland towards native villages. They used their iron tools to clear forests and establish farms.

Perception of Natives and Europeans on Forests

- Natives and Europeans had different perspectives on forests.
- Natives had a profound understanding of the forest, identifying paths invisible to the Europeans.

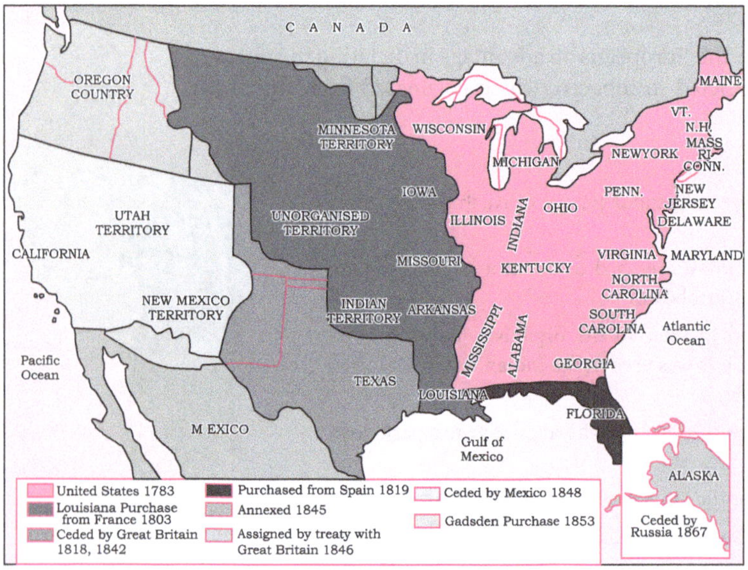

▲ *The Expansion of the USA*

- Europeans aimed to clear forests for agriculture.
- **Thomas Jefferson** wanted a nation inhabited by Europeans who cultivated small farms. He considered native farming methods uncivilised because they were focused on personal needs instead of profit.

Emergence of Canada and the USA

- In the late 18th century, Canada and the United States emerged as independent nations, occupying a relatively small portion of the land compared to their present territories. Over the next century, they significantly expanded their control over more territory.
- The United States acquired vast territories by purchasing land in the South (the Louisiana Purchase) from France and the Alaska from Russia. It expanded its Western border through wars with Mexico, forcing native Americans to relocate.

Change in Landscape of America

- The 19th century witnessed significant changes in the American landscape, largely driven by European settlers.
- European migrants from Britain and France sought to own property, as they were unable to inherit their father's land due to their young age.
- Later, many immigrants from Germany, Sweden and Italy, who had lost their land to large landowners in their home countries, came to America with the dream of owning their own farms.
- People from Poland were happy to work in the prairie grasslands, which reminded them of their homeland and were excited to buy large properties at low prices.
- These settlers actively developed agriculture by clearing land and introducing crops like rice and cotton, which were not suitable for cultivation in Europe. They also hunted wild animals, such as wolves and mountain lions, to protect their farms.
- The invention of **barbed wire**[4] in 1873 provided further security for their landholdings.

Slave Trade

- The hot climate of the Southern region made outdoor work difficult for Europeans.
- In South America, enslaved native Americans faced harsh conditions and high mortality rates while working on plantations. As a result, plantation owners in the United States look for slaves in Africa.
- Despite protests from anti-slavery groups, the slave trade continued, and many Africans were brought to the United States as slaves.
- Even after the slave trade was banned, Africans and their children who were already in the United States continued to live in slavery.

Abolition of Slavery

- The economies of the Northern states were not dependent on plantations or slavery. They opposed slavery and criticised the inhumane practice.
- This difference in economic systems and moral values contributed to the American Civil War (1861-1865), between the pro-slavery Southern states and the abolitionist Northern states.
- Although slavery was abolished after the Civil War, racial segregation still existed
- It wasn't until the 20th century that African Americans achieved civil liberties, ending segregation in schools and public transportation.

Problem of Canada

- The Canadian government faced a significant challenge following the British victory over France in 1763.
- The French settlers in Canada demanded autonomous political status. This issue was eventually resolved in 1867 by organising Canada as a confederation of autonomous states.

The Native Peoples Lose their Land

- The expansion of European settlements in the United States forced Native Americans to relocate, after signing land sale treaties. Despite receiving low compensation, many native American tribes were displaced.
- European settlers often engaged in dishonest practices by taking more land than agreed upon or paying less than promised.
- The actions of European settlers were not considered wrong by higher officials. For example, in Georgia, the **Cherokee tribe** was denied citizenship rights despite their efforts to learn English and adopt American customs.

---

4 **Barbed wire** It is a type of steel fencing wire constructed with sharp edges or points arranged at intervals along the strands.

- In 1832, Chief Justice John Marshall announced that the Cherokee tribe was a separate community with its own land, in which the laws of Georgia had no force. However, President Andrew Jackson, disregarded this ruling. He ordered the US Army to forcibly remove almost 15000 Cherokee people, from their land and relocate them to the Great American Desert. It is called as **Trail of Tears**.
- Those who took land from the tribes justified it by claiming that the natives did not deserve to occupy land they were not fully using. They also accused them of being lazy for not using their craft skills to produce goods for the market.
- Settlers criticised native Americans for not adopting European customs, such as learning English and dressing in European attire.

Exploitation of Natives by Europeans

- **Native Americans**[5] were repeatedly pushed westward, given new lands, and often displaced again if valuable resources like lead, gold or oil were found on their land.
- Different tribes had to share land that originally belonged to just one tribe. This caused fights between tribes, and they were confined to small areas known as 'reservations' often on land to which they had no previous connection.
- The forced relocations and marginalisation led to a series of rebellions from 1865 to 1890, which were ultimately suppressed by the US Army.
- In Canada, **Metis**[6] people also engaged in armed revolts between 1869 and 1885, but eventually gave up their resistance.

The Gold Rush and Growth of Industries

▲ *Moving to California as part of the Gold Rush*

- The discovery of gold in California in the 1840s encouraged many Europeans to come to the area in hopes of getting rich quickly. This event is known as the Gold Rush.
- This inflow of people contributed to the demand for labour, resulting in the recruitment of thousands of Chinese workers to construct railway lines across the continent.
- The railway lines were completed in the United States by 1870 and in Canada by 1885.
- An example of the economic opportunities created by the Gold Rush is Andrew Carnegie, a poor immigrant from Scotland who became one of the first millionaire industrialists in the United States.

Industrialisation in the USA and Canada

Industrialisation in USA and Canada had huge impacts in both the countries as follows

- In England, the Industrial Revolution was driven by the displacement of small peasants by large landowners, forcing them to seek employment in factories.
- In North America, industrialisation was motivated by different factors, such as the need for railway equipment to connect distant places and the desire for machinery to facilitate large-scale farming.
- Both the United States and Canada experienced significant industrial growth, with numerous industrial towns and factories developed across the continent.
- The United States, which had an underdeveloped economy in 1860, became a leading industrial power by 1890.

---

5 Native American The indigenous people of Americas.

6 Metis People of native European desert/origin.

- Large-scale agriculture also expanded in North America, as vast areas of land were cleared and divided into farms. The bison population wiped out by the late 19th century, ending the traditional hunting practices of native Americans.
- The United States completed its continental expansion by 1892, with the area between the Pacific and Atlantic Oceans divided into states. This westward expansion attracted European settlers for decades.
- Within a few years, the United States also established its own colonies in Hawaii and the Philippines, emerging as an imperial power.

Constitutional Rights

- The United States was shaped by the spirit of democracy that inspired settlers to fight for independence from European kings and nobles in the 1770s.
- The US Constitution covered the individual's right to property, protecting it from government interference. However, these democratic rights and property rights were initially limited to white men.
- In 2000, Canadian native **Daniel Paul** noted that Thomas Paine, a supporter of democracy during the American Revolution, viewed native and the French Americans as examples of how society could be organised.

Changes in the Lives of Natives

- Natives had serious health and education problems until the 1920s, as shown by Lewis Meriam's survey, 'The Problem of Indian Administration' in 1928.
- The **Indian Reorganisation Act of 1934** was enacted which gave natives the right to buy land.
- In the 1950s and 1960s, natives fought against government efforts to make them fit into European culture.
- The **Declaration of Indian Rights in 1954** allowed them to keep their reservations and traditions.
- In Canada, the government initially refused to recognise aboriginal rights in 1969.
- The natives protested against this decision which resulted in the Constitution Act in 1982 that acknowledged those rights.
- Even though their numbers decreased, natives were able to claim their rights and practise their culture, including their rights to sacred sites.

Quick Test 2

1. What were natives and settlers addicted to?
2. Who were the Cherokees?
3. Who was Andrew Carnegie?
4. Where did the USA set up its colonies?
5. In which year was 'The Declaration of Indian Rights' prepared?

6.4 Australia

- Australia has a long history of human habitation, dating back to approximately 40,000 years.
- The aboriginal people are a term for different indigenous groups who came to Australia from New Guinea, when it was linked to the continent by a land bridge.
- According to tribal traditions, their ancestors were always present in Australia, rather than migrating there.
- The past centuries were referred to as the "Dreamtime," a concept that was difficult for Europeans to understand as there was no difference in past and present.

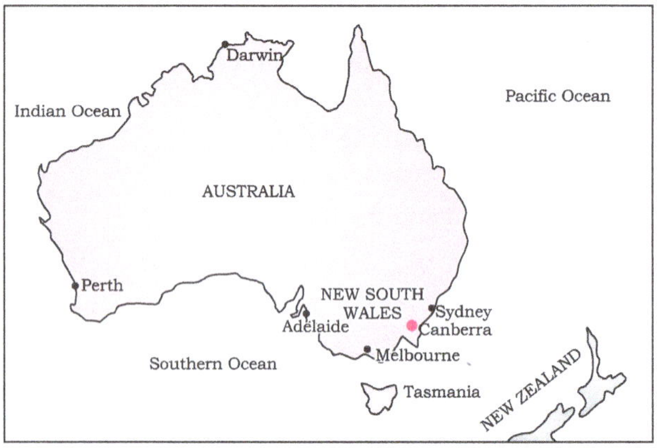

▲ *Australia*

Natives of Australia

- In the late 18th century, there were approximately 350 to 750 distinct native communities in Australia, each with its own unique language. Today, around 200 of these languages continue to be spoken.
- The **Torres Strait Islanders,** another significant group of indigenous people, inhabit the Torres Strait region in the North. They are not referred to as 'aborigine' because they are believed to have migrated from elsewhere and are considered a distinct racial group.
- In 2005, the Torres Strait Islander population made up approximately 2.4% of Australia's total population.

Initial Encounters of Settlers

- Australia was a sparsely populated continent, with most towns located along the coast due to the arid desert in the central region. The British first arrived in Australia in 1770.
- The initial interactions between European settlers and aboriginal people were described as friendly in Captain Cook's reports. However, after Captain Cook was killed by a native Hawaiian, relations between Europeans and aboriginal people got worse significantly.

Exploitation of Natives

- The native Australians faced significant exploitation and hardship during the 19th and 20th centuries, leading to a decline in their population by nearly 90%. This decline was attributed to **diseases introduced by Europeans,** loss of land and resources, and conflicts with settlers.
- The British first tried sending convicts to Brazil but stopped because of protests by native Americans. Instead, they deported convicts to the American colonies and later to Australia.
- Once they arrived, the convicts earned their freedom after serving their jail term and settled on the land, which pushed native Australians out. This caused conflicts and further marginalised the indigenous people.

Economic Development

- Australia's economic growth was similar to that of the United States during European settlement.
- Large-scale farms and mining stations were established over time, requiring significant labour inputs.
- Eventually, Australia also developed vineyards and wheat farming. These economic activities formed the foundation of the country's prosperity.
- In 1911, after the unification of the Australian states, the decision was made to build a new capital city. One suggested name was 'Woolwheat gold'. Ultimately, it was named Canberra, which comes from the native word Kamberra meaning 'meeting place'.

Discrimination Against Non-Whites

- Some Native Australians were employed on farms but the working conditions were often harsh and was similar to slavery.
- Chinese immigrants provided cheap labour in both Australia and the United States, but governments in these countries were hesitant to rely heavily on non-white labour and implemented policies to restrict Chinese immigration.

- Until 1974, there was concern in Australia about a potential inflow of dark-skinned people from South Asia or South-East Asia. To address this concern, the government implemented policies to limit non-white immigration.

6.5 Winds of Change

- In 1968, anthropologist **W.E.H. Stanner** delivered a lecture titled **The Great Australian Silence**, highlighting the lack of information and understanding about aboriginal history among Australians. This lecture inspired a growing interest in aboriginal culture and history.
- Since the 1970s, people have appreciated aboriginal communities for their unique cultures and perspectives on nature and climate, rather than seeing them just as subjects for study.
- Henry Reynolds' book, "***Why Weren't We Told?***," criticised the practice of writing Australian history as if it began with captain Cook's discovery. This led to several significant changes
  - **Establishment of University Departments** Universities began to establish departments dedicated to the study of Aboriginal cultures.
  - **Inclusion of Aboriginal Art** Art galleries expanded their collections to include aboriginal art.
  - **Dioramas and Interactive Exhibitions** Museums incorporated dioramas and other interactive exhibitions to showcase aboriginal culture.
  - **Indigenous Storytelling** Aboriginal people began writing their own life histories and sharing their stories.
- In **1974**, Australia officially adopted **multiculturalism as a policy**, recognising and respecting the diverse cultures of both indigenous Australians and immigrants from Europe and Asia.
- The concept of **human rights** gained prominence in the **1970s**, with discussions at the United Nations and other international organisations. This awareness led Australians to realise that their country lacked formal treaties with native Australians regarding land ownership, unlike the United States, Canada and New Zealand.
- The Australian government had always considered the land as ***terra nullius***, meaning it belonged to no one.
- Many mixed-race children were taken away from their native families, which was a sad part of history.
- People spoke out about these problems, leading to investigations and important decisions. The Australian government recognised that native Australians have a strong connection to their land and that their culture should be respected.
- They also apologised publicly for taking mixed-race children away from their families, admitting that it was wrong.

Quick Test 3

1. What were Torres Strait Islanders?
2. What name was given to the new capital of Australia in 1911?
3. What did Henry Reynolds condemn?
4. In which year was multiculturalism accepted in Australia?.
5. From which year the term 'Human Rights' was given a formal recognition in the meetings of the United Nations?

TIMELINE

Year	Event
Australia	
1606	Dutch travellers sight Australia
1642	Tasman land on the island later named Tasmania
1770	James Cook reached Botany Bay, named New South Wales
1788	British Penal Colony formed, Sydney founded
1850	Self-government granted to Australian colonies
1851	Chinese coolie immigration. Stopped by law in 1855
1851-1961	Gold rushes
1901	Formation of Federation of Australia, with six states
1911	Canberra established as capital
1948-75	Two million Europeans migrate to Australia
1974	'White Australia' policy ends, Asian immigrants allowed entry
1992	The Australian High Court (in the Mabo case) declares that *terra nullius* was legally invalid, and recognises native claims to land from before 1770.
1995	National Enquiry into the Separation of Aboriginal and Torres Strait Islander Children from their Families
1999	(26 May) 'A National Sorry Day' as apology for the children 'lost' from the 1820s to the 1970s
Quebec	
1497	John Cabot reached Newfoundland
1534	Jacques Cartier travels down the St Lawrence river and meets native peoples
1608	French found the colony of Quebec
Canada	
1701	French treaty with natives of Quebec
1763	Quebec conquered by the British
1774	Quebec Act
1791	Canada Constitutional Act
1837	French-Canadian rebellion
1840	Canadian Union of Upper and Lower Canada
1859	Canada Gold Rush
1867	Confederation of Canada
1869-85	Red River Rebellion by the Metis in Canada
1876	Canada Indians Act America
1885	Transcontinental railway linked East and West coasts
American Colonies	
1507	Amerigo de Vespucci's *Travels* published
1607	British found the colony of Virginia
1620	British found Plymouth (in Massachusetts)
USA	
1781	Britain recognised USA as an independent country
1783	British gave Mid-West to the USA
1803	Louisiana purchased from France
1825-58	Natives in USA moved to reserves
1832	Justice Marshall's judgement
1849	American Gold Rush
1861-65	American Civil War
1865-90	American Indian Wars
1870	Transcontinental railway
1890	Bison almost exterminated in America
1892	End of American frontier

Mind Map

DISPLACING INDIGENOUS PEOPLES

1 European Imperialism

- After 17th century, new countries (France, Holland & England) established their colonies in African, Asian and American continent.
- East India Company defeated local kings and annexed territories in South East Asia.
- English was the only official language, except in Canada where French was also spoken.

2 North America

The Native Peoples of North America

- Continent of North America extends from the Pacific Ocean to the Atlantic Ocean.
- The earliest inhabitants of North America came from Asia over 30,000 years ago.
- Native Americans lived in villages along rivers valleys.

The Gold Rush and the Growth of Industries

- In the 1840, traces of gold were found in the USA.
- Gold Rush led to development of infrastructure like railway lines in America.
- Rapid transportation system between distant places helped in growth of industrial Revolution in America.
- By 1890, USA was the leading industrial power in the world.

Entry of European Traders in North America

- Mississippi river was a trading point for exchange of handicrafts among tribes.
- Europeans traded for tribal products with tribes and supplied iron vessels, blankets, etc to Americans.

Mutual Perception between European Traders and Natives

- Europeans considered Americans as uncivilised.
- Poets like Wordsworth described them as living among wild.
- In 17th century, there was nationwide prosecution of Protestants and Catholics in Europe, so they migrated to America.
- New countries like Canada and America came into existence at the end of 18th century.
- Slavery was abolished after a Civil War in 1865.
- Canada was organised as Confederation of Autonomous state in 1867.

The Native Peoples Lose their Land

- Native were forced to sell their land in low prices as more and more European people migrated to America.
- Natives were displaced if mineral found on their land.

Constitution Rights

- Democratic rights like right to vote and property were limited only to white men.

3 Australia

- Aboriginals came from 'New Guinea' by land routes to Australia.
- Torres Strait islanders were living in the North part of Australia.
- Most of the early European settlers in Australia were convicts in England.
- Woolwheatgold name was suggested for the capital in 1911 but Canberra become the capital in 1913.

4 Changes in the Lives of Natives

- Indian Reorganisation Act of 1934, gave natives in reservation, the right to buy land and take loans.
- In 1982, a constitutional act accepted the aboriginal and treaty rights of natives.

The Winds of Change

- Scholars like W.E.H. Stanner raise their voice for 'Aboriginal rights' in Australia.
- From 1970 onwards, there was an eagerness to understand natives and their unique culture.
- From 1974, multiculturalism became the official policy in Australia, which gave equal rights to native and immigrant cultures.

NCERT Folder

Intext Questions

1. Discuss the different images that Europeans and native Americans had of each other and the different ways in which they saw nature.

Ans. The different perceptions that Europeans and native Americans had of each other were

- Europeans considered themselves to be civilised in terms of literacy, an organised religion and urbanism. For them, natives were uncivilised.
- Goods exchanged with the Europeans were considered as gifts by natives, but Europeans thought that these were commodities which can be used to become rich.
- Europeans saw natives as lazy and that natives do not use their skills to maximise production for the sake of market while natives saw Europeans as greedy.
- Natives respected the nature and saw it as a part of their life, but Europeans saw nature as means to increase their wealth. They exploited the nature by indiscriminate cutting of trees and killing of animals. Natives felt very uneasy about these things.

2. Comment on these two sets of population data.

	USA : 1820	*Spanish America : 1800*
Natives	0.6 million	7.5 million
Whites	9.0 million	3.3 million
Mixed Europeans	0.1 million	5.3 million
Blacks	1.9 million	0.8 million
Total	11.6 million	16.9 million

Ans. The above data represents the population composition in USA in 1820 and Spanish America in 1800. The population of USA in 1820 was inclined in the favour of whites. Natives and mixed Europeans were very less in number as compared to Whites. Blacks were also more in number than natives. It shows that there was large scale destruction of native people in USA in 1820.

Whereas, the population in Spanish America in 1800 had a majority of population of natives, followed by mixed Europeans, Whites and a minority population of Blacks. It was in equal proportions and except blacks, all other populations were in significant numbers.

3. Comment on the following statement by the American historian Howard Spodek: "For the indigenous [people] the effects of the American Revolution were exactly opposite to those of the settlers – expansion became contraction, democracy became tyranny, prosperity became poverty, and liberty became confinement."

Ans. The above statement by American historian Howard Spodek comments on the effects of American Revolution on both indigenous people and settlers. In the American Revolution, the 13 colonies of the America fought for independence from British and established democracy. They fought for the democratic rights and right to tax themselves but not by British. While settlers in these colonies wanted to expand themselves and enjoy liberty by getting independence after American Revolution, it became a curse to the natives or indigenous people. Settlers expansion meant natives were pushed to corner.

Settlers enjoyed democratic rights, but natives were not given right to vote and they did not have any right to property. Settlers prospered by taking land from natives which pushed them into poverty. While settlers enjoyed the liberty and freedom, natives were locked off in small areas called 'reservations' in the Western side and made to live in poor conditions without any freedom.

4. In 1911, it was announced that New Delhi and Canberra would be built as the capital cities of British India and of the Commonwealth of Australia. Compare and contrast the political situations of the native people in these countries at that time.

Ans. The political situation in India and Australia during 1911 was

India India was not yet given any political freedom in 1911. There was no responsible government present in India. British were trying to divide the Indians on the basis of religions through different legislations. People were not enjoying freedom, there were still many restrictions on press, civil services, government jobs, etc. In 1911, Indians were neither politically empowered nor enlightened to the levels of Australians.

Australia Self-government was granted to Australian colonies in 1850 itself. Australia was made dominion of the British empire in 1901. Responsible government was established before 1901 itself. People were already enjoying the freedom during 1911 in Australia. Australians were politically empowered by 1911 and have more political enlightenment.

Answer in Brief

1. Comment on any points of difference between the native peoples of South and North America.

Ans. The differences between the native peoples of South and North America were

South America	*North America*
They were highly organised e.g. Aztecs, Mayas and Incas.	They lived in bands, in villages along river valleys.
They cultivated corn, beans, squash, pumpkins, potatoes and other crops.	They ate fish and meat and cultivated vegetables and maize.
They generally got the food mainly from agriculture.	They often went on long journeys in search of meat, mainly that of bison.
They did extensive agriculture and produced surplus corn.	They did not attempt extensive agriculture.
They maintained well established kingdoms and empire.	They did not develop kingdoms and empires.
They built big cities and forts.	They did not build massive fort like buildings.

2. Other than the use of English, what other features of English economic and social life do you notice in 19th century USA?

Ans. In 19th century USA, besides the use of English, the features of English economic and social life were

- People were converted to Christianity. There was a wide spread of Christianity in USA and establishment of new Churches.
- Forests lands were cleared and large scale cultivation of crops was done. Agriculture was commercialised.
- Large scale hunting of bisons was done, so that they were almost destroyed.
- Slave trade happened. Many Africans were bought and enslaved in USA.
- Extensive mining was done. During Gold Rush, many Europeans came to America for gold and made wealth. Industrial towns grew and factories multiplied and by 1890, USA became major industrial power.

3. What did the 'frontier' mean to the Americans?

Ans. 'Frontier' meant the boundaries to the Americans. It was expanding due to the conquer policy of British.

From this, we can understand that for Americans frontier was not a fixed one, but it was constantly moving from time to time according to the convenience of Americans. They did not care about natives when shifting their frontiers.

4. Why was the history of the Australian native peoples left out of history books?

Ans. The history of the Australian native peoples left out of history books due to the following reasons

- Europeans always wrote about the history of Australia from European perspective. They wrote that Europeans discovered Australia and hardly mentioned about native people.
- If they wrote about native people, they talked about the way natives were hostile to Europeans.
- Europeans did not want future generations to know about the native peoples and if they do not write about the native peoples, then no one will question about the exploitation done by Europeans.

Answer in a Short Essay

5. How satisfactory is a museum gallery display in explaining the culture of a people? Give examples from your own experience of a museum.

Ans. A museum is an institution that cares for the collection of artefacts and other objects of cultural and historic importance. Museums are store houses of knowledge. So, when a museum gallery is displayed, it gives us an idea about the culture of people during past times.

My own experience of a museum is given in the following examples

- When I went to a museum in Rajasthan, I could see the kind of sarees women used to wear during those times. I also saw how local tribals lifestyle was so distinct from others. I saw different war instruments and weapons used by the soldiers and kings for battle.
- When I went to a museum in Delhi, I saw Indian crafts, wooden carvings, metal ware and paintings. Mud huts with painted walls and thatched roofs, courtyards, terracotta horses recreating village shrines, craftsmen at work are some of the elements that add to the rural ambience of the place.
- When I went to museum in Hyderabad, I saw the stone sculptures, bronze images, painted textiles (*Kalamkari*), wood carvings, jade carvings, metal ware, manuscripts, arms and armour, etc.

6. Imagine an encounter in California in about 1880 between four people: a former African slave, a Chinese labourer, a German who had come out in the Gold Rush and a native of the Hopi tribe and narrate their conversation.

Ans. The conversation between them would be

African Slave He would be talking about the inhuman practices of Europeans against the African slaves. He would talk about the civil liberties and human rights of African slaves.

Chinese Labourer Chinese labourer who must have been recruited to work in the Gold Rush, not knowing much local language would be in constant fear. He must have spoken very little because he was new to the America.

German Mostly he must be the big investor, so he would be showing arrogance and superiority over other people. He would be talking to others without any respect and must be boasting about the European advancement in economy.

Native of the Hopi Tribe He must be angry at others because all others are migrants who came to America and were reason for their distress. He must be talking in pair to all others and describe how everyone exploited them and made them strangers in their own homeland.

Exam Pattern Questions

Objective Type Questions

Multiple Choice Questions (MCQs)

1. In 1642 .... gave the name 'New Zealand' to some island which he first saw.

(a) Amerigo Vespucci (b) Tasman of Holland
(c) William Macleish (d) None of these

2. Native tribes in North America, though that time moved in .... **CBSE Diksha**

(a) Forward Way (b) Backward Way
(c) Circle (d) Day and Night

3. The oldest artefact found in America, an arrow-point is .... years old.

(a) 10,000 (b) 11,000
(c) 15,000 (d) 14,000

4. Many tribes that were forced to share the land originally occupied by one tribe, eventually got engaged into quarrels and were locked off in **CBSE Diksha**

(a) reservations (b) camps
(c) green house (d) farm sheds

5. The early settlers in South America were **CBSE Diksha**

(a) Portugal (b) English
(c) Spanish (d) French

6. Which famous philosopher called the Native people untouched by civilisation therefore uncivilised? **CBSE Diksha**

(a) Jean-Jacques Rousseau (b) Rudyard Kipling
(c) Nicolas de Condorcet (d) Voltaire

7. In this American President's 'dream', was a country populated by Europeans with small farms and the natives, who grew crops for **CBSE Diksha**

(a) John Adams (b) James Madison
(c) Thomas Jefferson (d) Andrew Jackson

8. In which colony did the French settlers demand an autonomous political status? **CBSE Diksha**

(a) Wisconsin (b) Canada
(c) Kentucky (d) Maine

9. Which president did not honour the decision of 1832 by Justice John Marshall which announced that the Cherokees were a distinct community? **CBSE Diksha**

(a) Andrew Jackson (b) Andrew Johnson
(c) James K. Polk (d) Theodore Roosevelt

10. Displacement of the 15000 Cherokees from Georgia to the Great American Deseret is called **CBSE Diksha**

(a) The Wounded Knee Massacre
(b) The Panic of 1837 Indian Removal
(c) Trail of Tears
(d) Night of Tears

11. Gold Rush was a phenomenon, experienced by the state of .... **CBSE Diksha**

(a) Nevada (b) California
(c) Arizona (d) Arkansas

12. The USA's railway was completed by ....

(a) 1850 (b) 1865 (c) 1870 (d) 1875

13. In which year a survey 'The Problems of Indian Administration' was published?

(a) 1828 (b) 1912
(c) 1928 (d) 1938

14. This act gave natives in reservations the right to buy land and take loans? **CBSE Diksha**

(a) Indian Reorganisation Act of 1934
(b) Virginia Declaration of Rights 1776
(c) Indian Cleaning Campaign 1837
(d) Indigenous protection Act

15. A number of native peoples, prepared this document through which they accepted the citizenship of the USA on condition that **CBSE Diksha**

(a) Virginia Declaration of Rights 1776
(b) Universal Declaration of Human Rights 1948
(c) Declaration of Rights 1954
(d) The Thirteenth Amendment 1865

16. This British colony was used as the Penal Colony/Exile Colony .... **CBSE Diksha**

(a) Fiji (b) New Zealand
(c) Hawaii (d) Australia

17. In which year Canberra was established as a capital of Australia?

(a) 1911 (b) 1917
(c) 1927 (d) 1931

18. Canberra word comes from the native word 'kamberra' which means ....

(a) working place (b) tourist spot
(c) meeting place (d) None of these

19. 1968 people were electrified by a lecture called .... delivered by anthropologist W.E.H. Stanner on the silence of historians about the aborigines. **CBSE Diksha**

(a) Great Australian Silence
(b) Black Elk Speaks Genocide of Native People
(c) Dreams That Kill
(d) Midnight dream

20. Who wrote the book 'Why Weren't We Told'?

(a) Tasman (b) WEH Stanner
(c) Henry Reynolds (d) None of these

21. Henry Reynolds in his powerful book .... , condemned the practice of writing Australian. **CBSE Diksha**

(a) Why Weren't We Told?
(b) Midnight Children
(c) Favoured Children
(d) Forgotten Children

22. In .... Britain recognises USA as an independent country.

(a) 1780 (b) 1785 (c) 1790 (d) 1781

23. Consider the following statements and choose the correct option.

(i) Spain and Portugal did not expand their American empires after 17th century.
(ii) Jean-Jacques Rousseau was a German philosopher.
(iii) First travellers from Europe came to settle in Mexico.

Codes

(a) Only (i) (b) Only (ii)
(c) Both (i) and (ii) (d) All of these

24. Consider the following statements and choose the correct option.

(i) At the end of 19th century, Canada and USA came into existence.
(ii) The economy in the Northern states of USA neither depend on plantations nor slavery.
(iii) The traces of gold were found in California in the 1890s.

Codes

(a) Only (i) (b) Only (ii)
(c) Both (i) and (ii) (d) All of these

25. Arrange in sequence.

(i) Gold Rushes
(ii) Self-government granted to Australian colonies
(iii) Chinese coolie immigration stopped by law

Codes

(a) (ii), (iii), (i) (b) (i), (ii), (iii)
(c) (ii), (i), (iii) (d) (iii), (ii), (i)

26. Identify the name of the person from the information given below.

(i) He was third President of the USA.
(ii) He was a contemporary of Wordsworth.
(iii) His dream was a country populated by Europeans with small farms.
(iv) In his view, the natives were uncivilised.

(a) John Adams (b) Thomas Jefferson
(c) James Madison (d) Andrew Jackson

27. Identify the name of the writer from the information given below.

(i) She is an Australian writer.
(ii) She was a champion of the rights of the Australian aborigines.
(iii) She wrote many moving poems about the loss created by keeping the white people and the natives apart.

(a) Helen Garner (b) Collen McCullough
(c) Judith Wright (d) Elizabeth Jolley

28. Trail of Tears: Cherokee :: Gold Rush: ....

(a) California (b) Australia
(c) Nevada (d) Hawaii

29. **Andrew Carnegie: Industrialist :: Thomas Jefferson: ....**

(a) Scientist (b) Explorer
(c) President (d) Philosopher

30. **Tasman: New Zealand :: Captain Cook: ....**

(a) Australia (b) Canada
(c) Hawaii (d) Alaska

31. **Torres Strait Islanders: Australia :: Native Americans: ....**

(a) Europe (b) America
(c) Asia (d) Africa

Assertion-Reason

32. **Assertion** (A) Thomas Jefferson dreamt of a country populated by the Europeans with small Farms.
Reason (R) Jefferson thought that the native people were uncivilised thus their extermination was justified.

Codes

(a) Both A and R are true and R is the correct explanation of A
(b) Both A and R are true, but R is not the correct explanation of A
(c) A is true, but R is false
(d) A is false, but R is true

33. **Assertion** (A) In 1867, Canada was organised as a confederation of autonomous states.
Reason (R) Canada was won by the British after a War with France.

Codes

(a) Both A and R are true and R is the correct explanation of A
(b) Both A and R are true, but R is not the correct explanation of A
(c) A is true, but R is false
(d) A is false, but R is true

Match the Following

34.

List I	List II
A. Lewis Meriam	1. Champion of Democracy
B. Thomas Paine	2. The Problem of Indian Administration
C. WEH Stanner	3. Discovered New South Wales
D. Captain Cook	4. The Great Australian Silence

Codes

	A	B	C	D		A	B	C	D
(a)	3	1	2	4	(b)	2	3	1	4
(c)	2	1	4	3	(d)	4	2	1	3

35.

List I	List II
A. Louisiana	1. Desert region
B. Fiji	2. Purchase from France
C. Nevada	3. Gained independence from Britain
D. Germany	4. Emerged as unified nation state

Codes

	A	B	C	D		A	B	C	D
(a)	2	3	1	4	(b)	4	2	1	3
(c)	3	4	2	1	(d)	2	1	4	3

Picture Based Questions

36. **The woman in the image given below belongs to which tribe?**

(a) Winnebago (b) Menominee
(c) Ho-Chunk Nation (d) Ojibwe

37. **Who are shown moving in black dress in the image below?**

(a) European settlers (b) Native of America
(c) Inhabitant of Mexico (d) None of these

Answers

1. (b) Tasman of Holland
2. (c) Circle
3. (b) 11,000
4. (a) reservations
5. (c) Spanish
6. (a) Jean-Jacques Rousseau
7. (c) Thomas Jefferson
8. (b) Canada
9. (a) Andrew Jackson
10. (c) Trail of Tears
11. (b) California
12. (c) 1870
13. (c) 1928
14. (a) Indian Reorganisation Act of 1934
15. (c) Declaration of Rights 1954
16. (d) Australia
17. (a) 1911
18. (c) meeting place
19. (a) Great Australian Silence
20. (c) Henry Reynolds
21. (a) Why Weren't We Told?
22. (d) 1781
23. (a) Only (i)
24. (b) Only (ii)
25. (a) (ii), (iii), (i)
26. (b) Thomas Jefferson
27. (c) Judith Wright
28. (a) California
29. (c) President
30. (a) Australia
31. (b) America
32. (a) Both A and R are true and R is the correct explanation of A
33. (b) Both A and R are true, but R is not the correct explanation of A
34. (c)
35. (a)
36. (a) Winnebago
37. (a) European settlers

Subjective Questions

Short Answer Type Questions

1. Discuss the contribution of East India Company in South Asia.

Ans. The contribution of the East India Company to South Asia was as follows

- In South Asia, the East India Company established themselves as political powers.
- They defeated local rulers and annexed their territories.
- They retained the older well-developed administrative system and collected taxes from landowners.
- They built railways to make trade easier, excavated mines and established big plantations.

2. Discuss about the geography of North America.

Ans. The North American continent extends from the Arctic Circle to the Tropic of Cancer, from the Pacific to the Atlantic Ocean. There is desert of Arizona and Nevada to the West of the Rocky mountains.

Further to the West, there are Sierra Nevada mountains, the Great Plains, the Great Lakes, the valleys of Mississippi and the Ohio and the Appalachian mountains in the East. Mexico is in the South. Canada is covered 40 per cent with forests.

There are many big industries in USA and Canada due to the availability of oil, gas and mineral resources in many areas. Wheat, corn and fruit are grown widely, and fishing is the major industry in Canada.

3. How did Anti-slavery Movement lead to civil liberties to slaves in North America?

Ans. The Anti-slavery Movement led to civil liberties to slaves in North America in the following ways

- Europeans could not work outdoors in the Southern region as it was too hot.
- The natives who were enslaved in South America to work in plantations had died in large numbers. So in USA, plantation owners bought slaves from Africa.
- Anti-slavery groups protest led to a ban on slave trade but the Africans and their children who were in the USA remained slaves.
- The economy in the Northern states of USA neither depended on plantations nor slavery. They wanted to end slavery and condemned the inhuman practice of it.
- There was a war between the states that wanted to continue slavery and those who wanted its abolition between 1861-65.
- Though slavery was abolished, it was only in the 20th century that the African Americans were able to win the battle for civil liberties.
- They ended the practice of discrimination in which Whites and non-Whites in schools and public transport were used to be segregated.

4. What goods did Europeans trade and exchange from natives for local products? Which products did they get addict to?

Ans. The European traders in the 17th century came to North America to trade in fish and furs from the natives who were experts in hunting. The natives held regular gatherings to exchange handicrafts which were unique to a tribe or food items not available in other regions. The Europeans gave blankets, iron vessels, guns and alcohol to the natives in exchange for local products.

The product that the natives got addicted to was alcohol. This was advantageous to Europeans because it helped them to dictate terms of trade. Similarly, Europeans got addicted to tobacco which was acquired from the natives.

5. Why and how Industrial Revolution happened in England and North America?

Ans. Industrial Revolution in England happened because the small peasants who were displaced, moved to towns for jobs in factories.

On the other hand, in North America, the industries were developed for different reasons. They manufactured railway equipment to link distant places with rapid transport, produced machinery which would make large-scale farming easier.
Both in USA and Canada, industrial towns and factories multiplied. The USA was an undeveloped economy in 1860 but became a leading industrial power in the world in 1890.

Large areas were cleared and divided into farms. Large scale agriculture was expanded.

6. Write a brief note on the Gold Rush and reasons for the growth of industries in North America.

Ans. **Gold Rush** The traces of gold were found in California in the 1840s. Thus, in order to make a quick fortune, thousands of Europeans came to America that led to the Gold Rush.
This led to recruitment of thousands of Chinese workers to build railway lines across the continent, which were completed by 1870 in USA and in Canada by 1885.

Reasons for the Growth of Industries in North America
In North America, the industries were developed for different reasons which were

- The industries manufactured railway equipment to link distant places with rapid transport.
- The industries produced machinery which would make large-scale farming easier.

7. What was the natives' reaction to the USA and Canada government's thought of ending all special provisions for the natives?

Ans. **Natives' Reaction to USA Government**
Governments of USA and Canada wanted to end special provisions for the natives in order to join them in mainstream i.e. adopt European culture. But natives did not want this. USA government prepared the Declaration of Indian Rights in 1954 in which a number of native peoples accepted citizenship of the USA but on a condition. The condition was that their reservations would not be taken away and their traditions would not be interfered with.

Natives' Reaction to Canada Government
In 1969, Canada government announced that they would not recognise aboriginal rights. In reaction, the natives in a well organised way, held a series of demonstrations and debates. Finally in 1982, Constitution Act accepted the existing aboriginal and treaty rights of the natives.

8. Discuss the exploitation of natives in Australia.

Ans. The natives in Australia, did not expect that in the 19th and 20th centuries, nearly 90 per cent of them would die due to germs, loss of their lands and resources, and in battles against the settlers.

The British also adopted same practice in the American colonies and stopped once they became independent. Later they continued same in Australia. Most of the convicts had been deported from England and these became the early settlers in Australia.

After their jail term ended, they were allowed to live as free people in Australia only if they would never return to Britain. These people now replaced natives without any hesitation and took their land for cultivation.

9. What were the economic developments happened in Australia?

Ans. The economic developments of Australia were similar to America under European settlers. These developments were as follows

- Large ship farms and mining stations were established over a long period of time and with the help of much labour, they started vineyards and wheat farming. All these economic activities formed the basis for the country's prosperity.
- In 1911, it was decided to build a new capital for Australia after the states were united. The name suggested at the time was Woolwheatgold, but finally it was called Canberra, which was derived from the native word 'kamberra' meaning meeting place.

10. Why government had termed Australia as the *terra nullius*? What were the two important decisions that were taken after the enquiries conducted against the atrocities committed against natives in Australia?

Ans. The government had always termed the land of Australia as *terra nullius* meaning it belongs to nobody.

The agitations around the questions related to atrocities against natives led to enquiries and to two important decisions that were

- To recognise that the natives had strong historic bonds with the land which was sacred to them and which should be respected.
- There should be a public apology for the injustice done to children in an attempt to keep white and coloured people apart.

11. "European imperialism played a key role in shaping the history of native populations in both America and Australia." Explain how European colonisation impacted the lives of natives in Australia.

Competency Based Que

Ans. European colonisation impacted the lives of natives in Australia in the following ways

- **Loss of Land** The arrival of European settlers in Australia led to the mass displacement of native populations, as their land was taken over for farming and settlements.
- **High Mortality Rates** Around 90% of the indigenous population died due to diseases introduced by Europeans, loss of resources and battles with settlers.
- **Exploitation of Labour** Native Australians were often forced to work in near-slavery conditions on farms, where harsh labour practices were common.
- **Cultural Erosion** Many native traditions and languages were lost as Europeans imposed their culture and way of life which further disconnected indigenous groups from their heritage.
- **Introduction of Convicts** Australia's population was heavily influenced by British convicts, who became settlers after serving their sentences, forcing the displacement of natives.

Long Answer Type Questions

1. Discuss about the history, lifestyle, languages and beliefs of native people of North America.

Ans. History of Native People of America

The earliest inhabitants of North America came from Asia over 30,000 years ago on a land- bridge across the Bering Straits and during the last Ice Age 10,000 years ago, they moved further South.

The oldest artefact found in America is an arrow point which is 11,000 years old. The population of natives started increasing about 5,000 years ago when the climate became more stable.

Lifestyle of Native People of America

Lifestyle of native people of America was as following

- The natives of North America lived in bands, in villages along river valleys.
- They ate fish and meat, and cultivated vegetables and maize.
- They often went on long journeys in search of meat, chiefly that of bison, the wild buffalo which roamed in the grasslands. They only killed as many animals as they needed for food.
- They did not do extensive agriculture so they could not produce surplus and thus they could not develop kingdoms and empires like in Central and South America.
- They did not own land and one of the important traditions of them was to make alliances, friendships and exchange gifts.
- They did not buy goods but got them as gifts.
- They held regular gatherings to exchange handicrafts unique to a tribe or food items not available in other regions. They did not attach value to the goods they exchanged with others. They considered those as gifts. They also grew crops for their own needs but not for sale or profit.

Language and Beliefs of Native People of America

- Various languages were spoken in North America, but they were not written down.
- They could read the land, understand the climates and different landscapes in the way literate people read written texts.
- They believed that time moved in cycles and each tribe had accounts about their origins and their earlier history which were passed on from one generation to the next.

2. Discuss the entry of European traders in North America. How did they change the landscape of the North America?

Ans. Entry of European Traders in North America

European traders reached the North coast of North America in the 17th century. The initial European traders came to North America to trade in fish and furs. They got whole hearted support from the natives who were experts in hunting. Europeans exchanged local products and gave the natives blankets, iron vessels, guns and alcohol. While natives thought these were gifts, Europeans looked at them as commodities which can earn profit for them.

After the European traders, Other traders also started coming to North America. Different groups of Europeans started being oppressed as they belonged to a different sect of Christianity like Protestants and Catholics.

Many of these left Europe and went to America to start a new life. Initially, this was not a problem because there was vacant land but later Europeans went further inland nearer to native villages and used their iron tools to cut down forests to lay out farms. This annoyed the native people.

Change in Landscape of North America

In the 19th century, the landscapes of America changed. These changes were as follows

- Land was treated differently by Europeans unlike natives. Migrants from Britain and France could not inherit their father's property as they were young, and therefore they wanted to own land in America.
- Later, lot of immigrants from Germany, Sweden and Italy who had lost their lands to big farmers, wanted to own farms in America.
- Poland people found prairie grasslands in the USA, similar to steppes of their homes and were very excited to buy huge properties at very low prices.
- They developed agriculture by clearing lands and introduced crops like rice and cotton which could not be grown in Europe, so that they could sell them for profit.

3. Discuss the European imperialism in detail. How did they extend their colonies in different continents?

Ans. **European Imperialism** The American empires of Spain and Portugal did not expand after the 17th century. It was other countries from Europe who started expanding themselves all around the world. France, Holland and England began to extend their trading activities, and established colonies in America, Africa and Asia.

Ireland was indirectly a colony of England because most of the landowners present in Ireland were English settlers. It was obvious that the prospect of profit drove people to establish colonies but there were differences in the nature of the control established by these imperialistic countries in their respective colonies.

The colonies were extended South Asia in the following ways

- In South Asia, the East India Company established themselves as political powers.
- They defeated local rulers and took over their territories.
- They used the older well-developed administrative system and collected taxes from the landowners.
- They also built railways to make trade easier.
- They excavated mines and established big plantations.
- In this way, they used South Asia as a golden goose to generate enormous amount of wealth.

The colonies were extended in Africa in the following ways

- In Africa, Europeans traded on the coast, except in South Africa, and only in the 19th century they ventured into the interior.
- European countries decided to divide up Africa as colonies for themselves, which shows the arrogance of the European imperialistic powers.

4. "Multiculturalism became the official policy in Australia." Discuss the transformation of Australian government from being exploitative and cruel to being apologetic to natives. What was the role of different people and institutions in this transformation? Competency Based Que

Ans. The transformation of Australian government can be explained in the following ways

- The Australian government did not recognise aboriginal rights and its attitude towards natives in land dealings was worse than the USA and Canada. It was in 1968, when WEH Stanner delivered a lecture titled 'The Great Australian Silence' which meant the silence of historians about aborigines. Natives had vast amount of stories, textile and painting and carving skills and this has to be understood and recorded and respected.
- Scholars like Henry Reynolds condemned the practice of writing Australian history starting from Captain Cook's discovery. He wanted historians to start writing the Australian history beginning with native people. After this, in universities, departments were started to study native cultures. Galleries of native art have been added to art galleries. Museums were enlarged to incorporate dioramas and imaginatively designed rooms explaining native culture. Natives also started writing their own life histories.
- In 1974, multiculturalism became the official policy in Australia which gave equal respect to native cultures and to the different cultures of the immigrants from Europe and Asia. From 1970s, when human rights were more emphasised at international organisations like United Nations. Another inhuman thing was, children of mixed blood were forcibly captured and separated from their native relatives.
- With agitations by natives and others, enquiries were set up and some important decisions were taken by Australian government. It was decided that natives historic bonds with land should be respected and there will be public apology for the injustice done to children in an attempt to keep white and coloured people apart.

5. Discuss the changes that were brought in the USA and Canada in order to provide legitimate rights to the natives.

Ans. The changes that were brought in the USA and Canada in order to provide legitimate rights to the natives were

Reservations In 1920s, things began to improve for the native peoples of the USA and Canada. A Survey named, "The Problem of Indian Administration" under social scientist Lewis Meriam was published in 1928. It showed the terribly poor health and education facilities for natives in reservations. White Americans now felt sympathy for the natives who were not able to follow their cultures and also denied the benefits of citizenship. This led to a landmark law in the USA, the Indian Reorganisation Act of 1934, which gave natives in reservations the right to buy land and take loans.

Declaration of Indian Rights In 1950s and 1960s, the USA and Canadian governments thought of ending all special provisions for the natives in the hope that they would join the mainstream and adopt European culture. This idea was opposed by natives. The USA government prepared the Declaration of Indian Rights in which a number of natives accepted citizenship of the USA on a condition that their reservations would not be taken away and their traditions would not be interfered.

Constitution Act In Canada, Government decided to end the recognition of aboriginal rights. In reaction to this, natives organised demonstrations and debates. Finally in 1982, the Constitution Act was introduced which accepted the existing aboriginal and treaty rights of the natives.

Assertion of Rights Natives in both the USA and Canada had reduced in numbers as compared to their number in the 18th century but they could now assert their rights and practice their culture. In Canada, they even had rights to their sacred lands which their ancestors did not have in 1880s.

6. "The experiences of Native Americans and Aboriginal Australians under European colonisation show both similarities and differences." Discuss the impact of European colonisation on the social, economic, and political systems of Native Americans and Aboriginal Australians, highlighting key differences and similarities. Competency Based Que

Ans. The impact of European colonisation on the social, economic, and political systems of Native Americans and Aboriginal Australians were as follows

(i) **Social Impact**

- **Displacement of Natives** Both Native Americans and Aboriginal Australians were displaced from their traditional lands by European settlers. In North America, natives were forced onto reservations, while in Australia, they were pushed into small, isolated areas.
- **Population Decline** The introduction of European diseases like smallpox drastically reduced the native populations in both regions.
- **Cultural Suppression** Both groups experienced the suppression of their cultures. Native Americans lost their land and way of life, while in Australia, the indigenous children were separated from their families.

(ii) **Economic Impact**

- **Resource Exploitation** European settlers exploited the resources of both continents. In North America, vast forests were cleared, and agriculture expanded at the expense of native lands. In Australia, European settlers introduced sheep farming, vineyards, and mining operations.
- **Labour Exploitation** Both native Americans and Aboriginal Australians were subjected to labour exploitation.

(iii) **Political Impact**

- **Loss of Autonomy** European colonisation led to the loss of political autonomy for both native groups. In America, native American tribes lost their sovereignty and were governed by European settlers, while in Australia, native political systems were entirely disrupted by the imposition of British rule.
- **Different Responses to Colonisation** While both groups resisted colonisation, the native Americans engaged in numerous wars and treaties with European settlers, such as the Cherokee's resistance in Georgia. In contrast, the Aboriginal Australians had fewer formal treaties or negotiations with the settlers, who largely disregarded their claims to land.

Key differences between the two were as follows

- **Cultural Preservation** While native Americans have largely been able to retain some cultural identity through treaties and reservations, the Aboriginal Australians faced more direct cultural erosion.
- **Political Response** The US government had formal policies, such as reservations and treaties with native Americans. However, in Australia, the government declared the land as *terra nullius* (belonging to no one) and largely ignored the political rights of the Aboriginal people until much later.

Source Based Questions

Read the sources given below and answer the following questions.

1. It was indicated on the stone tablets that the Hopis had that the first brothers and sisters that would come back to them would come as turtles across the land. They would be human beings, but they would come as turtles. So when the time came close the Hopis were at a special village to welcome the turtles that would come across the land and they got up in the morning and looked out at the sunrise.

They looked out across the desert and they saw the Spanish Conquistadores coming, covered in armour, like turtles across the land. So this was them. So they went out to the Spanish man and they extended their hand hoping for the handshake but into the hand the Spanish man dropped a trinket. And so word spread throughout North America that there was going to be a hard time, that may be some of the brothers and sisters had forgotten the sacredness of all things and all the human beings were going to suffer for this on the Earth.

- From a talk by Lee Brown, 1986

(i) **What was the belief of the Hopis? Whom did Hopis encounter?**

(ii) **What did Spanish man give and what did Hopis expect?**

(iii) **Why were all the human beings going to suffer on the Earth?**

Ans. (i) Hopis believed that the first brothers and sisters would come back to them but as turtles. Hopis encountered with Spanish Conquistadores.

(ii) Hopis expected for a handshake from Spanish man but he dropped a trinket. It meant that the Spanish colonisers wanted to control the Hopis.

(iii) Hopis thought that some of the brothers and sisters had forgotten the sacredness of all things due to which all the human beings have to suffer on the Earth.

2. It is interesting to note that another writer, Washington Irving, much younger than Wordsworth and who had actually met native people, described them quite differently.

'The Indians I have had an opportunity of seeing in real life are quite different from those described in poetry... Taciturn they are, it is true, when in company with white men, whose good will they distrust and whose language they do not understand; but the white man is equally taciturn under like circumstances.

When the Indians are among themselves, they are great mimics, and entertain themselves excessively at the expense of the whites...who have supposed them impressed with profound respect for their grandeur and dignity...The white men (as I have witnessed) are prone to treat the poor Indians as little better than animals.'

(i) **Who is the author of the passage? How did the author describe native Indians?**

(ii) **What was the behaviour of Indians when they were among themselves?**

(iii) **How did white men treat poor Indians?**

Ans. (i) Washington Irving is the author of the passage. The author described the native Indians as taciturn meaning they were reserved, quiet and did not talk much.

(ii) The behaviour of Indians when they were among themselves was that as they were great mimics, they used to entertain themselves at the expense of the whites.

(iii) The white men treated poor Indians as little better than animals.

3. In 1854, the President of the USA received a letter from a native leader, Chief Seattle. The President had asked the chief to sign a treaty giving a large part of the land they lived on to the American government. The Chief replied:

'How can you buy or sell the sky, the warmth of the land? The idea is strange to us. If you do not own the freshness of the air and the sparkle of the water, how can one buy them? Every part of the Earth is sacred to my people. Every shining pine-needle, every sandy shore, every mist in the dark woods, every clearing and every humming insect is holy in the memory and experience of my people. The sap which courses through the trees carries the memories of the red man...

So, when the Great Chief in Washington sends word that he wished to buy our land, he asks much of us. The Great Chief sends word that he will reserve us a place so that we can live comfortably. He will be our father and we will be his children. So we will consider your offer to buy our land. But it will not be easy. For this land is sacred to us.

The shining water that moves in the streams and rivers is not just water but the blood of our ancestors. If we sell you land, you must remember that it is sacred and you must teach your children that it is sacred and that each ghostly reflection in the clear water of the lakes tells of events and memories in the life of my people. The water's murmur is the voice of my father's father...'

(i) **What did President of the USA write letter for?**
(ii) **Why was the idea of selling land strange to the native leader?**
(iii) **What did President promise the native leader?**

Ans. (i) The President of the USA wrote letter to a native leader, asking him to sign a treaty giving a large part of the land they lived on to the American government.

(ii) For native leader it was strange because one cannot buy or sell sky, the warmth of the land. One cannot own the freshness of the air and the sparkle of the water.

(iii) President promised that he will reserve some place to the native people where they can live comfortably.

4. 'Aboriginal production had been dramatically disturbed by the British presence. The arrival of a thousand hungry mouths, followed by hundreds more, put unprecedented pressure on local food resources.

So what would the Daruk people have thought of all this? To them such large-scale destruction of sacred places and strange, violent behaviour towards their land was inexplicable. The newcomers seemed to knock down the trees without any reason, for they were not making canoes, gathering bush honey or catching animals.

Stones were moved and stacked together, clay dug up, shaped and cooked, holes were made in the ground, large unwieldy structures built. At first they may have equated the clearing with the creation of a sacred ceremonial ground...Perhaps they thought a huge ritual gathering was to be held, dangerous business from which they should steer well clear. There is no doubt the Daruks subsequently avoided the settlement, for the only way to bring them back was by an official kidnapping.'

-(P Grimshaw, M Lake, A McGrath, M Quartly, Creating a Nation

(i) **What was Daruk people's reaction to British?**
(ii) **What did newcomers expect British to do with the knocked down trees?**
(iii) **What did they do before large structures were built?**

Ans. (i) Daruk people were astonished and could not understand the large scale destruction of sacred places and strange, violent behaviour towards their land by the British.

(ii) Daruks thought that newcomers knocked trees for making canoes, gathering bush honey or catching animals, but they were not doing anything like that.

(iii) Before building large structures the stones were moved and arranged together, clay was dug up shaped and cooked and holes were made in the ground.

5. Kathy my sister with the torn heart,
I don't know how to thank you
For your dreamtime stories of joy and grief
Written on paperbark.
You were one of the dark children
I wasn't allowed to play with-
Riverbank campers, the wrong colour
(I couldn't turn you white.)
So it was late I met you,
Late I began to know
They hadn't told me the land I loved
Was taken out of your hands.'

- 'Two Dreamtimes', written for Oodgeroo Noonuccal

(i) **What does the author mean by 'dark children?'**
(ii) **Why was author not allowed to play with Kathy? What was the author thanking Kathy for?**
(iii) **What happened to riverbank campers land?**

Ans. (i) 'Dark children' refers to those who are from a different racial or cultural background, in this case, it refers to the indigenous people whom the speaker was not allowed to associate with.

(ii) Since Kathy was dark girl, the author was not allowed to play with her. The author was thanking Kathy for her dreamtime stories of joy and sadness written on a paperbark tree.

(iii) The riverbank campers land was taken away or occupied by the white people forcibly.

Map Based Questions

1. Locate the following locations on the American map.

(i) Mexico (ii) Florida (iii) New York (iv) Georgia (v) California

Ans.

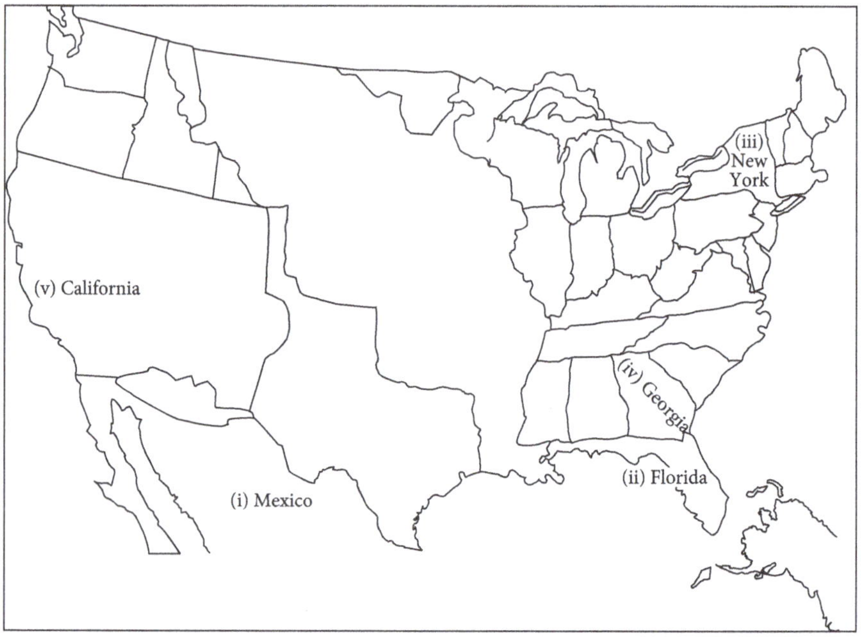

2. Locate the following locations on the Australian map.

(i) Darwin (ii) Perth (iii) Melbourne (iv) Sydney (v) Canberra

Ans.

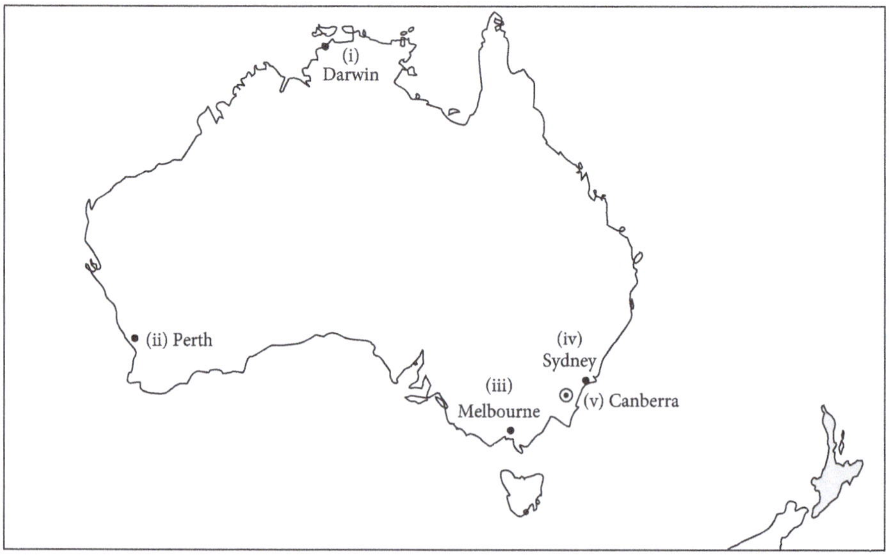

SELF ASSESSMENT TEST

Objective Type Questions

1. 'Australia' comes from the Latin word 'Austral' which means ....
   (a) South (b) North (c) East (d) West
2. The USA bought Alaska from
   (a) Canada (b) Mexico (c) Russia (d) China
3. What was one significant change in the study and presentation of native cultures from the 1970s?
   (a) Aboriginal culture was studied only as a curiosity.
   (b) Native cultures were understood and recorded as distinct and respected communities.
   (c) The study of native cultures was banned in universities.
   (d) Indigenous art was removed from public galleries.
4. Match the Following

	List I		List II
A.	Sydney was founded	1.	1607
B.	Recognition of America as separate nation by Britain	2.	1788
C.	Britain found the colony of Virginia	3.	1791
D.	Canada Constitutional Act	4.	1781

Codes

	A	B	C	D		A	B	C	D
(a)	3	1	4	2	(b)	4	3	2	1
(c)	2	4	1	3	(d)	4	2	1	3

Short Answer Type Questions

5. How did natives of a North America lose their land? What were their sufferings?
6. How did the trading companies make themselves into political powers in South Asia?
7. How did the USA and Canada reach their present territorial limits?
8. What was the demand of French settlers in Canada? How was it solved?
9. Most of the towns are along the coast in Australia. Comment.
10. There was a non-white policy in Australia to keep non-white people out. Discuss.

Long Answer Type Questions

11. Why a lot of Europeans hurried to America in the hope of making a quick fortune?
12. Explain the arrival of aborigines in Australia. What are their characteristics?
13. The European traders changed the landscapes of Australia in the 19th century. Discuss.
14. In what ways did the Constitutional Act of 1982 in Canada address the issues surrounding oboriginal rights and treaty rights? How has the situation for native peoples in the United States and Canada changed since the 1880s regarding their cultural rights and land claims?

7

CHAPTER

In the early 19th century, East Asia was dominated by China under the Qing dynasty, while Japan was a relatively small and isolated island nation.
This chapter will explore how Japan rapidly transformed itself into a modern nation-state, established an industrial economy, and even built a colonial empire.

YOUR STUDY GOALS

7.1 History of Japan and China
7.2 Japan
7.3 China
7.4 Modernisation in Japan and China
7.5 The Story of Taiwan
7.6 The Story of Korea

YOUR PRACTICE GOAL

- Objective Type Questions (25 Qs ; MCQs, A-R, Matching, Picture Based)
- Subjective Questions (17 SAs, 7 LAs)
- Source Based Questions (6 Qs)
- Map Based Questions (2 Qs)

Paths to Modernisation

7.1 History of Japan and China

- In China and Japan, rulers used to keep records and write about their families' history.
- **Sima Qian** (145-90 BCE) is regarded as one of the greatest historians of early China.
- Due to the influence of Chinese culture, Japan also placed great importance on history. The **Meiji government** created a department in 1869 to gather information and write a favourable account (to praise) of the Meiji Restoration.
- A wide range of written materials, including official histories, scholarly writings, popular literature and religious tracts are available due to the high respect for the written word and literary ability.
- Printing and publishing were important industries in the pre-modern period, allowing for the tracking of book distribution in 18th-century China and Japan.

Views of Modern Scholars

- Modern scholars like **Liang Qichao** in China and **Kume Kunitake** (1839-1931) in Japan laid the foundations for modern scholarship.
- Writings from European travellers (**Marco Polo** (1254-1324), **Mateo Ricci** (1552-1610), **Luis Frois** (1532-97)) and 19th-century Christian missionaries provide valuable historical insights.
- **Joseph Needham's** work on history of science in China and **George Sansom's** studies on Japanese history has provided detailed research.
- Many works of Chinese and Japanese scholars have been translated into English, providing global perspectives of these countries.

▲ East Asia

Naito Konan (1866-1934)

- **Naito Konan** was a famous Japanese scholar who studied China. His work has influenced many other scholars around the world.
- Naito Konan used new ways of studying history that were developed in the West. He also had experience as a journalist. He helped start a **Department of Oriental Studies** in Kyoto University in 1907.
- In his book "***Shinaron***, (on China 1914)" he suggested that China should improve its local communities. He believed that a new kind of government, where people have more power, would end the rule of the aristocracy.

Quick Test 1

1. Who is considered the greatest historian of early China?
2. Who are the pioneers of modern history in Japan?
3. What was the contribution of Joseph Needham and George Sansom?
4. Who was Naito Konan?

7.2 Japan

- Japan is a group of islands consisting of four main islands: **Honshu, Kyushu, Shikoku** and **Hokkaido**.
- The Okinawan chain, located in the Southernmost part of Japan, is at the same latitude as the Bahamas. Over half of the land area of the main islands is mountainous.
- Japan is situated in an earthquake-prone region, which has significantly affected the architecture of Japan.
- The majority of Japan's population is Japanese, with small **Ainu** and **Korean** minorities. The latter group was forcibly brought to Japan during the colonial period.
- **Rice** is a staple crop in Japan and **fish** is a major source of protein. Raw fish such as **sashimi or sushi**, is considered healthy. The Japanese people traditionally did not engage in animal rearing.

The Political System in Japan

- Japan was ruled by an emperor, but the imperial court lost its power to the **shoguns**[1] by the 12th century. The shoguns ruled in the name of the emperor.

1 Shogun They were default rulers of Japan, though formally appointed by the Emperor.

- Members of the **Tokugawa family** held the position of shogun from 1603 to 1867.
- The country was divided into 250 domains ruled by lords called ***daimyo***[2].
- The shogun made sure that the ***daimyo*** lived in **Edo (modern Tokyo)** to prevent them from causing trouble and also controlled the major cities and mines.
- The shogun and *daimyo* were served by the **samurai**[3].

Three key changes were brought in Japan in the late 16th century which laid the foundation of the future development

(i) Only the samurai were allowed to carry swords, ensuring peace and order by disarming the peasantry.

(ii) *Daimyo* were ordered to live in the capitals of their domains, limiting their autonomy.

(iii) Land surveys were conducted to identify owners and taxpayers, and land productivity was assessed to ensure a stable revenue base (income).

A New Policy launched by the Government

- The Japanese government launched the "***Fukoku-Kyohei***" (rich country, strong army) **policy**, recognising the need for economic development and military strength to avoid becoming a colony like India.
- This policy aimed to create a sense of nationhood among the people and transform them from subjects into citizens.

Government Built the Emperor System

- The government established the **emperor system**, sending officials to study European monarchies to model their own system.
- The emperor, believed to be related to the Sun Goddess, was very important. His birthday was a national holiday, and he wore European-style military clothes.
- The government made new rules using the emperor's name. The **Imperial Rescript on Education 1890** told people to learn, help others and work together.

Economic Growth

- The capitals of *daimyo* grew, making **Edo** the world's most populous city by the 17th century. **Osaka** and **Kyoto** were also important cities.
- By the mid-17th century, Japan had at least six castle-towns with populations over 50,000.
- The growth of cities promoted the development of a commercial economy, leading to the creation of financial and debt systems.
- Status was no longer based only on birth or social class; instead, personal achievements were valued. This shift helped create a lively urban culture, where the growing merchant class enjoyed theatre and the arts.
- The popularity of reading increased, allowing gifted writers to earn a living through their writing.
- In Edo, people could 'rent' a book for the price of a noodle bowl, indicating the widespread accessibility and affordability of literature.

Economic Development and Trade in Japan

- Japan imported luxury items like silk from China and textiles from India. It had to pay for these imports with gold and silver. To solve this issue, the Tokugawa government limited the export of precious metals.
- To reduce dependence on imports, Japan developed its own silk industry in **Nishijin**, Kyoto. **Nishijin silk** gained popularity for its high quality.

---

2 *Daimyo* They were lords who controlled domains in Japan.

3 Samurai It represents the warrior class.

- The growing use of money and the creation of a rice stock market showed Japan's economic progress. These changes indicated a move towards a more market-driven economy.

Nishijin

- Nishijin is a quarter or township in Kyoto. In the 16th century, it had a weavers' guild (association) with 31 households.
- By the end of the 17th century, the community grew to over 70,000 people.
- **Sericulture** was encouraged by an order in 1713. It required the use of only domestic yarn. Nishijin specialised in producing the most expensive products.
- Silk production contributed to the rise of a class of regional entrepreneurs who challenged the Tokugawa order.
- When foreign trade began in 1859, Japan's silk exports became a significant source of profit for an economy that was struggling to compete with Western goods.

Social and Intellectual Changes in Japan

- The study of ancient Japanese literature led to a questioning on the extent of Chinese influence on Japanese culture.
- Some scholars argued that Japan had a unique cultural essence long before contact with China.
- Early Japanese classics like ***Tale of the Genji*** and **origin myths**, portrayed the islands as creations of the gods and the emperor as a descendant of the Sun Goddess. These books highlighted the country's indigenous traditions.

The Meiji Restoration by Perry in Japan

- In 1853, the United States sent **Commodore Matthew Perry** (1794-1858) to Japan. He asked the Japanese government to sign a treaty for trade and diplomatic relations. Japan was important because it was located on the way to China.
- Japan was seen as a good market for American goods. American large ships also needed a stop to get refuelled in the Pacific.
- Japan had maintained a **policy of isolation**[4], with only the Holland trading with the country.
- Perry's arrival and demands forced Japan to remove its isolationist policy and enter into trade agreements with the United States and other Western powers.
- The arrival of foreign ships ended the Tokugawa shogunate and brought the emperor back to power in Japan.
- This event, known as the **Meiji Restoration**, marked a significant turning point in Japan's history.

▲ *Commodore Perry as seen by the Japanese*

Impact of Perry's Arrival on Japanese Politics

- The arrival of Commodore Perry led to the re-emergence of the emperor as a significant figure in Japanese politics.
- A movement to remove the shogunate grew stronger, and in 1868, the emperor was taken to Edo (now Tokyo).
- Edo was made the capital of Japan and renamed Tokyo, meaning **Eastern Capital**.

▲ *Perry's Ship*

4 Policy of isolation A national policy that involves avoiding political and economic ties with other countries.

Reforms Introduced in Meiji

Educational Reforms

- A new school system was implemented in the 1870s, making schooling compulsory for both boys and girls. By 1910, schooling became nearly universal.
- Tuition fees were kept minimal, and the curriculum was modelled like Western systems.
- In the 1870s, there was a strong emphasis on loyalty to the emperor and the study of Japanese history.
- The Ministry of Education controlled the curriculum, textbooks selection and teacher's training.
- Moral culture was taught, and children were encouraged to respect their parents, be loyal to the nation and become good citizens.

Phonetic Alphabets

In 6th century, Japanese borrowed their written script from Chinese. They developed two phonetic alphabets as their language is very different from Chinese, namely –

(i) Hiragana (considered as feminine as used by women writers in Heiare period like Murasaki)

(ii) Katakana

Administrative Reforms

- The Meiji government imposed a new administrative structure and reorganised village and domain boundaries to unite the nation.
- Administrative units needed enough revenue to support local schools and health services. They also had to serve as recruitment centers for the military.
- **Compulsory military service** was introduced for all young men over the age of twenty. A modern military force was developed.
- A **legal system** was established to regulate political groups, control meetings and impose strict censorship.
- The military and bureaucracy were placed under the direct command of the emperor.

Reforms for Modernising Economy

- An agricultural tax was charged to raise funds.
- The first railway line between **Tokyo** and **Yokohama** was built in 1870-1872.
- Textile machinery was imported from Europe, and foreign technicians were recruited to train Japanese workers and teach at universities and schools. Japanese students were also sent abroad for training.
- Modern banking institutions were established in 1872.
- To increase trading by Japanese ships, important ship builders companies like Mitsubishi and Sumitomo were helped through subsidies and tax benefits.
- Large business organisations controlled by individual families called ***zaibatsu***, dominated the economy until after the Second World War.
- Japan's population increased from 35 million in 1872 to 55 million in 1920. To reduce population pressure, the government encouraged migration. People migrated to the Northern island of **Hokkaido**. It was a large self-ruling area inhabited by the indigenous **Ainu people**. Japanese people also migrated to Hawaii, Brazil and other Japanese colonies.
- Industrialisation led to a shift towards urban living. The urban population increased from 21% in 1925 to 32% in 1935.

Conditions of Industrial Workers in Japan

- The number of people working in manufacturing increased dramatically from 700,000 in 1870 to 4 million in 1913.

- Many workers were employed in units without machinery or electric power, indicating a dependence on traditional methods.
- Over half of the employees in modern factories were women. In 1886, women organised the **first modern strike**. While the number of male workers increased after 1900, the number of women exceeded men until the 1930s.
- Factory size began to increase, with the number of factories employing over 100 workers rising from 1,000 in 1909 to over 2,000 by 1920 and 4,000 by the 1930s.
- There were 550,000 workshops that employed less than 5 employees.
- Small workshops helped families stay together, just like the emperor's family system. This system focused on national unity and loyalty.

▲ *Workers in a textile factory*

Protest against Pollution

- The rapid and unregulated growth of industry and the increasing demand for natural resources like timber led to significant environmental degradation in Japan.
- In 1897, **Tanaka Shozo**, a member of the first House of Representatives, led the first major protest against industrial pollution.

Tanaka Shozo: A Pioneer of Environmental Activism (1841-1913)

- Tanaka Shozo, the son of a farmer, actively involved in the **Popular Rights Movement** in the 1880s, advocating for constitutional government. His efforts led to his election as a member of the first diet.
- He led a significant protest against the pollution of the Watarase River by the Ashio Copper Mine, which affected over 100 square miles of farmland and impacted thousands of families.
- The company was forced to take steps to reduce pollution because of public protests. This helped the environment and allowed people to harvest crops normally again by 1904.

Aggressive Nationalism in Japan

- The Meiji Constitution established a limited franchise, restricting voting rights to a selected group of citizens and created a Diet[5] with limited powers.
- Despite the imperial restoration, political parties emerged and formed cabinets between 1918 and 1931. However, these cabinets were eventually replaced by national unity cabinets, which were formed by politicians from different parties.
- The emperor remained the commander of the armed forces, and from 1890, this was interpreted to mean that the army and navy had independent control.
- The fear of Western domination led to a strengthening of the military and expansion of Japan's colonial empire.

Views of Japanese Intellectuals on Relations of Japan with Other Countries

- According to ***Fukuzawa Yukichi***, a leading intellectual during the Meiji era, Japan must 'expel Asia.' He meant that Japan should give up its Asian traits and become part of the Western world.
- The next generation of intellectuals opposed the complete acceptance of Western ideas and advocated for building national pride based on indigenous values.
- **Miyake Setsurei (1860-1945)**, a philosopher, argued that each nation should develop its unique talents to contribute to world civilisation.
- Many intellectuals wanted Japan to be based on democracy, not military power. They were influenced by Western ideas of freedom and equality.

▲ *The novelty of electric goods : a rice-cooker*

5 Diet It refers to a German word for Parliament

- **Ueki Emori** (1857-1892), a leader of the Popular Rights Movement, called for a constitutional government. He admired the ideas of natural rights and popular sovereignty from the French Revolution.
- Ueki also believed in liberal education to help individuals grow. Some people even wanted women to have the right to vote. This pressure from the movement led the government to announce a Constitution.

Daily Life in Japan

▲ *A Toaster*

- The traditional patriarchal household system, where multiple generations lived together under the authority of the head of the house, began to decline.
- As more people became rich, new family structures emerged, with the nuclear family becoming popular.
- The nuclear family (The new home or homu in Japanese) consisted of a husband and wife, with the husband as the breadwinner and the wife as the homemaker.
- The concept of the nuclear family led to a demand for new types of domestic goods, family entertainments and housing.
- Construction companies offered affordable housing options in the 1920s.

Overcoming Modernity

- In the 1930s and 1940s, Japan started aggressive wars to grow its empire in China and other areas of Asia. During the Second World War when Japan attacked the United States at **Pearl Harbour**.

▲ *An American Grill*

- During this period, the Japanese government imposed many restrictions on society. People who disagreed were punished and sent to prison. At the same time, patriotic groups, including many women's organisations, were created to support the war effort.
- A famous meeting called **Overcoming Modernity** took place in 1943. It focused on Japan's challenge of dealing with Western influence while keeping its own modern identity.
- **Moroi Saburo**, a musician argued to rescue music from the art of sensory stimulation and to restore it as an art of the spirit.
- **Nishitani Keiji**, a well-known philosopher, explained 'modernity' as the combination of three key Western ideas: the **Renaissance**, the **Protestant Reformation** and the **development of natural sciences.**
- Nishitani believed that Japan had a responsibility to create a new world order called **Greater East Asia**. He stressed the importance of combining science and religion to achieve this new vision.

Japan's Re-emergence as a Global Economic Power

- Japan's defeat in the Second World War and its failed attempt to establish a colonial empire led to its demilitarisation.
- Japan introduced a new Constitution under the US-led Occupation (1945-1947).
- The new Constitution, including **Article 9**, renounced the use of war as an instrument of state policy.
- A number of reforms were implemented, including agrarian reforms, the re-establishment of trade unions, and efforts to break up the ***zaibatsu***.
- Political parties were revived and the first post-war elections were held in 1946, marking the **first time when women voted in Japan**.

Rebuilding of Japanese Economy

- Japan's rapid economic recovery after its defeat in the Second World War is often referred to as the **post-war miracle**.
- The post-war Constitution made Japan more democratic by increasing political participation.

- The social unity that existed before the war became stronger, leading to closer cooperation among the government, bureaucracy and industry.
- The Japanese economy was also supported by the United States. The economy benefited from the increased demand due to the Korean and Vietnamese wars.
- The **1964 Tokyo Olympics** showed Japan's economic growth and its emergence as a global player.

▲ *Tokyo before and after the Second World War*

- The introduction of the high-speed ***Shinkansen*** bullet train network in 1964 demonstrated Japan's ability to produce better and cheaper goods through advanced technology.

Environmental Challenges

- Industrialisation in Japan led to environmental problems, including pollution and health hazards. Civil society movements emerged in the 1960s to address these issues, demanding government action and compensation for victims.
- Cadmium poisoning, Mercury poisoning cause Minamata disease in 1960s and other problems by air pollution in the early 1970s affected Japan badly.
- Japan implemented strict environmental regulations, which led to improvements in environmental conditions.
- Interest in environmental issues declined in the mid-1980s due to the country's strong environmental controls.

Quick Test 2

1 What was Nishijin famous for?
2 Who was Tanaka Shozo?
3 Who were Moroi Saburo and Nishitani Keiji ?
4 Which disease is caused due to Mercury Poisoning?
5 Give an example of the environmental problem in Japan in the 1960s.

7.3 China

- China, a vast continental country, encompasses various climatic zones. A significant portion of its landscape is mountainous, and it has three major river systems: the **Yellow river** (Huang He), the **Yangtse river** (Chang Jiang, the world's third-longest river) and the **Pearl river**.
- The modern history of China revolves around **three primary pillars** as follows
    - To regain its sovereignty.
    - To end the humiliation of foreign occupation.
    - To achieve equality and development for its people.
- Three major groups have played significant roles in Chinese political debates:
    - Reformers like **Kang Youwei** (1858-1927) and **Liang Qichao** (1873-1929) attempted to adapt traditional Chinese ideas to address the challenges posed by the West.
    - Inspired by ideas of Japan and the West, Republican revolutionaries like Sun Yat-sen, the first President of the Republic of China, tried to overthrow the monarchy and establish a democratic republic.
    - The **Chinese Communist Party (CCP)** aimed to eliminate age-old inequalities and throw out foreign influence from China.

China's Culture

- The majority of people in China are **Han**, but there are also many other ethnic groups, such as **Uighur, Hui, Manchu** and **Tibetan**.
- Chinese (Putonghua) is the major language, but there are also significant regional dialects such as **Cantonese** (Yue) and **Shanghainese** (Wu), as well as other minority languages.
- China's large area and different regions have resulted in unique food traditions. Southern or Cantonese cuisine is especially famous, featuring popular dishes like **dim sum**[6], pastries and dumplings.
- Wheat is the staple food in Northern China, while both rice and wheat are consumed in Eastern China.
- Szechuan cuisine, known for its spiciness, was influenced by spices brought by Buddhist monks along the Silk Route and chilli peppers introduced by Portuguese traders.

China's Encounter with West

- The modern history of China started in the 16th and 17th centuries when it began to interact with Western countries.

▲ *The Opium War*

- Jesuit missionaries brought Western sciences like astronomy and mathematics to China. Although the initial effects were small, these early interactions led to future developments.
- The British East India Company forced China to buy opium, which led to the First Opium War (1839-1842). This weakened the **Qing dynasty's** power and increased demands for reform and change.
- Reformers such as **Kang Youwei** and **Liang Qichao** saw the need to protect China from colonisation and strengthen its systems.
- They pushed for modernising the government, creating a new army, establishing an educational system and setting up local assemblies to support constitutional government.

Debates and Views of China about Colonised Nations

- The partition of Poland in the 18th century strongly influenced Chinese thinkers. The phrase '**to Poland us**' (*bolan wo*) became a popular saying in China to describe a divided and oppressed nation.
- In **1903, Liang Qichao,** a prominent Chinese thinker, believed that China could only resist Western influence by recognising itself as a unified nation. He criticised India for being ruined by the East India Company, which he viewed as a foreign entity. He accused Indians of betraying their own people and being under British control.
- These arguments were important to ordinary Chinese people, especially when the British used Indian soldiers to fight against China.
- Many Chinese thinkers believed that traditional Confucian values, which focus on good behaviour, practical wisdom, and social relationships, were not allowing new ideas and changes.
- **Confucianism**[7] influenced how people viewed life, set social standards, and shaped political beliefs, making it a major problem in modernisation.

Japanese Influence on Chinese Modernisation

- Chinese students were sent to study in Japan, Britain and France to learn about modern subjects and bring back new ideas. Many of these students, who studied in Japan in the 1890s, became leading republicans and played a significant role in China's modernisation.

---

6 **Dim Sum** It is a cuisine that literally means 'touch your heart'.
7 **Confucianism** It was a philosophy which was concerned about good conduct, practical wisdom and proper social relationships.

- The Chinese borrowed even Japanese translations of European words like **justice, rights** and **revolution**, demonstrating the influence of Western ideas.
- The **Russo-Japanese War in 1905** led to the removal of the centuries-old Chinese examination system, which had been used to select candidates for the elite ruling class.

Republican Revolution

- Sun Yat-sen (1866-1925), a visionary leader and the founder of modern China, led the removal of the Manchu dynasty in 1911, establishing the Republic of China.
- Sun Yat-sen introduced the **Three Principles of the People** (San min Chui), which guided his vision for China. These are as follows
  (i) **Nationalism** The goal was to overthrow the Manchu dynasty, seen as a foreign rule, and to remove other foreign imperialists from China.
  (ii) **Democracy** Establishing a democratic government.
  (iii) **Socialism** Controlling money and making land ownership fair.
- On **4th May, 1919**, an angry demonstration was held in Beijing to protest the decisions of the post-war conference.
- Even though China was on the winning side with Britain, it didn't get back the lands that were taken from it. This protest started a bigger movement that brought many Chinese people together. Following were the demands of the May Fourth Movement
  - Use of simple language in writing.
  - Abolishing the practice of foot-binding and the subordination of women.
  - Equality in marriage.
  - Economic development to end poverty.
- The Republican Revolution led to a period of political instability and crisis. The **Guomindang** (National People's Party) and the **Chinese Communist Party** (CCP) emerged as significant forces, seeking to unify the country and bring stability.

The Guomindang and its Political Philosophy

- Guomindang's political philosophy was based on Sun Yat-sen's ideas. They identified **clothing, food, housing** and **transportation** as the four essential needs of the people.
- **Chiang Kai-shek** (1887-1975) took over from Sun Yat-sen as the leader of the Guomindang and focused on several reforms and policies. He led a **military campaign** to defeat warlords and get rid of the Communist Party.
- He promoted a secular and rational version of Confucianism while also emphasising traditional values for women, including chastity (purity), appearance, speech and work.
- The Guomindang mainly had support from cities, and industrial growth was slow and limited.
- **Shanghai** became a hub for modern development, but the industrial working class was small, with most workers involved in small trades. Women, in particular, faced low wages and difficult working conditions.
- The spread of schools and universities contributed to social and cultural change. **Peking University**, established in 1902, played a significant role in promoting new ideas. The popular magazine ***Life Weekly***, edited by **Zao Taofen**, reflected these changing trends.

- New ideas and leaders, such as **Mahatma Gandhi** and **Kemal Ataturk**, were introduced to Chinese readers through publications like 'Life Weekly'.
- Despite its efforts, the Guomindang failed to unify the country due to its narrow social base and limited political vision.
- The party's neglect of the peasantry and the growing social inequalities contributed to its downfall.
- The Guomindang focused more on military control instead of solving the people's issues, which made the population feel more distant from them.

The Rise of the Chinese Communist Party

- In 1937, the Japanese invasion of China forced the Guomindang to withdraw, leading to a long war that weakened the country. From 1945 to 1949, prices increased by 30% each month, severely affecting the lives of everyday people.
- Rural China faced two major crises which contributed to the growing dissatisfaction with the Guomindang government. These were
  (i) **Ecological Crisis** There were major environmental problems like soil exhaustion, deforestation and floods.
  (ii) **Socio-Economic Crisis** Rural communities faced severe economic difficulties due to unfair land ownership, debt, outdated technology and poor communication systems.
- **The Chinese Communist Party (CCP)** was founded in 1921 after the Russian Revolution.
- The success of the Russian Revolution had a significant impact worldwide, leading to the establishment of the **Comintern** (Third International) by leaders like Lenin and Trotsky in March 1918. The Comintern aimed to promote a global revolution to end exploitation.
- The CCP was initially supported by the Comintern and the Soviet Union. The CCP followed traditional Marxist beliefs, thinking that the urban working class should lead a revolution.
- Initially, its ideas appealed to people in various countries. However, over time, the CCP became a tool for Soviet interests and was dissolved in 1943.

Mao Zedong : An Important Leader of Communist Party (1893-1976)

- **Mao Zedong** focused on the peasants for his revolutionary ideas. By getting the peasants involved, he helped the CCP become a strong political group and win against the Guomindang.
- From 1928 to 1934, Mao Zedong and the CCP set up a base in the **Jiangxi mountains**. They stayed there and fought back against attacks from the Guomindang.
- The CCP organised a strong **peasant council**, known as a **Soviet**, through the confiscation and redistribution of land. This strategy mobilised the peasantry and strengthened the CCP's base of support.
- Unlike other leaders, Mao Zedong stressed the need for an independent government and army, rejecting foreign influence and control.
- Mao Zedong was aware of the problems faced by women and supported the formation of rural women's associations.
- He introduced a **new marriage law** that removed arranged marriages, prohibited the purchase and sale of marriage contracts, and simplified divorce procedures.

The Long March

- The Guomindang blocked the Communists' Soviet forces, forcing them to find a new base. This led to the Long March (1934-35), a tough 6,000-mile journey to Shanxi.
- In their new base in Yanan, they focused on ending warlordism, making land reforms, and fighting foreign imperialism. This gave them a strong support from the people.
- During the tough years of war, the Communists and Guomindang worked together. However, after the war ended, the Communists gained power, and the Guomindang was defeated.

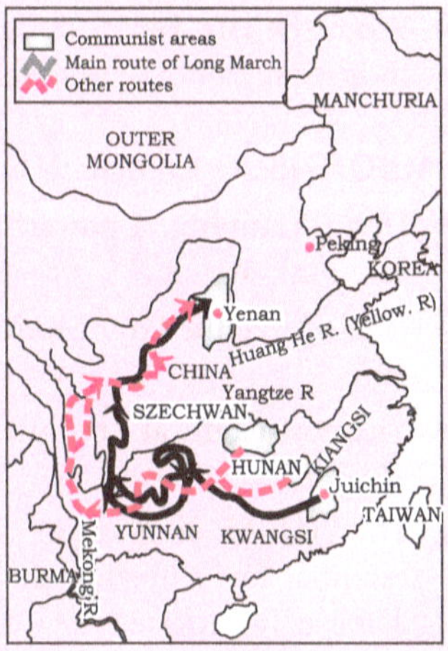

Establishing the New Democracy : 1949-65

- The **People's Republic of China**, established in 1949, was based on the principles of the New Democracy, which aimed to include all social classes.
- The government took control of key sectors of the economy and gradually phased out **private enterprise** and land ownership. In 1953, the government announced a new program of socialist[8] transformation.
- The **Great Leap Forward**, launched in 1958, was a policy aimed at rapid industrialisation. People were encouraged to set up small-scale steel furnaces in their backyards to contribute to industrial production.
- **Rural communes** were established, covering a significant portion of the farm population. These communes collectively owned and cultivated land, promoting agricultural cooperation.
- Mao Zedong mobilised the masses to achieve the party's goals. He emphasised the creation of a **socialist man** with five loves: the fatherland, the people, labour, science and public property.
- Mass organisations were established for various groups, including farmers, women and students like the All-China Democratic Women's Federation and the All-China Students Federation.
- The commune system faced challenges, and leaders like **Liu Shaochi** (1896-1969) and **Deng Xiaoping** (1904-97) attempted to modify it. The steel produced in backyard furnaces was often unsuitable for industrial use.

Great Proletarian Cultural Revolution

- The Great Proletarian Cultural Revolution, launched in 1965 by Mao Zedong, was a response to growing dissatisfaction and criticism within the Chinese Communist Party.
- The conflict arose between those who supported Mao's vision of creating a **'socialist man'** and those who objected to his prioritisation of ideology over expertise.
- The Cultural Revolution was a time of political unrest in China. **Red Guards** (students and soldiers) were used to attack old traditions and ideas. People were forced to learn from the masses and focus on political beliefs rather than skills. There was no room for discussion and debate.

Effect of Cultural Revolution

- The Cultural Revolution left China in a state of confusion and uncertainty. It weakened the Communist Party, severely disturbed the economy and educational system, and weakened social bonds and harmony.

---

8 Socialist A socialist is a person who believes that society, instead of private companies, should own or control important goods and services.

- From the late 1960s, the government emphasised the need for better social behaviour and a strong industrial economy to make China a powerful country by the year 2000.

Reforms in China from 1978

- **Deng Xiaoping**, a powerful leader, kept the Communist Party in control but also introduced a new economic system.
- He declared the **Four Modernisations** (science, industry, agriculture and defence) as the party's goals in 1978.
- The post-Cultural Revolution era witnessed an exciting inflow of new ideas, similar to the May Fourth Movement.
- The Fifth Modernisation poster, which appeared on 5th December, 1978, argued that democracy was essential for achieving the other goals of modernisation, such as science, industry, agriculture and defense. It criticised the Communist Party for its failure to address poverty and sexual exploitation.
- Many intellectuals called for greater transparency and an end to **ossified dogmas** (*su shaozhi*), which referred to fixed principles. These calls for reform gained momentum in 1989, on the 70th anniversary of the May Fourth Movement.
- Students demonstrated at Tiananmen Square in Beijing, demanding political reforms. However, the protests were brutally suppressed by the government, leading to widespread criticism around the world.

Post-reform Period in China

- The post-reform period in China witnessed various debates on the best path for development. The dominant view, supported by the Communist Party, emphasised strong political control, economic liberalisation, and integration into the global market.
- The critics questioned the excessive focus on the market, highlighting the growing inequalities between social groups, regions and genders, which were contributing to social tensions.
- There was a re-emergence of interest in traditional Confucian ideas, with some arguing that China could achieve modernisation by following its own cultural traditions rather than blindly copying the West.

Quick Test 3

1. Who were Kang Youwei and Liang Qichao?
2. What was San Min chui?
3. In which year was the Great Leap Forward Movement launched?
4. Who launched the Great Proletarian Cultural Revolution?
5. Mention any one reform in China from 1978.

7.4 Modernisation in Japan and China

China and Japan, instead of becoming like each other, have found their own paths to become modern. The histories of China and Japan reveal how different historical conditions led them into contrasting paths and build themselves as independent and modern nations.

Japan's Path to Modernisation

- Japan successfully maintained its independence and included traditional skills and practices into its modernisation efforts.
- The modernisation in Japan was led by a small group of powerful people. This led to a strong sense of nationalism and a government that did not allow people to disagree.

- Japan's past as a colonial power caused problems at home and abroad. Although Japan learned from Western powers, it also tried to find its own solutions.
- There were two contrasting perspectives on Japanese nationalism
  (i) **Liberation of Asia** Many Japanese hoped to liberate Asia from Western domination.
  (ii) **Imperial Expansion** Others justified Japan's imperial ambitions as a means to assert its power and influence.

Japanese Way of Transformation

- The changes in Japan were not just about bringing back old traditions. They also involved finding new ways to use these traditions. For example, the Meiji school system was based on European and American ideas, but it also taught Japanese students to be loyal to the emperor.
- The changes in Japanese family life and daily routines show how foreign and Japanese ideas were mixed together. These changes were not just a return to old ways but a new way of using traditions in a modern society.

China's Path to Modernisation

- China's path to modernisation was different from that of other countries. The foreign imperialism and a weak Qing dynasty led to social and political problems. These problems included fighting, stealing and natural disasters, which made life very difficult.
- China changed a lot in the 19th and 20th centuries. People rejected old ways of life and wanted a new and strong China.
- The Communist Party wanted to end poverty and make women equal. They promised a better future, but the government was very strict.
- They made China's economy better, but there are still problems like inequality and lack of freedom. China's journey to become modern has been difficult and has both good and bad parts.

7.5 The Story of Taiwan

- **Taiwan** was a **Japanese colony** from 1895 until the end of World War II. The ***Cairo Declaration*** (1943) and the ***Potsdam Proclamation*** (1949) restored sovereignty to China. However, the Chinese Civil War resulted in the defeat of the Guomindang (GMD) by the Communist Party, leading to the establishment of the **People's Republic of China** in mainland China.
- Chiang Kai-shek and his followers retreated to Taiwan, where they established the **Republic of China**.
- In February 1947, massive demonstrations in Taiwan led to the formation of the GMD, a political party.
- Under Chiang Kai-shek's strict government, free speech and political opposition were not allowed, and local people were kept out of power. However, the GMD did make land reforms that helped farming and modernised the economy.
- By 1973, **Taiwan's Gross National Product** (GNP) ranked second in Asia, following Japan. The country's economy, heavily dependent on trade, continued to grow steadily. The gap between the rich and poor began to decline, indicating a more equal distribution of wealth.

Transformation of Taiwan into Democracy

- The transformation process of Taiwan to a democracy started slowly after the death of Chiang in 1975.
- It became stronger when martial law was lifted in 1987 and opposition parties were allowed to exist legally.

- The local Taiwanese were brought to power by the first free elections. As Taiwan is considered as part of China, full diplomatic relations and embassies are not possible in Taiwan. Therefore, most countries have only trade missions with it.

Reunification of Taiwan

- The reunification of Taiwan with mainland China remains a complex and unresolved issue. Although relations between China and Taiwan have improved, with more trade and travel between them, China believes that Taiwan should be part of China again.
- China would only allow Taiwan to have some control over its own government if Taiwan agreed to be part of China.

7.6 The Story of Korea

Beginning of Modernisation

- After years of political interference, imperial Japan took control of Korea as its colony in 1910 by defeating the **Joseon Dynasty** (1392-1910).

▲ *Koreans celebrate their Independence from Japan in 1945*

- The Korean people were upset by Japan's suppression of their culture and the forced efforts to make them adopt Japanese ways. They protested around the country against colonial rule and set up a provisional government. They also sent delegations to appeal to foreign leaders at different international meetings held in Cairo, Yalta and Potsdam Conferences.
- The Japanese colonial rule ended after 35 years in August 1945, after Japan was defeated in the Second World War.
- After liberation, the Korean Peninsula was temporarily divided along the **38th parallel** with the Soviets managing the North and the UN managing the South. This division became permanent as separate governments were established in both North and South Korea in 1948.

The Korean War

- The Korean War began in June 1950 when South Korea received support from the United Nations forces led by the United States, while North Korea was supported by communist China.
- The Korean War became a proxy war of the Cold War era. The war ended in July 1953 with an **armistice agreement**, but the Korean Peninsula remained divided.

Effects of the Korean War

- The Korean War resulted in massive casualties and property damage.
- The war delayed the development of a free-market economy in South Korea.
- Increased national expenses and currency issuance during the war led to inflation and rising prices.
- Industrial facilities built during the colonial period were severely damaged or destroyed.
- South Korea became heavily dependent on economic assistance from the United States.

Unrest in South Korea

- Following the Korean War, **Syngman Rhee** was elected president in 1948, but his administration was marked by political instability and public dissatisfaction.
- The **rigged election**[9] of 1960 led to the April Revolution, which forced Rhee to resign. However, the new Democratic Party government could not meet the people's demands because of internal conflicts.

9 **Rigged election** It involves illegal interference with the process of an election.

- Reform movements and student protests grew stronger, but military authorities opposed them.
- Eventually, a military **coup**[10] led by **General Park Chung-hee** overthrew the Democratic Party government in May 1961, marking a major change in South Korean politics.

Rapid Industrialisation under Strong Leadership

- Park Chung-hee became President in 1963 and introduced a government-led economic policy which focused on exports to boost South Korea's economic growth.
- The government focused on supporting large corporations, expanding employment opportunities, and enhancing the country's competitiveness.
- Korea's economic strategy shifted from Import Substitution Industrialisation (ISI) to a focus on exports.
- Initially, the government supported labour-intensive light industries like textiles and garments. In the late 1960s and 1970s, the focus shifted to value-added heavy and chemical industries, such as steel, non-ferrous metals, machinery, shipbuilding, electronics and chemical production.

The New Village (*Saemaul*) Movement

- The New Village Movement, launched in 1970, aimed to empower rural communities and modernise the agricultural sector in South Korea.
- By encouraging and mobilising rural people to participate in the development of their villages, the movement aimed to improve living conditions and promote rural development.
- Later, the scope of the New Village Movement expanded to include urban areas and neighbourhoods near industrial plants, reflecting its broader impact on South Korean society.

Factors Contributing to South Korea's Economic Growth

- Korea benefited from strong leadership, well-trained bureaucrats and a capable workforce. Ambitious entrepreneurs responded positively to government incentives, increasing exports and developing new industries.
- Korea's high literacy rate and educated workforce facilitated its economic development.
- Korea's open economic policy allowed for the absorption of advanced institutions and technologies from other countries.
- Foreign investment and high domestic savings rates contributed to the development of the heavy industrial sector. **Remittances**[11] from South Korean workers overseas also provided a boost to the overall economy.

Continued Economic Growth and Calls for Democratisation

- In October 1972, Park Chung-hee introduced the **Yusin Constitution**. This made the presidency permanent and gave the president complete control over laws and government. The Constitution also allowed the president to amend any law as an **emergency measure**.
- Korea faced **a second oil crisis** in 1979 due to overinvestment in the heavy chemical industry.
- Students, scholars and opposition groups demonstrated against the Yusin Constitution, expressing their disagreement with Park Chung-hee's authoritarian rule.
- In October 1979, the Park administration came to an end with Park Chung-hee assassination.
- Chun Doo-hwan's administration successfully raised economic growth rates from 1.7% in 1980 to 13.2% in 1983. This impressive growth was accompanied by a significant reduction in inflation.
- In December 1979, a military coup led by Chun-Doo-hwan was organised. In May 1980, students and citizens of many cities demanded democracy. The military crushed the democracy movement. This movement for democracy is known as the **Gwangju Movement** as it was mainly developed in **Gwangju city**.

---

10 Coup A sudden, illegal and often violent change of government.

11 Remittance It is the money that is sent to the family or friends by a migrant worker.

- This movement was crushed and Chun became the president through an indirect election under the Yusin Constitution.
- The economic development fostered by the Chun administration led to improvements in education, living standards and media advancements. As a result, the public became more aware of their political rights.

Korean Democracy

- The death of a university student by torture in May 1987 led a large-scale pro-democracy movement in South Korea.
- The government's refusal to conduct a proper investigation into the incident increased public anger and strengthened the movement.

▲ *Demonstrators during the June Democracy Movement of 1987*

- Students and the middle class actively participated in the **June Democracy Movement**, demanding political reforms.
- The growing pressure from the public forced the Chun Doo-hwan's administration to amend the Constitution, allowing for direct presidential elections.

The Strengthening of Democracy in South Korea

- The first direct presidential election in South Korea was held in December 1987, marking a significant milestone in the country's transition to democracy. Military leader **Roh Tae-woo** was elected President.
- In 1990, Roh Tae-woo's party and the opposition party led by Kim Young-sam formed a large ruling party, demonstrating a commitment to cooperation and democratic principles.
- Kim Young-sam's election as President in 1992 further solidified democracy in South Korea. His presidency marked the end of decades of military rule and led to a new era of civilian leadership.

Administration under Kim

- Kim Young-sam's government continued to focus on exporting products, which helped Korean companies become successful worldwide. The government focused on building up heavy and chemical industries, as well as electronics, to enhance the country's economic competitiveness.
- In 1996, under increasing pressure for neoliberal reforms, South Korea joined the **Organisation for Economic Cooperation and Development** (OECD). This membership required the country to further open its markets and strengthen its international competitiveness.
- Due to rising trade deficits, poor management by financial institutions, and reckless business operations by conglomerates, South Korea faced a foreign currency crisis in 1997. The country received emergency financial support from the International Monetary Fund (IMF) to address the crisis.
- In response to the crisis, the government implemented various reforms to improve the country's economic constitution. Citizens actively contributed to foreign loan repayment through the **Gold Collection Movement**.

Presidents of Korea

- In December 1997, Kim Dae-jung was elected as the President.
- In 2008, conservative Lee Myung-bak was elected as the President, following the progressive Roh Mu-hyun administration.
- In 2012, conservative **Park Geun-hye** was elected as the **first female President**. She was the daughter of Park Chung-hee. At first she got support from the people, but in October 2016, she faced nationwide protest, which led to her impeachment and removal from office in March 2017.
- In May 2017, Moon Jae-in was elected as the President.

Quick Test 4

1. Why did Chiang Kai-shek flee to Taiwan in 1949?
2. Which countries exerted increasing foreign pressure on Korea during the late 19th century?
3. In which year was the New Village (Saemaul) Movement introduced?
4. What was the key political event that helped solidify Park's power in 1972?

TIMELINE

Year	Event
Japan	
1603	Tokugawa Ieyasu established the Edo shogunate
1630	Japan closed its country to Western Powers except for restricted trade with the Dutch
1854	Japan and the USA concluded the Treaty of Peace, ending Japan's seclusion.
1868	Restoration of Meiji.
1872	Compulsory education system. First railway line between Tokyo and Yokohama.
1889	Meiji Constitution was enacted
1894-95	War between Japan and China
1904-05	War between Japan and Russia
1910	Korea was annexed, remaining a colony until 1945
1914-18	First World War
1925	Universal male suffrage
1931	Japan's invasion of China
1941-45	The Pacific War
1945	Atomic bombs dropped on Hiroshima and Nagasaki
1946-52	US-led occupation of Japan. Reforms to democratise and demilitarise Japan
1956	Japan becomes a member of the United Nations
1964	Olympic Games were held in Tokyo, the first time in Asia
China	
1644-1911	Qing dynasty
1839-60	Two Opium Wars
1912	Sun Yat-sen founded Guomindang
1919	May Fourth Movement
1921	Chinese Communist Party (CCP) founded
1926-49	Civil Wars in China
1934	Long March
1949	People's Republic of China established. Chiang Kai-shek founded the Republic of China in Taiwan
1962	China attacked India over the border dispute
1966	Cultural Revolution
1976	Death of Mao Zedong and Zhou Enlai
1997	Hong Kong was returned to China by Britain

Mind Map

PATHS TO MODERNISATION

1 Japan

The Political System in Japan
- Between 1603 to 1867, members of Tokugawa family held the position of Shogun.
- Country was divided into 250 domains under the powerful feudal lord called Daimyo.
- Samurai was the warrior class, who served to both Shogun and Daimyo.
- Land survey helped in identification of owner and land productivity.

Daily Life in Japan and Overcoming Modernity
- Nuclear family system replaced the joint family system.
- Philosopher 'Nishitani Keiji' argued that Japan's moral energy helped it to escape colonisation.

Japan's Re-emergence as a Global Economic Power
- Japan's aim to establish colonial empire was destroyed by bombardment at Hiroshima and Nagasaki.
- Japan was demilitarised by US led operations and a new constitution with 'no war clause' was adopted.

Views of Japanese Intellectuals on Relations of Japan with Other Countries
- Fukuzawa Yukichi expressed that Japan must shed its Asian characterstics and become part of the West.
- Some philosophers emphasised that Japan's political system should be based upon democracy only.

The Meiji Restoration by Perry in Japan
- USA sent Matthew Perry to open diplomatic and trade relations with Japan.
- In 1868, a movement removed the Shogun from power and made the 'Edo' as capital, later renamed to 'Tokyo'.
- Government launched a policy with slogan 'Fukoku Kyohei', meaning rich country, strong army.
- Meiji Constitution was based upon restricted franchise.

Reforms for Modernising Economy
- Modernisation fund was raised through levying agricultural tax.
- Japan's first railway line was between Tokyo & Port Yokohama.
- Government encouraged migration of population to newer areas of Japan.
- Number of workshops increased to 5,50,000 by 1940.

2 China

Republican Revolution
- Sun Yat Sen overthrew Manchu empire and established the foundation of modern China.
- Guomindang (The National People's Party) and CCP emerged as major parties which united the country.

The Rise of Chinese Communist Party
- CCP was based upon the ideas of Russian Revolution and it was founded in 1921.
- Mao Zedong emerged as a major leader and followed a radical approach.
- Mao simplified marriage laws and encouraged rural women's association.

Establishing the New Democracy: 1949-65
- People's Republic of China government was established in 1949, which followed 'New Democracy Principle'.
- Great leap forward movement launched in 1958 to encourage rapid industrialisation.
- Mao launched the Great Proletarian Revolution to suppress dissent among party and society.

Reforms in China from 1918
- Deng Xiaopings introduced economic reforms.
- Fifth modernisation (call for democracy) was suppressed in Tianenmen protest of 1989.
- Economic liberalisation encouraged growth but widened inequalities.
- Traditional ideas of Confucianism was revived.

The Story of Taiwan
- In 1949, Chiang Kai-Shek fled to China after defeated by CCP.
- Land reforms and modernisation boosted Taiwan's economy, making its economy second only to Japan in Asia by 1973.
- Taiwan transitioned to democracy after Chiang's death in 1975.

3 The Story of Korea

Beginning of Modernisation and a Post War Nation
- Japan annexed Korea in 1910 and ended its colonial rule in August 1945.
- 38th parallel divided North and South Korea.
- During Korea war of 1950, North Korea was supported by USSR & China while South Korea by US led forces.

Korean Democracy & IMF Crises
- South Korea transitioned to democracy with 1987 elections.
- The 1997 financial crises led to IMF support and national efforts in Korea.

NCERT Folder

Intext Questions

1. Contrast the encounter of the Japanese and the Aztecs with the Europeans.

Ans. Encounter of the Japanese with the Europeans
Japanese encountered with Portuguese first among Europeans. The only Western country with which Japan traded was Holland. They knew about the British establishment of colonies in their neighbourhood. Rather than ignoring European ideas, they wanted to learn them and adopt the new technologies offered by the Europeans. They imported textile machinery from Europe.

Encounter of the Aztecs with the Europeans
The encounter of Aztecs with the Europeans was not good. Aztecs after giving shelter to Spaniards, thought that they gave shelter to a monster. Spaniards fought against Aztecs and destroyed their villages and killed their people. Spaniards conquered Mexico by defeating Aztecs in two years and established their colony there.

2. Would you agree with Nishitani's definition of 'modern'?

Ans. The philosopher Nishitani Keiji defined 'modern' as the unity of three ideas of Western thought i.e. the Renaissance, the Protestant Reformation and the rise of natural sciences.

I would not agree with everything about Nishitani's definition of modern. For example, if we take India, as early as in Gupta period, our scientists had invented zero, formulated many mathematics theorems, proved that Sun being centre of the universe and Earth rotating on its own axis.

If we take China, it was aware of printing technology long before Western people knew about it. In fact most of the Westerners learnt many things from Indians, Chinese and Arabs. So, modernity is not just unity of three ideas of Western thought.

3. Does this painting give you a clear sense of the significance of the Opium War?

Ans. The painting does not give a clear sense, but it gives a rough idea about the significance of the Opium War. It provides us with basic knowledge that British fought Opium wars against Chinese in order to solve their balance of trade problems. From the painting we can make out that, British destroyed Chinese ships and defeated them in the war, forcing their terms and conditions on Chinese and dominating it.

4. How does a sense of discrimination unite people?

Ans. The sense of discrimination unites people. It is true and this can be proved with numerous examples from the history. Some of them were

- When third estate people were discriminated in France, it led to the unity of the common people and revolt against the kings, nobles and clergy leading to French Revolution.
- In India, when soldiers were discriminated against their British counterparts, it led to the India's First War of Independence in 1857.

The reasons behind unity of people when there is discrimination were

- Discrimination gives rise to a common cause among the people. It creates a common enemy for the oppressed people. Thus, they unite together to fight the common enemy.
- Discrimination promotes inhuman practices like black's segregation in USA or apartheid in South Africa or untouchability in India. To fight for justice and to gain dignity, the people who are affected get united to get back their legitimate rights.

Answer in Brief

1. What were the major developments before the Meiji restoration that made it possible for Japan to modernise rapidly?

Ans. The major developments before the Meiji restoration that made it possible for Japan to modernise rapidly were

- Peasantry were disarmed and only *Samurai* were allowed to carry swords. This ensured peace and order.
- The *Daimyo* were ordered to live in capitals of their domains, each with a large degree of autonomy.
- Land surveys identified owners and taxpayers and graded land productivity to ensure a stable revenue base.
- The *Daimyo's* capitals became bigger and cities of Japan became some of the most populated in the world.

- Individual's merit was valued more than his status.
- Culture of patronising theatre and the arts started. People started reading extensively.
- Silk industry was developed in Nishijin. Stock market was created.
- Social and intellectual changes like study of ancient Japanese literature, helped Japanese to feel proud about their history.

2. Discuss how daily life was transformed as Japan developed.

Ans. Japan's transformation into a modern society can be seen also in the changes in everyday life in the following ways

- The patriarchal household system compromised many generations living together under the control of the head of the house, but as more people became affluent, new ideas of the family spread.
- Nuclear family became prevalent, where husband and wife lived as breadwinner and homemaker respectively. This new concept of domesticity in turn generated demands for new types of domestic goods, new types of family entertainment and new forms of housing.

3. How did the Qing dynasty try and meet the challenge posed by the Western powers?

Ans. The Qing dynasty tried to meet the challenges posed by Western powers by establishing a new administrative system, setting up local assemblies, sending students abroad and protesting against Western missionaries, etc.

However, the Qing dynasty could not meet the challenges posed by the Western powers. It demanded for reforms but its position weakened after Opium War (1839-42). This was the failure of Qing dynasty which led to the emergence of Civil War in China.

4. What were Sun Yat-sen's three principles?

Ans. Sun Yat-sen's three principles were as follows

(i) **Nationalism** Overthrowing the Manchu who were seen as a foreign dynasty, as well as other foreign imperialists.

(ii) **Democracy** Establishing democratic government.

(iii) **Socialism** Regulating capital and equalising landholdings.

5. How did Korea deal with the foreign currency crisis in 1997?

Ans. Korea faced a foreign currency crisis in 1997, due to increasing trade deficits, poor management by financial institution and reckless business operations by corporations. The crisis was dealt through emergency financial supports provided by the International Monetary Fund (IMF).

To improve the country's economic condition simultaneous efforts were also made by the citizens. They actively contributed towards foreign loan repayment through the Gold Collection Movement.

Answer in a Short Essay

6. Did Japan's policy of rapid industrialisation lead to wars with its neighbours and destruction of the environment?

Ans. It is true that Japan's policy of rapid industrialisation led to wars with its neighbours and destruction of the environment.

Effects on Relations with Neighbours were as follows

Japan government launched its new policy 'Fukoku–Kyohei' meaning rich country and strong army. To achieve this, it started rapid industrialisation policy.

Japan followed closed economy approach for 250 years. It was only after Meiji restoration that Japan adopted the open economy approach and Japan was modernised in all sectors including transportation, education, administration, communication and industrialisation.

Japan become highly developed in first half of 20th century. As Japan became highly industrialised it also entered into a race of imperialism in order to meet its increasing demands for raw material and market.

Increasing aspiration for imperialism resulted in war with China in 1894 and with Russia (1904-1905).

Effects on Environment were as follows

The demand for raw material used in industries resulted in exploitation of natural resources. In this way, industrialisation had an adverse impact on the environment also.

Further Japan's emphasis on industrialisation affected the environment as cadmium poisoning and mercury poisoning in minamata were some of the effects of the rapid industrialisation.

7. Do you think that Mao Zedong and the Communist Party of China were successful in liberating China and laying the basis for its current success?

Ans. Yes, I think that Mao Zedong and the Communist Party of China were successful in liberating China and laying the basis for its current success. It was done in the following ways

- The Communist Party of China (CCP) was founded in 1921. Mao Zedong emerged as a major CCP leader who based his revolutionary programme on the peasantry.
- Mao's success made the CCP a powerful political force that ultimately won against the Guomindang. A strong peasants' council was organised united through confiscation and redistribution of land.

- Mao also stressed the need for an independent government and army. He also supported rural women's associations.
- In 1949, the Peoples Republic of China government was established. It was based on the principles of the New Democracy i.e. an alliance of all social classes.
- Under Mao Leadership, the Great Leap Forward Movement was launched in 1958 and through it the country was united to industrialise rapidly.
- People were encouraged to set up steel furnaces in their backyards. In the rural areas, people's communes were started. Mao was able to mobilise the masses to attain the goals set by the Party.

Thus, we can see that, the present status of China as one of the leading global powers is due to the foundations laid by Mao Zedong in early period.

8. Did economic growth in South Korea contribute to its democratisation?

Ans. During the Chun administration economy grew remarkably. It grew from 1.7 per cent in 1980 to 13.2 per cent by 1983. At that time inflation also became low. This economic growth has contributed to democratisation in the following ways

- It led to urbanisation in Korea.
- It improved education levels of the citizens.
- It caused media advancements.
- It helped to grow citizen's self awareness about political rights.
- It resulted into demands for a constitutional amendment. The Chun administration was forced to make a revision to the Constitution which allowed direct elections. With this amendment a new Chapter of Korean democracy began.

Exam Pattern Questions

Objective Type Questions

Multiple Choice Questions (MCQs)

1. At the beginning of the 19th century East Asia was dominated by ....

(a) Japan (b) China (c) Russia (d) England

2. Who is considered as the greatest historian of early China?

(a) Sima Qian (b) Liang Qichao
(c) Kume Kunitake (d) Mateo Ricci

3. The term Fukoku-kyohei means

(a) rich country (b) strong army
(c) dictatorship (d) Both (a) and (b)

4. .... developed two phonetic alphabets *viz, hiragana* and *katakana*.

(a) Chinese (b) Japanese (c) Mongolian (d) Korean

5. When did male workers in Japan begin to outnumber women?

(a) After 1950s (b) After 1930s
(c) After 1890s (d) None of these

6. Who participated in the popular rights movement and launched the first agitation against industrial pollution in 1897?

(a) Tanaka Shozo (b) Mateo Ricci
(c) Naito Konan (d) None of these

7. After the Second World War, Japan rebuilt its economy and by the .... emerged as a major economic power.

(a) 1950s (b) 1960s
(c) 1970s (d) 1980s

8. Which of the following step (s) was/were taken to industrialise Japan?

(a) Foreign technicians were employed to train workers.
(b) Japanese students were sent abroad to learn new emerging skills.
(c) Textile and other machineries were imported from Europe.
(d) All of the above

9. When did the Chinese Communist Party emerge victorious from the Civil War?

(a) 1940 (b) 1945
(c) 1949 (d) 1950

10. The radical idea(s) proposed by Mao Zedong was/were

(a) stressed the need for an independent government and army.
(b) supported the emergence of rural women's associations.
(c) promulgated a new marriage law that forbade arranged marriages.
(d) All of the above

11. **The Long March in China was started in**

(a) 1940s (b) 1920s
(c) 1930s (d) None of these

12. **Consider the following statements and choose the correct option.**

I. Sima Qian (145-90BCE) is considered the greatest historian of early China.
II. Naito Konan was a leading Japanese scholar of Italy.
III. Osaka is the largest island of Japan.

Codes

(a) Only I (b) Only II
(c) Both I and II (d) All of these

13. **Consider the following statements and choose the correct option.**

I. The Japan Government launched a policy with the slogan Fukoku-Kyohei.
II. Japan imported luxury goods like silk from India and textiles from China.
III. Silk industries was developed in Tokyo.

Codes

(a) Only I (b) Only II
(c) Both I and II (d) All of these

14. **Arrange in sequence**

(i) Japan's invasion of China
(ii) The First World War
(iii) The Pacific War

Codes

(a) (ii), (i), (iii) (b) (i), (iii), (ii)
(c) (iii), (i), (ii) (d) (i), (ii), (iii)

15. **Identify the name of the scholar from the information given below.**

(i) He was a leading Japanese scholar of China.
(ii) He helped establish the Department of Oriental Studies in Kyoto University in 1907.
(iii) He saw in Chinese history strengths that would make it modern and democratic.
(iv) He thought that Japan had an important role to play in China but he underestimated the power of Chinese nationalism.

Options

(a) Sakuma Shozan (b) Naito Konan
(c) Takashi Higuchi (d) Katsu Kaishu

16. **Identify the name of the political figure from the information given below.**

(i) He was the self-taught son of a farmer.
(ii) He participated in the Popular Rights Movement in the 1880s, a movement demanding constitutional government.
(iii) He was elected member to the first diet.
(iv) He believed that ordinary people should not be sacrificed for industrial progress.

Options

(a) Hirohito (b) Toyotemi Hideyoshi
(c) Hideki Tojo (d) Tanaka Shozo

Assertion-Reason

17. Assertion (A) The Peoples Republic of China Government was established in 1949.

Reason (R) The Guomindang blockade of the communists Soviet forced the party to seek a base.

Codes

(a) Both A and R are true and R is the correct explanation of A
(b) Both A and R are true, but R is not the correct explanation of A
(c) A is true, but R is false
(d) A is false, but R is true

18. Assertion (A) Chiang Kai-shek defeated by the CCP fled in 1949 to Taiwan and established there the Republic of China.

Reason (R) Chiang Kai-shek wanted to establish 'New Democracy' in Taiwan.

Codes

(a) Both A and R are true and R is the correct explanation of A
(b) Both A and R are true, but R is not the correct explanation of A
(c) A is true, but R is false
(d) A is false, but R is true

Match the Following

19.

List I	List II
A. Sima Qian	1. Leading Japanese scholar of China
B. Naito Konan	2. Popular Rights Movement
C. Tanaka Shozo	3. Greatest historian of early China
D. Ueki Emori	4. Demanded Constitutional government in Japan

Codes

	A	B	C	D		A	B	C	D
(a)	3	1	2	4	(b)	2	3	1	4
(c)	2	1	3	4	(d)	4	2	1	3

20.

List I	List II
A. Sun Yat-sen	1. Life Weekly
B. Zao Taofen	2. Founder of Modern China
C. Lenin	3. Elected as first President of South-Korea
D. Syngman Rhee	4. Third International

Codes

	A	B	C	D		A	B	C	D
(a)	2	3	1	4	(b)	4	2	1	3
(c)	3	4	2	1	(d)	2	1	4	3

Picture Based Questions

21. What is the name of the ship depicted in the below image?

(a) Perry's ship
(b) Donald's ship
(c) Emperor ship
(d) Ship of coins

22. What does the below picture depict?

(a) Women's car pool
(b) European women
(c) Women in Europe's winters
(d) Women preparing for a play

23. Which of the following has been depicted in the below image?

(a) Korean War
(b) Boxer Rebellion
(c) Opium War
(d) Chinese Civil War

24. The first modern industrial strike in Japan shown in the image below was led by

(a) 1847 by automobile workers
(b) 1902 by coal miners
(c) 1886 by women industrial worker
(d) None of the above

25. The Long March shown in the image below launched in China aimed for

(a) popularisation of communist ideas in China under the Mao Zeadong.
(b) popularisation of democratic ideas in China under the Sun Yat-Sen.
(c) development of modern industrial base on the Capitalist ideals.
(d) None of the above

Answers

1. (b) China
2. (a) Sima Qian
3. (d) Both (a) and (b)
4. (b) Japanese
5. (b) After 1930s
6. (a) Tanaka Shozo
7. (c) 1970s
8. (d) All of the above
9. (c) 1949
10. (d) All of the above
11. (c) 1930s
12. (a) Only I
13. (a) Only I
14. (a) (ii), (i), (iii)
15. (b) Naito Konan
16. (d) Tanaka Shozo
17. (b) Both A and R are true, but R is not the correct explanation of A
18. (c) A is true, but R is false
19. (a)
20. (d)
21. (a) Perry's ship
22. (a) Women's car pool
23. (c) Opium War
24. (c) 1886 by women industrial worker
25. (a) Popularisation of communist ideas in China under Mao Zeadong.

Subjective Questions

Short Answer Type Questions

1. Discuss the vibrant culture of appreciating theatre and arts in Japan.

Ans. A vibrant culture emerged in the towns of Japan in the following ways

- The fast growing class of merchants enjoyed theatre and the arts.
- Gifted writers now could earn living solely by writing because people enjoyed reading.
- For instance in Edo, people could rent a book for the price of a noodles bowl which shows that reading had become popular and gives an idea into the scale of printing.
- Printing was done with woodblocks. The Japanese did not like the regularity of European printing.

2. What were the different thoughts of scholars on learning new ideas from Europe? What did the slogan 'Fukoku- kyohei' mean and what did Japanese need to achieve this?

Ans. Different thoughts of scholars on learning new ideas from European were as follows

Many scholars and leaders wanted to learn from the new ideas in Europe rather than ignore them as the Chinese were doing.

Others sought to exclude the Europeans even while being ready to adopt the new technologies they offered.

Some argued for a gradual and limited opening to the outer world.

Fukoku-kyohei A policy with the slogan fukoku-kyohei (rich country, strong army) was launched by the government, because it realised that they need to develop Japan's economy and build a strong army, otherwise they would be subjugated like India. To achieve this, they needed to create a sense of nationhood among the people and transform them into citizens from subjects.

3. Discuss the significance of the weavers' guild in Nishijin during the 16th century.

Ans. Nishijin is a quarter in Kyoto. In the 16th century, it had a weavers guild of 31 households. But by the end of 17th century, the community numbered over 70,000 people. Sericulture spread and was encouraged by an order in 1713 that only domestic yarn was to be used. Nishijin specialised only in the most expensive products. Silk production helped the growth of a class of regional entrepreneurs who challenged the Tokugawa order and when foreign trade started in 1859, Japan's silk exports became a major source of profit for the economy struggling to compete with Western goods. The silk from Nishijin came to be known as the best in the world.

4. Discuss the new school system in Japan.

Ans. The new school system in Japan was as following

- From the 1870s, the new school system had begun to be built in Japan.
- Schooling was made compulsory for boys and girls and by 1910 almost universal. Tuition fees was minimal.
- The curriculum was based on Western models. While there was an emphasis on modern ideas, stress was also placed on loyalty and the study of Japanese history.
- The Ministry of Education exercised control over the curriculum and in the selection of textbooks, as well as in teachers' training.

- Moral culture was taught and texts encouraged children to respect their parents, be loyal to the nation and become good citizens.

5. Who was Tanaka Shozo? Discuss his role in demanding a constitutional government in Japan.

Ans. Tanaka Shozo (1841-1913) was a son of a farmer who became a major political figure. He participated in the Popular Rights Movement in 1880s, a movement demanding constitutional government.

He was elected member to the first Diet Parliament. He believed that ordinary people should not be sacrificed for industrial progress.

He launched the first agitation against industrial pollution in 1897 with 800 villagers in a mass protest forcing the government to take action. The Ashio Mine (copper mine) was polluting the Watarase river ruining 100 square miles of farmland and affecting thousand of families. The agitation forced the company to take pollution-control measures so that by 1904 harvests were normal.

6. Discuss the increasing power of army in Japan.

Ans. The Japan government focused on increasing the power of the army as it realised that if they don't develop their economy and build strong army, they would face the prospect of being subjugated. From 1890s, the army and the navy had independent control. The emperor was the commander of the forces. In 1899, the Prime Minister ordered that only serving generals and admirals could become ministers.

The strengthening of the military, together with the expansion of Japan's colonial empire was connected with the fear that Japan was at the mercy of Western powers. This fear was used to silence opposition and military expanded and higher taxes were levied to fund the armed forces.

7. State-centered nationalism found full expression in the 1930s and 1940s. Discuss. **Competency Based Que**

Ans. In the 1930s and 1940s, state-centered nationalism was at its peak. Japan launched wars to extend its empire in China and other parts of Asia, leading to a war that merged into the Second World War after Japan attacked the USA at Pearl Harbour.

The government became stricter during this period. People who disagreed with the government were punished or put in jail. Patriotic groups, including many women's organisations, were formed to support the war. During this period, the size of factories also began to increase. Factories employing more than a hundred workers, just over 1000 in 1909, increased to over 4000 by the 1930s and there were 550,000 workshops in 1940s that employed less than five employees.

8. Was transformation of social and political institutions and daily life in Japan just about reviving traditions? Explain.

Ans. In Japan, the transformation of social and political institutions and daily life was not just about reviving traditions or carefully preserving them, but creatively using in new and different ways. For example, Meiji school system was based on European and American practices and introduced new subjects, but the main motto of the curriculum was to make citizens loyal.

A course on morals that laid importance on loyalty to the emperor was compulsory. Even changes in the family and daily life of Japanese, show how foreign and indigenous ideas were brought together to create something new.

9. What were the three changes brought in the late 16th century in Japan?

Ans. The three changes that were brought in Japan in the late 16th century were

- The peasantry was disarmed and only the *Samurai* could carry swords. This ensured peace and order.
- The *Daimyo* were ordered to live in the capitals of their domains, each with a large degree of autonomy.
- Land surveys identified owners and taxpayers and graded land productivity to ensure a stable revenue base.

10. Explain the 'emperor system' in Japan.

Ans. The new government in Japan built 'emperor system.' Japanese scholars used this term because emperor was part of the system, along with the bureaucracy and the military, that exercised the power. Officials were sent to study the European monarchies on which they planned to model their own system.

The emperor would be treated with respect as he was considered a direct descendant of the Sun Goddess. His birthday became a national holiday. He wore Western-style military uniforms and edicts were issued in his name to set up modern institutions.

11. The beginning of modern China can be traced to its first encounter with the West in 16th and 17th centuries. Discuss. **Competency Based Que**

Ans. The beginning of modern China can be traced to its first encounter with the West in the 16th and 17th centuries when Jesuit missionaries introduced Western sciences such as astronomy and mathematics. Though the immediate impact is limited, it led to events that gathered momentum in the 19th century. During this period, Britain used force to expand its profitable trade in opium leading to the first Opium War.

The 19th and 20th centuries saw a rejection of traditions and a search for ways to build national unity and strength. The CCP and its supporters wanted to end the tradition which kept the masses in poverty, the women subjugated and the country undeveloped.

12. What did Qing reformers do to introduce new ideas and institutions?

Ans. The Qing reformers had done several things to introduce new ideas and institution. These were

- Students were sent to study in Japan, Britain and France, to get trained in modern subjects and bring back new ideas.
- Many Chinese students went to Japan in the 1890s. They not only brought back new ideas but also became leading republicans.
- The Chinese borrowed even Japanese translations of European words such as justice, rights and revolution because they used the same ideographic script, a reversal of the traditional relationship.
- The centuries-old Chinese examination system that gave candidates entry into the elite ruling class was abolished.

13. What were the outcomes of the Cultural Revolution?

Ans. The outcomes of Cultural Revolution were as follows

- The Cultural Revolution led to the beginning of a period of crisis, weakened the Communist Party and severely disrupted the economy and educational system. From the late 1960s, the shift began to turn. In 1975, the Communist Party once again laid emphasis on greater social discipline and the need to build an industrial economy so that China could become a power before the end of the century.
- The Cultural Revolution was followed by a process of political changes. Deng Xiaoping kept party control strong while introducing a socialist market economy. In 1978, the party declared its goal as the Four Modernisations. They were to develop science, industry, agriculture and defence. Debate was allowed as long as the party was not questioned.

14. What was Fifth Modernisation? Describe about the Tiananmen Square incident.

Ans. **Fifth Modernisation** A wall poster appeared on 5th December 1978 in China. It declared that without democracy the other modernisations meant nothing.

It criticised the CCP for not solving the problem of poverty or ending sexual exploitation, even mentioned cases of such abuse from within the party.

Tiananmen Square Incident

In 1989, many intellectuals called for a greater transparency and an end to 'ossified dogmas' which means principles on the 70th anniversary of the May Fourth Movement. For this reason, students demonstrated at Tiananmen Square in Beijing and it was brutally oppressed. The incident was strongly criticized around the world.

15. What are the marked physical contrasts between China and Japan?

Ans. Difference between physical features of China and Japan are as follows

China	Japan Shade it
China is a large continental country that has many climatic zones.	Japan is a group of islands.
It is dominated by three important river systems i.e. the Yellow river (Huang He), the Yangtse river (Chang Jiang which is the third longest river in the world) and the Pearl river.	Honshu, Kyushu, Shikoku and Hokkaido are the four largest islands of Japan.
Large part of the country is mountainous.	More than half of the land area of main islands is mountainous.

16. "Chinese debates were marked by the views of three groups." Discuss. Competency Based Que

Ans. Chinese debates were marked by the views of three groups which were

- The early reformers such as Kang Youwei or Liang Qichao who tried to use traditional ideas in new and different ways to meet the challenges posed by the West.
- Republican revolutionaries such as Sun Yat- sen, the first President of the Republic, who were inspired by ideas from Japan and the West.
- The Communist Party of China which wanted to end age-old inequalities and drive out the foreigners.

17. What were the different views regarding the ways to develop China?

Ans. There were different views regarding the ways to develop China during the post-reform period. These were

- Strong political control, economic liberalisation and integration into the market were the dominant views supported by the party.
- Critics questioned the stress on the market and mentioned the growing inequalities between social groups, regions and men and women which were creating social tensions.
- There was a growing revival of earlier so-called traditional ideas of Confucianism. It was argued that China could build a modern society by following its own traditions, without imitating the West.

Long Answer Type Questions

1. What was the role of Meiji reform in modernising the Japan's economy? What were the demographic changes that happened in Japan due to economic reforms and Japanese government's reaction to it?

Ans. The role of Meiji reforms in modernising the Japan's economy were as follows

- Funds were raised by levying an agricultural tax for investing in the other sectors of economy.
- Japan's first railway line between Tokyo and the port of Yokohama was built in 1870-72.
- Textile machinery was imported from Europe and foreign technicians were employed to train workers, as well as to teach in universities and schools, and Japanese students were sent abroad.
- In 1872, modern banking institutions were launched.
- Companies like Mitsubishi and Sumitomo were helped through subsidised and tax benefits to become major shipbuilders, so that Japanese trade was from now carried in Japanese ships.

Demographic Changes in Japan

The demographic changes also happened in Japan due to economic changes. The population was 35 million in 1872 and it increased to 55 million in 1920. Within Japan, there was a shift to towns as industry developed. By 1925, around 21 per cent of the population lived in cities and in 1935, it went up to 35 per cent.

Reaction of Japanese Government

To reduce the population pressure, the government actively encouraged migration. First, they were sent to Northern island of Hokkaido which was largely an autonomous area where the indigenous people called the Ainu lived. Then, they were sent to Hawaii and Brazil and other areas of colonial empire of Japan.

2. "The Guomindang despite its attempt to unite the country failed." Look at the statement and discuss about the role of Sun Yat-sen and Chiang Kai-shek. Why did Guomindang fail to unite the country? **Competency Based Que**

Ans. Role of Sun Yat-Sen

In 1911, republic was established under Sun Yat-sen. He was regarded as the founder of modern China. He introduced a programme called Three Principles. They were nationalism, democracy and socialism.

Sun Yat-sen's ideas became the foundation for the political philosophy of the Guomindang. They identified the 'four great needs' as clothing, food, housing and transportation.

Role of Chiang Kai-shek

After the death of Sun Yat-sen, Chiang Kai-shek emerged as the leader of the Guomindang. He launched a military campaign to control the warlords, regional leaders who had taken over authority forcibly and to eliminate the Communists. Chiang supported a secular and rational ' this-worldly' Confucianism, but also sought to militarise the nation. He urged people to develop habit and instinct for unified behaviour. He encouraged women to cultivate the four virtues i.e. purity, appearance, speech and work and recognised their role as confined to the household.

Guomindang Failed to Unite the Country

The Guomindang despite attempting to unite the country failed to do so because of its narrow social base and limited political vision.

The Guomindang social base was in urban areas. Industrial growth was slow and limited. Only small people were employed in modern industries such as shipbuilding. Most of the people in towns were petty urbanites, traders and shopkeepers. Urban workers, especially women earned very low wages. Working hours were long and conditions of work were bad.

A major principle in Sun Yat-sen's programme i.e. regulating capital and equalising land, was never carried out because the Guomindang party ignored the peasantry and the rising social inequalities. It sought to impose military order rather than address the problems faced by the people.

3. "Japan and China, the two industrial societies far from becoming like each other have found their own paths to becoming modern." Look at the statement and discuss in detail about the paths took by both the countries to achieve modernisation. **Competency Based Que**

Ans. Japan was successful in retaining its independence and using traditional skills and practices in new ways. But its elite-driven modernisation generated an aggressive nationalism. It helped sustain a repressive regime that suppressed dissent and demands for democracy. It established a colonial empire that left a legacy of hatred in the region as well as changed internal developments.

Japan's programme of modernisation was carried out in an environment dominated by Western imperial powers. While it imitated them, it also attempted to find its own solutions. Japanese nationalism was marked by these different compulsions. Many Japanese hoped to liberate Asia from Western domination, but for others, these ideas justified building an empire. Japan has modernised itself without losing its traditions. It used creative, new and different ways to preserve these traditions.

On the other hand, Chinese path to modernisation was very different from Japan. Foreign imperialism and a weak dynasty, weakened the government control and resulted in breakdown of political and social order. Warlordism, banditry, civil war, Japanese invasion and natural disasters took a heavy toll on Chinese. During 19th and 20th centuries, the Communist Party of China and its supporters fought to put an end to traditions, which they thought were responsible for country being undeveloped. On one side, they called for power to the people, but built a highly centralised state. The Communist Party successfully removed centuries-old inequalities, spread education and raised consciousness among the people. The party has later carried out market reforms and successfully made China economically powerful.

4. Discuss Chiang Kai-shek's role in Taiwan and the transformation of Taiwan that took place after the death of Chiang Kai-shek. What are the dynamics of relationship between China and Taiwan?

Ans. Role of Chiang Kai-shek in Taiwan

In 1949, Chiang Kai-shek was defeated by the Communist Party, thus he fled to Taiwan with over US $300 million in gold reserves and packs of priceless art treasures and established the Republic of China.

The Guomindang under Chiang Kai-shek established a repressive government which banned free speech and political opposition. It also excluded local population from high positions. But they carried out land reforms which increased agricultural productivity and modernised the economy so that by 1973 Taiwan had Gross National Product second highest in Asia after Japan. The gap between the rich and poor was steadily declining.

Transformation of Taiwan

There was dramatic transformation of Taiwan into a democracy. It began after the death of Chiang in 1975 and gained speed when army law was removed in 1987 and opposition parties were legally permitted. The first free elections began the process of bringing local Taiwanese to power.

Relationship between China and Taiwan

Many countries have only trade missions in Taiwan. Full diplomatic relations and embassies are not possible as Taiwan is considered to be part of China. The question of re-unification of Taiwan with the mainland China remains a problematic issue but, relations between China and Taiwan have been improving. Taiwanese trade and investments in the mainland are massive and travel has become easier.

China's relationship with Taiwan will be good as long as Taiwan does not take up any move to gain independence.

5. What steps did Meiji government take to integrate the nation? What were the outcomes of those steps or measures ?

Ans. The steps or measures taken by Meiji Government to integrate the nation were as follows

- It imposed a new administrative structure by altering old village and domain boundaries. The administrative unit had to have adequate revenue to maintain local schools and health facilities, along with recruitment centre for the military.
- All young men over twenty had to do a period of military service. A modern military force was developed.
- A legal system was set up to regulate the formation of political groups, control the holding of meetings and impose strict censorship. In all these measures, the government had to face opposition.
- The military and the bureaucracy were put under the direct command of the emperor. This meant that even after a Constitution was enacted, these two groups remained outside the control of the government.

Outcomes of these measures were as follows

- Government faced opposition in all these measures.
- The army pressed for a vigorous foreign policy to acquire more territory which led to wars with China and Russia, and Japan won both of them.
- Japan developed economically and acquired a colonial empire that suppressed the spread of democracy at home and put it in collision with people it colonised.

6. "The rapid rebuilding of the Japanese economy after its shattering defeat was called a post-war miracle." Look at the statement and discuss in detail how Japan after getting defeated in Second World War bounced back to become an economic power? Competency Based Que

Ans. After getting defeated in Second World War, Japan revived its power by the following post-war changes:

- Under the US-led occupation (1945-47), Japan was demilitarised and a new Constitution was introduced. This had a no-war clause that renounces the use of war as an instrument of state policy.
- Agrarian reforms, the re-establishment of trade unions and an attempt to dismantle the *Zaibatsu* or large monopoly houses that dominated the Japanese economy were also carried out.
- Political parties were revived and the first post-war elections were held in 1946 where women voted for the first time.
- The Constitution was democratised. Japanese were inherently had a great tradition of popular struggles and intellectual engagement which broadened political participation.

- The social cohesion of the pre-war years was strengthened, allowing for a close working of the government, bureaucracy and industry. US support along with the demand created by the Korean and the Vietnamese wars also helped the Japanese economy.
- The 1964 Olympics held in Tokyo, showed how within 20 years Japan had rebuilt itself.
- Japan also built the network of high-speed Shinkansen or bullet trains which ran at 200 miles per hour in 1964 and now their speeds are around 300 miles per hour. This represents the ability of the Japanese to use advanced technologies to produce better and cheaper goods.

Today, Japan is one of the major powers of the world politically, economically and technologically. Thus, we can say that the rapid rebuilding of the Japanese economy after its shattering defeat was called a post-war miracle.

7. "Communists established themselves in power and the Guomindang was defeated." Explain. **Competency Based Que**

Ans. Communists rose to power in the following ways

- The Communist Party of China was founded in 1921 soon after the Russian Revolution. The Russian success had a powerful influence all around the world.
- Mao Zedong emerged as a prominent leader in the Communist Party. He followed a revolutionary programme which was based on the peasantry. In this attempt, he became successful and thus made the Communist Party a powerful political force which ultimately won against the Guomindang.
- Mao Zedong camped from 1928 to 1934 in Jiangxi region in the mountains to secure themselves from Guomindang attacks. He organised a strong peasants' council called Soviet. It was united through confiscation and redistribution of land.
- He was sympathetic to women's problems. He supported rural women's associations, introduced a new marriage law that did not allow arranged marriages, stopped purchase or sale of marriage contracts and simplified divorce.

Guomindanag was defeated in the following ways

- The defeat of Guomindang was started when it created a blockade against the Communists' Soviet. This forced communists to look for another base.
- Due to blockade, the communists led the famous Long March, a tiring journey of 6,000 miles to Shanxi. Here, the Communists formed a new base in Yanan and further developed their programme to end warlordism, carry out land reforms and fight foreign imperialism. This won Communists a strong social base.
- In the difficult years of the war, the Communists and the Guomindang worked together but after the end of the war, the Communists established themselves in power and the Guomindang was defeated.
- Finally, the Peoples Republic of China government was established in 1949 by the Communists.

Source Based Questions

1. Read the source given below and answer the following questions.

A fictionalised diary of the Heian court written by Murasaki Shikibu, the Tale of the Genji became the central work of fiction in Japanese literature. That period saw the emergence of many women writers, like Murasaki, who wrote in the Japanese script, while men wrote in the Chinese script, used for education and government. The novel depicts the romantic life of Prince Genji and is a striking picture of the aristocratic atmosphere of the Heian court. It shows the independence that women had in choosing their husbands and living their lives.

(i) Who wrote the Tale of the Genji? What was the novel about?

(ii) How does The Tale of Genji depict the Heian court's aristocratic atmosphere?

(iii) What was social message it had in it?

Ans. (i) Murasaki Shikibu wrote the Tale of the Genji. The novel depicts the romantic life of Prince Genji and was a striking picture of the aristocratic atmosphere of the Heian court.

(ii) The novel depicts the Heian court's aristocratic atmosphere through its detailed portrayal of courtly life, social interactions and romantic arrangements.

(iii) It showed the independence that women had in choosing their husbands and living their lives. This is a social message that novel gives.

2. Read the source given below and answer the following questions.

The Japanese had borrowed their written script from the Chinese in the 16th century. However, since their language is very different from Chinese they developed two phonetic alphabets – *hiragana* and *katakana*. *Hiragana* is considered feminine because it was used by many women writers in the Heian period (such as Murasaki). It is written using a mixture of Chinese characters and phonetics so that the main part of the word is written with a character – for instance, in 'going', 'go' would be written with a character and the 'ing' in phonetics.

The existence of a phonetic syllabary meant that knowledge spread from the elites to the wider society relatively quickly. In the 1880s, it was suggested that

Japanese develop a completely phonetic script, or adopt a European language. Neither was done.

(i) **What did Japanese borrow from Chinese? What did Japanese do to the script as their language was very different from Chinese?**

(ii) **Why was *hiragana* considered feminine? How was *hiragana* written?**

(iii) **What was the key difference between the Japanese language and Chinese that led to creation of *hiragana*?**

Ans. (i) The Japanese had borrowed their written script from the Chinese in the 16th century. Japanese language was very different from Chinese and so the Japanese developed two phonetic alphabets.

(ii) *Hiragana* was considered feminine because it was used by many women writers in the Heian period. *Hiragana* was written using a mixture of Chinese characters and phonetic symbols.

(iii) The key difference was that Japanese and Chinese were structurally very different languages, so the Japanese needed a more suitable system for writing their own language, which led to the creation of the phonetic alphabets, *hiragana* and *katakana*.

3. Read the source given below and answer the following questions.

Fukuzawa Yukichi (1835-1901)

Born in an impoverished samurai family, he studied in Nagasaki and Osaka learning Dutch and Western sciences and later, English. In 1860, he went as a translator for the first Japanese embassy to the USA. This provided material for a book on the West, written not in the classical but in the spoken style that became extremely popular. He established a school that is today the Keio Univeristy. He was one of the core members of the Meirokusha, a society to promote Western learning.

In the Encouragement to Learning (*Gakumon no susume*, 1872-76) he was very critical of Japanese knowledge: ' All that Japan has to be proud of is its scenery'. He advocated not just modern factories and institutions but the cultural essence of the West-the spirit of civilisation. With this spirit it would be possible to build a new citizen. His principle was: 'Heaven did not create men above men, nor set men below men.'

(i) **What was Fukuzawa Yukichi's background before becoming a prominent individual?**

(ii) **Where did Yukichi work first? How was he related to Meirokusha?**

(iii) **What was Yukichi critical about and what was his principle?**

Ans. (i) Fukuzawa Yukichi was born into an impoverished samurai family. Despite being from a humble background, he studied in Nagasaki and Osaka, learning Dutch, Western sciences and later English.

(ii) Yukichi went as a translator for the first Japanese embassy to the USA.

Meirokusha was a society to promote Western learning and Yukichi was one of the core members of this society.

(iii) Yukichi was critical about Japanese knowledge and even said that Japan has to be proud of only its scenery. Yukichi's principle was 'Heaven did not create men above men, nor set men below men.'

4. Read the source given below and answer the following questions.

Moga : An abbreviation for 'modern girl'. It represented the coming together in the 20th century of ideas of gender equality, a cosmopolitan culture and a developed economy. The new middle-class families enjoyed new forms of travel and entertainment. Transport in cities improved with electric trams, public parks were opened from 1878, and department stores began to be built.

In Tokyo, the Ginza became a fashionable area for *Ginbura*, a word combining 'Ginza' and 'burbura' (walking aimlessly). The first radio stations opened in 1925. Matsui Sumako, an actress, became a national star with her portrayal of Nora in the Norwegian writer Ibsen's A Doll's House. Movies began to be made in 1899 and soon there were a dozen companies making hundreds of films. The period was one of great vitality and the questioning of traditional norms of social and political behaviour.

(i) **How did the middle-class families enjoy modern life in early 20th century Japan?**

(ii) **What became fashionable in Tokyo? Who was Matsui Sumako?**

(iii) **Why was this period of great importance?**

Ans. (i) New middle-class families enjoyed new forms of travel, entertainment and improved urban infrastructure trams as electric trans and departmental stores which reflected the growth of Japan's economy and modernisation.

(ii) In Tokyo, the Ginza became a fashionable area for *Ginbura*, a word combining *Ginza* and *burbura* (walking aimlessly).

Matsui Sumako was an actress. She became a national star after she was portrayed as Nora in Ibsen's A Doll's House.

(iii) This period was of great importance because there was questioning of traditional norms of social and political behaviour. Movies began to be made during this period and soon there was a dozen of companies making hundreds of films.

5. Read the source given below and answer the following questions.

Entry to the elite ruling class (about 1.1 million till 1850) had been largely through an examination. This required writing an eight-legged essay [pa-ku wen] in classical Chinese in a prescribed form. The examination was held twice every three years, at different levels and of those allowed to sit only 1-2 per cent passed the first level, usually by the age of 24, to become what was called 'beautiful talent'. At any given time before 1850 there were about 526,869 civil and 212,330 military provincial (*sheng-yuan*) degree holders in the whole country.

Since there were only 27,000 official positions, many lower-level degree holders did not have jobs. The examination acted as a barrier to the development of science and technology as it demanded only literary skills. In 1905, it was abolished as it was based on skills in classical Chinese learning that had, it was felt, no relevance for the modern world.

(i) How could one enter elite ruling class? What did exam contain?

(ii) What was the number of degree holders in the whole country before 1850 and why they did not have jobs?

(iii) What was the defect in the examination and how it was corrected?

Ans. (i) The entry into the elite ruling class was based on an examination. The examination required writing an eight-legged essay in classical Chinese in a prescribed form.

(ii) Before 1850, there were about 526,869 civil and 212,330 military provincial degree holders in the whole country. As there were only 27000 officals positions, many lower-level degree holders did not have jobs.

(iii) The defect in the examination was that it demanded only literary skills, so it acted as the barrier to the development of science and technology.

In 1905, it was corrected by abolishing it as it was based on skills in classical Chinese learning that had no relevance for the modern world.

6. Read the source given below and answer the following questions.

Shanghai in 1935: Buck Clayton, a black American trumpet player, in Shanghai with his jazz orchestra lived the life of the privileged expatriates. But he was black and once some white Americans assaulted him and his orchestra members and threw them out from the hotel they played in. Thus, though American, he had greater sympathy for the plight of the Chinese being himself a victim of racial discrimination.

Of their fight with white Americans where they emerged victorious he writes, 'The Chinese onlookers treated us like we had done something they always wanted to do and followed us all the way home cheering us like a winning football team.'

On the poverty and hard life of the Chinese, Clayton writes, 'I would see sometimes twenty or thirty coolies pulling a big heavy cart that in America would be pulled by a truck or horses. These people seemed to be nothing but human horses and all they would get at the end of the day was just enough to get a couple of bowls of rice and a place to sleep. I don't know how they did it.'

(i) Who was Buck Clayton? What did Chinese people want at the end of the day according to Clayton?

(ii) What happened to Buck Clayton?

(iii) Why was Buck Clayton cheered by Chinese?

Ans. (i) Buck Clayton was a Black American trumpet player in Shanghai. According to him, Chinese people just wanted a couple of bowls of rice and a place to sleep at the end of the day.

(ii) Clayton and his orchestra members were attacked by some White Americans and they threw them out from the hotel where they played in.

(iii) The Chinese onlookers felt happy and cheered them when Buck Clayton and his team fought back with White Americans and emerged victorious.

Map Based Questions

1. Locate the following locations in the East Asia map.

(i) Manchuria (ii) Tokyo (iii)Kyoto

(iv) Hiroshima (v) Nagasaki

Ans.

2. Identify the following locations marked on the map of Japan.

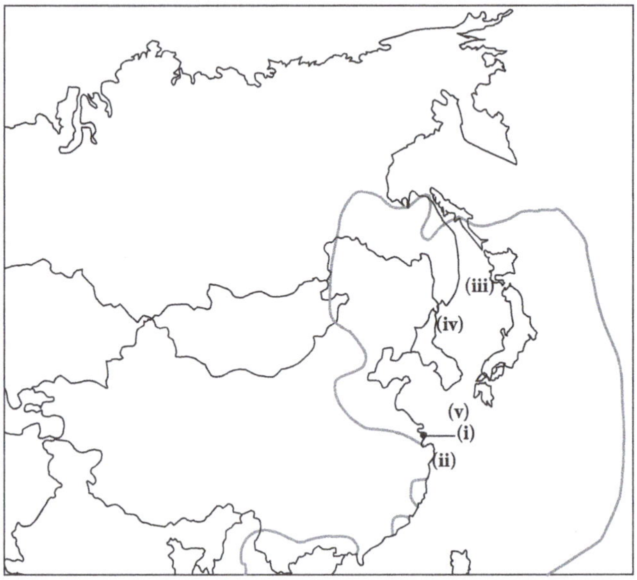

Ans.

SELF ASSESSMENT TEST

Objective Type Questions

1. Which republic was established in 1911 after the decline of Manchu Empire?
   (a) China (b) Japan (c) Korea (d) Mongolia
2. When did the USA send Commodore Matthew Perry to Japan?
   (a) 1750 (b) 1850 (c) 1853 (d) 1870
3. Which political party was known as the Guomindang?
   (a) Communist Party of China
   (b) Chinese Nationalist Party
   (c) Democratic Progressive Party
   (d) Qing Imperial Party
4. Match the following.

List I	List II
A. Zaibatsu	1. Rulers of Japan
B. Shogun	2. Large business organisations controlled by individuals
C. Daimyo	3. Political and moral philosophy
D. Confucianism	4. Lords who controlled domains in spring

Codes

	A	B	C	D		A	B	C	D
(a)	3	1	4	2	(b)	2	1	4	3
(c)	2	1	3	4	(d)	4	2	1	3

Short Answer Type Questions

5. Examine how the Chinese food reflects regional diversity.
6. Discuss the changes in the 16th century Japan which laid the pattern for future development.
7. Internal discontent coincided with demands for trade and diplomatic relations. Discuss.
8. What were the features of the new school system that began to built from the 1870s?
9. What role did the Meiji reforms play in modernising the economy of Japan?
10. Discuss the different views of Japanese intellectuals on Japan's relations with other countries.

Long Answer Type Questions

11. Discuss the role and responsibilities of the Shogun during the Tokugawa period in Japan.
12. How did Japan's awareness of European colonial expansion influence its approach to modernisation?
13. What were the long term effects of Japan's post-war reforms on its political and economic systems?
14. Sun Yat-sen's ideas became the basis of the political philosophy of the Guomindang. Discuss.

Project Work

Meaning of Project

The word project comes from the Latin word 'Projectum' which means 'before an action'. At school level, a project is a research assignment given to a student which generally requires a larger amount of effort and more independent work that is involved in a normal assignment. It requires students to undertake their own fact finding endeavours, either from library, or from the internet or by means of primary data collection. A project report should

- be handwritten
- have diagrammatic presentation
- have topics with suitable headings
- be concise and clear
- have a length of 25 to 30 pages
- end up with conclusion

Utilities of Making a Project

Following points state the uses/utility of project work

(*i*) To provide information about the development and growth of institutions, business products, and government activities.

(*ii*) To provide information to the consumers about the price of commodities, quality and uses, etc of a product as per their interest.

(*iii*) It is helpful in estimating the preference of consumers for petrol car or diesel car, telephone or mobile phone, etc.

(*iv*) Project report is helpful for the shareholders, who may be interested in knowing the earning of an enterprise and possibility of getting dividend.

(*v*) To help in the policy formulation about the economic and social development of any country.

Thus, we can say that project work may help marketers, shareholders, economists, consumers and government in effective and efficient decision-making.

Elements of Project Report

A good project report should contain the following elements

Title Page

This should include the project title, name of the company on which you are conducting your research and name of the student. You can also list the name of your school, class and subject teacher.

Acknowledgement

It is usual to thank those individuals, who have provided particularly useful assistance, technical or otherwise, during your project.

Content Page

This should list the main sections and sub-sections of your report. Choose self-explanatory titles with their respective pages and use double spacing for clarity.

Introduction

This is one of the most important components of the project report. It should begin with a clear statement of what the project is about, so that the nature and scope of the project can be understood by a reader. It should summarise everything which you set out to achieve and provide a clear summary of the project's background, relevance and main contributions. The introduction should set the context for the project and should provide the reader with a summary of the key things to look out for in, the remainder of the report.

Background

The background section of the report should set the project into action, it specifies the problem of the company, what remedial actions were taken by the company and what are its effects.

Body of Report

The central part of the report usually consists of three or four sections detailing the technical work undertaken during the project. The structure of these sections is highly project dependent.They can reflect the chronological development of the project. It includes the detailed description regarding the matter of the project.

Evaluation

This might involve quantitative and qualitative evaluation such as expressibility, functionality, ease-of-use, etc of a product. At some point, you should also evaluate the strengths and weaknesses of what you have done. It includes certain questionnaires, sampling test which help in evaluating the result on the basis of truths and facts.

Conclusion

The conclusion should list the things, which have been learnt as a result of the work you have done. It shows the ultimate response of the project undertaken by a student. It should be expressive and impressive so that a reader would clearly evaluate the result and rated you on the basis of your presentation.

Bibliography

In this section, you should mention the details of all the secondary sources, *i.e.*, magazines, newspapers, reports, internet links, etc. used for developing the project.

Project Work on Genghis Khan

Name : ....

Class : ....

Roll No. : ....

Subject : ....

School : ....

Submitted by ....

Submitted to ....

Acknowledgement

I would like to extend my sincere and heartfelt obligation towards all those who have helped me in making this project. Without their active guidance, help, cooperation and encouragement, I would not have been able to present the project on time.

I am extremely thankful and pay my gratitude to my teacher Mr/Ms .... for his/her valuable guidance and support for completion of this project.

I extend my gratitude to my Principal Mr/Ms .... for the moral support extended during the tenure of the project.

I also acknowledge with a deep sense of reverence, my gratitude towards my parents, other faculty members of the school and friends for their valuable suggestions given to me in completing this project.

Date...........

....

Name of Student

Certificate

This is to Certify that the project work

.... is the bonafide

work of .... (Name of the student) who

carried out the work under my supervision

....

Name and Signature of
Teacher/Supervisor

Contents

Piecing Together the Past of Genghis Khan

Birth of Genghis Khan

Genghis Khan (Temujin) was probably born on 1162 CE near the Onon river in the North of present-day Mongolia. He was the founder and first Great Khan of the Mongol Empire. "The Secret History of the Mongols" reports that Temujin was born grasping a blood clot in his fist, a traditional sign that he was destined to become a great leader. He was the second son of his father Yesugei who was a Kiyad chief prominent in the Khamag Mongol confederation and an ally of Toghrul of the Keraite tribe. Temujin was the first son of his mother Hoelun. "According to the Secret History of the Mongols", Temujin was named after the Tatar chief Temujin-uge whom his father had just captured.

Early Life and Family of Genghis Khan

Genghis Khan was the son of Yesugei, the chieftain of the Kiyat, a group of families related to the Borjigid clan. His father was murdered at an early age and his mother, Oelun-eke, raised Temujin, his brothers and step-brothers in great hardship. He had three brothers Hasar, Hachiun and Temuge, one sister Temulen, and two half-brothers Begter and Belgutei.

The following decade was full of reversals – Temujin was captured and enslaved and soon after his marriage, his wife, Borte, was kidnapped, and he had to fight to recover her. During these years of hardship he also managed to make important friends. The young Boghurchu was his first ally and remained a trusted friend; Jamuqa, his blood-brother (anda), was another. Temujin also restored old alliances with the ruler of the Kereyits, Tughril/Ong Khan, his father's old blood-brother.

Wives and Children

As previously arranged by his father, Temujin married Borte of the Onggirat tribe when he was around 16 years old in order to form alliances between their two tribes. Soon after the marriage, Borte was kidnapped by the Merkits. Temujin rescued her with the help of his friend and future rival, Jamukha, and his protector, Toghrul of the Keraite tribe. She gave birth to a son, Jochi (1185-1226), nine months later, clouding the issue of his parentage.

Despite speculation over Jochi, Borte would be Temujin's only empress, though he did follow tradition by taking several morganatic wives. (A morganatic marriage is a marriage between people of unequal social ranks).

Borte had three more sons, Chagatai (1183-1242), Ogedei (1186-1241), and Tolui (1191-1232). Genghis later took about 500 secondary wives and "consorts", but Borte continued to be his life companion. He had many other children with those other wives, but they were excluded from succession, only Borte's sons being considered to be his heirs. However, a Tatar woman named Yisui, taken as a wife when her people were conquered by the Mongols, eventually came to be given almost as much prominence as Borte, despite originally being only one of his minor wives. The names of at least six daughters are known, and while they played significant roles behind the scenes during his lifetime, no documents have survived that definitively provide the number or names of daughters born to the consorts of Genghis Khan.

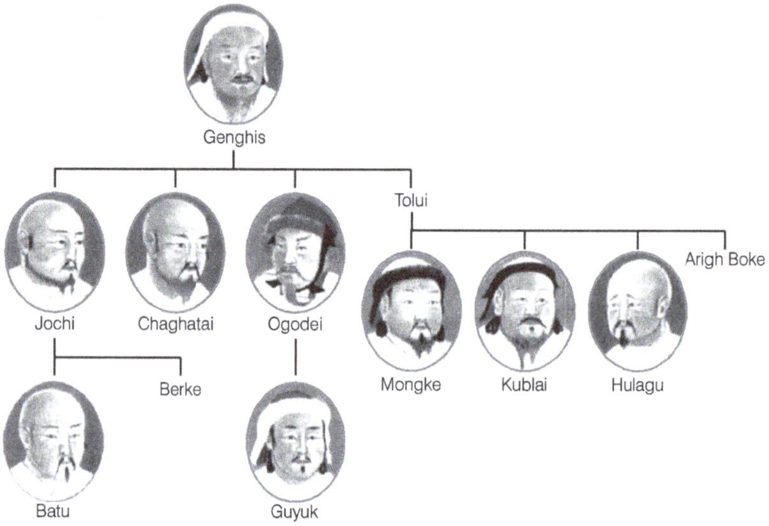

The Mongol Dynasty

Religion of Genghis Khan

Genghis Khan was a tengrist (a follower of the Tengri religion), but was religiously tolerant and interested in learning philosophical and moral lessons from other religions. He consulted Buddhist monks, Muslims, Christian missionaries and the Taoist monk Qui Chuji.

Genghis Khan, and the following Yuan Emperors forbade Islamic practices like Halal butchering, forcing Mongol methods of butchering animals on Muslims, and other restrictive decrees continued. Muslims had to slaughter sheep in secret. Genghis Khan explicitly called Muslims and Jews "slaves", and demanded that they follow the Mongol method of eating rather than the Halal method.

The Career of Genghis Khan

Through the 1180s and 1190s, Temujin remained an ally of Ong Khan and used the alliance to defeat powerful adversaries like Jamuqa, his old friend who had become a hostile foe (an enemy). It was after defeating him that Temujin felt confident enough to move against other tribes: the powerful Tatars (his father's assassins), the Kereyits and Ong Khan himself in 1203 CE.

The final defeat of the Naiman people and the powerful Jamuqa in 1206 CE, left Temujin as the dominant personality in the politics of the steppe lands. It was a position that was recognised at an assembly of Mongol chieftains (quriltai) where he was proclaimed the 'Great Khan of the Mongols' (Qa'an) with the title Genghis Khan, the 'Oceanic Khan' or 'Universal Ruler'.

Just before the quriltai of 1206 CE, Genghis Khan had reorganised the Mongol people into a more effective, disciplined military force (see following sections) that facilitated the success of his future campaigns. The first of his concerns was to conquer China, divided at this time into three realms: the Hsi Hsia people of Tibetan origin in the North-Western provinces; the Jurchen whose Chin dynasty ruled North China from Peking; the Sung dynasty who controlled South China.

By 1209 CE, the Hsi Hsia were defeated, the 'Great Wall of China' was breached in 1213 CE and Peking sacked in 1215 CE. Long drawn-out battles against the China continued until 1234 CE but Genghis Khan was satisfied enough with the progress of his campaigns to return to his Mongolian homeland in 1216 CE and leave the military affairs of the region to his subordinates.

After the defeat in 1218 CE of the Qara Khita who controlled the Tien Shan mountains North-West of China, Mongol dominions reached the Amu Darya, and the States of Transoxiana and Khwarazm. Sultan Muhammad, the ruler of Khwarazm, felt the fury of Genghis Khan's rage when he executed Mongol envoys. In the campaigns between 1219 CE and 1221 CE the great cities – Otrar, Bukhara, Samarqand, Balkh, Gurganj, Merv, Nishapur and Herat surrendered to the Mongol forces. Towns that resisted were devastated.

At Nishapur, where a Mongol prince was killed during the siege operation, Genghis Khan commanded that the 'town should be laid waste in such a manner that the site could be ploughed upon; and that in the exaction of vengeance [for the death of the prince] not even cats and dogs should be left alive'.

Military Campaigns of Genghis Khan

Western Xia Dynasty

During the 1206 CE political rise of Genghis Khan, the Mongol Empire created by Genghis Khan and his allies shared its Western borders with the Western Xia dynasty of the Tanguts. To the East and South was the Jin dynasty, founded by the Manchurian Jurchens, who ruled Northern China as well as being the traditional overlords of the Mongolian tribes for centuries.

Genghis Khan organised his people, army, and his State to first prepare for war with Western Xia, or Xi Xia, which was close to the Mongolian lands. He correctly believed that the more powerful young ruler of the Jin dynasty would not come to the aid of Xi Xia. When the Tanguts requested help from the Jin dynasty, they refused. Despite initial difficulties in capturing its well-defended cities, Genghis Khan managed to force the emperor of Xi Xia to submit to vassal status.

Battle between Mongol Warriors and the Chinese

Jin Dynasty

In 1211 CE, after the conquest of Western Xia, Genghis Khan planned again to conquer the Jin dynasty. Wanyan Jiujin, the field commander of the Jin army, made a tactical mistake in not attacking the Mongols at the first opportunity. Instead, the Jin commander sent a messenger, Mingan, to the Mongol side, who defected and told the Mongols that the Jin army was waiting on the other side of the pass. At this engagement fought at Yehuling, the Mongols massacred hundreds of thousands of Jin troops.

In 1215 CE, Genghis besieged, captured, and sacked the Jin capital of Zhongdu (modern-day Beijing). This forced the Jin ruler, Emperor Xuanzong, to move his capital South to Kaifeng, abandoning the Northern half of his empire to the Mongols.

Between 1232 and 1233 CE, Kaifeng fell to the Mongol under the reign of Genghis's third son, Ogedei Khan. The Jin dynasty collapsed in 1234 CE, after the siege of Caizhou.

Genghis Khan Entering Beijing

Project Work

Qara Khitai

Kuchlug, the deposed Khan of the Naiman confederation that Temüjin defeated and folded into his Mongol Empire, fled West and usurped the khanate of Qara Khitai (also known as the Western Liao, as it was originally established as remnants of the Liao dynasty). Genghis Khan decided to conquer the Qara Khitai and defeat Kuchlug, possibly to take him out of power.

By this time the Mongol army was exhausted from ten years of continuous campaigning in China against the Western Xia and Jin dynasty. Therefore, Genghis sent only two tumen (20,000 soldiers) against Kuchlug, under his younger General, Jebe, known as "The Arrow".

With such a small force, the invading Mongols were forced to change strategies and resort to inciting internal revolt among Kuchlug's supporters, leaving the Qara Khitai more vulnerable to Mongol conquest. As a result, Kuchlug's army was defeated West of Kashgar. Kuchlug fled again, but was soon hunted down by Jebe's army and executed.

By 1218 CE, as a result of the defeat of Qara Khitai, the Mongol Empire and its control extended as far West as Lake Balkhash, which bordered Khwarazmia, a Muslim State that reached the Caspian Sea to the West and Persian Gulf and the Arabian Sea to the South.

Death of Genghis Khan

Genghis Khan died in August 1227 CE, during the fall of Yinchuan, which is the capital of Western Xia. The exact cause of his death remains a mystery and is variously attributed to being killed in action against the Western Xia, illness, falling from his horse, or wounds sustained in hunting or battle. According to "The Secret History of the Mongols",

Genghis Khan fell from his horse while hunting and died because of the injury. He was already old and tired from his journeys. The Galician-Volhynian Chornian alleges he was killed by the Western Xia in battle, while Marco Polo wrote that he died after the infection of an arrow wound he received during his final campaign.

Later Mongol chronicles connect Genghis's death with a Western Xia princess taken as war booty. One chronicle from the early 17th century even relates the legend that the princess hid a small dagger and stabbed him, though some Mongol authors have doubted this version and suspected it to be an invention by the rival Oirads.

Years before his death, Genghis Khan asked to be buried without markings, according to the customs of his tribe. After he died, his body was returned to Mongolia and presumably to his birthplace in Khentii Aimag, where many assume he is buried somewhere close to the Onon river and the Burkhan Khaldun mountain (part of the Kentii mountain range).

According to legend, the funeral escort killed anyone and anything across their path to conceal where he was finally buried. The Genghis Khan Mausoleum, constructed many years after his death, in his memorial, but not his burial site.

Successors of Genghis Khan

The succession of Genghis Khan was already a significant topic during the later years of his reign, as he reached old age. The long running paternity discussion about Genghis's oldest son Jochi was particularly contentious because of the seniority of Jochi among the brothers.

According to traditional historical accounts, the issue over Jochi's paternity was voiced most strongly by Chagatai. In the "Secret History of the Mongols", just before the invasion of the Khwarezmid Empire by Genghis Khan, Chagatai declared before his father and brothers that he would never accept Jochi as Genghis Khan's successor. In response to this tension and possibly for other reasons, Ogedei was appointed as successor.

Ogedei

Ogedei Khan, born Ogedei (1186-1241 CE) was the third son of Genghis Khan and second Great Khan (Khagan) of the Mongol Empire. He continued the expansion that his father had begun and was a world figure when the Mongol Empire reached its farthest extent West and South during the invasions of Europe and Asia.

Jochi

Genghis Khan was aware of the friction between his sons (particularly between Chagatai and Jochi) and worried of possible conflict between them if he died. He therefore decided to divide his empire among his sons and make all of them Khan in their own right, while appointing one of his sons as his successor.

Chagatai was considered unstable due to his temper and rash behavior, because of statements he made that he would not follow Jochi, if he were to become his father's successor. Tolui, Genghis Khan's youngest son, was not suitable since in Mongol culture, youngest sons were not given much responsibility due to their age.

If Jochi were to become successor, it was likely that Chagatai would engage in warfare with him and collapse the empire. Therefore, Genghis Khan decided to give the throne to Ogedei. Ogedei was seen by Genghis Khan as dependable in character and relatively stable and down to earth and would be a neutral candidate that might defuse the situation between his brothers.

Jochi died in 1226, during his father's lifetime. Some scholars, notably Ratchnevsky, have commented on the possibility that Jochi was secretly poisoned by an order from Genghis Khan. Rashid al-Din reports that the great Khan sent for his sons in the spring of 1223, and while his brothers heeded the order, Jochi remained in Khorasan. Juzjani suggests that the disagreement arose from a quarrel between Jochi and his brothers in the siege of Urgench. Jochi had attempted to protect Urgench from destruction, as it belonged to territory allocated to him as a fief.

He concludes his story with the clearly apocryphal statement (of doubtful authenticity) by Jochi: "Genghis Khan is mad to have massacred so many people and laid waste so many lands. I would be doing a service if I killed my father when he is hunting, made an alliance with Sultan Muhammad, brought this land to life and gave assistance and support to the Muslims."

Juzjani claims that it was in response to hearing of these plans that Genghis Khan ordered his son secretly poisoned; however, as Sultan Muhammad was already dead in 1223 CE, the accuracy of this story is questionable.

Genghis Khan and three of his four Sons

Conclusion

When we remember Genghis Khan today the only images that appear in our imagination are those of the conqueror, the destroyer of cities and an individual who was responsible for the death of thousands of people. But for the Mongols, Genghis Khan was the greatest leader of all time. He united the Mongol people, freed them from interminable tribal wars and Chinese exploitation, brought them prosperity, fashioned a grand transcontinental empire and restored trade routes and markets that attracted distant travellers like the Venetian Marco Polo.

Today, after decades of Soviet control, the country of Mongolia is recreating its identity as an independent nation. It has seized upon Genghis Khan as a great national hero who is publicly venerated and whose achievements are recounted with pride. At a crucial juncture in the history of Mongolia, Genghis Khan has once again appeared as an iconic figure for the Mongol people, mobilising memories of a great past in the forging of national identity that can carry the nation into the future.

Viva Voce Questions

1. ***When was Genghis Khan born?***
Ans. Genghis Khan was probably born in 1162 CE.

2. ***When was Temujin proclaimed as Genghis Khan?***
Ans. It was in 1206 CE when he was awarded the title of the 'Universal Ruler' (i.e. Genghis Khan).

3. ***What were the names of Genghis Khan's and Borte's sons?***
Ans. Genghis Khan's and Borte's had four sons namely; Jochi, Chaghatai, Ogodei and Tolui.

4. ***Who was Toghrul of the Keraite tribe?***
Ans. Toghrul was the protector of Genghis Khan.

5. ***How was China divided during the Genghis Khan campaigns?***
Ans. During the Genghis Khan campaigns, China was divided into three realms: Hsi Hsia, Jurchen and The Sung dynasty.

6. ***Who were Hsi Hsia?***
Ans. Hsi Hsia were the people of Tibetan origin in the North-Western provinces of China.

7. ***Who did no participate in Genghis Khan's military campaigns?***
Ans. Jochi, Genghis Khan's eldest son, did not participate in his father's military campaigns from 1222 CE until his death in 1227 CE.

8. ***What do you understand by the term ulus?***
Ans. That term ulus refers to newly conquered but not fixed territories.

9. ***When was Jin Dynasty collapsed?***
Ans. The Jin Dynasty collapsed in 1234 CE, after the siege of Caizhou.

10. ***When was Genghis Khan died?***
Ans. Genghis Khan died in August 1227 CE.

SAMPLE QUESTION PAPER 1

A Highly Simulated Sample Question Paper for CBSE Class XI

(SOLVED)

HISTORY

General Instructions

- Question paper comprises five Section: A, B, C, D and E. There are 34 questions in the question paper. All questions are compulsory.
- Section A: Question numbers 1 to 21 are MCQs of 1 mark each.
- Section B: Question numbers 22 to 27 are Short Answer Type Questions, carrying 3 marks each. Answer to each question should not exceed 60-80 words.
- Section C: Question number 28 to 30 are Long Answer Type Questions, carrying 8 marks each. Answer to each question should not exceed 300-350 words.
- Section D: Question number 31 to 33 are Source Based Questions with three sub questions and are of 4 marks each.
- Section E: Question number 34 is Map based, carrying 5 marks that includes the identification and location of significant test items. Attach the map with the answer book.
- There is no overall choice in the question paper. However, an internal choice has been provided in few questions. Only one of the choices in such questions have to be attempted.
- In addition to this, separate instructions are given with each section and question, wherever necessary.

Time : 3 hours **Max. Marks : 80**

FULLY SOLVED

Section A

(1 × 21 = 21)

(Objective Type Questions)

1. Identify the European astronomer who brought the elements of turning point in European science, with the help of following information. (1)

- He believed opposite of what Christians had believed about the Earth.
- He asserted that the planets including the Earth, rotate around the Sun.

(a) Nicolo Martini (b) Martin Luther (c) Copernicus (d) Galileo Galilei

2. Who among the following crowned Charlemagne as Holy Roman Emperor? (1)

(a) Pope Leo I (b) Pope Leo II (c) Pope Leo III (d) Pope Leo IV

3. Match the following. (1)

	List I (Mesopotamian Site)		List II (Famous For)
A.	Uruk	1.	Important city
B.	Assur	2.	Clay Tablet
C.	Abu Salabikh	3.	First Capital City
D.	Babylon	4.	First evidence of wall outlines

Codes

	A	B	C	D		A	B	C	D
(a)	3	4	2	1	(b)	4	1	3	2
(c)	2	3	4	1	(d)	1	2	3	4

4. Which one of the following statements is the correct explanation of 'Richness of Japan' ? **(1)**

(a) Japan imported goods like silk from China and textile from India.
(b) An emperor had ruled Japan from Kyoto.
(c) The Japanese did not like the regularity of European printing.
(d) Japan demanded more trade relaxation from China.

5. Identify the given image from the following options. **(1)**

(a) Mt Fuji
(b) Mt Kilimanjaro
(c) Manaslu Range
(d) A Ranch in Colorado

FULLY SOLVED

6. Which among the following statements is true ? **(1)**

(a) French found the colony of Quebec in 1808.
(b) Britain recognised USA as an independent country in 1781.
(c) The word Esettler was used for Dutch in South America.
(d) The French setup its colonies in Hawaii and Philippines.

7. The term 'Hades' means **(1)**

(a) the gates of hell
(b) the land of heaven
(c) the land of slaves
(d) None of these

8. Match the following. **(1)**

	List I		List II
A.	The Paris Academy	1.	1662
B.	The Royal Society in London	2.	1670
C.	Academy of Sciences in Paris	3.	1349
D.	University in Florence	4.	1673

Codes

	A	B	C	D
(a)	1	2	3	4
(b)	2	1	4	3
(c)	2	4	3	1
(d)	3	4	2	1

9. Find out the correct chronological order of the following. **(1)**

I. Quebec Act
II. Canada Constitutional Act
III. Quebec conquest by the British
IV. French treaty with natives of Quebec

Codes

(a) II, III, IV, I
(b) IV, III, II, I
(c) IV, III, I, II
(d) III, I, IV, II

10. Given below are two statements, one labelled as Assertion (A) and the other labelled as Reason (R).

Assertion (A) Christians had believed that the Earth was a sinful place and the heavy burden of sin made it immobile.

Reason (R) Copernicus suggested that the Earth stood at the center of the universe around which moved the celestial planets. (1)

Codes

(a) Both A and R are true and R is the correct explanation of A
(b) Both A and R are true, but R is not the correct explanation of A
(c) A is true, but R is false
(d) A is false, but R is true

11. Complete the following with the correct option. (1)

Thomas More : England, Martin Luther : ……

(a) France (b) Germany (c) Italy (d) USA

12. Which among the following pairs is correctly matched? (1)

	Postion		Function
(a)	Clergy	-	Religious function/activities
(b)	Abbeys	-	Religious communities to spread the sect
(c)	Nobles	-	Agricultural labourers on the field
(d)	Serf	-	Those who had control over land

13. Given below are two statements, one labelled as Assertion (A) and the other labelled as Reason (R).

Assertion (A) In the 15th and early 16th centuries, many scholars in universities in North Europe were attracted to humanist ideas.

Reason (R) In almost every part of Europe, peasants began to rebel against the taxes imposed by the Church.

Codes (1)

(a) Both A and R are true and R is the correct explanation of A
(b) Both A and R are true, but R is not the correct explanation of A
(c) A is true, but R is false
(d) A is false, but R is true

14. Consider the following statements and select the correct answer from the following options. (1)

I. The woman's head was sculpted in white marble at Uruk before 3000 BC.
II. The eyes and eyebrows of the woman's head were made of lapis lazuli and shell.
III. The Uruk woman's head is considered as the world famous piece of sculpture.

Codes

(a) I and II (b) II and III (c) I and III (d) I, II and III

15. The Mongol Khans belonged to a variety of different faiths. Choose the correct option among the following. (1)

I. Buddhist II. Christian
III. Shaman IV. Islam

Codes

(a) I and II only (b) I, III and IV only
(c) II and IV only (d) All of these

16. Which among the following countries came into existence at the end of the 18th century? (1)

(a) Canada (b) Indonesia (c) China (d) Korea

17. Who among the following was not the natural son of Augustus? (1)

(a) Justin I (b) Plutarch
(c) Tiberius (d) Apollo

FULLY SOLVED

18. Which among the following options is correct? (1)
(a) The fall of Roman Empire caused occupation of Italy, Spain and France by Germans.
(b) The term 'noble' is used by historians to describe the legal, economic and socio-political relationship in Europe.
(c) Sicily, a province of Roman Empire had two extensive coastlines.
(d) In 1596 AD, Clovis and the Franks converted to Christianity.

19. Find out from the following pairs which one is not correctly matched. (1)
(a) 1837 – Canada Gold Rush
(b) 1825 – Natives in USA moved to reserves
(c) 1803 – Louisiana purchased from France
(d) 1849 – American Gold Rush

20. Which act gave right to natives to buy land and take loans in USA? (1)
(a) Human Rights Act, 1970
(b) The Indian Reorganisation Act, 1934
(c) Declaration of Indian Rights, 1954
(d) Multi Culturalism Act, 1974

21. What was the name of influential symposium, that in 1943 debated about being modernity without the help of West? (1)
(a) Outclass Modernity
(b) Rising Eastern World
(c) Overcoming Modernity
(d) Overcoming Westernity

Section B (3 × 6 = 18)

(Short Answer Type Questions)

22. What is the need for a social organisation in urban cities? (3)

Or

Discuss the system of writing of Mesopotamians and their literacy levels.

23. What was the position of women in merchant families in Europe? (3)
24. Discuss the primitive methods used in farming by European people initially. (3)
25. How landscapes of America changed drastically in the 19th century? (3)
26. Explain the story behind the 'Trail of Tears'. (3)
27. What were the outcomes of the Cultural Revolution? (3)

Or

Was transformation of social and political institutions and daily life in Japan just about revining traditions? Explain.

FULLY SOLVED

Section C (8 × 3 = 24)

(Long Answer Type Questions)

28. "Roman historians have a rich collection of sources to use for reconstruction of the history". Justify this statement by listing different sources. Explain about each type of the sources.

Or

Discuss the position of women in the Roman Empire. (8)

29. Discuss the changes that were brought in the USA and Canada in order to provide legitimate rights to the natives. (8)

Or

"The Guomindang despite its attempt to unite the country failed." Look at the statement and discuss the role of Sun Yat-sen and Chiang Kai-shek. Why did Guomindang fail to unite the country?

30. In pre-industrial age of poor technological communications, what skills were deployed by the Mongols to administer and control such a vast empire and handle diverse social and religious groups?

Or Discuss the evolution of *'yasa'*. How did it help Mongols to unite and create a universal empire? (8)

Section D (4 × 3 = 12)

(Source Based Questions)

31. Read the following source carefully and answer the questions that follow. (4)

The Warka Head

This woman's head was sculpted in white marble at Uruk before 3000 BCE. The eyes and eyebrows would probably have taken lapis lazuli (blue) and shell (white) and bitumen (black) inlays, respectively. There is a groove along the top of the head, perhaps for an ornament. This is a world-famous piece of sculpture, admired for the delicate modelling of the woman's mouth, chin and cheeks and it was modelled in a hard stone that would have been imported from a distance.

(i) What was the gender of Warka Head? What was it made of? (1)

(ii) List different materials used for eyes and eyebrows of Warka Head. Why was there a groove along the top of the head? (1)

(iii) In which city was Warka Head sculpted? Which stone was used for this sculpture? (2)

32. Read the following source carefully and answer the questions that follow. (4)

'How many valiant men, how many fair ladies, (had) breakfast with their kinfolk and the same night supped with their ancestors in the next world! The condition of the people was pitiable to behold. They sickened by the thousands daily, and died unattended and without help.

Many died in the open street, others dying in their houses, made it known by the stench of their rotting bodies. Consecrated churchyards did not suffice for the burial of the vast multitude of bodies, which were heaped by the hundreds in vast trenches, like goods in a ships hold and covered with a little Earth.'

(i) What was author referring to in the passage? (1)

(ii) Why was condition of the people pitiable? (1)

(iii) What does the line "consecrated churchyards did not suffice for the burial of the vast multitude of bodies" in the passage mean? (2)

33. Read the following source carefully and answer the questions that follow. (4)

William Tyndale (1494-1536), an English Lutheran who translated the Bible into English in 1506, defended Protestantism thus:

'In this they be all agreed, to drive you from the knowledge of the scripture, and that ye shall not have the text thereof in the mother-tongue, and to keep the world still in darkness, to the intent they might sit in the consciences of the people, through vain superstition and false doctrine, to satisfy their proud ambition, and insatiable covetousness and to exalt their own honour above king and emperor, yea, and above God himself. Which thing only moved me to translate the New Testament. Because I had perceived by experience, how that it was impossible to establish the lay-people in any truth, except the scripture were plainly laid before their eyes in their mother-tongue that they might see the process, order, and meaning of the text.

(i) Who was William Tyndale? (1)

(ii) What were the objectives of William Tyndale to translate the Bible into English? (1)

(iii) Why did William Tyndale want to translate the New Testament? (2)

FULLY SOLVED

Section E

(Map Based Question)

34. I. On the given map of Italy, locate the following with appropriate symbols. (1 × 5 = 5)

(i) Florence (ii) Rome *Or* Padua (iii) Corsica

II. On the same map of Italy, two seas have been marked as A and B. Identify them.

FULLY SOLVED

Answers

1. (c) Copernicus
2. (c) Pope Leo III
3. (c) 2 3 4 1
4. (a) Japan imported goods like silk from China and textile from India.
5. (d) A Ranch in Colorado
6. (b) Britain recognised USA as an independent country in 1781
7. (a) the gates of hell
8. (b) 2143
9. (c) IV, III, I, II
10. (c) A is true, but R is false
11. (b) Germany
12. (b) Abbeys – Religious communities to spread the sect
13. (b) Both A and R are true, but R is not the correct explanation of A
14. (d) I, II and III
15. (d) All of these
16. (a) Canada
17. (c) Tiberius
18. (a) The fall of Roman Empire caused occupation of Italy, Spain and France by Germans.
19. (a) 1837 - Canada Gold Rush
20. (b) The Indian Reorganisation Act of 1934
21. (c) Overcoming Modernity
22. The need for a social organisation in urban cities is due to following reasons
    - Fuel, metals, various stones, wood, etc come from many different places for city manufacturers. Thus, organised trade and storage is needed.
    - Deliveries of grain and other food items from the village to the city, and food supplies need to be stored and distributed.
    - Many activities need to be coordinated and a system is needed where some people command and others obey.

    Or

    Mesopotamians writing involved cuneiform signs. Cuneiform means wedge-shaped, broad at based and narrow at top.
    - These cuneiform signs represented not as consonant or vowel (like s or a in the English alphabets), but syllables (like -put-, or -la- , or -in-). So the signs that a Mesopotamian scribe had to learn ran into hundreds.
    - The scribe further had to handle a wet tablet and get it written before it dried. This shows system of writing was not only a skilled craft but also a huge intellectual achievement conveying the system of sounds in visual form using a language.
    - As there were hundreds of signs to learn and most of them being complex, very few Mesopotamians could read and write.
23. Position of women in merchant families was
    - Shopkeepers were often assisted by their wives in running the shop.
    - Wives looked after business when their men were away on work.
    - The early death of a merchant forced his widow to perform a larger public role. For example, Isabella d'Este (1474-1539) was a famous woman, who ruled the state while her husband was absent.

24. Agricultural technology was very primitive initially in Europe. Methods used by European people were
    - Peasants used wooden plough, drawn by oxen. This plough could at best scratch the surface of the Earth and affect the productivity of the soil.
    - Agriculture became labour intensive. For example, fields had to be dug by hand, often once in four years.
    - Ineffective method of crop rotation was in use. The land was divided in half, one field was planted in autumn with winter wheat, while the other field was left empty.
    - Rye was planted on the piece of empty land in the next year while other half was put to empty. This system deteriorated the soil slowly.
25. The landscapes of America changed drastically in the 19th century. The Europeans treated the land differently from the natives. Some of the migrants from Britain and France were younger sons who would not inherit their fathers' property, and therefore were eager to own land in America. Later, there were waves of immigrants from countries like Germany, Sweden and Italy who wanted farms they could own.
26. The 'Trail of Tears' refers to the forced relocation and movement of Cherokees. In 1832, an important judgement was announced by the US Chief Justice, John Marshall that the Cherokees were a distinct community. They were occupying thin own territory in which the laws of Georgia had no force and they have certain rights in some matters. But US President Andrew Jackson ordered the US army to evict the Cherokees from their land and drive them to the Great American Desert. Due to this 15000 people had to relocate and many died due to harsh weather, diseases and saturation. This event was then known as Trail of Tears.
27. The outcomes of Cultural Revolution were as follows
    - The Cultural Revolution led to beginning of a period of crisis, weakened the Communist Party and severely disrupted the economy and educational system. From the late 1960s, the tide began to turn. In 1975, the Communist Party once again laid emphasis on greater social discipline and the need to build an industrial economy so that China could become a power before the end of the century.
    - The Cultural Revolution was followed by a process of political changes. Deng Xiaoping kept party control strong while introducing a socialist market economy. In 1978, the Party declared its goal as the Four Modernisations. They were to develop science, industry, agriculture and defence. Debate was allowed as long as the Party was not questioned.

Or

In Japan, the transformation of social and political institutions and daily life was not just about reviving traditions or carefully preserving them, but creatively using in new and different ways. For example, Meiji school system was modelled on European and American practices and introduced new subjects, but the main motto of the curriculum was to make citizens loyal.

A course on morals that laid importance on loyalty to the emperor was compulsory. Even changes in the family and daily life of Japanese, show how foreign and indigenous ideas were brought together to create something new.

28. The rich collection of sources that Roman historians used for reconstruction of history can be broadly divided into three groups. They are
    - **Textual Sources** It include histories of the period written by contemporaries which are usually called 'Annals' because the narrative is constructed year-by-year basis. Letters, speeches, sermons, laws and others are part of textual sources that historians used.
    - **Documentary Sources** It include mainly inscriptions and papyri. Inscriptions were usually cut on stone, so a large number of them survived in both Greek and Latin.

      The papyrus was a reed like plant which is processed to produce a writing material that was very widely used in everyday life. Thousands of contracts, accounts, letters and official documents survive 'on papyrus' and have been published by scholars who are called 'papyrologists'.
    - **Material Sources/Remains** It include a very wide collection of items that mainly archaeologists discover by excavation and field survey, buildings, monuments and other kinds of structures, pottery, coins, mosaics and even entire landscapes using aerial photography.

Or

Women enjoyed relatively better position in Roman empire. After marriage, wife was not transferred to husband's authority but she retained full rights in the property of her natal family. Though, woman's dowry went to husband for the duration of the marriage, she still remained primary heir of her father and becomes an independent property owner after her father's death. Thus, Roman women enjoyed considerable rights in owning and managing property. This shows that as per the law, married couple was not one financial entity but two and the wife enjoyed complete legal independence.

Divorce was also relatively easy. A notice of intent to dissolve the marriage either by husband or wife is enough for divorce. Males married in twenties or early thirties and women married in the late teens or early twenties, so there was an age gap between husband and wife and this would have encouraged a certain inequality. As marriages were generally arranged, women were subjected to domination by their husbands.

For example, Augustine, the great catholic bishop from North Africa tell about how his mother was regularly beaten by his father and it was same with other women too.

Thus, we can see that on one hand women enjoyed good amount of independence but on the other, they also faced violence.

29 The changes that were brought in the USA and Canada in order to provide legitimate rights to the natives were

- **Reservations** In 1920s, things began to improve for the native peoples of the USA and Canada. A Survey named, The Problem of Indian Administration under social scientist Lewis Meriam was published in 1928. It showed the terribly poor health and education facilities for natives in reservations. White Americans now felt sympathy for the natives who were not able to follow their cultures and also denied the benefits of citizenship. This led to a landmark law in the USA, the Indian Reorganisation Act of 1934, which gave natives in reservations the right to buy land and take loans.
- **Declaration of Indian Rights** In 1950s and 1960s, the USA and Canadian governments thought of ending all special provisions for the natives in the hope that they would join the mainstream and adopt European culture. This idea was opposed by natives. The USA government prepared the Declaration of Indian Rights in which a number of natives accepted citizenship of the USA on a condition that their reservations would not be taken away and their traditions would not be interfered.
- **Constitution Act** In Canada, Government decided to end the recognition of aboriginal rights. In reaction to this, natives organised demonstrations and debates. Finally in 1982, the Constitution Act was introduced which accepted the existing aboriginal and treaty rights of the natives.
- **Assertion of Rights** Natives in both the USA and Canada had reduced in numbers as compared to their number in the 18th century, but they could now assert their rights and practice their culture. In Canada, they even had rights to their sacred lands which their ancestors did not have in 1880s.

Or

Role of Sun Yat-sen

In 1911, republic was established under Sun Yat-sen. He was regarded as the founder of modern China. He introduced a programme called Three Principles. They were nationalism, democracy and socialism.

Sun Yat-sen's ideas became the foundation for the political philosophy of the Guomindang. They identified the 'four great needs' such as clothing, food, housing and transportation.

Role of Chiang Kai-shek

After the death of Sun Yat-sen, Chiang Kai-shek emerged as the leader of the Guomindang. He launched a military campaign to control the warlords, regional leaders who had taken over authority forcibly and to eliminate the Communists. Chiang advocated a secular and rational 'this worldly' Confucianism, but also sought to militarise the nation. He urged people to develop habit and instinct for unified behaviour. He encouraged women to cultivate four virtues i.e. chastity, appearance, speech and work and recognise their role confined to the household.

Guomindang Failed to Unite the Country

The Guomindang despite its attempt to unite the country failed to unite the country because of its narrow social base and limited political vision. The Guomindang social base was in urban areas. Industrial growth was slow and limited. Only small people were employed in modern industries such as shipbuilding. Most of the people in towns were petty urbanites, traders and shopkeepers. Urban workers, especially women earned very low wages. Working hours were long and conditions of work were bad.

A major principle, in Sun Yat-sen's programme i.e. regulating capital and equalising land, was never carried out because the Guomindang party ignored the peasantry and the rising social inequalities. It sought to impose military order rather than address the problems faced by the people.

30. The skills deployed by the Mongols to administer and control such a vast empire diverse social and religious groups were

- Genghis Khan worked to systematically erase the old tribal identities of the different groups who joined his confederacy. He altered the old steppe order and divided old tribal groupings and distributed their members into new military units. So now a military contingent had people from different groups and this integrated them into a single group with an identity derived from Genghis Khan.
- Genghis Khan rewarded his loyalists. He publicly honoured some of them as his blood-brothers (*anda*). Some others were given special ranking as his bondsmen (*naukar*), a title that marked close relationship with the master. The old rankings were removed and new aristocracy derived its status from a close relationship with the Great Khan of the Mongols.
- The new military contingents were kept under the control of his four sons. He also assigned the responsibility of governing newly conquered people to his four sons. This decentralised the power and also provided a sense among all the family members that everyone is sharing the power. This feeling was further strengthened by *quriltais* i.e. assembly of chieftains where all decisions were collectively taken. He also declared that which son was going to access the throne after him, which made it easy for avoiding future rebellions.
- Genghis Khan also developed rapid courier system that connected distant areas of his regime. This was further refined and developed by later Great Khans to keep a check on developments at the farthest end of their regime across the continental landmass.
- Mongol Khan themselves belonged to multiple faiths like Shaman, Buddhist, Christian and Islam, but they never imposed their personal beliefs on public policy. They recruited administrators and armed contingents from people of all ethnic groups and religions. Thus, their empire was multi-ethnic, multi-lingual and multi-religious.
- Genghis Khan has laid foundation and given a direction to his descendants which helped Mongols to administer and control such a vast empire. Their tolerance to all religions and ethnicities also helped them to keep the empire intact.

Or

Evolution of *Yasa*

As per the research of David Ayalon, *yasa* was the code of law that Genghis Khan had promulgated at the *quriltai* in 1206. It had elaborated on the complex ways in which the memory of the Great Khan was shaped by his successors.

In its earliest formulation, the term was written as *yasaq* which meant law, decree or order. *Yasaq* was concerned about administrative regulations like the organisation of the hunt, the army and the postal system. By the middle of 13th century, Mongols started using the term *yasa* in a more general sense to mean the 'legal code of Genghis Khan'.

Significance of *Yasa* in uniting Mongols and creating a Universal Empire

By the middle of the 13th century, Mongols had emerged as a unified people and created the largest empire, the world had ever seen. They ruled over sophisticated urban societies with their respective histories, cultures and laws. The one way in which they could protect their identity and distinctiveness was through a claim to a sacred law given to them by their ancestor. The *yasa* gave them this identity and distinctiveness.

The *yasa* was a compilation of all the customary traditions of Mongol tribes, but they referred it as Genghis Khan's code of law to give it a status equivalent to that of laws given by Moses and Solomon. Thus, this authoritative code could be imposed on their subjects.

The *yasa* served to unite the Mongol people around a body of shared beliefs and acknowledged the love towards Genghis Khan and his descendants. Though, they absorbed different aspects of settled lifestyle, *yasa* gave them confidence to retain their ethnic identity and impose their 'law' on their defeated subjects.

Thus, the powerful ideology which was inspired by the vision of Genghis Khan became important in the construction of a Mongol universal empire.

31. (i) It was a women's head. It was made of white marble and it is a world famous piece of sculpture admired for delicate modelling of the woman's mouth, chin and cheeks.

(ii) Lapis lazuli, shell and bitumen were used for eyes and eyebrows. The groove along the top of the head was perhaps for an ornament.

(iii) The Warka Head is sculpted in Uruk before 3000 BCE. It was modelled in a hard stone that would have been imported.

32. (i) In the passage, author was referring to epidemic that was killing several thousands of people and the havoc it is creating.

(ii) The condition of people was pitiable because thousands of people were getting sick daily and dying unattended and without any help.

(iii) It means that many people were died during the plague and the burial ground in churchyard was not sufficient to bury huge number of bodies which were in hundreds.

33. (i) William Tyndale was an English Lutheran who translated the Bible into English in 1506 and defended Protestantism.

(ii) The objectives of William Tyndale to translate the Bible into English were

- To make available the copies of the Bible to the layman.
- To expose the malpractices indulge by the Church on the name of the text written in it (Bible).

(iii) William Tyndale wanted to translate the New Testament because common people will know the real truth and meaning of the scripture only when the scripture is translated in their mother tongue.

34.

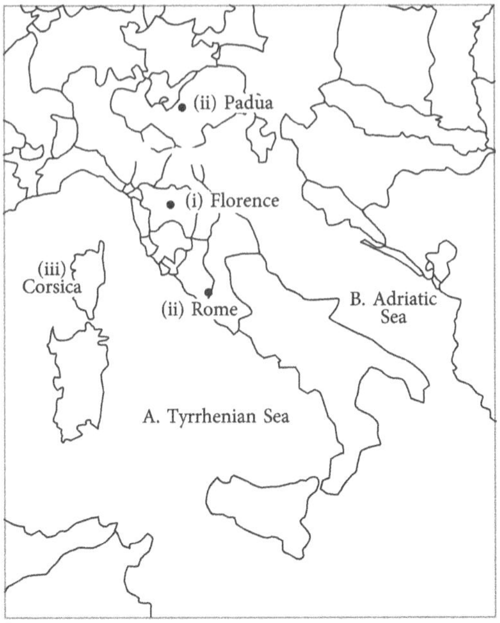

FULLY SOLVED

SAMPLE QUESTION PAPER 2

A Highly Simulated Sample Question Paper for CBSE Class XI

(UNSOLVED)

HISTORY

General Instructions

- Question paper comprises five Section: A, B, C, D and E. There are 34 questions in the question paper. All questions are compulsory.
- Section A: Question numbers 1 to 21 are MCQs of 1 mark each.
- Section B: Question numbers 22 to 27 are Short Answer Type Questions, carrying 3 marks each. Answer to each question should not exceed 60-80 words.
- Section C: Question number 28 to 30 are Long Answer Type Questions, carrying 8 marks each. Answer to each question should not exceed 300-350 words.
- Section D: Question number 31 to 33 are Source Based Questions with three sub questions and are of 4 marks each.
- Section E: Question number 34 is Map based, carrying 5 marks that includes the identification and location of significant test items. Attach the map with the answer book.
- There is no overall choice in the question paper. However, an internal choice has been provided in few questions. Only one of the choices in such questions have to be attempted.
- In addition to this, separate instructions are given with each section and question, wherever necessary.

UNSOLVED

Time : 3 hours **Max. Marks : 80**

Section A

(1 × 21 = 21)

(Objective Type Questions)

1. Identify the site of earliest history with the help of following information. (1)

- A team of Britain was sent to this site to find the story of Holy Bible.
- Exploration of this site in 1960s found that many stories of old Testament were true.

(a) Inca (b) Mesopotamia (c) Israel (d) Egypt

2. Who among the following had popularised Luther's ideas in Switzerland? (1)

(a) Ulrich Zwingli (b) Copernicus (c) Thomas Moore (d) None of these

3. Match the following. (1)

List I	List II
A. Francesco Barbaro	1. Society of Jesus
B. Lorenzo Valla	2. Defended the acquisition of wealth as a virtue
C. Niccolo Machiavelli	3. Criticised the Christian commandment against pleasure.
D. Ignatius Loyola	4. The Prince

Codes

	A	B	C	D
(a)	3	1	2	4
(b)	2	4	1	3
(c)	3	2	4	1
(d)	2	1	4	3

4. Which of the following statements is the correct explanation of 'empire'? **(1)**

(a) Sense of material location
(b) Sense of imperial location
(c) Sense of societal power
(d) Sense of military power

5. Identify the given image from the following options. **(1)**

(a) Emperor Constantine
(b) Emperor Minerva
(c) Emperor Caesar
(d) None of these

6. Cardinal Gasparo Contarini writes about the democratic government of his city state in **(1)**

(a) The Last Supper (1495)
(b) Canterbury Tales (1390)
(c) The Commonwealth and Government of Venice (1534)
(d) The Civilisation of the Renaissance in Italy (1860)

7. In which part of the Europe by the end of the 13th century, the warm summer of the past 300 year paved way for bitterly cold summers? **(1)**

(a) North
(b) South
(c) East
(d) West

8. Choose the correct option among the following in the context of North American continent **(1)**

I. It extends from the Arctic circle to the Tropic of Cancer.
II. Rocky mountains is located in the East.
III. Mexico is located in the South.

Codes

(a) I and II only
(b) II and III only
(c) I and III only
(d) I, II and III

9. Arrange in sequence.

(i) Use of iron
(ii) Establishment of the Assyrian Kingdom
(iii) Assyrian empire
(iv) Rule of Assurbanipal

Codes

(a) (ii), (i), (iii), (iv)
(b) (i), (ii), (iv), (iii)
(c) (iv), (iii), (ii), (i)
(d) (i), (iii), (iv), (ii)

10. Given below are two statements, one labelled as Assertion (A) and the other labelled as Reason (R).

Assertion (A) In 1867, Canada was organised as a confederation of autonomous states.
Reason (R) Canada was won by the British after a war with France.
Codes **(1)**

(a) Both A and R are true and R is the correct explanation of A
(b) Both A and R are true, but R is not the correct explanation of A
(c) A is true but, R is false
(d) A is false but, R is true

UNSOLVED

11. Complete the following with correct option. (1)

Serf : Slaved cultivators, Noble : ....

(a) Poor middle class
(b) Rich aristocrats
(c) Subordinate rulers
(d) None of these

12. Which among the following pairs is correctly matched? (1)

	Event		Year
(a)	Louisiana purchase from France	–	1803
(b)	Texas coded by Britain	–	1853
(c)	Gadsden purchase	–	1842
(d)	California purchase from Spain	–	1845

13. Given below are two statements, one labelled as Assertion (A) and the other labelled as Reason (R). (1)

Assertion (A) One of the ways that merchants spent their money was by making donations to Churches.

Reason (R) From the 12th century, large Churches called Cathedrals were being built in France.

Codes

(a) Both A and R are true and R is the correct explanation of A
(b) Both A and R are true , but R is not the correct explanation of A
(c) A is true, but R is false
(d) A is false, but R is true

14. Consider the following statements and select the correct answer from the following options. (1)

I. The Manchu empire was overthrown and a republic established in 1911.
II. On 4th May, 1992, demonstration was held in Beijing to protest against the post-war peace conference.
III. The Guomindang and the CCP emerged as major forces in China.

Codes

(a) II and III (b) I and II (c) I and III (d) I, II and III

UNSOLVED

15. Who wrote the book 'Why Weren't We Told' ? (1)

(a) Tasman
(b) WEH Stanner
(c) Henry Reynolds
(d) None of these

16. Match the following. (1)

List I	List II
A. Sima Qian	1. Japanese scholar of China
B. Liang Qichao	2. The greatest historian of early China
C. Naito Konan	3. The pioneer of modern history in Japan
D. Marco Polo	4. European trarveller

Codes

	A	B	C	D
(a)	2	3	1	4
(b)	4	3	2	1
(c)	1	2	3	4
(d)	3	2	4	1

17. Against whom the Mongols waged their successful war in North China? (1)

(a) Qing dynasty
(b) Chin dynasty
(c) Zhou dynasty
(d) Tang dynasty

18. Which of the following options is correct? (1)

(a) Ghazan Khan was the first Il-Khanid ruler to convert to Islam.
(b) Chinese and Persian secretaries deployed in India during 12th century AD.
(c) Toluyid branch was more adept in present day Russia.
(d) Genghis Khan's code of law was originated in South East Asia.

19. Find out from the following pairs, which is not correctly matched. (1)

(a) Sun Yat Sen – Founder of Modern China
(b) Zao Taofen – Life weekly
(c) Lenin – Third International
(d) Syngman Rhee – Elected as first President of China

20. What does the literal meaning of 'Monolith' refers to? (1)

(a) Deciphered language (b) Roman gladiators
(c) Large block of stone (d) Tablet block of clay

21. The government had always turned the land of Australia as 'terra nullius', which means (1)

(a) Belonging to government (b) Belonging to poor people
(c) Belonging to nobody (d) Belonging to everybody

Section B (3 × 8 = 18)

(Short Answer Type Questions)

22. Describe the 'early and late empire' of the Roman empire. (3)

Or

Discuss the different reasons for the revival of Italian cities.

23. What did Qing reformers do to introduce new ideas and institutions? (3)

24. How did Feudalism develop in England in medieval period? (3)

25. Explain the term 'Aborigines' and their significance in Australia. (3)

26. How did Anti-slavery Movement lead to civil liberties to slaves in North America? (3)

27. What were the three orders and explain how they played a significant role in shaping European society? (3)

Or

How the subject Anthropology helped in understanding about the native people across the world?

Section C (8 × 3 = 24)

(Long Answer Type Questions)

28. "The rapid succession of emperors in the 3rd century is an obvious symptom of the strains faced by the empire in this period". Look at the statement and discuss the crisis that occurred in the 3rd century. (8)

Or

Explain the 'Gold Rush' and its impacts on the people's lives.

29. How attentive was the government to the conditions of work of women and children? Did it pass any laws? If passed, discuss them in detail. How did industrialists try to circumvent laws? (8)

Or

What do understand by the 'democratic spirit'? How the United States gained independence through the same?

30. Mention the important events after the death of Genghis Khan. (8)

Or

The most valuable research on the Mongols was done by Russian scholars. Explain in the context of the given statement.

Section D
(4 × 3 = 12)

(Source Based Questions)

31. Read the following source carefully and answer the questions that follow. (4)

The Palace at Mari of King Zimrilim (1810–1760 BCE)

The great palace of Mari was the residence of the royal family, the hub of administration, and a place of production, especially of precious metal ornaments. It was so famous in its time that a minor king came from North Syria just to see it, carrying with him a letter of introduction from a royal friend of the king of Mari, Zimrilim. Daily lists reveal that huge quantities of food were presented each day for the king's table: flour, bread, meat, fish, fruit, beer and wine. He probably ate in the company of many others, in or around courtyard, paved white.

You will notice from the plan that the palace had only one entrance, in the North. The large, open courtyards were beautifully paved. The King would have received foreign dignitaries and his own people in audience hall, a room with wall paintings that would have awed the visitors. The palace was a sprawling structure, with 260 rooms and covered an area of 2.4 hectares.

(i) What was great palace of Mari used for? How many entrances did the palace had and in which direction? (1)

(ii) What was mainly produced in great palace of Mari? (1)

(iii) What were the varieties of food that king had each day? Whom did king receive in audience hall? (2)

32. Read the following source carefully and answer the questions that follow. (4)

In the 12th century, Abbess Hildegard of Bingen wrote: 'Who would think of herding his entire cattle in one stable – cows, donkeys, sheep, goats, without difference? Therefore, it is necessary to establish difference among human beings, so that they do not destroy each other. God makes distinctions among his flock, in heaven as on Earth. All are loved by him, yet there is no equality among them.'

(i) Who is the author of the passage? What is the author trying to convey through the passage? (1)

(ii) Why is it necessary to establish difference? (1)

(iii) What analogy did author use to justify inequality? (2)

33. Read the following source carefully and answer the questions that follow. (4)

"Art" is embedded in nature; he who can extract it, has it...Moreover, you may demonstrate much of your work by geometry. The more closely your work abides by life in its form, so much the better will it appear. No man shall ever be able to make a beautiful figure out of his own imagination unless he has well stored his mind by much copying from life.' - Albrecht Durer (1471-1528)

The sketch by Durer (Praying Hands) gives us a sense of Italian culture in the 16th century, when people were deeply religious, but also had a sense of confidence in man's ability to achieve near perfection and to unravel the mysteries of the world and universe.

(i) What is the name of the artist mentioned in the passage? What are the views of this artist on art? (1)

(ii) When can a man make a beautiful figure? (1)

(iii) What does Praying Hands sketch describe? (2)

Section E (1 × 5 = 5)

(Map Based Question)

34. I. Mark the following locations on the map of Central Asia.

(i) Samarqand (ii) Karakorum (iii) Turfan *Or* Nishapur

II. On the same map of Central Asia, two locations are marked as A and B. Identify them.

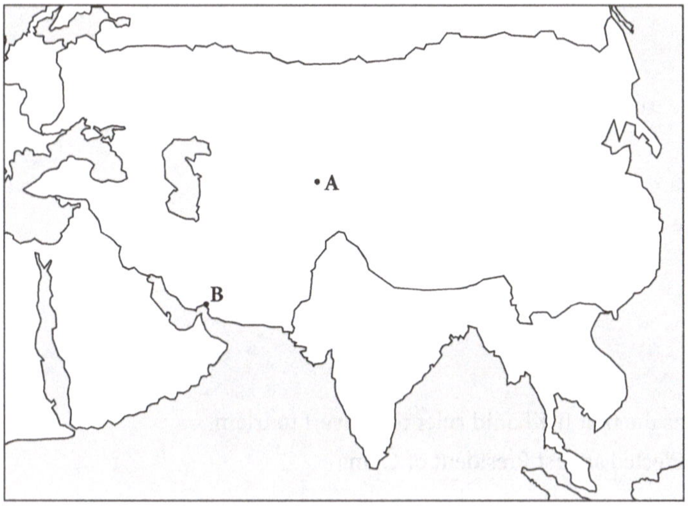

Answers

1. (b) Mesopotamia
2. (a) Ulrich Zwingli
3. (c) 3241
4. (a) Sense of material location
5. (a) Emperor Constantine
6. (c) The Commonwealth and Government of Venice (1534)
7. (a) North
8. (c) I and III only
9. (a) (ii), (i), (iii), (iv)
10. (b) Both A and R are true, but R is not the correct explanation of A
11. (b) Rich aristocrats
12. (a) Louisiana purchase from France - 1803
13. (a) Both A and R are true and R is the correct explanation of A
14. (c) I and III
15. (c) Henry Reynolds
16. (a) 2314
17. (b) Chin dynasty
18. (a) Ghazan Khan was the first Il-Khanid ruler to convert to Islam.
19. (d) Syngman Rhee-Elected as first President of China
20. (c) Large block of stone
21. (c) Belonging to nobody
34.

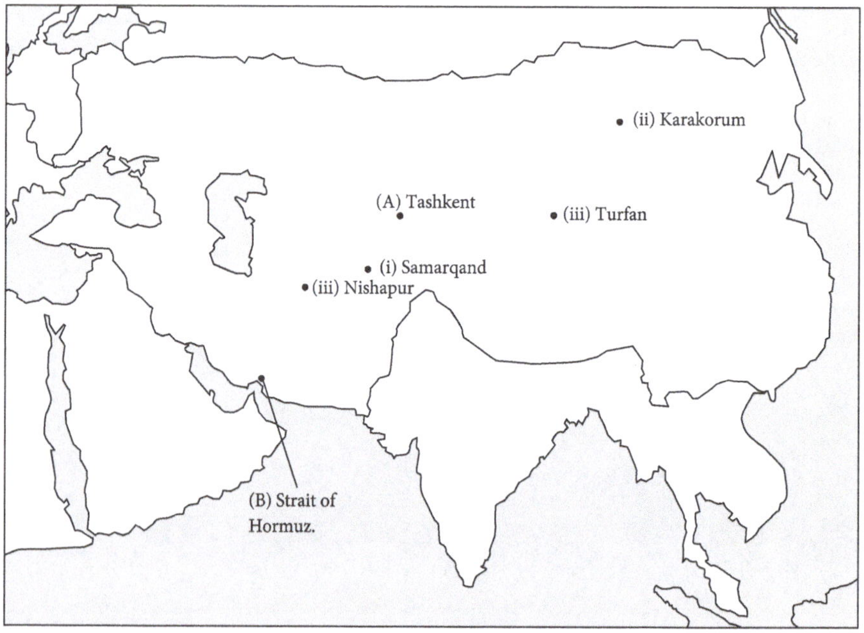

SAMPLE QUESTION PAPER 3

A Highly Simulated Sample Question Paper for CBSE Class XI

(UNSOLVED)

HISTORY

General Instructions

- Question paper comprises five Section: A, B, C, D and E. There are 34 questions in the question paper. All questions are compulsory.
- Section A: Question numbers 1 to 21 are MCQs of 1 mark each.
- Section B: Question numbers 22 to 27 are Short Answer Type Questions, carrying 3 marks each. Answer to each question should not exceed 60-80 words.
- Section C: Question number 28 to 30 are Long Answer Type Questions, carrying 8 marks each. Answer to each question should not exceed 300-350 words.
- Section D: Question number 31 to 33 are Source Based Questions with three sub questions and are of 4 marks each.
- Section E: Question number 34 is Map based, carrying 5 marks that includes the identification and location of significant test items. Attach the map with the answer book.
- There is no overall choice in the question paper. However, an internal choice has been provided in few questions. Only one of the choices in such questions have to be attempted.
- In addition to this, separate instructions are given with each section and question, wherever necessary.

Time : 3 hours **Max. Marks : 80**

UNSOLVED

Section A

(1 × 21 = 21)

(Objective Type Questions)

1. Identify the name of the site from the information given below. (1)

(i) It was one of the earliest temple towns, in which depictions of armed heroes and their victims were found.

(ii) The site was continuously occupied from about 4200 BCE to about 400 CE.

(iii) The site came to have a defensive wall at a very early date.

(iv) By about 2800 BCE, it had expanded to 400 hectares.

(a) Uruk (b) Ur (c) Mari (d) Mohenjodaro

2 In which year, Canberra was established as a capital of Australia? (1)

(a) 1911 (b) 1917 (c) 1927 (d) 1931

3 Match the following. (1)

	List I		List II
A.	Augustus	1.	Built the city of Dara
B.	Anastasius	2.	First emperor
C.	Constantine	3.	Separated civilian from military functions
D.	Diocletian	4.	Introduced new denomination called Solidus

Codes

	A	B	C	D
(a)	3	1	2	4
(b)	2	1	3	4
(c)	2	1	4	3
(d)	4	2	1	3

4. Consider the following statements and choose the correct option. (1)

I. Marc Bloch was one of the earliest scholars from France who worked on feudalism.
II. Feudalism developed in England from 13th century.
III. The Catholic Church was not a powerful institution and didn't depend on the king.
IV. Serfs, physically challenged and women could become priests.

Codes

(a) Only I (b) Only II (c) Both I and II (d) Both III and IV

5. Identify the picture given below. (1)

(a) Archaeologists moved to Florida
(b) Dreams of poor European immigrants
(c) Immigrants welcomed by the USA
(d) Moving to California for Gold Rush

6. The term 'fukoku kyohei' means (1)

(a) rich country
(b) strong army
(c) dictatorship
(d) Both (a) and (b)

7. Who was called as 'the Marchesa of Mantua' during renaissance in Italy? (1)

(a) Cassandra Fedele (b) Isabella D'este (c) Martin Luther (d) Ulrich Zwingli

8. Fill in the blank. (1)

During the period of ...., new monarchs in Spain arrived.

(a) 1461-1559 (b) 1474-1556 (c) 1485-1547 (d) 1495-1545

9. Find out the correct chronological order from the following options. (1)

I. Sack of Rome by the Visigoths
II. Arab invasion of Spain
III. Invasion of Italy by Lombards
IV. Capture of Eastern Roman territories by the Persians

Codes

(a) IV, II, I, III (b) II, III, I, IV (c) I, III, IV, II (d) IV, III, I, II

10. Given below are two statements, one labelled as Assertion (A) and the other labelled as Reason (R). (1)

Assertion (A) The great urban centres that lined the shores of the Mediterranean (Carthage, Alexandria, Antioch were the biggest among them) were the true bedrock of the imperial system.

Reason (R) It was through the cities that 'government' was able to tax the provincial countrysides which generated much of the weath of the empire.

Codes

(a) Both A and R are true and R is the correct explanation of A
(b) Both A and R are true, but R is not the correct explanation of A
(c) A is true, but R is false
(d) A is false, but R is true

11 Complete the following with the correct option. (1)

Ashurbanipal : King of Syria, Zimrilim : ....

(a) King of Ur (b) King of Uruk
(c) King of Mari (d) King of Babylon

12 Match the following. (1)

List I	List II
A. Louisiana	1. Desert region
B. California	2. Purchased from French
C. Nevada	3. Ceded by Mexico
D. Quebec	4. Province of Canada

Codes

	A	B	C	D		A	B	C	D
(a)	2	3	1	4	(b)	4	2	1	3
(c)	3	4	2	1	(d)	2	1	4	3

13 Given below are two statements, one labelled as Assertion (A) and the other labelled as Reason (R). (1)

Assertion (A) Native people were friendly and welcoming to settlers.

Reason (R) In the 18th century, Western Europeans defined 'civilised' people in terms of literacy, an organised religion and urbanism.

Codes

(a) Both A and R are true and R is the correct explanation of A
(b) Both A and R are true, but R is not the correct explanation of A
(c) A is true, but R is false
(d) A is false, but R is true

14. Consider the following statements and select the correct answer from the following options. (1)

I. One of the first novel, Don Quixote written in Spanish in 1605 AD.
II. First printed book appeared in Europe.
III. Coffee from South America is drunk in Europe for the first time in 1517 AD.

Codes

(a) I and II (b) II and III
(c) I and III (d) I, II and III

UNSOLVED

15. Who said these lines, "I am not on the side of the Persian peasantry. If there is a purpose in pillaging them all, there is no one with more power to do this than I"? (1)

(a) Ghazan Khan (b) Genghis Khan
(c) Ogodei (d) Chaghatai

16. In Mesopotamia, writing was used for (1)

(a) keeping records, making dictionaries. (b) giving legal validity to land transfer.
(c) narrating the deeds and reforms of the king. (d) All of the above

17. The territories of Hopi was annexed by the (1)

(a) Spanish conquistadores (b) English settlers
(c) Portuguese (d) None of these

18. Who participated in the popular rights movement and launched the first agitation against industrial pollution in 1897? (1)

(a) Tanaka Shozo (b) Mateo Ricci
(c) Naito Konah (d) None of these

19. Find out from the following pairs, which one is not correctly matched. (1)

(a) Meiji Constitution – 1889 (b) Foundation of Guomindang – 1912
(c) Japan-USA Treaty of Peace – 1945 (d) Japan's Invasion of China – 1931

20. The Mongol army consisted of people recruited from (1)
(a) different ethnic, religious and linguistic group.
(b) herdsman from Mongolia only.
(c) people belonging to the Mongoloid race only.
(d) None of these

21. Which of the following statements about Canberra is correct? (1)
(a) It's meaning is meeting place.
(b) It is known for 'Gold mines'
(c) It is known for 'white men place'.
(d) It's meaning is 'right place'.

Section B (3 × 6 = 18)

(Short Answer Type Questions)

22. What were the reasons that led to the emergence of monarchies? (3)

Or

Discuss the minstrels and the life of Serfs.

23. In the late sixteenth century, three changes laid the pattern for futre development. Describe these changes in the context of Japan. (3)

24. How did Francesco Petrarch contribute to the development of humanism? (3)

25. Mention the differences between 'Red Indians' and Native Americans. (3)

26. How River Euphrates played a significant role in Mesopotamian culture? (3)

27. State the significance of the growth in trade and towns in the period of Renaissance. (3)

Or

In what ways painting enriched during Renaissance period?

Section C

(Long Answer Type Questions)

28. The Empire had a substantial economic infrastructure of harbours, mines, quarries, brickyards, olive oil factories, etc. Explain the economic expansion of Roman Empire in the context of this statement. (8)

Or

Explain the urbanisation in Mesopotamia and also mention their temples and God.

29. Explain the history, lifestyle, languages and beliefs of native people of North America. (8)

Or

Discuss the entry of European traders in North America. How did they change the landscape and demography of the North America?

30. "Genghis Khan has spent most of his life in military combat. His military achievements were astounding". Justify the statement and discuss his various conquests. (8)

Or

The Mongols were diverse body of people, linked by similarities of language. Explain the social background of the Mongols.

Section D

(Source Based Questions) (4 × 3 = 12)

31. Read the following source carefully and answer the questions that follow. (4)

In Benedictine monasteries, there was a manuscript with 73 chapters of rules which were followed by monks for many centuries. Here are some of the rules they had to follow:

Chapter 6: Permission to speak should rarely be granted to monks.

Chapter 7: Humility means obedience.

Chapter 33: No monk should own private property

Chapter 47: Idleness is the enemy of the soul, so friars and sisters should be occupied at certain times in manual labour, and at fixed hours in sacred reading.

Chapter 48: The monastery should be laid out in such a way that all necessities be found within its bounds: water, mill, garden, workshops.

(i) What is the passage describing about? What is the enemy of the soul? (1)

(ii) Mention two rules that monks should follow. (1)

(iii) How monastery should be built? (2)

32. Read the following source carefully and answer the questions that follow. (4)

Giovanni Pico Della Mirandola (1463-94), a humanist of Florence, wrote on the importance of debate in On the Dignity of Man (1486).

'For [Plato and Aristotle] it was certain that, for the attainment of the knowledge of truth they were always seeking for themselves, nothing is better than to attend as often as possible the exercise of debate. For just as bodily energy is strengthened by gymnastic exercise, so beyond doubt in this wrestling-place of letters, as it were, energy of mind becomes far stronger and more vigorous'.

(i) Who is the author of the passage? What did the author write about? (1)

(ii) What did GP Della Mirandola say about the importance of debate in 'On the Dignity of Man'? (1)

(iii) What is the analogy used by the author to describe the importance of debate? (2)

33. Read the following source carefully and answer the questions that follow. (4)

A leading Japanese scholar of China, Naito Konan's writings influenced scholars worldwide. Using the new tools of Western historiography Naito built on a long tradition of studying China as well as bringing his experience as a journalist there. He helped establish the Department of Oriental Studies in Kyoto University in 1907. In Shinaron [on China (1914)], he argued that republican government offered the Chinese a way to end aristocratic control and centralised power that had existed since the Sung dynasty (960-1279) a way to revitalise local society where reform must begin.

(i) Which scholar used new tools of Western historiography? (1)

(ii) Why Naito established the Department of Oriental Studies in Kyoto University in 1907? (1)

(iii) What did Naito argue about in his Shinaron? (2)

UNSOLVED

Section E

(1 × 5 = 5)

(Map Based Question)

34 I. Locate the following locations on the map of Western Europe given below.

(i) St Denis (ii) Madrid (iii) Vienna *Or* London

II. On the same outline map, two locations have been marked as 'A' and 'B'. Identify them.

UNSOLVED